The Commerce of Louisiana during the French Régime, 1699–1763

N. M. MILLER SURREY

Introduction by GREGORY WASELKOV

THE UNIVERSITY OF ALABAMA PRESS
Tuscaloosa

The University of Alabama Press
Tuscaloosa, Alabama 35487-0380

Manufactured in the United States of America

Published by The University of Alabama Press, 2006

∞

The paper on which this book is printed meets the minimum requirements of American National Standard for Information Science—Permanence of Paper for Printed Library Materials, ANSI Z39.48-1984.

Library of Congress Cataloging-in-Publication Data

Miller Surrey, N. M. (Nancy Maria), 1874–1941.
The commerce of Louisiana during the French regime, 1699–1763 / N.M. Miller Surrey ; introduction by Gregory Waselkov.
p. cm.
Originally published Columbia University, 1916.
Includes bibliographical references and index.
ISBN-13: 978-0-8173-5296-7 (pbk. : alk. paper)
ISBN-10: 0-8173-5296-1
1. Louisiana—Commerce—History. 2. Mississippi River Valley—Commerce—History. I. Title.
HF3025.S8 2006
382.09763—dc22

2006003733

ISBN-13: 978-0-8173-8413-5 (electronic)

Cover Illustration: Cotton cultivation and processing on a French colonial plantation in the West Indies, Denis Diderot and Jean Le Rond d'Alembert, eds., *Encyclopédie*, vol. 18 (Paris: Briasson, David, Le Breton, and Durand, 1762).

The Commerce of Louisiana during the French Régime, 1699–1763

CONTENTS

PREFACE

Histories of Louisiana under the rule of France have been little more than narratives of events. None has given primary attention to the development of institutions. The present contribution, begun in 1909 as a seminar paper, is intended within the field chosen to remedy this omission.

In elaborating the theme an effort has been made to bring together all that is pertinent and available in French and English records. Every library in the United States likely to contain material on the subject has been visited. As the chief source of information naturally is France itself, the stores of the archival centres and the libraries there have been freely drawn upon. The work, in fact, is based, very largely, on unpublished documents.

For suggestions, criticism and guidance in the performance of my task I am greatly indebted to William R. Shepherd, of Columbia University, under whom it was carried on. To him I express my sincere gratitude. I desire to convey my sense of appreciation, also, to Mr. Waldo Leland, of the Carnegie Institution of Washington, and to M. Abel Doysié, of Paris, for aid in utilizing the French archives. To librarians and others who have placed their collections at my disposal I am duly thankful for the many courtesies received.

N. M. Miller Surrey
New York, April 1916

INTRODUCTION TO THE NEW EDITION

Nancy Maria Miller Surrey's dissertation on commerce in the early eighteenth-century French colony of *La Louisiane* appeared in print on the eve of the American entry into World War I. From our twenty-first century perspective, her fascination with one of Europe's minor colonies of a distant era might seem oddly disengaged from the earthshaking developments of her own day. For American historians of the late nineteenth and early twentieth centuries, however, studying earlier episodes of colonialism was not idle, ivory-tower intellectualism. In 1916 a handful of European nations—Great Britain, France, Holland, Germany, Belgium, Spain, Portugal, and Italy—still dominated much of the world's lands, people, and commerce through their overseas colonial empires. The United States had engaged in its own highly controversial colonizing ventures—the Indian wars, the war with Mexico (1846–1848), the war with Spain (1898)—in the course of the nineteenth century. Our country arose from former colonies and in turn imposed colonialism on others. Nothing could be more central to the historical study of the United States than an analysis of colonialism in all its varied forms and repercussions.

Most American historical studies written in the early and mid-nineteenth century concentrated on the British colonies of the eastern seaboard, the original thirteen colonies, and particularly the most populous of those, Massachusetts and Virginia. Historians initially took little interest in the French, Spanish, Dutch, Swedish, and Russian colonies that once existed within the bounds of the future United States. One might point to Francis Parkman as a notable exception, considering the public fascination his works generated in the history of New France.[1] For Parkman, though, the French served essentially as foils and worthy foes of the ultimately victorious British, whose conquest of the continent comprised the central story. The discipline of history, for much of the nineteenth century, remained outcome driven. Britain defeated France in the Seven Years' War; British culture and laws and the English language provided the basis for much of American culture and laws and language; and from the British colonies of Massachusetts and Virginia came many influential early Americans: statesmen, scientists, even historians. Consequently, historians who wanted to understand how their United States came to be, created narratives tracing the nation's origins directly back from an Anglo-dominated present.

Despite the popular appeal of that approach (which retains a surprisingly strong following among professional historians to this day), several serious flaws gradually became apparent to the increasingly professionalized historians of the late nineteenth century. To state only the most obvious problem with "outcome-driven" history, even the most committed Anglophile could see the United States was not simply Great Britain replicated at a new spot on the globe. The American people have diverse origins, and much of that diversity appeared in colonial times. American culture and laws and language are themselves diverse and derive from complex interactions of multiple (often competing) societies, ethnicities, and religions. Historians began to look at the nation's history as a remarkably multifaceted process in which the American environment, its native peoples, and numerous immigrant peoples all played important roles. Among the most influential of this new kind of historian was Frederick Jackson Turner, who first outlined his geographically influenced frontier theory of American history in 1892.[2] Simultaneously, interest in regional histories rose dramatically at universities in Texas, California, and other locations far removed from old academic centers in the East. Long-neglected colonies of the Spanish and French, colonies that once encompassed the bulk of the North American continent in their territorial claims, now demanded serious attention from scholars. Since much of the primary documentation for America's colonial past lay in European, Mexican, and Cuban archives, exploring and indexing those archival collections became a priority. Nancy Miller Surrey undertook her graduate tutelage with the first generation of American historians overtly committed to the study of American colonial history in all its cultural and ethnic complexity.

Born on January 16, 1874, in rural DeWitt County, central Illinois, Nancy Maria Miller attended the University of Chicago, where she obtained a Bachelor of Science degree in 1903. One year later she married Franklin Surrey, a native of Massachusetts (born in 1876), who had earned B.A. and M.A. degrees at Dartmouth College in 1899 and 1902. The couple henceforth used the compound (and un-hyphenated) surname Miller Surrey. Though commonplace in our time, such an exchange of names was unusual in 1904 and must have reflected Nancy's strong will and modern sense of personal identity, as well as Frank's enlightened attitude toward women. Because the conventions of that era demanded a single surname for official purposes, the Library of Congress cataloged her publications under "Surrey," and that is where her works appear in most bibliographies. However, in deference to her own clear preference in the matter, "Miller Surrey" is employed for this edition of her major work.

By 1907 Nancy and Frank resided in Madison, Wisconsin, where she enrolled at the University of Wisconsin for the M.A. program in American history. Frank supported them by teaching physics at Madison High School but took summer graduate courses at the university (field unknown). In 1908 she published a short note on Ohio's judicial policy toward juvenile delinquency in *The American Political Science Review*, an outcome of her coursework for a minor in political science at Wisconsin. That brief article, her first, appeared under the name "N. M. Miller Surrey," a by-line she used in all subsequent publications. In 1909 Nancy completed her masters' degree requirements with a thesis, "History of Education in the Old Northwest to 1800," directed by Frederick Jackson Turner. Immediately afterward the couple moved to New York City, where Nancy entered Columbia University as a Ph.D. candidate in American history under the direction of William R. Shepherd.[3]

A few years earlier Shepherd had published, under the auspices of the Carnegie Institution of Washington, the first guide to Spanish archival material for American historical researchers.[4] Circumstantial evidence suggests that Shepherd obtained Carnegie support for his new student to assist with the compilation of a calendar of documents in the French archives relating to the Mississippi Valley. An organizational meeting for the calendar had taken place in December 1907 in Madison, Wisconsin, where Miller Surrey surely heard of the proposed project. Precisely when her own participation began is unknown, but she may have become an assistant to M. Abel Doysié, project director, as early as 1909. Nancy Miller Surrey must have spent considerable time in Paris just prior to the outbreak of World War I, because her 1914 dissertation is based almost entirely on primary sources from French archives, documents unavailable in the United States for another two decades (except, in some instances, as transcriptions at the Library of Congress). Columbia University published her remarkable dissertation, *The Commerce of Louisiana during the French Régime, 1699–1763*, in 1916 as volume 71 of "Studies in History, Economics and Public Law," the same series in which Shepherd's own dissertation had appeared twenty years before.[5]

Despite her first-rate dissertation and book, illustrious mentors, and impeccable academic pedigree, with diplomas from three of the country's most prestigious universities, Nancy Miller Surrey never obtained an academic appointment. Perhaps the then-prevalent prejudice against women in higher education frustrated a search for a faculty position. Her use of gender-neutral initials instead of her first name in all formal publications could have been a tactic to circumvent biases facing female professional historians in the early twentieth century. At 42, her age may also have been considered a drawback. But this is all speculation. None of her published writings reveal aspirations for a teaching post (and any extant personal correspondence has not been located). Miller Surrey may have been most happy at work among the colonial archival records she came to know so thoroughly. In any event, she remained actively engaged in French colonial history for another dozen years. In 1917 she contributed book reviews to two of the premier history journals, *The Journal of American History* and *The American Historical Review.* The University of Wisconsin's alumni directory listed her residence two years later as 593 Riverside Drive, New York City, where she was occupied with "Historical Research."

Indeed, from 1919 until 1924, "Mrs. N. M. Miller Surrey, of New York" kept extremely busy compiling and editing, on behalf of the Carnegie Institution of Washington, the calendar of Parisian archival sources begun before the war. The magnitude of that task must surely have required her return to Paris sometime during that period. In 1926 and 1928, the Carnegie's Department of Historical Research distributed her 1,783-page typescript, *Calendar of Manuscripts in Paris Archives and Libraries Relating to the History of the Mississippi Valley to 1803,* in two planograph volumes to major libraries around the country. Although copies are now difficult to come by, Miller Surrey's monumental *Calendar* remains an invaluable tool for anyone studying French colonization in the midcontinent. Key subject terms are provided for each of the approximately 29,000 referenced documents from twenty French archival collections, ample proof of the indefatigable Dr. Miller Surrey's tenacity and her skills as a translator and researcher.[6]

By 1930, at the age of 56, Nancy Miller Surrey's career as a historian had come to an end. In May a federal census enumerator interviewed her and Frank at the same Manhattan apartment they occupied a decade previous. While Frank (to whom she had dedicated *Commerce*) still taught high school, Nancy now listed her occupation as farm manager. As the Great Depression settled over the country, she returned to her agrarian roots, brushed off skills gained at the University of Chicago, and commuted to the outskirts of New York City (maybe to Long Island) to apply modern methods of truck farming. According to historian Carl J. Ekberg, the Miller Surreys resided for a time in Cedartown, rural northwest Georgia, where Nancy worked as a "dairy and scientific farmer," perhaps as participants in one of the New Deal relief programs of the mid-1930s. If so, they did not stay long in the South and had returned by 1941 to New York City, where Nancy died on May 16 at the age of 67.[7]

Nancy Miller Surrey's major work, *The Commerce of Louisiana during the French Régime, 1699–1763,* remains an essential reference on French colonial America ninety years after its original publication. Few historical texts remain relevant nearly a century afterward, but *Commerce* continues to deserve a place on the bookshelves of discerning readers for several reasons.

First, Miller Surrey relied almost entirely on primary

sources, most of which remain unpublished to this day. For modern-day students and historians, *Commerce* still serves as an authoritative introduction to the principal archival documentation of French colonial Louisiana. Second, Miller Surrey was a skillful translator. For *Commerce* she extracted the gist of literally thousands of manuscript pages by deciphering hundreds of often difficult handwriting styles, puzzling over the meanings of ancient texts obscured by faded inks or decayed paper or insect damage, parsing reams of misspelled or ungrammatical or just plain bad French, and interpreting it all in English for the benefit of American readers. And, equally important as the other two reasons, Miller Surrey wrote *Commerce* in simple, clear, elegant English, as accessible to modern readers as it was to her contemporaries.

Commerce begins with a brief overview of colonial Louisiana's geography (natural, political, and administrative), followed by a lengthy discussion of the waterways and the boats and ships upon which the colonists relied for transport and communication. Miller Surrey's analysis of French Louisiana's formal economic organization appears in chapters VII-XI, which remains the most succinct description of this complex topic and the most innovative portion of her book. In 50 pages she explains the fiscal structure of a colony chronically short of specie, lacking valuable export commodities and investment capital, intermittently prohibited from trading with neighboring British and Spanish colonies, excluded from the lucrative beaver trade by Canadian monopoly, and mismanaged on several occasions by corrupt public officials. Credit, consisting principally of bills of exchange drawn on the perpetually overextended colonial treasury, kept Louisiana afloat through the numerous wars and other crises of the colony's 64-year existence.

Miller Surrey devotes the rest of her book, another 300 pages, to domestic trade and to the various commercial networks linking Louisiana to France; the Illinois country; New France (Canada); the French West Indies; the Spanish colonies of Mexico, New Mexico, Texas, Florida, and Cuba; and neighboring English colonies. At her most analytical, Miller Surrey offers many insights on the privileges, gratuities, and monopolies exercised by French merchants in their highly profitable transactions with colonial officials. These chapters are particularly rich in detail about the agricultural commodities, forest products, and peltries that constituted the bulk of exports, and the imported foodstuffs and munitions, cloth, liquor and other manufactured goods consumed by the colonists and the Indians who came to depend on trade with the French. In fact, every chapter of *Commerce* contains abundant references to material culture, which explains the book's continuing appeal to folklorists, archaeologists, living history reenactors, and others readers concerned with the artifacts of French Louisiana.

In *Commerce,* Miller Surrey carefully notes those rare but highly suggestive instances when official records documented illicit trade, accomplished particularly by smuggling contraband aboard royal supply ships to evade customs duties and by the diversion of goods from the royal storehouses to private trade. Modern historians and archaeologists are just beginning to realize what Miller Surrey discovered so many decades ago—the critically important role of illicit trade in the economy of French Louisiana.[8]

Commerce undeniably remains a valuable work of reference and a source of ideas for future research. But every book is a product of its time. Over those many years since 1916 scholars have busily pursued numerous leads pioneered by Miller Surrey; in some cases their work now supercedes hers. At times her language is dated (particularly her use of the term "savage," following the French colonists' usage of *sauvage,* "wild," for "Indian"). In other instances, we know the precocious Nancy Miller Surrey committed the occasional error (usually by following errors in her colonial sources).[9] Those rare failings aside, how have historians and other scholars responded to and built upon her seminal book?

Initial reviews in professional and popular historical journals were uniformly positive, complementing Miller Surrey's original archival research and readable style. One reviewer chastised her for the lack of an index. Another, writing for *The Nation,* a popular journal distributed by the *New York Evening Post,* thought the book "admirable," but wondered whether "an entire chapter devoted to the subject of Boats . . . [is] really more than the reader is likely to have any use for."[10] However, her peers, the small cadre of French colonial scholars, accepted her work as authoritative and comprehensive. The detail she lavished on Boats and other topics made her book immediately valuable as a reference, and largely explains its continuing usefulness today. Rather than developing the themes she explored, most of Miller Surrey's contemporaries instead invested their energies in other aspects of French regime history. Preparing English translations of French documents became very popular. For instance, beginning in 1918, Henry P. Dart published a calendar of Superior Council proceedings in quarterly installments for many years in *The Louisiana Historical Quarterly.* Miller Surrey frequently cited the minutes of Superior Council meetings, which document policy and judicial decisions of the governor, *ordonnateur,* and other colonial leaders. In Mississippi, Dunbar Rowland (who had been instrumental in initiating the Paris archives calendar project that had supported Miller Surrey during her dissertation research) collaborated with Albert Godfrey Sanders between 1927 and 1932 to translate and publish three volumes of French colonial records relating to his state.[11]

Apart from these and other translation projects, a new generation of scholars began to examine the colonial histories of specific French communities, often with a particular emphasis on economics. At The University of Alabama Daniel Thomas submitted a thesis in 1929 on Fort Toulouse, a French military and trading outpost in the Creek Indian nation. Natalia Belting studied the Illinois country, breadbasket of lower Louisiana, for her path-breaking dissertation, *Kaskaskia Under the French Regime,* published in 1948. Both authors emulated Miller Surrey by detailing the material world of the colonists and considering the commercial role of their respective settlements, in addition to the military and political themes then standard fare for American historians. In Canada, Alice Jean Lunn employed a similar approach to investigate the economics of eighteenth-century New France for her 1942 dissertation at McGill University.[12]

Until recently, French scholars have shown little interest in the Louisiana colony, with the singular exception of Marcel Giraud, who set about systematically writing a narrative history of that overlooked overseas possession of the *ancien régime.* For forty years, beginning in the 1950s, Giraud methodically mined the French archives as no one had done since Miller Surrey. His slower pace enabled him to detect errors in earlier works, such as her mistaken belief that Antoine Crozat's monopoly had been unprofitable. (She was misled by Crozat's own complaints, preserved in the Paris archives.) Giraud never finished his monumental task, completing five volumes reaching only to 1731 before his death at the age of 93. Furthermore, Giraud wrote political history; he was not a practitioner of the Annales School, which Miller Surrey, with her more eclectic interests, somewhat anticipated. However, Giraud's epic project did inspire French archivists to issue for American and French researchers two guides to the official correspondence between the king's ministers and various officials in colonial Louisiana.[13]

In 1968 AMS Press reprinted *Commerce* in facsimile (once

again without an index). The reappearance of Miller Surrey's masterpiece, more than a half century after its original publication, signaled renewed interest in French colonial Louisiana among American readers. Translation projects, which had fallen out of fashion during the Great Depression, underwent a revival. In 1975 Polyanthos Press published a calendar of Governor Vaudreuil's papers, which had been captured by a British warship during the Seven Years' War and eventually found their way to the Huntington Library in San Marino, California. Two years later Margaret Kimball Brown and Lawrie Cena Dean published the Kaskaskia notarial records in translation, an invaluable reference to the appearance and social structure of a French colonial village in the Illinois country. In the mid-1980s Patricia Galloway brought to completion two more volumes of colonial records begun fifty years earlier by Dunbar Rowland and A. G. Sanders.[14]

Other scholars began to explore realms of commercial history hardly touched since Miller Surrey's day. Louise Dechêne's innovative study of Montreal merchants placed those entrepreneurs at the heart of French trade ties to interior Indian tribes of the *Pays d'en Haut.* Dale Miquelon and John G. Clark's volumes on the merchants of Rouen and La Rochelle showed how research in the archives of the French Atlantic ports could illuminate aspects of colonial commerce not revealed in state archives of the metropole. Since neither considered Louisiana in any detail, who knows what finds await the curious researcher there and in St. Lo, Nantes, Bordeaux, Marseilles, and other locations? Due to the widespread availability of microfilm reprint editions and the increasing number of classic studies in digital form accessible on the Internet, modern scholars can also refer more easily than did Miller Surrey to rare eighteenth-century French publications, such as Jacques Savary des Bruslons' invaluable summary of French commerce published in 1713.[15]

Archaeologists have only seriously explored within the last

thirty years the subterranean evidence of Louisiana's colonial commerce. Due to vagaries of preservation in the soil, important categories of material culture such as cloth and foodstuffs are poorly represented in the archaeological record. In some regards, though, excavated artifacts provide less ambiguity on the variety and quality of materials imported to the colony than do the written records consulted so long ago by Nancy Miller Surrey. These two very different sources of data complement each other for a fuller, more accurate view of colonial life. Analysis of trade goods found at town sites of the Tunica and Creek Indians, for example, reveal the changes occurring in Native American cultures through contact with the French. Likewise, investigations of the ruins of Cahokia and Fort de Chartres in the Illinois country and Mobile, Port Dauphin, and New Orleans in the south are beginning to answer questions on adaptations and accommodations made by the French in their efforts to cope with the challenges posed by their new homeland. A recent dissertation by Shannon Lee Dawdy, "La Ville Sauvage: 'Enlightened' Colonialism and Creole Improvisation in New Orleans, 1699–1769," demonstrates how the melding of written and artifactual evidence offers an exciting new approach to the history of French colonial Louisiana.[16]

Great strides have also been made recently in historical studies of the Indians who populated the lands claimed by the French as *La Louisiane.* Despite their modern reputation for skillfully coexisting with the native peoples of the Americas, the French fielded their share of inept administrators who mistreated and antagonized the Indians upon whom the colony depended for military and commercial alliances. The successes and failures of French-Indian contacts at a personal level have been brilliantly explored by Richard White in his influential volume *The Middle Ground* and by Daniel Usner in *Indians, Settlers, and Slaves in a Frontier Exchange Economy.*

Arnaud Balvay has lately focused inquiry on the critical relations between Indians and soldiers of the colonial garrisons, the *troupes de la Marine,* in his Sorbonne dissertation "*L'épée et la plume.*" [17]

Similarly our understanding of Africans in French Louisiana has been revolutionized in recent years by two books, Gwendolyn Midlo Hall's *Africans in Colonial Louisiana* and Ira Berlin's *Many Thousands Gone.* They argue compellingly that enslaved Africans developed a unique creole culture in Louisiana that endured until the social disruptions accompanying transfer of the region to the United States and the resumption of slave imports from the southern states. Historians have also begun to consider the new social order created by colonists. Morris Arnold's books on colonial Arkansas, Carl Ekberg's on the Illinois country, and Dawdy's dissertation on New Orleans document efforts by colonists to establish identities distinct from that of continental France. In *Chasing Empire across the Sea,* Kenneth Banks has dissected the elaborate system of communication developed to maintain ministerial contact with (and, ostensibly, control over) these remote colonial outposts.[18] Nancy Miller Surrey would perhaps be amazed at the creative directions taken by historians of French régime Louisiana. But more likely she would be intrigued by the research findings of these kindred spirits. I hope she would also take justifiable pride in the foundational role of her own work, which has contributed so directly to our current state of knowledge.

This edition of Nancy Miller Surrey's *The Commerce of Louisiana during the French Régime, 1699–1763* reproduces the 1916 edition, with the addition of a new index. Readers may notice discrepancies in spelling between Miller Surrey's text and some index entries. Most result from Miller Surrey's reliance on the colonial documents, which contain many misspellings. For instance, she wrote "Fort St. Louis de la Mobile" (p. 70), instead of the correct "Fort Louis de la Mobile," because that error occurs in the official correspondence. Many French names used in her book have since become standardized in American historical writings, something that was not the case in her day, nor in colonial times, when individuals might change the spelling of their own names at will. However, most entries direct readers to the diverse items exchanged by merchants engaged in commerce in French Louisiana. I hope this index eases modern readers' explorations of Nancy Miller Surrey's pioneering scholarship.

—Gregory A. Waselkov

Notes to the Introduction

1. For instance, Francis Parkman, *The Conspiracy of Pontiac and the Indian War after the Conquest of Canada* (Boston, MA: Charles C. Little and James Brown, 1851); *Pioneers of France in the New World* (Boston, MA: Little, Brown & Co., 1865); *The Jesuits in North America in the Seventeenth Century* (Boston, MA: Little, Brown & Co., 1867; *The Discovery of the Great West* (Boston, MA: Little, Brown & Co., 1869).

2. Frederick Jackson Turner, The Significance of the Frontier in American History, in *Annual Report of the American Historical Association for the Year 1893,* pp. 199–227 (Washington, D.C.: Government Printing Office, 1894).

3. Carl J. Ekberg, Foreword to *The Commerce of Louisiana during the French Régime, 1699–1763,* facsimile reprint edition (Ville Platte, LA: Provincial Press, 2001), v. Date of birth from Graduate Department admissions application forms, September 24, 1907, and September 29, 1908, Archives and Records Management Services, University of Wisconsin–Madison (ARMS, UWM). On Franklin Surrey, Wisconsin Summer Session admissions form, ARMS, UWM. N. M. Miller Surrey, Juvenile Delinquency, *The American Political Science Review* 2 (4 November 1908), 574–575. He also attended Harvard for a time; *Harvard*

University Directory (Boston, MA: Harvard Alumni Association, 1913). Nancy Maria Miller Surrey, History of Education in the Old Northwest to 1800 (unpublished M.A. thesis, Department of History, University of Wisconsin, 1909). A "Vita" appended to a 1968 reprint of *Commerce* noted that she took courses and seminars from J. Franklin Jameson (at the University of Chicago), F. J. Turner and C. R. Fish (at the University of Wisconsin), and professors Shepherd, Dunning, Giddings, Robinson, and Osgood (at Columbia University). See N. M. Miller Surrey, *The Commerce of Louisiana during the French Régime, 1699–1763* (New York: AMS Press, 1968), 477. A book notice published in 1917 states that her dissertation research began in 1909; Notes, *The Nation* 104 (2704, 26 April 1917), 497.

Sue Moore assisted with historical research on Nancy Miller Surrey's personal history. I am grateful for her generous help, and for research kindly performed by Helene Androski (Ask Memorial), David Null (University Archivist), and Phyllis Holman Weisbard (Women's Studies Librarian), all with the University of Wisconsin–Madison.

4. William R. Shepherd, *Guide to the Materials for the History of the United States in Spanish Archives* (Washington, D.C.: Carnegie Institution of Washington, 1907). Also see his related major works, "The Spanish Archives and their Importance for the History of the U.S.," in *Annual Report of the American Historical Association for 1903* (Washington, D.C.: Government Printing Office, 1904), 145–183; *Latin America* (New York: Henry Holt & Co., 1914); *Hispanic Nations of the World, a Chronicle of Our Southern Neighbors* (New Haven, CT: Yale University Press, 1919).

5. N. M. Miller Surrey, "History of the Calendar of Documents in the Archives of Paris Relating to the Mississippi Valley," *The Louisiana Historical Quarterly* 7 (4 October 1924), 551–563. In this article a self-effacing Miller Surrey never spells out her own role in the compilation and editing of the *Calendar,* which clearly was substantial. N. M. Miller Surrey, "The History of Commerce and Industry in Louisiana during the French Régime" (unpublished Ph.D. dissertation, Department of History, Columbia University, 1914); Eleventh List of Doctoral Dissertations in Political Economy in Progress in American Universities and Colleges, *The American Economic Review* 4 (2 June 1914), 525–526. N. M. Miller Surrey, *The Commerce of Louisiana during the French Régime, 1699–1763,* Studies in History, Economics and Public Law 71 (1), whole

number 167 (New York: Columbia University, 1916), 7; William Robert Shepherd, *History of Proprietary Government in Pennsylvania,* Studies in History, Economics and Public Law 6, whole number 16 (New York: Columbia University, 1896).

6. N. M. Miller Surrey, Review of *French Colonial Question, 1789–1791,* by Mitchell B. Garrett, in *The Journal of American History* 4 (2 September 1917), 231–232; and N. M. Miller Surrey, Review of *Spanish and French Rivalries in the Gulf Region of the United States,* by William Edward Dunn, in *The American Historical Review* 23 (1 October 1917), 182–183. *University of Wisconsin Alumni Directory, 1849–1919* (Madison: University of Wisconsin, 1921), 330; Meeting of the American Historical Association at St. Louis, *The American Historical Review* 27 (3, April 1922), 419; N. M. Miller Surrey (Mrs. F. M. Surrey), History of the Calendar of Documents, 558-563, and *Calendar of Manuscripts in Paris Archives and Libraries Relating to the History of the Mississippi Valley to 1803,* two vols. (Washington, D.C.: Department of Historical Research, Carnegie Institution of Washington, 1926–1928). Also see her article, "The Development of Industries in Louisiana During the French Regime, 1673–1763," *The Mississippi Valley Historical Review* 9 (3 December 1922), 227–235. The *Calendar* project was directed by J. Franklin Jameson, director of the Department of Historical Research at the Carnegie, and Waldo G. Leland, an independent researcher working in the Paris archives. An inquiry to the Carnegie Institution of Washington uncovered no records of Nancy Miller Surrey's employment or involvement there in the *Calendar* project.

For later published guides to the French archives that incorporate sources identified by Miller Surrey and the other staff of the *Calendar* project, see Waldo G. Leland, *Guide to Materials for American History in the Libraries and Archives of Paris,* vol. 1, *Libraries* (Washington, D.C.: Carnegie Institution of Washington, 1932), and Waldo G. Leland, John J. Meng, and Abel Doysié, *Guide to Materials for American History in the Libraries and Archives of Paris,* vol. 2, *Archives of the Ministry of Foreign Affairs* (Washington, D.C.: Carnegie Institution of Washington, 1943). See "Historical News," *The American Historical Review* 32 (2 January 1927), 409, on the *Calendar,* which is "reproduced by the planograph rather than by type. . . . The edition is small; copies have been sent gratuitously to the libraries in which a manual is most likely to be of use."

7. 1930 United States Census, New York City, Manhattan Borough Schedule, Ward Pt. A W 21, Block H, House Number 593. Ekberg, Foreword, x, citing Jocelyn K. Wilk, Assistant Director, Columbia University Archives & Columbiana Library, New York. *Wisconsin Alumnus,* 92 (7 July 1941), 361. Franklin Miller Surrey's date and place of death have not been determined.

8. Gregory A. Waselkov, *Old Mobile Archaeology* (Tuscaloosa: The University of Alabama Press, 2006), 34, 47; James Pritchard, *In Search of Empire: The French in the Americas, 1670–1730* (Cambridge, UK: Cambridge University Press, 2004), 201–208. The final sentence of *Commerce* reads: "When the war ended in 1763, the illicit trade had not lost any of its significance."

9. On "sauvage," see John Francis McDermott, *A Glossary of Mississippi Valley French, 1673–1850,* Washington University Studies–New Series, Language and Literature 12 (St. Louis, MO: 1941), 136. Miller Surrey mistakenly thought Bienville established Fort Toulouse in 1714, instead of 1717, following an earlier incorrect secondary source on the matter (p. 343).

10. Reviews of *Commerce* in Irving B. Richman, *The American Historical Review* 22 (3 April 1917), 714–715; Notes, *The Nation* 104 (2704, April 26, 1917), 497; Isaac Lippincott, *The Journal of Political Economy* 25 (2 February 1917), 209–210; Grace King, *The Louisiana Historical Quarterly* 5 (1 January 1922).

11. Dunbar Rowland and Albert Godfrey Sanders, editors and translators, *Mississippi Provincial Archives, French Dominion, 1729–1740,* vol. 1 (Jackson: Mississippi Department of Archives and History, 1927); *Mississippi Provincial Archives, French Dominion, 1701–1729,* vol. 2 (Jackson: Mississippi Department of Archives and History, 1929); *Mississippi Provincial Archives, French Dominion, 1704–1743,* vol. 3 (Jackson: Mississippi Department of Archives and History, 1932).

12. Thomas revised his thesis for publication in 1960 in the *Alabama Historical Quarterly,* and that version has been reissued as Daniel H. Thomas, *Fort Toulouse: The French Outpost at the Alabamas on the Coosa,* with a new introduction by Gregory A. Waselkov (Tuscaloosa: The University of Alabama Press, 1989). Natalia Maree Belting, "Kaskaskia Under the French Regime," *Illinois Studies in Social Sciences* 29 (3, 1948). Alice Jean E. Lunn, "Economic Development in New France, 1713–1760" (unpublished Ph.D. dissertation, Department of History, McGill

University, 1942); *Développement économique de la Nouvelle France, 1713–1760,* translated by Brigitte Monel-Nish (Montreal, PQ: Les Presses de l'Université de Montréal, 1986).

13. Marcel Giraud, *Histoire de la Louisiane Française,* vol. 1, *Le Règne de Louis XIV* (1698–1715) (Paris: Presses Universitaires de France, 1953); *Histoire de la Louisiane Française,* vol. 2, *Années de Transition* (1715–1717) (Paris: Presses Universitaires de France, 1958); *Histoire de la Louisiane Française,* vol. 3, *L'époque de John Law* (1717–1720) (Paris: Presses Universitaires de France, 1966); *Histoire de la Louisiane Française,* vol. 4, *La Louisiane après le système de Law (1721–1723)* (Paris: Presses Universitaires de France, 1974); *A History of French Louisiana,* vol. 1, *The Reign of Louis XIV, 1698–1715,* translated by Joseph C. Lambert (Baton Rouge: Louisiana State University Press, 1974); *A History of French Louisiana,* vol. 2, *Years of Transition, 1715–1717,* translated by Brian Pearce (Baton Rouge: Louisiana State University Press, 1993); *A History of French Louisiana,* vol. 5, *The Company of the Indies, 1723–1731,* translated by Brian Pearce (Baton Rouge: Louisiana State University Press, 1991). See Henry Folmer, *Review of Histoire de la Louisiane Française,* vol. 2, *Années de Transition (1715–1717),* by Marcel Giraud, in *The American Historical Review* 64 (1 October 1958), 188. Marie-Antoinette Menier, Étienne Taillemite, and Gilberte de Forges, *Correspondance à l'arrivée en provenance de la Louisiane,* vol. 1 *(articles C13A 1 à 37),* (Paris, France: Archives Nationales, 1976), and vol. 2 *(articles C13A 38 à 54, C13B 1, C13C 1 à 5),* (Paris, France: Archives Nationales, 1983). One recent book by a French scholar (an example of the small but sustained interest in colonial Louisiana that exists today in France) revisits the feud between Governor Kerlérec and Ordonnateur Rochemore, documented at length by Miller Surrey. See Hervé Gourmelon, *Le chevalier de Kerlérec, 1704–1770: L'affaire de la Louisiane* (Spézet, France: Keltia Graphic, 2003).

14. Bill Barron, *The Vaudreuil Papers: A Calendar and Index of the Personal and Private Records of Pierre de Rigaud de Vaudreuil, Royal Governor of the French Province of Louisiana, 1743–1753* (New Orleans, LA: Polyanthos, 1975). Margaret Kimball Brown and Lawrie Cena Dean, translators and editors, *The Village of Chartres in Colonial Illinois, 1720–1765* (New Orleans, LA: Polyanthos, 1977). Rowland Dunbar, A. G. Sanders, and Patricia Kay Galloway, editors and translators, *Mississippi*

Provincial Archives, French Dominion, 1729–1748, vol. 4 (Baton Rouge: Louisiana State University Press, 1984); *Mississippi Provincial Archives, French Dominion, vol. 5, 1749–1763* (Baton Rouge: Louisiana State University Press, 1984).

15. Louise Dechêne, *Habitants et Marchands de Montréal au XVIIe siècle* (Paris, France: Les Éditions Plons, 1974); *Habitants and Merchants in Seventeenth-Century Montreal,* translated by Liana Vardi (Montreal, PQ: McGill-Queen's University Press, 1992). Dale Miquelon, *Dugard of Rouen: French Trade to Canada and the West Indies, 1729–1770* (Montreal, PQ: McGill-Queen's University Press, 1978). John G. Clark, *La Rochelle and the Atlantic Economy during the Eighteenth Century* (Baltimore, MD: Johns Hopkins University Press, 1981). Jacques Savary, *Le Parfait négociant ou instruction générale pour ce qui regarde le commerce des marchandises de France, et des pays estrangers, 7eme édition, par Jacques Savary des Bruslons,* two vols. (Paris: Michel Guignard et Claude Robustel, [1675] 1713).

16. Jeffrey P. Brain, "Tunica Treasure," *Papers of the Peabody Museum of Archaeology and Ethnology 71* (Cambridge, MA: Harvard University, 1979). John A. Walthall, editor, *French Colonial Archaeology: The Illinois Country and the Western Great Lakes* (Urbana: University of Illinois Press, 1991). John A. Walthall and Thomas E. Emerson, eds., *Calumet and Fleur-de-Lys: Archaeology of Indian and French Contact in the Midcontinent* (Washington, D.C.: Smithsonian Institution Press, 1992). Waselkov, *Old Mobile Archaeology.* Shannon Lee Dawdy, "La Ville Sauvage: 'Enlightened' Colonialism and Creole Improvisation in New Orleans, 1699–1769" (Ann Arbor: Ph.D. dissertation, Departments of Anthropology and History, University of Michigan, 2003).

17. Richard White, *The Middle Ground: Indians, Empires, and Republics in the Great Lakes Region, 1650–1815* (Cambridge, UK: Cambridge University Press, 1991). Daniel H. Usner, Jr., *Indians, Settlers, and Slaves in a Frontier Exchange Economy: The Lower Mississippi Valley before 1783* (Chapel Hill: University of North Carolina Press, 1992). Arnaud Balvay, "L'épée et la plume: Amérindiens et soldats des troupes de la Marine en Louisiane et au Pays d'en Haut (1683–1763)" (Paris: Ph.D. dissertation, département d'histoire, Université de Paris I—Panthéon-Sorbonne/Université Laval, 2004).

18. Gwendolyn Midlo Hall, *Africans in Colonial Louisiana: The De-*

velopment of Afro-Creole Culture in the Eighteenth Century (Baton Rouge: Louisiana State University Press, 1992). Ira Berlin, *Many Thousands Gone: The First Two Centuries of Slavery in North America* (Cambridge, MA: Belknap Press, 1998), 77–92, 195–210. Morris S. Arnold, *Colonial Arkansas, 1686–1804: A Social and Cultural History* (Fayetteville: University of Arkansas Press, 1991). Carl J. Ekberg, *French Roots in the Illinois Country: The Mississippi Frontier in Colonial Times* (Urbana: University of Illinois Press, 1998). Kenneth Banks, *Chasing Empire across the Sea: Communications and the State in the French Atlantic, 1713–1763* (Montreal, PQ: McGill-Queen's University Press, 2002). Dawdy, *La Ville Sauvage.*

CHAPTER I

Introduction

THE province of Louisiana under French rule included, roughly speaking, the whole of the valleys of the Mississippi and Mobile rivers. To the northeast of this area lay the colony of New France where the chief occupation of the people was the fur trade. Every one from the governor down to the humblest inhabitant was interested directly or indirectly in the expansion of this trade, a fact that led to explorations in search of new centers for its development.

Governor Frontenac, acting upon the advice of the intendant, an experienced fur trader, appointed Joliet, a tactful, intelligent man, a native of Quebec who had mastered more than one of the numerous Indian languages, to take up the work of pushing forward exploration and the fur trade. With Father Marquette and a few other companions, Joliet, May 17, 1673, left Michilimackinac for the west, and June 17 of the same year reached the Mississippi at the mouth of the Wisconsin river. They entered and passed down that river to latitude 33° 40′ and returned to the starting place by way of the Illinois river and Lake Michigan, thereby making known to the French much of the Mississippi and all of the Illinois river.[1]

The reports of these men concerning the great fertility of the soil, the mildness of the climate, the abundance of

[1] *The Jesuit Relations and Allied Documents,* vol. lix, pp. 89-107, 159.

game of all kinds, and the docility of the Illinois Indians gave considerable stimulus to French interest in the Mississippi valley. Father Marquette made a second voyage to the Illinois region for the purpose of establishing a mission there. This undertaking was crowned with success in 1675 by the founding on the upper Illinois river among the Kaskaskia Indians of a mission which he named the Immaculate Conception.[1] Two years later Allouez took charge of the mission and from that time onward missionary work was carried on regularly among the Illinois Indians.[2]

The traders, too, were soon again in the Illinois country. On May 12, 1678, La Salle received a patent from the king to carry on trade and exploration in the west. He started for the territory assigned him the next year, but found so many obstacles to be overcome that it was January, 1680, before he reached the Illinois. On arriving at Lake Peoria he began the construction of a fort which he called Crèvecoeur, and from here as a starting point he proposed to explore the Mississippi above and below the mouth of the Illinois river.

Hennepin was placed in charge of the exploration of the upper Mississippi. Leaving Fort Crèvecoeur February 29, 1680, he passed down the Illinois and up the Mississippi to where the river is obstructed by falls. These he named in honor of Saint Anthony of Padua, passed around them and continued his exploration on up the river to the source in Lake Issati (*sic*), sixty leagues to the west of Lake Superior.[3]

[1] *The Jesuit Relations and Allied Documents*, vol. lix, pp. 185-191, 235.

[2] *Ibid.*, vol. lx, pp. 163-167; vol. lxv, p. 69.

[3] Margry, *Découvertes et Établissements des Français dans l'Ouest et dans le Sud de l'Amérique Septentrionale*, vol. i, pp. 477-481.

Soon after the departure of Hennepin from Crèvecoeur, La Salle set out overland for Fort Frontenac and was not at his Illinois station again until December, 1681. In a short time he left this post and passed on down the Illinois in order to begin exploring the lower Mississippi. This he found full of floating ice and he was forced to delay his descent until navigation was safe. On April 9, 1682 he reached the mouth of the river, planted a cross, took possession of the valley in the name of the king of France and named the country Louisiana. After this formality La Salle started on the return voyage and reached the Illinois villages July 15, 1682. Fort Crèvecoeur, during his absence, had been entirely destroyed. He left eight of his men there and with the remainder went by land to Lake Michigan where he met Tonty, whom he sent with nine men to join those he had at Crèvecoeur. La Salle went on to Michilimackinac and, as soon as it was possible for him to make the journey, joined his men at Lake Peoria. Under his guidance a new fort was constructed on a rocky prominence well guarded by nature and now called Starved Rock, not far from the present city of Utica, Illinois. This post he named Fort St. Louis. Leaving it under the command of Tonty, he went to Quebec, reaching that place November 13, 1683, and early the next year set sail for France, in order to get permission to return by way of the Gulf of Mexico to plant a colony on the lower Mississippi.[1]

La Salle secured the consent and aid of the crown for the undertaking and in February, 1685, was at Matagorda Bay, Texas, near which, on the Garcitas river, he built a fort that he named "Fort of St. Louis Bay."

[1] Margry, *op. cit.*, vol. i, pp. 502, 519-520, 549-570.

Hardships and insubordination followed. On March 9, 1687, while on a journey in search of the Mississippi, La Salle was assassinated by one of his own men.[1] This act ended a colonizing enterprise that had added nothing to the settlement and very little to the exploration of the Mississippi valley.

After La Salle's efforts in the Illinois country in 1682, French military and commercial occupation was not again discontinued. La Barre, who succeeded Frontenac as governor of New France, however, hated La Salle and tried hard to destroy the latter's work in the Illinois country; but fortunately his efforts met with small success.[2] Until after the migration of the Kaskaskia Indians to the region between the Kaskaskia and Mississippi rivers in the autumn of 1700, in order to escape the onslaughts of the Iroquois and Fox Indians, as well as to be in closer touch with the new French settlement on the Gulf coast, Tonty and La Forest were established at Fort St. Louis on the upper Illinois river.[3]

In 1698 the crown again took up the work of colonizing the lower Mississippi valley, and sent out an expedition under Iberville, a native of New France. In the early part of the next year he reached the Gulf of Mexico, selected a location on Biloxi Bay and built on the site a post which he named Biloxi.[4] The new settlement had a hard struggle to keep itself alive. It was in an unhealthy situation surrounded by a morass, and was

[1] Margry, *op. cit.*, vol. iii, pp. 106-120, 318-335; *The Mississippi Valley Historical Review*, vol. ii, pp. 165-182.

[2] Parkman, *Count Frontenac and New France under Louis XIV*, vol. i, pp. 76-92.

[3] *Jes. Rel.*, vol. lxv, p. 101.

[4] La Harpe, *Journal Historique de l'Établissement des Français à la Louisiane*, pp. 4-7; Margry, vol. iv, pp. 213-296.

not on a waterway that led to the interior of the country. Consequently, in 1702, Iberville gave orders for the foundation of a new settlement on the west side of the Mobile river, about 18 leagues from the sea. Here a fort was built and named "Fort St. Louis de la Mobile." This location Iberville thought superior to that of Biloxi, since it brought the French into much easier communication with the Indians of the Mobile valley, with the French in the Illinois country and with the Spanish of Pensacola. Moreover he claimed for the new settlement a good harbor which could be entered easily and was naturally defended.[1]

It was soon discovered that the site for the new post was not well chosen. The land on which it was located was low and subjected to inundations, a circumstance which in 1711 led to the removal of the settlement to the mouth of the Mobile river, eight leagues nearer the sea. Around this fort there grew up a village called Mobile which early became the capital of the province.[2] The new post was not far enough inland to combat successfully English aggression; therefore, in 1714, For Toulouse was built on the upper waters of the Alabama river.[3] To the same end, in 1736, Fort Tombecbée was erected on the river of the same name, not far from the Choctaw.[4] During the French period these two posts mark the frontier of settlement in this region.

The discovery of an English vessel a short distance up the Mississippi river, in 1700, caused the French to construct a fort on the lower waters of that river. A site

[1] *Jes. Rel.*, vol. lxv, p. 179; Margry, vol. iv, pp. 533-534, 603; Le Page du Pratz, *Histoire de la Louisiane*, vol. i, pp. 268-269; La Harpe, p. 38.

[2] Margry, vol. v, pp. 481, 482, 484; La Harpe, pp. 107-108.

[3] *Historical Collections of Louisiana and Florida*, vol. i, p. 128.

[4] Le Page du Pratz, vol. ii, p. 255.

on the south side was selected and a rough fort, called Fort Mississippi, was built eighteen leagues from the mouth. This post, which was not abandoned until 1705, had five or six houses for the soldiers and a small but neat house for the commandant, Bienville.[1]

War at home occupied too much of the attention of France for the proper development of its infant colony of Louisiana. Consequently in 1712, in return for exclusive rights of trade in the province, Antoine Crozat, an energetic and successful French merchant, took over the work. A desire on his part to reap immediate and substantial returns from the smallest possible investment of capital doomed the venture to financial failure. In 1717 he gave the province back to the crown, which at once granted it to the Company of the West with substantially the same privileges as had been given to Crozat. Under the new patent, however, Louisiana was made to include the Illinois country as well.

The interest of the Company of the West in establishing trade with the Spanish of New Mexico caused a movement of settlement westward. In 1717 New Biloxi was founded on the Gulf coast,[2] and a site was selected for a new village, to be named New Orleans. Here a settlement was begun in 1718,[3] which later replaced Mobile as the capital of the colony, and in 1723 had a few log cabins along the river front "put up without order."[4]

Louisiana, in 1721, was divided into nine military dis-

[1] *Jes. Rel.*, vol. lxv, p. 161; La Harpe, p. 19.

[2] Margry, vol. v, p. 548.

[3] *Ibid.*, vol. v, p. 549; La Harpe, p. 142.

[4] *Records of the American Catholic Historical Society of Philadelphia*, vol. x, p. 202.

tricts.[1] The growth of settlement in three of those districts, Mobile, Biloxi and Alibamon, has already been described. In the district of New Orleans, in 1722, Fort Balise was built for the purpose of commanding the mouth of the Mississippi, and from there to within ten leagues of New Orleans the land was low, marshy and unfit for occupation. At that distance below the village, however, settlements began to appear separated from each other by only a few miles.[2] The same condition existed above New Orleans. At ten leagues above the capital, extending for five or six leagues along the west bank of the Mississippi, were three villages of German settlers.[3] Before the end of the French control of Louisiana, New Orleans grew to be a comparatively large town, surrounded on all sides by farms and plantations.[4] In 1721, furthermore, there was a fort (St. Pierre) in the Yazoo district on the river of the same name. Not many settlers took up land near it, because of Indian hostility.[5]

Fort Rosalie, ninety-five leagues up the Mississippi river from New Orleans, was the center of the Natchez district. This fort, begun in 1700 and finished in 1716, was splendidly located on high fertile ground which, before the Indian massacre, was considered one of the best locations on the lower Mississippi. After the Natchez revolt, settlement in this region grew slowly notwithstanding the situation was most desirable.[6] Some fifty leagues below Fort Rosalie there was a cluster of fertile

[1] La Harpe, p. 296.

[2] *Jes. Rel.*, vol. lxix, p. 209; *Hist. Coll. La.*, pt. iii, p. 181.

[3] *Jes. Rel.*, vol. lxix, p. 215. [4] *Ibid.*, pp. 211, 215.

[5] La Harpe, pp. 310, 330.

[6] Le Page du Pratz, vol. iii, p. 230; Margry, vol. v, pp. 573-574; *Hist. Coll. La.*, pt. iii, p. 21.

farms stretching out for some distance along the west bank of the river, called Pointe Coupée.[1]

North of the Natchez lay the Arkansas district with a fort, begun by Tonty in 1685, near the mouth of the Arkansas river. From here to the Illinois country, one hundred and fifty leagues, there was not a single permanent French settlement along this part of the Mississippi,[2] though the forts of St. Francis (1739) thirty leagues above the Arkansas, St. Martin (1738) a little farther up the river on an island of the same name, l'Assomption (1739) at the mouth of the Margot river (Wolf river), and Prud'homme (1719) forty leagues above, had been established, and had survived for short periods of time.[3]

The exploration of the country to the west of the Mississippi was begun in 1700, when Bienville and St. Denis made a voyage of discovery up the Red river. Later they conducted further explorations in this part of Louisiana, and in time St. Denis, through Texas, reached New Mexico. La Harpe, Du Tisné, Vérendrye and others extended this work as far as the Rocky Mountains. In 1717 Fort Natchitoches, seventy leagues above the mouth of the Red river, was erected, and as was the case at the other French posts, a village slowly grew up around it. Natchitoches continued to the end of the French régime to be the only French settlement in this part of Louisiana.[4]

[1] *Jes. Rel.*, vol. lxix, p. 215.

[2] *Ibid.*, p. 217.

[3] *Journal de la Guerre du Micissippi contre les Chicachas, en 1739 et finie en 1740, etc.*, pp. 37-40; Le Page du Pratz, vol. ii, p. 291; La Harpe, p. 305; Jefferys, *The Natural and Civil History of the French Dominions in North and South America*, pt. 1, p. 143; Margry, vol. v, p. 403; *Delisle's Map*, 1718; Collot, *A Journey in North America*, vol. ii, p. 28.

[4] Margry, vol. vi, pp. 193-305, 309-315, 583-612; La Harpe, pp. 30, 130-131.

The Illinois country, as has been shown, was quite well known to the people of New France before the beginning of colonization on the lower Mississippi. There were no permanent settlements made until 1700, when both Cahokia and Kaskaskia were begun.[1] Later settlements were made at Fort Chartres (1720), St. Anne (1719), St. Philippe (1726), and Prairie du Rocher (1722). Across the Mississippi river, one mile from its western bank, southwest from Kaskaskia, were St. Geneviève (1732), and near Cahokia, Prairie du Pont (1760).[2]

These settlements were surrounded by an outer ring of frontier posts. At Lake Peoria on the north there had been a few settlers almost continuously since the time of La Salle. They cultivated the soil to some extent, but for the most part were interested in the Indian trade.[3] To the south of the settlements was Fort Massac (1710 or 1711), a Jesuit mission and fortified trading post. This post was situated upon the Ohio, about forty miles from its mouth, and was placed there to protect the French from the marauding Cherokee.[4] As early as 1714 Charville, a trader, sent out by Crozat's agents on the Gulf, went among the Indians on the Cumberland river and established a trading post on the

[1] *Jes. Rel.*, vol. lxv, pp. 101, 263, 264; vol. lxiv, p. 278; *Early Voyages Up and Down the Mississippi*, pp. 60-65.

[2] *Jes. Rel.*, vol. lxv, pp. 101-105; vol. lxix, p. 221; La Harpe, p. 243; *Archives Nationales, Colonies, Série* C^{13}, vol. xxxv, fol. 126; *Early Western Travels*, vol. iv, p. 266; *Transactions of the Illinois State Historical Society*, No. 8, p. 105; No. 10, pp. 58-61.

[3] *A. N., C., Sér.* C^{13}, vol. xxix, fol. 85; *Jes. Rel.*, vol. lxiv, p. 161, note 29; Blanchard, *History of Illinois*, p. 55.

[4] *Trans. Ill. Hist. Soc.*, No. 8, 1903, pp. 38-64; *Chicago Historical Society Collections*, vol. iii, p. 55.

site of the present city of Nashville.[1] In 1756 a new fort was begun at the mouth of Cherokee river and was named l'Ascension (Ft. Massac), but the work was stopped owing to the lack of funds.[2] Fort Ouiatanon on the upper Wabash marked the frontier on the east. Here a fort was built (1719 or 1720) to give protection to the French from the assaults of the Iroquois.[3] Later it was found necessary to build Fort Vincennes (1733 or 1734) on the lower Wabash in order to keep out the English traders.[4]

In 1721 the Spanish from New Mexico and their Indian allies threatened the French settlements from the west. This danger, together with the news that the Spanish were about to begin the erection of a fort upon the Kansas river, caused the authorities of Louisiana to send an order to the Illinois country to stop this aggression. Accordingly Fort Orleans (1724) was constructed not far from the mouth of the Grand river. This frontier post was established with a double purpose: to check the advance of the Spaniards, if need be, though preferably to build up a trade with them; and secondly for the conclusion of alliances and the establishment of trade with the neighboring Indians. Fort Orleans, however, did not prosper, and it was soon suggested that the garrison be reduced to eight men.[5]

[1] Ramsey, *The Annals of Tennessee*, p. 45; Winsor, *The Mississippi Basin*, p. 87.

[2] Villiers du Terrage, *Les Dernières Années de la Louisiane Française*, p. 79.

[3] *Documents Relating to the Colonial History of the State of New York*, vol. ix, p. 894; *Indiana Historical Society Publications*, vol. ii, p. 329.

[4] *A. N., C., Sér.* C^{13}, vol. xviii, fols. 70-88; *Sér.* F^{3}, vol. xxiv, fol. 241.

[5] *Ibid., Sér.* C^{13}, vol. xi, fols. 366-368; Margry, vol. vi, p. 452; Le Page du Pratz, vol. iii, p. 142.

The Company of the West, in 1719, gave way to the Company of the Indies. This corporation continued in control of the province of Louisiana until 1731, when it relinquished its powers to the crown. Bienville, being the most prominent as well as the most influential man in Louisiana, soon became governor. Struggles with the other colonial officials finally led to Bienville's recall in 1742 and the naming of Vaudreuil, a native of New France, as governor of Louisiana in his place. The new governor had tact, good judgment and much dignity, a combination which enabled him to govern the province with as little friction, perhaps, as was possible, and to leave it for a higher colonial post in 1752.

Governor Kerlérec, who succeeded Vaudreuil, was a man of ability and integrity, but from the start he was handicapped in his administration of the colony. He was forced to begin his work after the close of one, and at the beginning of another and much longer, war. He had the misfortune to be obliged to work with several "ordonnateurs," or finance officers, and finally with one whom he could neither direct nor restrain. Against great odds he managed to give the colony as good a government as could reasonably be expected under the circumstances, and was recalled only when Louisiana passed, in 1763, under Spanish and English control.

CHAPTER II

WATERWAYS

THE huge valley lying between the Great Lakes on the north, the Gulf of Mexico on the south, the Appalachian range on the east, and the Rockies on the west, is drained by the Mobile and Mississippi river systems, and a few single rivers flowing directly or undirectly into the Gulf of Mexico. For the smaller boats of the time these rivers furnished highways to almost every part of the region. Nine of the chief rivers of the Mississippi system, together with the principal rivers of the Alabama network, afford sixteen thousand miles of navigable waterways. To this mileage, however, should be added that supplied by a large number of smaller rivers and streams used in making exploring and trading expeditions. The navigable rivers of the Mississippi valley, indeed, opened to the French "such a scene of inland navigation as cannot be paralleled in any other part of the world."[1]

Within the Mississippi valley there are various places where the headwaters of the two systems are not far apart. Such intervening stretches of land the French called "portages," or carrying places. From the Tombigbée branch of the Mobile system it is possible to pass over a portage of three miles to the Tennessee river, and by another branch of the same system and a similar carriage almost

[1] Colden, *The History of the Five Nations of Canada*, vol. ii, pp. 36-37.

directly to the lower Mississippi.[1] The hostility of the Chickasaw who were in control of the territory in which it was located rendered it impossible, however, for the French ever to make a free use of the former of these two connections.

Then, too, New Orleans through lake and stream had water communication with Mobile. At times when Lake Pontchartrain overflowed its banks it afforded an uninterrupted watercourse. At all other times, however, a carriage over the bars at the head of the lake was necessary.[2]

The waterways of Louisiana were rendered still more serviceable by the discovery of many convenient portages from one to another branch of the same river system. For example, a trader was able to pass from a branch of the Wisconsin river over short portages to the Rock and Illinois rivers, thus shortening the route to his place of destination.[3]

In order further to increase the utility of these natural highways, the French on the lower Mississippi constructed canals, either for the purpose of making a more direct route to the Gulf of Mexico, or of joining the Mississippi with the bayous at the rear of the settlements. These connections with the Mississippi were used for the transportation of lumber. In 1724 one large landholder across the river from New Orleans alone had between eight and ten miles of such canals.[4] For his own and

[1] Winsor, *The Westward Movement*, p. 522, map; *Transactions of the Alabama Historical Society*, vol. ii, p. 44.

[2] *A. N., C., Sér.* C^{13}, vol. ix, fol. 62; *A Topographical and Statistical Account of the Province of Louisiana*, p. 24.

[3] Colden, vol. ii, pp. 36-37; Parrish, *Historic Illinois, etc.*, p. 105.

[4] *Archives, Bibliothèque du Département des Colonies, Série* G^1, vol. 464; Hutchins, *An Historical, Narrative and Topographical Description of Louisiana and West Florida*, p. 415.

the use of the public as well, the entrepreneur of public works (*entrepreneur des travaux du roi*) established water connection between New Orleans and Barataria Bay. This canal, twenty-five feet wide and a little more than three leagues long, was finished in 1739 and in 1741 the colony was deriving considerable benefit from it through the exportation of lumber over the route.[1] As early as 1723 it was proposed to construct a canal between St. Jean Bay and Lake Pontchartrain.[2] The work was begun in 1728; but it was some years later before there was a direct waterway through canal, lake and stream between the capital and Mobile.[3]

The internal advantages of this network of waterways did not exceed, in any respect, its external possibilities. The Mississippi afforded close connections with the Spanish provinces on the west, and was in such proximity to the rivers of the Arctic region as to cause them also to be claimed by the French.[4] A number of the branches of the St. Lawrence system, too, took their rise near the source of the Mississippi, thereby affording to the French colonies in North America good highways for intercolonial intercourse.

The expedition of Joliet and Marquette resulted in the discovery and use of the Fox-Wisconsin portage which Marquette states was about "2700 paces" in length.[5] This distance, however, was variable; continuous water passage from one to the other was available during a period of freshets. In the dry season the portage was about a

[1] *A. N., C., Sér.* C^{13}, vol. xxiv, fols. 31-32; vol. xxv, fols. 193-194, 268-272; vol. xxvi, fols. 17.

[2] *Ibid.*, vol. vii, fol. 260.

[3] *Ibid.*, vol. xi, fols. 20, 122; vol. xiii, fols. 82-83.

[4] Margry, vol. vi, pp. 510-512.

[5] *Jes. Rel.*, vol. lix, p. 105.

mile and a half wide.[1] The shortness of the portage and the directness of the journey from New France through Michilimackinac to the Mississippi made this route attractive to the French traveler and trader.

By 1699, the very year that the first permanent settlement was made in Louisiana, the Fox-Wisconsin portage had become practically closed on account of the hostilities of the Fox Indians.[2] They made it impossible in fact to establish a military post along this route, and as a result the French were able to use the portage only during the short intervals of inter-tribal peace. At the same time the Fox-Dakota alliance closed the communication with the Mississippi by way of Michilimackinac, Lake Superior and the St. Croix portage.[3] Thereupon the French changed the course of their voyages and went from Michilimackinac to the Illinois by the waterway leading from the south end of Lake Michigan.

Here there was a choice of several routes: one by way of the two Calumet rivers, over a portage either to the Des Plaines, the north, or to the Kankakee, the south, branch of the Illinois river; another by the Chicago-Des Plaines route; a third by the St. Joseph river which of itself affords two waterways. Of the first two routes the second was the better known, and hence was more frequently used by the French. From about 1685 a French post called Miamis, had been in existence at the mouth of the Chicago river.[4] Marquette, in fact, made his return

[1] Winsor, *The Miss. Basin*, pp. 22-23, map; Carver, *Travels through the Interior Part of North America in the years 1766, 1767 and 1768*, map.

[2] *Early Voyages, etc.*, p. 49.

[3] Winsor, *op. cit.*, p. 22; Carver, map.

[4] Charlevoix, *A Voyage to North America, etc.*, vol. ii, pp. 127, 139-140; Winsor, *op. cit.*, p. 24; Hennepin, *A New Discovery of a Vast Country in America*, vol. i, p. 22, map; *Jes. Rel.*, vol. lix, p. 161, note,

voyage by the Chicago-Des Plaines route over a portage a little more than a mile in length.[1] St. Cosme, on finding the Fox-Wisconsin highway blocked by unfriendly Indians, says he "was obliged to take the Chicago route." He followed this river until it is "lost in the prairie," whereupon, in order to reach the Illinois he found it necessary to make two short portages.[2] The carrying-place varied from four to nine miles in length according to the season of the year. Sometimes during the spring freshets it was not over a mile, and when the water was exceptionally high a canoe could pass from one river system to the other.[3] Charlevoix, however, states that he rejected this route because he had been told that in summer the Des Plaines river was too shallow at times to be used for canoes.[4] In that case the length of the portage would be as much as ten or twelve miles. The Iroquois-Fox alliance, however, pushed the Illinois Indians southward and caused the abandonment by the French of Fort St. Louis on the upper Illinois river.[5] This movement left the Chicago route unguarded and consequently the French travelers became a prey to hostile Indians. The route then gradually fell into disuse and by 1718 was so nearly given up as to find no place on the French maps of the period.[6]

pp. 313-314; *Early Voyages, etc.*, p. 51, note; *Collections and Researches made by the Michigan Pioneer and Historical Society*, vol. xix, p. 6; *Deslisle's Map*, 1718.

[1] *Jes. Rel.*, vol. lix, p. 161, note; *Early Voyages, etc.*, p. 51.

[2] *Early Voyages, etc.*, pp. 49-54.

[3] *Jes. Rel.*, vol. lix, p. 161, note 41; Winsor, *op. cit.*, p. 24.

[4] Charlevoix, *op. cit.*, vol. ii, p. 139.

[5] *Early Voyages, etc.*, pp. 58-59; Andreas, *The History of Chicago*, vol. i, p. 91.

[6] *Delisle's Map*, 1718, N. Y. Pub. Lib.; Le Gac, *Mémoire d'après les Voyages sur la Louisiane*, map, 1722, Newberry Lib., Chicago.

Once more travelers from Michilimackinac to the Illinois country were forced to shift the course of their voyages farther to the east.[1] They now went up the St. Joseph river, from which they passed over a portage, varying according to the season of the year from about three to five miles in length, to the Kankakee, the south fork of the Illinois river.[2] In 1711 a mission station was erected on the St. Joseph sixty leagues from its mouth, and the following year the French constructed at the mission a military post which they occupied to the end of their control in the Mississippi valley.[3] This waterway to the Illinois country was further protected in the early part of the eighteenth century by the Miami Indians who checked the advance of the Iroquois, thereby affording travelers over the St. Joseph-Kankakee route some degree of security.[4] It was possible, though usually undesirable because of the circuitousness of the course, to go from the St. Joseph over a portage of nine miles to the Wabash river, down which one could pass to the Mississippi and thence by way of the latter to the Illinois country.[5] The St. Joseph, therefore, formed a link in each of three routes from New France to that region. The third ran from Montreal by way of Lake Erie and the Maumee river to the St. Joseph, and then to the Kankakee and Illinois.[6]

[1] *Pennsylvania Archives, Second Series,* vol. vi, pp. 54-55.

[2] Charlevoix, *op. cit.*, vol. ii, p. 139; Baker, "The St. Joseph-Kankakee Portage," in *Northern Indiana Historical Society Publications,* p. 24; *Coll. and Res. Mich. Pio. and Hist. Soc.*, vol. x, p. 248.

[3] *Jes. Rel.*, vol. lix, p. 314, note; Baker, *op. cit.*, pp. 20, 36.

[4] Winsor, *op. cit.*, p. 26.

[5] *Ibid.;* Hulbert, *Historic Highways of America,* vol. vii, p. 175.

[6] *Delisle's Map,* 1718; Margry, vol. ii, pp. 97, 98, 244, 248; Vergennes, *Mémoire Historique et Politique sur la Louisiane,* p. 83.

With the growth of settlement on the lower Mississippi, intercourse with New France yearly became more frequent, and consequently led to the use of the Maumee-Wabash-Kankakee route, which was known perhaps as early as 1656[1] and was certainly known to both La Salle and Allouez.[2] In 1682 La Salle writes of it as the shortest and most direct, though because of hostile Iroquois, the most dangerous route from New France to the Illinois.[3] This waterway, therefore, was not in general use until the Miami Indians had repulsed the Iroquois-Fox alliance and located themselves upon it about 1715.[4] From 1718 onward the route was definitely marked out on the French maps, and was the principal highway between New Orleans and Detroit, Montreal and Quebec.[5] In order to give further protection to it, the French established and garrisoned Fort Ouiatanon on the upper Wabash river, which added security and gave great impetus to travel over the Wabash-Maumee route.[6] Later they found it necessary to establish Fort Vincennes on the lower Wabash, in order to defend themselves against the English traders who were now rapidly making inroads into French territory.[7] This route, on account of the military protection thus given and its short portage

[1] Winsor, *op. cit.*, p. 26; Benton, *The Wabash Trade Route in the Development of the Old Northwest*, J. H. U. Studies, vol. xxi, p. 12; *The American Antiquarian*, vol. i, p. 223, Sanson's Map.

[2] Benton, *op. cit.*, p. 12; Margry, vol. ii, p. 98.

[3] Margry, vol. ii, pp. 244, 296; Winsor, *op. cit.*, p. 26.

[4] *Doc. Rel. Col. Hist. N. Y.*, vol. ix, pp. 890, 894; *Reports and Collections of the State Historical Society of Wisconsin*, vol. viii, p. 242; Winsor, *op. cit.*, p. 26.

[5] Jefferys, pt. i, p. 134, map.

[6] *Ind. Hist. Soc. Pub.*, vol. ii, No. 8, pp. 329, 330; *Doc. Rel. Col. Hist. N. Y.*, vol. ix, pp. 891, 894.

[7] *Penn. Col. Papers*, p. 194; Dunn, *Indiana*, pp. 45-55.

of only about nine miles, continued throughout the French period to be the highway most frequently used between Louisiana and New France.[1]

The more eastern branches of the Mississippi taking their rise close to the St. Lawrence system were of little use to the French since they were almost entirely under the control of the Iroquois. The route most frequently followed by the Indians on entering the Mississippi valley was by way of Lake Erie to the Sandusky river, from this river over a portage of about a mile to the Scioto river and thence directly to the Ohio.[2] The Indians made use also of a route from Lake Erie by way of the Cuyahoga river which they ascended to its forks. Here they either passed up the west branch of that river to the head of navigation and made a portage of about eight miles to the east fork of the Muskingum river, or passed up the east branch of the Cuyahoga to a portage connection with Big Beaver creek which flows into the Ohio about thirty miles below Pittsburg.[3] Over these, and no doubt over some other less frequented routes, the traders from New York followed the Indians into the Mississippi valley.

There were connections between the Mississippi and the rivers of the Atlantic coast plain, also, that were convenient for the traders. Pennsylvania, through the Susquehanna and the Juniata, had good portage communication with the Allegheny branch of the Ohio, while Virginia had access to another and even more direct

[1] *Board of Trade Papers*, vol. x, pt. 2, 1718-1720, Penn. Hist. Soc. Trans., Vergennes, p. 84; *Coll. and Res. Mich. Pio. and Hist. Soc.*, vol. xix, p. 5.

[2] *Doc. Rel. Col. Hist. N. Y.*, vol. ix, p. 886.

[3] *An Account of the Remarkable Occurrences in the Life of Col. James Smith, etc.*, Ohio Valley Hist. Series, No. 5, pp. 56, 172, note.

route by way of the Potomac river to the Monongahela branch.[1] The Carolina rivers, too, allowed for comfortable portages with the Tennessee, Cumberland and Alabama rivers.[2] With the exception of Fort Toulouse on the upper water of the Alabama, however, the vastness of the province and the existence of the Chickasaw-Iroquois alliance made it impossible for the French to protect these entrances to Louisiana by military posts. Therefore they became English, rather than French, highways into the Mississippi valley.

The waters of the Gulf of Mexico, the chief connection of Louisiana by sea with the outside world, were shallow for a considerable distance from the coast. The whole of the Louisiana coast, in fact, was skirted by a "barrier-beach," "little banks of sand forming a sort of double coast at a distance of twenty-five to thirty toise from the shore."[3] Moreover the whole of the coast "was so flat, that it could hardly be seen at a distance of two leagues and it is not easy to get up to it."[4]

Mobile Bay, however, which was about thirty miles long and from four to eight miles wide and deep enough for all the largest boats, could be entered with comparative ease.[5] As a rule European vessels did not pass up the bay. Landing places were poor, and the Mobile and its branches were too narrow and winding to make it possible for sea-going vessels to go far inland.[6] Therefore,

[1] Ellet, *The Physical Geography of the Mississippi Valley*, pp. 6-9.

[2] Winsor, *op. cit.*, pp. 19-20.

[3] Chaville, "La Voyage en Louisiane," 1720-1724, in *Journal de la Société des Américanistes de Paris*, 1903, vol. iv, p. 124.

[4] Raynal, *A Philosophical and Political History of the Settlement and Trade of the Europeans in the East and West Indies*, vol. v, p. 253.

[5] Chaville, vol. iv, p. 124; Margry, vol. vi, pp. 532-533.

[6] Charlevoix, *History and General Description of New France*, vol. vi, pp. 36, 38, 39.

Dauphin Island, a part of the "barrier-beach," was used as a landing place.[1]

Biloxi Bay could be entered only by shallops not in excess of a hundred tons. Larger boats could go no nearer Biloxi than five leagues. Here, however, they found good anchorage in the roadstead in front of Ship Island, also a part of the "barrier-beach."[2] To go inland from Biloxi it was necessary to pass up narrow shallow streams so clogged in places with floating logs as to necessitate a resort to portages.[3]

The shallowness of the water along the coast caused the Mississippi river to enter the Gulf of Mexico through a number of mouths, all of which were more or less obstructed by sand bars. In 1700 it was claimed there was not more than eleven feet of water in any of the various mouths and in most of them much less.[4] "These openings," it was said, "are constantly changing and most of them have but little depth of water."[5] To the west of the mouth of the Mississippi the French made no use of the Gulf coast as harbors, except occasionally in their attempts to build up a trade with the Spanish in Mexico.

[1] La Harpe, pp. 94, 105, 107, 108, 110, 128, 131, 132.

[2] *Jes. Rel.*, vol. lxv, p. 165; Charlevoix, *op. cit.*, vol. vi, p. 39.

[3] Margry, vol. v, pp. 620-621; *Jes. Rel.*, vol. lxv, p. 171.

[4] *Jes. Rel.*, vol. lxv, p. 171; Raynal, vol. v. p. 253.

[5] Raynal, vol. v, p. 253.

CHAPTER III

NAVIGATION

WITH the exception of the Chickasaw who were much afraid of the water,[1] the French on their entrance into the Mississippi valley found the Indians using the rivers as highways.[2] This example probably had its influence upon the white travelers, yet the physiography of the country was undoubtedly the determining factor which caused them to adopt and continue to use the same mode of travel, notwithstanding the fact that in making such voyages hindrances almost innumerable had to be overcome.

In passing down the Mississippi the French found the current at the mouth of the Missouri powerful and impetuous; a little farther down stream a rocky cliff extended into the river and formed a whirlpool where the water was constantly boiling up, whirling around and lashing itself into foam against the shores.[3] Continuing the descent, they found enormous floating trees, with dangerous currents near them, high dense woods on the banks keeping out the winds,[4] and many other obstacles

[1] *The Present State of the Country and Inhabitants, European and Indians of Louisiana on the North Continent of America*, 1744, p. 8.

[2] Colden, vol. ii, pp. 36-37; *Jes. Rel.*, vol. lviii, p. 97.

[3] *Early Voyages, etc.*, pp. 65, 68; *Jefferys*, pt. i, p. 138.

[4] *Jes. Rel.*, vol. lxv, pp. 109-161; Pittman, *The Present State of the European Settlements on the Mississippi*, pp. 36-37.

such as sand bars, permanent islands, wooded islands,[1] "planters"[2] and "sawyers,"[3] any one of which could easily and often did put their boats out of commission.[4] Moreover, throughout the course there were few camping or landing places and the many bends in the river, varying from three to eight miles, made the journey by water double the distance by land. One traveler in relating his voyage down stream says "we boxed the compass in three hours travel, and went half around in going two leagues." Necessarily, therefore, navigation on the Mississippi was for the French "slow, tedious and very difficult."[5]

To all these difficulties must be added the bodily discomforts from tornadoes, heavy rains, excessive heat, scarcity of food and drinking water, black flies, gnats and mosquitoes.[6] The torture of the mosquito alone is said by one traveler to have been so intense that every thing else in comparison with it seemed "only a recreation." He believed "the plagues of Egypt were not more cruel," and asserted that the "little insect had caused more swearing since the French came to the Mississippi than had been done before that time in all the

[1] These were places where large quantities of drift-wood had been arrested and matted together.

[2] "Planters" were trunks of trees firmly fastened by their roots to the bottom of the river and appearing no more than about one foot above water when at medium height. The largest boats running against these would not move them.

[3] "Sawyers" were trunks of trees also fastened to the bottom, but yielding to the force of the current and appearing and disappearing like the movements of a saw.

[4] *Jes. Rel.*, vol. lxv, pp. 111, 153; Bossu, vol. ii, pp. 113-114; Hutchins, p. 412; *A. N., C., Sér.* C^{13}, vol. xi, fol. 33.

[5] *Jes. Rel.*, vol. lxv, pp. 137, 159, 161.

[6] *Ibid.*, pp. 111, 113, 127, 137, 155, 161; vol. lxvii, p. 291.

rest of the world." Be that as it may, a swarm of mosquitoes set out with the traveler in the morning; at night when he landed it was "mosquitoes' hour."[1]

From the mouth of the Missouri to the falls of St. Anthony, travel was somewhat less strenuous. Here the many bends and numerous islands greatly abated the force of the current. On the other hand there were in this stretch of the Mississippi two rock obstructions that formed rapids,—one near the mouth of the Rock river some fifteen miles in length, the other a short distance above the Des Moines river about eleven miles long,[2] which at low water interrupted navigation. At such times travelers were forced to "discharge their boats and get into the water and push them along with their hands."[3]

On the tributaries of the Mississippi the navigation was very similar to that on the main river above the mouth of the Missouri. All but the Missouri were shallow except during flood times, and above the rapids, usually, it was necessary to make the voyage in boats smaller than those used below the falls.[4] Belief indeed was expressed in Louisiana that the difficulties attendant upon these journeys would prevent the establishment of trade between the different parts of the province. On this point Governor Cadillac writes:

Is it to be expected that for any commercial or profitable purpose boats will ever be able to run up the Mississippi

[1] *Jes. Rel.*, vol. lxvii, pp. 293-297.

[2] Leveret, "The Lower Rapids of the Mississippi River," in *Proceedings of the Iowa Academy of Science*, 1898, vol. vi, p. 74.

[3] Margry, vol. v, pp. 411-412; Jefferys, p. 135.

[4] Jefferys, p. 136; *Jes. Rel.*, vol. lix, p. 107; Hennepin, *A New Discovery, etc.*, vol. i, pp. 186, 221-226; Charlevoix, *A Voyage to No. Am., etc.*, vol. ii, pp. 139-140; *Early Voyages, etc.*, p. 171.

into the Wabash, the Missouri, or the Red rivers? One might as well try to bite a slice off the moon. Not only are these rivers as rapid as the Rhône, but in their crooked courses they imitate to perfection a snake's undulations. Hence, for instance, on every turn of the Mississippi it would be necessary to wait for a change of wind, could it be had, because this river is so lined up with woods that very little wind has access to its bed.[1]

Fortunately for Louisiana this sort of opinion was not prevalent. As early as 1700 boats were making voyages from the Illinois country to the Gulf of Mexico. All the voyages, however, did not start from the Illinois country. In 1700 La Sueur left Biloxi to go up the Mississippi to the mines supposed to be located upon the upper waters of that river.[2]

The growth of settlement in the Illinois country and on the lower Mississippi caused a proportional increase in the voyages between these two places. Throughout the period of French occupation single boats from time to time made voyages to all parts of Louisiana, yet by far the larger number of expeditions, especially between New Orleans and the Illinois country, were made by convoys of from two to twenty or more boats.[3] Not infrequently a number of armed men were designated by the government to accompany the little fleet as a guard, the size of which varied with the degree of danger attendant upon the voyage and the number of men in the colony available for such work. Before starting on the journey this military escort appointed one of its own

[1] Lowry and McCardle, *A History of Mississippi, etc.*, p. 36.

[2] Margry, vol. v, pp. 402-415.

[3] Pittman, p. 36; *Kerlérec's Report*, 1758, p. 69; Bossu, vol. i, pp. 33, 113; Margry, vol. v, p. 358; *A. N., C., Sér. C[13]*, vol. xiii, fols. 85-86; *Rec. Am. Cath. Hist. Soc. Phila.*, vol. x, p. 206.

men as a leader, or asked the officials to give them one whose duty it was to take charge of the guard, to name the men who were to be on duty during meal time and during the encampment for the night, and in general to give commands. In 1732 twenty men were given as a military escort for four pirogues of "voyageurs" going from New Orleans to the Illinois country.[1]

Whoever made these journeys soon learned that the best time to leave the Illinois country for New Orleans was about the beginning of February, when the water was high and flowing at the rate of something like five miles an hour, which would give an advantage of three miles an hour over a voyage made during low water.[2] Then, too, as at this time of year the land on both sides of the Mississippi was flooded, and the Indians were engaged in hunting, both circumstances helped to insure the traveler against Indian attacks.[3]

In order to avoid the impetuous currents and to reach the Illinois country before winter set in, convoys going up stream usually left New Orleans sometime between August and November. In most cases enough time was thus given for the journey and for a stay of sufficient length to dispose of the cargo and to take on another for the return trip at flood times.[4] Occasionally, however, the allotted time was not adequate, and the convoy was forced to encamp and wait for the ice to break in the spring before completing the voyage.[5] During this

[1] *A. N., C., Sér.* C^{13}, vol. xiv, fol. 48; *Sér.* F^{3}, vol. xxiv, fol. 361; Pittman, p. 36.

[2] Pittman, pp. 36-37.

[3] *The Olden Times,* vol. i, p. 319.

[4] *A. N., C., Sér.* C^{13}, vol. viii, fols. 451-461; *Sér.* F^{3}, vol. xxiv, fol. 361; Bossu, vol. i, pp. 33, 111, 158; Pittman, p. 36.

[5] Bossu, vol. i, p. 158.

stay of the boatmen in the Illinois country there was a safe and comfortable harbor for the boats on the Kaskaskia river where they could be anchored while preparations were being made for the return trip.[1]

The convoys were owned both by private parties and by the colonial government. Bienville, in 1722, sent out an order to all the posts along the river between New Orleans and the Illinois country to give every possible protection to the government convoys,[2] which even with this help in many cases were managed badly. The captains in charge of the convoys were often selfish and dishonest men who sought chiefly to advance their own interests; moreover the amount of merchandise carried was thought to be too small for the number of men in the crew; consequently before 1723 the "inspecteur" of the colony had made two journeys to the Illinois country for the purpose of finding ways and means of making the river service more efficient.[3] The government, notwithstanding these irregularities, sent out annually two convoys made up of seven or eight boats each, one of which left New Orleans in the fall, the other in the spring.[4] During the intercolonial wars, the officials were obliged to supplement the regular convoys by extra ones.[5]

When hostilities began between the French and English on the upper Ohio, convoys carrying food and ammunition, were annually sent out from the Illinois country to Fort Du Quesne. These convoys left in time to pass the falls of the Ohio at time of high water; other-

[1] *A. N., C., Sér.* C^{13}, vol. xxxv, fol, 128.

[2] La Harpe, p. 314.

[3] *A. N., C., Sér.* C^{13}, vol. viii, fols, 451-461.

[4] *Ibid.;* Pittman, p. 36.

[5] Bossu, vol. i, p. 33.

wise they were put to the trouble of a portage, Before the war had been long in progress similar convoys went up the Wabash to the French troops in Canada.[1] These, however, did not prevent others leaving the Illinois for New Orleans just as they had done before the rupture with the English.[2] During the war it was necessary to provide much larger companies of soldiers in order to give adequate protection to the boatmen.[3]

The added war dangers proved to be no more of a deterrent to these persevering Frenchmen than the natural obstacles attendant upon the way had been when such journeys were first undertaken, and each year many boats passed up and down the Mississippi between the Illinois country and New Orleans. Moreover, the boat traffic on the Mississippi between the capital and the neighboring settlements reached considerable proportions before the end of the French control of Louisiana. Trips were made down the river with supplies for the weekly market and for fête days, while boats were sent to the capital with large cargoes of lumber and other colonial products.[4] From New Orleans, also, frequent journeys were undertaken by way of lake and stream to Mobile and from here up the rivers to Forts Toulouse and Tombecbée.[5]

All along the Mississippi where there were settlements on both banks of the river numerous boats were used only in plying from shore to shore.[6] In the Illinois

[1] Bossu, vol. i, p. 179; *Kerlérec's Report*, 1758, pp. 69-70; *A. N., C., Sér. C[13]*, vol. xxxvii, fols. 188-190; *Trans. Ill. Hist. Soc.*, No. 11, p. 222.

[2] *A. N., C., Sér. C[13]*, vol. xxxviii, fol. 26; *Sér. B*, vol. lxiii, fol. 608.

[3] Pittman, p. 36; Bossu, vol. i, p. 33; *Chalmer's Papers Relating to the Indians, 1750-1775*, N. Y. Pub. Lib.

[4] *A. N., C., Sér. C[13]*, vol. xiv, fol. 138.

[5] *Ibid.*, vol. xxii, fols. 46-50; vol. xxiv, fol. 159.

[6] Le Page du Pratz, vol. ii, p. 186.

country there were also two ferries, one at Cahokia, the other between Kaskaskia and St. Geneviève. Both were in use at the time that France relinquished control of the province; the latter having been in operation since 1727, some years before the settlement of St. Geneviève was begun. The ferry at Cahokia made it possible in 1763 for the French settlers who wished to migrate from the English to the Spanish part of Louisiana to take with them all their movable property.[1]

Difficulties to navigation were not wholly confined to that between the different settlements of Louisiana. In the north the ice often blocked the water routes. In such cases the canoe, when the wind was favorable, was converted into an ice-boat. One traveler writes: "instead of putting the canoe into the water, we placed it upon the ice, over which the wind, which was in our favor, and a sail made it go as on water. When the wind failed us, in place of paddles we used ropes to draw it along, as horses draw carriages."[2] Tonty, in the Illinois country, says: "the river being frozen we made sledges and dragged our baggage thirty leagues below the villages of Illinois."[3] In the south the natural formation of the Gulf coast, as shown above, provided few landing places for the vessels coming to the colony and even in fair weather a ship might easily be stranded for days on low-lying sand-bars. If the misfortune occurred at the time of a violent storm it was certain to cause the vessel's destruction.[4]

In 1717 a storm entirely choked up the harbor at

[1] Breese, *The Early History of Illinois, etc.*, App., p. 290; *Trans. Ill. Hist. Soc.*, No. 12, pp. 217-218.

[2] *Jes. Rel.*, vol. lx, pp. 151, 161.

[3] *Hist. Colls. La.*, pt. i, p. 59.

[4] *A. N., C., Sér.* C^{13}, vol. xvii, fols. 29-30, 100-102.

Dauphin Island. One day a vessel on entering found twenty-one feet of water in the channel through which it passed. Two days later, on attempting to pass out over the same course, it stuck in the sand and had to be unloaded and taken out through a different channel where there was not above ten feet of water.[1] Nothing like this had occurred since the French had established themselves on the Mobile, but the experience contributed much to the founding of New Biloxi. At this new post vessels were obliged to anchor in the roadstead in front of Ship Island. From this point the cargo was carried to New Biloxi in smaller boats and from here up the Manchac, where a second transfer was necessary in order to get supplies to the colonists located in the interior settlements.[2]

The growing importance of the establishments along the Mississippi river each year made it more and more desirable that the ships from France should land their loads in closer proximity to these places. To this end Bienville, in 1722, in the face of violent opposition, succeeded in having New Biloxi abandoned. This act did away with the only depot on the Gulf coast in which merchandise destined for the Mississippi settlements was received, and therefore forced the boats to sail directly to New Orleans.[3]

New perils were thus added to the long dangerous sea voyage. At the mouth of the Mississippi the vessels were in danger of collision with huge floating logs that came rushing down the river with great force.[4] Having

[1] Margry, vol. v, p. 548; La Harpe, p. 132.

[2] *A. N., C., Sér.* C^{13}, vol. x, fol. 158.

[3] Margry, vol. v, pp. 639-646.

[4] Raynal, vol. v, p. 253.

escaped these hazards, it required even greater vigilance to pass safely the bars which, almost from the beginning of their occupation of Louisiana the French knew were located in all of the numerous mouths of the Mississippi.[1]

In order to find the way to improve conditions at the mouth of that river, in 1717 the home government ordered the royal engineer and director of the Company to make soundings for the purpose of ascertaining the length of the bars and the depth of the water over them, and the course and rapidity of the current. This information, together with the date on which the investigations were made, were to be sent to France.[2] The next year the command was again given, along with an order to the Louisiana engineer, to try to remove the bars by means of iron dredges, of which the French government sent over six, together with four grappling-irons. These contrivances were to be passed over the bars in order to stir up the mud and thus cause it to pass out of the channel with the flow of the water.[3]

In 1719 more explicit orders concerning the improvement of conditions at the mouth of the Mississippi were sent out. The engineer was told to examine the bars with the idea of their removal, either by means of dredges or other similar devices, or by dykes or other water obstructions, whereby the bulk of the water would be sent through one channel, thereby increasing the force of the current and causing it to clear its own channel. The engineer was directed to erect at the entrance of the river two small towers sufficiently high so that they could be seen at a considerable distance during the day

[1] *Jes. Rel.*, vol. lxv, p. 171; Pittman, p. 35.

[2] Margry, vol. v, pp. 598-599.

[3] *Ibid.*, pp. 602-603.

and on which throughout the night lights were always to be kept burning. He was further instructed to make an exact map of the channels, along with which he was to send to France an estimate of the work necessary to make them navigable.[1] Accordingly the engineer, after making the needful soundings, sent in a report to the home government, in 1722, stating that the lighthouses at the entrance of the river were in operation, and that it was believed that the river itself could be made to remove permanently all the bars at the entrance. The cost of the work to accomplish it he believed would not be great.[2] Notwithstanding this favorable report nothing further, at this time, was done toward the removal of the obstructions to the navigation of the Mississippi.

Sixteen years later, in 1738, the royal engineer reported as follows:

There are daily changes at the mouth of the river and the Balise bar. It has been remarked that, when the winter is short and the north wind has not prevailed much, these changes become more perceptible and the water is not so deep. This may proceed from the existence of two other passes, through which water runs with more rapidity than in the one which is called the Balise. . . . To obviate this inconvenience, the India Company, some twelve years since, had caused to be constructed iron harrows (herses), which were dragged over the bar, but this expedient had its disadvantages . . . . it removed the soft mud, and left the sand, which, forming a solid and compact body, would, in time, not only have interfered with the passage of ships, but have prevented it altogether. This caused the harrows to be abandoned. As the ships of the company were large, and could not pass

[1] Margry, vol. v, pp. 609, 612-613.

[2] *Ibid.*, pp. 632-633; La Harpe, pp. 247-248; Bernard, *Recueil de Voyage au Nord*, vol. v, p. 33.

without being lightened, a small vessel (flute) was left stationed on the Balise bar, to receive part of the cargoes, and the spot where this vessel happened to be anchored, deepened gradually to twenty-five feet. From this fact the inference has been drawn, that, to deepen entirely the Balise, it would be proper to have a vessel drawing eighteen feet, in the hold of which brick wells should be constructed. By alternately pumping water into and out of this well, the vessel would rise and sink at will; and by running her up and down over the bar, it is evident that she would cut a channel through. It is true this would be expensive, but the utility of the measure would be incalculable.[1]

The home government seems not to have acted upon this ingenious method of clearing the Balise channel. War at home was occupying too much of the time of the French officials for them to consider this colonial work. The Balise channel continued to be the one most commonly made use of, but it was necessary to keep a pilot constantly employed in making soundings.

This royal pilot was stationed at the Balise to be in readiness to meet the ships and conduct them over the bars.[2] In his report to the home government in 1750, the chief pilot there wrote:

For these twenty-five years during which I have been employed here in the piloting vessels in and out, I rarely took them out by the same way in which I took them in; and these changes generally happened in October when this river has not much current.[3]

Nothing further was done to remove the obstructions. When it passed them, a ship could go on up the river

[1] Gayarré, *History of Louisiana,* vol. i, pp. 500-502.

[2] Pittman, p. 35; *Jes. Rel.,* vol. lxix, p. 205.

[3] Gayarré, *op. cit.,* App., ii, p. 361.

where there was sufficient depth of water for any of the ocean vessels. At eight leagues from the mouth, however, there was a bend which made it necessary for a boat to wait for a favorable wind. During a delay that might vary from a day to a month, the ship could make fast to a tree on bank and "haul close."[1] From this point boats found no further obstacle in the way to New Orleans, above which sea-going vessels rarely passed.

[1] Pittman, p. 35; Le Page du Pratz, vol. ii, pp. 257, 259.

CHAPTER IV

Boats

The French began to navigate the Mississippi and its tributaries in boats closely resembling those used by the Indians of the lake region. Joliet and his companions made their voyage of discovery down the Mississippi in two canoes "built of birch-bark, cedar splits, and ribs of spruce covered with yellow pine pitch, so light and strong, that they could be carried across portages on the shoulders of four men."[1] By 1700 there were many of those canoes plying up and down the rivers of the Mississippi valley. Usually they were put together with bark and splits, yet it was not unknown for the Indians, and French as well, to make them out of large buffalo hides, stretched over a framework of willow poles. These were called "bull-boats." They were used chiefly in emergencies and could be made large enough to carry five or six persons across the lake or river.[2]

Canoes were referred to by the French as "two-place," "three-place," etc. according to the number of men in the crew. A "two-place" canoe was from twelve to fourteen feet long and could carry, in addition to its human freight, from three to four hundred pounds of merchandise, whereas a "four-place" canoe was as much as twenty feet long, and had a capacity, similarly, of from

[1] Shea, *Discovery and Exploration of the Mississippi Valley*, p. 7.

[2] *A., B. N., Fr.*, vol. 12224, fols. 109-164; Margry, vol. iv, p. 607; vol. v, p. 357; Chittenden, *The American Fur Trade of the Far West*, vol. i, p. 35.

one thousand to two thousand pounds. Besides these smaller boats the French early began the construction of larger vessels which they called "master canoes" (*canots maîtres*). These were about thirty-six feet long and large enough to carry fourteen persons and a corresponding amount of freight. They were usually four feet wide by two anda half feet deep in the middle, and two at the bow and stern.[1] Sometimes they had seats, placed a little lower in the canoe than the cross-pieces that held the boat in shape. La Salle, in fact, began the construction at Fort Crèvecoeur in 1683 of a "mastercanoe" that was forty two feet keel by twelve feet beam.[2]

Bark canoes had no rudders and the boatmen propelled them by the "force of their arms with some paddles."[3] Sometimes when the wind was favorable, a sail, made of thin birch-bark and fastened to upright poles placed in holes in the cross-bars of the boat, was used.[4] Canoes of this sort were admirably suited to river navition where there were no rapids, and where portagages from one river to another were necessary.[5] Their use, however, was by no means limited to the upper waters of the rivers. Many of them found their way to the Gulf coast and in fact were employed in every part of Louisiana.[6]

[1] *Trans. Ill. Hist. Soc.*, No. 10, pp. 131-132; Hennepin, *A New Discovery of a Vast Country, etc.*, vol. i, pp. 36-37; Le Page du Pratz, vol. ii, pp. 49-50.

[2] *Doc. Rel. Col. Hist. N. Y.*, vol. ix, p. 383; *Colls. Ill. Hist. Lib.*, vol. i, pp. 88-89.

[3] Hennepin, *op. cit.*, vol. i, p. 37.

[4] Le Page du Pratz, vol. ii, p. 50.

[5] Chaville, *op. cit.*, vol. iv, p. 137; *Colls. Ill. Hist. Soc., Va. Ser.*, vol. i, p. xviii.

[6] Margry, vol. iv, p. 607; vol. v, p. 357; Kalm, *Travels in North America*, vol. ii, pp. 299-315; vol. iii, p. 15.

Because of the different materials available for the construction of boats, the Indians south of the Ohio gave the French a different model, a "dug-out" made from the trunk of a large cotton-wood tree. In 1673 Marquette saw many such vessels, one Indian village alone having two hundred and eighty.[1] Scarcely was Biloxi established when the settlers began to make boats similar to those used by the southern Indians. In 1700 they finished twelve, from thirty to thirty-five feet long.[2] Le Sueur no doubt used some of these on his voyage to the Illinois country, where they proved to be curiosities to the Illinois Indians who had seen only the bark canoes and a few Indian "dug-outs."[3]

The French, however, did not confine themselves wholly to the cotton-wood, but made "dug-outs" from the trunks of several different kinds of trees, of which the cypress was the most highly prized.[4] Constructed in this fashion the boats necessarily varied in size, the smaller ones being so narrow as not to be able to bear a sail. In a strong wind the water frequently dashed over them.[5] The larger-sized vessels, however, were from forty to fifty feet long by three to five feet wide and could carry thirty men. In freight capacity they ranged from one ton to forty-five or fifty tons. As a rule the French called such boats "pirogues" and frequently also, "canoes."[6]

[1] *Jes. Rel.*, vol. lviii, p. 97.

[2] *A. N., C., Sér.* C^{13}, vol. i, fol. 307.

[3] *Hist. Colls. La. and Fla.*, vol. i, p. 65.

[4] Le Page du Pratz, vol. i, p. 320; vol. ii, p. 31; Charlevoix, *A Voyage to N. Am.*, vol. ii, p. 177.

[5] Margry, vol. v, p. 381; Charlevoix, *op. cit.*, vol. ii, p. 177.

[6] Le Page du Pratz, vol. ii, pp. 33-34; Margry, vol. v, pp. 419-420; *Jes. Rel.*, vol. lviii, p. 97; Dumont, vol. i, p. 64.

A pirogue had seats for the rowers and for the coxswain. Usually it was guided by an oar attached to the stern; in other cases, a more pretentious rudder, made of planks was used.[1] It was propelled by oars, aided by a sail if the wind were favorable.[2] The Company of the Indies during its control of the province owned many boats of this kind.[3] In 1737, however, the royal government decreased the number by introducing into the river service a larger boat of different construction.[4]

By far the most of the pirogues were owned by private persons. Because of their simple construction they could be easily built. When there was a shortage in the government supply, private pirogues made up the deficiency, especially between New Orleans and the Illinois country where they were always more numerous than any other kind of boat.[5] It was not uncommon for twenty to thirty of them to pass from the Illinois to the capital in a single convoy; usually the number was much smaller. In Louisiana, where communication was largely carried on by boat, the general usefulness of the pirogue enabled it to maintain its popularity throughout the French period.[6] The very simplicity of construction, however, gave almost no market for such boats, even if in 1735 five of them did sell for four hundred and ten livres.[7]

Another boat in general service on the Mississippi

[1] Dumont, vol. i, pp. 62-63.

[2] Charlevoix, *op. cit.*, vol. ii, p. 177; Raynal, vol. v, p. 252.

[3] *A. N., C., Sér.* C^{13}, vol. vii, fol. 40.

[4] *Ibid.*, vol. xxii, fols. 18-20.

[5] *Ibid.*, vol. vi, fol. 299; vol. xiv, fol. 48; vol. xxxiv, fols. 291-296; *Sér. B*, vol. lxiii, fol. 608.

[6] *Ibid., Sér.* C^{13}, vol. xv, fols. 133-136; vol. xvi, fol. 300; vol. xxxiv, fols. 291-296; Margry, vol. v, p. 419; vol. vi, p. 244.

[7] *A. N., C., Sér.* C^{13}, vol. xx, fols. 250-251.

was the "cajeu." This was made of strong canes bound tightly together in such a way as to form a light vessel useful in making crossings from one bank of the river to the other. These boats were so easily constructed that they filled the place in the south that the "bull-boats" did in the north.[1] The boats used in the Illinois country for such crossings were pirogues sawed lengthwise into two equal parts with a broad flat piece of timber inserted in the middle in order to give greater beam to the vessel so that horses and cattle could be carried across the river with greater safety.[2]

Neither the bark canoe nor the pirogue answered fully the needs of the province; hence variations from these types soon began to appear. As early as 1700, in fact, Iberville had proposed the construction of light flat boats (*bateaux plats*) on which to carry large quantities of buffalo wool and hides from the interior down the Mississippi to the Gulf of Mexico.[3] Eight years later a contract for a flat boat was let to a shipwright and thirteen inhabitants of Mobile. This vessel drew one foot of water empty and three or four when loaded to its full capacity of about thirty tons, and was used upon the Gulf of Mexico[4] as a "transport-boat."[5] In 1709, the same carpenter built a second flat boat of about twelve tons burden and intended for the builder's own use in a trade he hoped to establish with Tampico and other Spanish towns.[6]

[1] Le Page du Pratz, vol. ii, p. 186.

[2] *Trans. Ill. Hist. Soc.*, No. 12, pp. 217-218; Breese, *The Early History of Ill., etc.*, App., p. 290; Hall, *Notes on the Western States*, p. 218.

[3] Margry, vol. iv, p. 376.

[4] The French used this term for the boats carrying merchandise from sea-going vessels to the settlements, and also from Louisiana to the West Indies or Mexico.

[5] *A. N., C., Sér.* C^{13}, vol. ii, fols. 193-211. [6] *Ibid.*, fols. 395-403.

The number ot such boats did not increase rapidly. An inventory of the royal property in Louisiana in 1718 shows only two of fifteen tons, three of four, and one of two tons capacity, the two largest being in very bad condition.[1] On the arrival of the new director of the Company in August of the same year he made a report to the home government of the condition of the province, and in this communication stated there were twenty-four or twenty-five flat boats ready to be used in carrying settlers from the vessels that brought them from France to their "concessions" along the Mississippi. This number does not seem to have been sufficient, for in 1719 Bienville was ordered by the Company to have a number of new ones constructed, and the work was begun soon after at Mobile, Biloxi and New Orleans.[2] When the work of transportation had slackened, he sent seven of them, with crews of nine or ten men each, from Biloxi by way of the mouth of the Mississippi to New Orleans on a voyage of inspection.[3]

In 1737 the colonial officials considered it advisable to increase the number of flat boats and to place them on the New Orleans-Illinois route. The contract, let to the lowest bidder, fell to certain settlers along the Mississippi. Fifty large vessels, forty by nine by four feet, each of twelve tons burden, to be finished in the month of October, 1738, were provided for.[4] A boat of this type, be it said, was not a flatboat or "broad-horn" of the later period of Mississippi boat traffic, for it had a sharp bow and stern and was of light draft and narrow

[1] *A. N., C., Sér. C[13]*, vol. v, fol. 182.

[2] Margry, vol. v, p. 571; Kalm, vol. iii, p. 15; *A., B. A. É., Mémoires et Documents, Amérique*, vol. i, fol. 107.

[3] *A. N., C., Sér. C[13]*, vol. vi, fol. 11.

[4] *Ibid.*, vol. xxii, fols. 18-20.

beam. It was made of several pieces of timber with a broad flat bottom, was larger than a canoe and of greater capacity than the large pirogue.[1] Toward the end of the French period in Louisiana, however, a boat resembling a flatboat of the present day began to be used on the Mississippi and its tributaries. This was called a "*radeau*" and served principally as a freight boat and for heavy and bulky merchandise in general.[2]

The French also made use of shallops (*chaloupes*). As early as 1704 two of these boats were at Biloxi, and in 1707 were brought into the transport service.[3] Before 1722 they had been placed on the lower Mississippi, where they were used for different kinds of work. Most of the boats in that part of Louisiana were broken to pieces by a violent storm that visited the Gulf region in August; of the government shallops only two remained.[4] The number, however, was soon increased, and in 1727 such boats were making voyages up the Mississippi to New Orleans with from twelve to fifteen passengers,[5] and five years later it was proposed that shallops tow ocean vessels from the Balise to New Orleans.[6] In 1746 a shallop of sixty tons, manned by a crew of five or six sailors, was owned and used on the Gulf of Mexico by a settler who had a cattle ranch on Deer Island.[7] Then, too, shallops were utilized by sea-going vessels for

[1] Kalm, vol. iii, p. 16; *Early Western Travels*, vol. xxvi, p. 61.

[2] Bossu, vol. i, p. 35.

[3] Béranger, p. 103; *A. N., C., Sér.* C^{13}, vol. i, fols. 468-470; vol. ii, fols. 5-32.

[4] *A. N., C., Sér.* C^{13}, vol. vi, fol. 340.

[5] *Relations du Voyage des Dames Réligieuses Ursulines de Rouen à la Nouvelle Orléans*, p. 32.

[6] *A. N., C., Sér.* C^{13}, vol. xv, fols. 54-56.

[7] *Ibid.*, vol. xxx, fol. 254.

all sorts of purposes, such as lifting anchor and doing rescue work in time of peril. Shallops, thus employed, were of about four tons capacity and varied in number from one to three for each vessel.[1] Even the "brigantins" on the river were sometimes provided with a shallop to help raise the anchor.[2]

Just what kind of boat it was that passed under the name of shallop in Louisiana is not easy to determine. As the name "canoe," at times, was applied to the pirogue, so shallop, in the same way, became also a term used indifferently for all medium-sized, and sometimes even for larger, boats. In structure, it seems to have followed closely the flatboat, differing from it no doubt only in some minor detail.

As early as 1713 an overseer of shallops was suggested by the "ordonnateur," and the next year two such officers were appointed, each of whom received for his services thirty livres a month.[3] Penicaut, from whose writings so much knowledge of the early history of the colony of Louisiana has been derived, was a maker and repairer of shallops, a term which in this case was applied to boats of all kinds, even including the large pirogues owned by the government.[4]

In an enumeration of boats used in Louisiana in 1704, it was stated "there are three shallops, one of which is a felouque'" (*felucca*).[5] Here again the term shallop is employed in the larger meaning. This type of boat had been in use in Louisiana since its foundation, for Iberville,

[1] *A. N., C., Sér.* C^{13}, vol. iii, fols. 287-309; vol. xxxiv, fol. p. 119.

[2] *Ibid.*, vol. xxxiv, fol. 119.

[3] *Ibid.*, vol. iii, fols. 262-263; 287-309.

[4] Margry, vol. v, p. 584; Kalm, vol. iii, p. 15.

[5] *A. N., C., Sér.* C^{13}, vol. i, fols. 468-470.

in 1700, speaks of sending his "felouque" into the interior of the country.[1] The "felouque" was a small, swift-sailing ship propelled by both oars and lateen sails, resembling in general the shallop, yet built in such a way that the helm could be used indifferently at either end of the boat. The number of these feluccas was increased from time to time, but they seem never to have become popular. For the most part its use was confined to the lower Mississippi and Gulf of Mexico, where it was employed in coasting voyages and for transport service.[2]

The larger boats in use in Louisiana were "bateaux," "brigantins," "barques," "keel-boats," "traversiers," "caiches," and frigates. "Bateaux" and "traversiers" were general terms. For example, any vessel making frequent voyages between places not far apart might be called a "traversier," regardless of its particular form. In 1704 there were two "traversiers," each of fifty tons capacity and with complete armament, making voyages from Louisiana to Mexico.[3] Such trips continued from time to time until one of the "traversiers," in 1706, ran too close to the shore and was wrecked off the coast not far from Biloxi.[4] In 1722 the "traversiers" then in the province, when not engaged in making journeys to the West Indies, were employed as "transport-boats" (*bâtiments de transport*). For this work, however, they were not well adapted, since they could get no nearer the shore than three-fourths of a league, thereby making it necessary to transfer the merchandise to shallops in order to land it.[5] The term "traversier" continued in

[1] Margry, vol. iv, pp. 363-364.

[2] *A., B. A. É., Am.*, vol. i, fol. 88.

[3] *A. N., C., Sér. C*[13], vol. i, fols. 387-396, 468-470.

[4] *Ibid.*, vol. ii, fols. 5-32, 57-59. [5] *Ibid.*, vol. vi, fols. 288-289.

use throughout the French period, but after the resumption of royal rule it was employed much less frequently.

"Bateau" had a still more general use. As a name it could be applied to any sort of small boat whether propelled by sails or oars, or by both sails and oars. Moreover, the term was used quite as often in reference to boats on the river as to those on the open sea. The French wrote "brigantin," "barque" or "bateau" more or less indifferently in referring to one and the same craft.[1] The application of the term "bateau," furthermore, may be shown by an account of the vessels in lower Louisiana that were mentioned as such.

In 1709, for example, the clerk of the province proposed to buy a "bateau" for the royal service. It was to be used in making voyages to Vera Cruz, and hence was simply a "traversier." Before the government had closed the bargain, however, Bienville and d'Artaguette bought it for fifteen hundred livres and put it on this service as a private enterprise. By 1713 two trips to Vera Cruz are recorded for it.[2] In 1711 a "bateau" of fifty tons was bought by the authorities for two thousands livres. This vessel was intended for a similar service between the West Indies and the colony.[3] In 1712 a "bateau" of thirty-five tons owned by a settler on Dauphin Island was brought from France. It had been necessary for the owner to secure a permit for himself, his Canadian companions and the boat itself, because an exclusive trading privilege had just been granted to Crozat, and the crown wished to protect that privilege.[4] A "bateau"

[1] *A. N., C., Sér. C[13]*, vol. ii, fols. 57-69; vol. iii, fols. 245-248; *A., B. A. É., Am.*, vol. i, fols. 81-129.

[2] *A. N., C., Sér. C[13]*, vol. iii, fols. 66; vol. v, fols. 257-259.

[3] *Ibid.*, vol. ii, fols. 586-602.

[4] *Ibid., Sér. B*, vol. xxxiv, fols. 127, 131.

in a colony where a boat of fifty tons cost more than one of two hundred in Europe, it was felt, would be an advantage rather than a hindrance to Crozat.[1] In 1717 a "bateau," "La Catherine," was bought by the government for two thousand livres for service in Louisiana.[2] There were already at Mobile a "bateau" of between sixty and seventy tons, and another of from twenty-five to forty, and still others elsewhere, all of them badly in need of repairs.[3]

For some time before the Company surrendered its right to the crown it had neither increased nor repaired the "bateaux" of Louisiana. Consequently the royal government found it necessary almost immediately to appropriate ten thousand livres for the construction of new, and the repair of old, vessels of the sort in the province.[4] This need for boats was enhanced, moreover, by the storm that destroyed many ships in lower Louisiana.[5] Among those lost was one wrecked off Horn Island while en route from New Orleans to Mobile by way of the Balise. After the storm there was but one royal "bateau" fit for service.[6] Salmon, the "ordonnateur," attempted to buy others in the West Indies to take the place of those lost, but was not successful. An Englishman came to Mobile about the same time and offered to sell a "bateau" of one hundred tons; a society organized for the purpose of establishing trade with the West Indies agreed to take it, but the owner did not return with the vessel to complete his share of the bargain.[7] This same year the provincial government

[1] *A. N., C., Sér.* C^{13}, vol. iii, fol. 605.

[2] *Ibid., Sér. B,* vol. xxxix, fol. 70.

[3] *A., B. A. É., Am.,* vol. i, fols. 107-108.

[4] *A. N., C., Sér.* C^{13}, vol. xiii, fols. 268-270; vol. xv, fols. 54-56.

[5] *Supra.*

[6] *Ibid.,* vol. xvii, fols. 53-54.

[7] *Ibid.,* vol. xvi, fol. 83.

bought at Vera Cruz a "bateau" of between sixty and seventy tons, which was called "L'Aigle Noir" and was to be a "traversier" along with an old "brigantin," the "St. Louis".[1]

Scarcely had the crown provided "bateaux" for official service in Louisiana when it was discovered that they were used more for the private trade of the government staff than for public purposes. To put an end to this abuse, Salmon issued an ordinance making it illegal for any official to convert such boats to private uses.[2] There were, however, not enough "bateaux" in the province, even though employed exclusively for official objects. A recommendation, therefore, was sent to the home government, in 1735, requesting it to have the needful boats constructed, each of from fifty to one hundred and fifty tons capacity, for the service in Louisiana.[3] The request being ignored, the colonists themselves made some attempts at increasing the number. In 1737 a "bateau" of fifty tons, "La Marie Elisabeth," from Bordeaux, was condemned by the colonial officials as unseaworthy. A settler bought it and with the aid of a ship carpenter made it again ready for use and at once freighted it for Martinique. This gain, however, was offset by the loss the same year of a "bateau" of sixty tons, "La Marguerite," which was wrecked off Horn Island on its return voyage from Cape Français (Cape Haitien). This vessel, too, was owned by a colonist and, when wrecked, was returning to Louisiana from its second journey that year to the West Indies.[4]

[1] *A. N., C., Sér. C^{13}*, vol. xvi, fols. 122-124; vol. xvii, fols. 167-169.

[2] *Ibid., Sér. A*, vol. xxiii, October 18, 1734.

[3] *Ibid., Sér. C^{13}*, vol. xx, fols. 57-60.

[4] *Ibid.*, vol. xxii, fols. 173-175, 182.

In 1740 a storm again passed over lower Louisiana causing great loss in boats of all kinds. A large "bateau" with its captain and four of the best negro sailors in the colony foundered while on its way from Mobile to New Orleans.[1] In order to have new ships built in place of the old ones lost, the crown the next year sent to Louisiana a ship carpenter. The deplorable state of the French finances, however, prevented the grant of further aid.[2] In 1749 the home government was again asked to increase the number of Louisiana "bateaux," especially for the New Orleans-Mobile lake and river route where the need was the greatest. Here there was but one boat of the kind and that was quite unfit for service.[3]

On the Mississippi between New Orleans and the Illinois country, the term "bateau" was used as early as 1717. In that year two small vessels of the sort were sent from France on the ship, "La Dauphine," and destined for service on the Mississippi. Others were soon added, but the supply seems never to have equaled the demand.[4] A "bateau" of sixteen tons, built at New Orleans for voyages between the capital and the Illinois country, was finished in 1733. When about ready to begin its maiden trip and while still at anchor, it was struck and badly damaged by a tree floating swiftly down stream. Repairs were at once begun and the boat started up the Mississippi early in 1734.[5] There was need for more such "bateaux" on this course,

[1] *A. N., C., Sér. C*[13], vol. xxvi, fols. 127-130.

[2] *Ibid., Sér. B*, vol. lxxii, fol. 9.

[3] *Ibid., Sér. C*[13], vol. xxxiv, fols. 118-119.

[4] *Ibid.*, vol. v, fol. 99; Margry, vol. vi, p. 244.

[5] *A. N., C., Sér. C*[13], vol. xix, fols. 8-10.

yet the home government did nothing in the matter until the outbreak of the Chickasaw War, when it became necessary to increase the number immediately. At the request of Bienville, in 1737, the "ordonnateur" placed a contract for the construction of fifty "bateaux," forty by nine feet, which were to cost one thousand five hundred and fifty livres each. The caulking, iron-work, rigging, gearing etc., brought the price up to three thousand four hundred and forty livres. The boats were to be finished by March, 1738.[1] The "bateaux" for the New Orleans-Illinois service were put in repair in 1746[2] and again in 1748, before they were allowed to leave the town.[3]

The "bateau" was used, also, on other rivers of the province. In 1739 boats of the kind were passing from Mobile up the river to Fort Toulouse, Fort Tombecbée, and to New Orleans.[4] Three years later Dubreuil, "entrepreneur of public works," launched a "bateau" of forty tons to be used carrying stone down the Mobile from a quarry five leagues above.[5] The number of voyages between New Orleans and the other parts of the province, furthermore, was greatly increased by additions to the military forces, compelling the "ordonnateur," in 1752, to enlarge correspondingly the number of boats on the river service. Six thousand livres, accordingly, was appropriated for the construction of new and the repairing of old "bateaux."[6]

[1] *A. N., C., Sér. C[13]*, vol. xx, fols. 176-179.

[2] *Ibid.*, vol. xxx, fol. 23.

[3] *Ibid.*, vol. xxxii, fols. 196-197.

[4] *Ibid.*, vol. xvii, fols. 100-102; vol. xxii, fols. 46-50.

[5] *Ibid.*, vol. xxvii, fol. 134.

[6] *Ibid.*, vol. xxxvi, fol. 285.

The final war between the French and English led to the employment of "bateaux" on the Ohio and Wabash rivers. Convoys of fifteen or sixteen such boats made annual trips from the Illinois country up the Ohio to Fort Du Quesne, and also up the Wabash with supplies for the troops in New France.[1]

[1] *Kerlérec's Report*, 1758, p. 70; Pittman, p. 36; *Trans. Ill. Hist. Soc.*, No. 11, pp. 222-223; No. 8, p. 111; *North American Review*, vol. xlix, p. 77.

CHAPTER V

Boats (Continued)

Passing now to a consideration of certain specific types of vessels, it may be said that a "barque" was a boat too small to be rigged with the same kind of sails and in the same way as those used on a "brigantin". As early as 1704 a "barque" of fifty tons was built and launched in Louisiana, the sails having been brought from France.[1] In 1707, one such boat was all that was needed for the service of the colony on the Gulf of Mexico.[2] By 1713 "barques" were in use on the Mississippi river. Here they were supplied with oars as well as with masts and sails. Ranging in capacity from forty-five to fifty tons, they were used as freighters.[3] In 1751, six boats of the sort left New Orleans for the Illinois country with four companies of troops (400 men) and large supplies of merchandise.[4]

The term "brigantin" was first applied in 1707 to a Louisiana boat of about fifty tons burden.[5] By 1713, another of from sixty to seventy tons had been added. It was small enough to pass some distance above Fort St. Louis de la Mobile, and yet large enough to make sea voyages to Tampico, Havana and Vera Cruz for cargoes of domestic animals and flour, and required only twelve men

[1] *A. N., C., Sér.* C^{13}, vol. i, fols. 468-470.

[2] *Ibid.*, vol. ii, fols. 57-69.

[3] *Ibid.*, vol. iii, fols. 209-310.

[4] Bossu, vol. i, p. 33.

[5] *A. N., C., Sér.* C^{13}, vol. ii, fols. 5-32.

to man it.[1] The next year a "brigantin" was sent from Mobile up the Mississippi after supplies of corn for the garrison. Not being able to secure the quantity needed, the vessel was later despatched to Vera Cruz to buy flour, a voyage which under favorable conditions required two months.[2] In 1717 the "brigantin", "Le Neptune", was sent from France with supplies for the province and directed to remain permanently in Louisiana. It was even intended for the navigation of the Mississippi as far as the Illinois country; but a voyage of the sort seems never to have been accomplished.[3]

An inventory taken in 1718 of the vessels in Louisiana shows several "brigantins". There was one of from twenty-five to forty tons at Mobile, another at Biloxi of from thirty to thirty-five tons, and "Le Pinère", between New and Old Biloxi. Though stranded and badly worm-eaten, all of them were capable of being repaired and put afloat ready for further service, except the one at Biloxi. Besides these there were at New Orleans two "brigantins" of fifteen and eighteen tons, respectively, and a large one of fifty tons which was in a state of decay.[4] Of these boats only one seems to have born an individual name.

Before 1731 the Company of the Indies had begun in Louisiana the construction of a "brigantin", forty-five by nineteen by nine feet, and of seventy-six tons capacity. The Company, however, never completed the boat, which was taken over by the crown and launched in December, 1733, under the name "La Louisiane".[5] At this time the "brigantin" "St. Louis", was in use at New Orleans but was very old and almost unfit for sea voyages and later in

[1] *Ibid.*, vol. iii, fols. 126-140, 186, 245-248.

[2] *Ibid.*, fols. 511-533, 561-606.

[3] Margry, vol. v, p. 596.

[4] *A.*, *B. A. É.*, *Am.*, vol. i, fols. 81-129.

[5] *A. N.*, *C.*, *Sér.* C^{13}, vol. xv, fol. 19; vol. xvii, fols. 100-101; vol. xix, fols. 8-10.

the year was lost while returning from a voyage to Mobile by way of the Mississippi.[1] Another "brigantin" plied on the river and lake route between New Orleans and Mobile. By 1749 this boat had grown too old for effective work, and the crown was asked to put in its place a new vessel of from eighty to ninety tons burden and not drawing above nine feet of water when loaded to its full capacity. It was desired to have the boat fitted up with masts and sails and provided with an extra set of sails, ropes, cables and anchors, as well as a shallop for raising the anchor, and armed with eight cannon.[2]

Few "caiches" (ketches) and frigates were ever in use in Louisiana. Of the former, one was brought from France in 1718 and used in the transport service at Biloxi.[3] About this time also there was at New Orleans a frigate of 150 tons burden and carrying sixteen cannon. Although vessels of this sort were intended primarily for warlike purposes, they were, at times, used to carry both freight and passengers. The arrangement of the sails and the employment of the cannon were the features differentiating such ships from the others in service.[4]

About 1742 the "keel-boat" began to be used on the Mississippi. This was a smaller vessel than the "bateau" and of lighter construction. It was usually from sixty to seventy feet long, with a breadth of beam of from fifteen to eighteen feet. The keel extended from bow to stern and the boat drew, usually, only from twenty to thirty inches of water. Most of the boats of this kind were of English construction and in the English service.[5]

[1] *A. N., C., Sér. C*[13], vol. xiv, fol. 38; vol. xv, fols. 55-56; vol. xix, fols. 8-10.

[2] *Ibid.*, vol. xxxiv, fols. 118-119. [3] *A., B. A. E., Am.*, vol. i, fol. 87.

[4] *Ibid.*, fol. 107; *A. N., C., Sér. B*, vol. lxix, fols. 106-107.

[5] Hall, pp. 218-219; Kalm, vol. iii, p. 15; *Early Western Travels*, vol. xxvi, pp. 60-61.

In 1723 it was proposed to put on the New Orleans-Illinois route a "galère" of from fifty to sixty tons burden and a smaller, or "demi-galère". It was claimed that the "galère" would be a decided improvement over the flat boat (bateau plat) and pirogue in use on the Mississippi. On these craft the cargo, when not under cover, was often badly damaged by heavy rains, whereas on the "galère" there were decks below which the merchandise could be stored and kept dry. An appeal was made to the home government for carpenters for the work; but it was unheeded, and the ships were not built.[1]

Notwithstanding the many different kinds of boats in use on the rivers of Louisiana, there was no great variety in the way they were propelled. From the largest to the smallest, all were rowed both up and down stream. Sails, to be sure, were used whenever it was possible, yet that sort of motor power could never, on a river voyage, be depended upon.[2] During times of low water resort was made to "punting". On either side of the vessel a boatman at the bow thrust a pole into the water till it struck bottom. With the poles, in this position, the men pushed upon them, at the same time walking toward the stern, and in this way the boat was moved forward. When the stern was reached the poles were pulled out of the water, carried to the bow, again planted and the process was repeated.[3]

After 1750, "cordelling" or towing was employed. In order to keep the cable from catching on the bushes along the shore, it was passed through a hole in the top of a high mast placed a little forward of the centre of the boat, and

[1] *A. N., C., Sér. C*[13], vol. vii, fol. 40.

[2] Pittman, pp. 36-37; Raynal, vol. v, p. 253; Bossu, vol. i, p. 33.

[3] Hall, p. 221; *Early Western Travels*, vol. xxvi, pp. 60-61; Moses, *Illinois, etc.*, vol. i, p. 105.

the end of the line fastened to the bow. The boat was then pulled forward by from twenty to thirty men strung along on the shore. Sometimes the shore end of the cable was attached to a tree and the men on board the boat did the pulling.[1] Another sort of towing was in use on the lower Mississippi, where vessels were pulled from the Balise to New Orleans by shallops.[2]

The number of men composing the crew on the different kinds of river boats varied greatly, even on those of the same construction and size. It frequently happened that there were not enough sailors in the entire province to man them adequately. Many were manned by owners of both boat and cargo.[3] In 1713 a "barque" of from forty-five to fifty tons required a crew of twenty men for a voyage up the Mississippi.[4] At Mobile, in 1733, there were twelve negroes who were sailors on the "bateau" that passed from that place up the river to Fort Toulouse, Fort Tombecbée, and to New Orleans. Though efficient sailors, their number was far too small; hence the colonial officials requested the home government to increase the supply.[5] The shortage continuing, in 1751 a further request was made for more sailors for the New Orleans-Illinois route. The negroes belonging to the government had grown old. There had never been more than one negro for each "bateau", consequently, since about twenty-four men were needed, it usually fell to the soldiers to do the rowing.

[1] Hall, pp. 218, 221; *Early Western Travels,* vol. xxvi, pp. 60-61; Moses, vol. i, p. 105.

[2] *A. N., C., Sér.* C^{13}, vol. xv, fols. 54-56.

[3] *Ibid., Sér. B,* vol. xci, fol. 8; Margry, vol. v, p. 357; vol. vi, pp. 358-359, 435.

[4] *A. N., C., Sér.* C^{13}, vol. iii, fols. 245-248.

[5] *Ibid.,* vol. xxiv, fols. 158-160.

Besides their pay as such, they received a small " gratification " varying in amount with the length of the voyage.[1] Each " bateau ", for the most part, was provided with a captain, yet it was not uncommon for a number of boats to be sent out under the command of a single officer.[2]

The pay of the sailors on the river boats is difficult to determine. Le Sueur paid some Canadian " vagabonds " 500 livres (French money) for a year's labor. This, however, included work as hunters as well as boatmen.[3] In 1714 sailors were receiving twenty-four livres a month.[4] On a boat of twenty-five tons, the construction of which was proposed in 1725, the captain was to receive forty livres a month, for a period of six months, and the sailors twenty.[5] This amount may be regarded as a fair average.

The time necessary for a voyage from New Orleans to the Illinois country varied from three to four months, whereas the return trip could be made in from twelve to twenty-five days.[6] A voyage from the Illinois to Fort Du Quesne required three months going up, and twelve days down stream.[7] Boats proceeding from New Orleans to Mobile by the lake route took four days,[8] while those going by way of the Mississippi, with favorable winds, could arrive at the Balise in about the same time. The sharp bend in the river made it necessary for the vessels to wait for a

[1] *A. N., C., Sér. C*[13], vol. xxxv, fols. 8-12.

[2] *Ibid.*, vol. vi, fol. 11; vol. viii, fols. 451-461; Pittman, p. 36.

[3] Margry, vol. vi, pp. 68-69.

[4] *A. N., C., Sér. C*[13], vol. iii, fols. 287-309.

[5] *Ibid.*, vol. viii, fols. 451-461.

[6] *Ibid.*; Pittman, p. 36.

[7] *Kerlérec's Report*, 1758, p. 70; *The Present State of the Country etc.*, 1744, p. 31.

[8] *A. N., C., Sér. C*[13], vol. vii, fol. 31.

change of wind, a circumstance, as above observed,[1] that might prolong the voyage to New Orleans anywhere from a day to a month.[2] The canoes usually went at the rate of four miles an hour down stream; but from daybreak to dusk, if provided with a sail and having a favorable wind, they were able to make from thirty to thirty-five leagues, and on lakes sometimes more.[3] The larger boats with say approximately twenty men could go about six or seven leagues a day up stream.[4] The rate of progress, however, was in direct proportion to the size of the crew.

It seems fitting to conclude this description of the boats of Louisiana with some account of the vessels plying between the province and France. During the period up to 1763 more than one hundred different ships were engaged. Some of them made a few voyages to Louisiana and were then transferred to the service of other French colonies. The voyages of a considerable number extended over many years, in a few cases as long as thirty. These vessels, however, rarely came year after year, and in only one case did the same ship undertake two voyages in a single year.[5] The number of French vessels sent to Louisiana, the irregularity of their visits and the colony's commercial history in this respect may be illustrated by the following diagram:

[1] *Supra*, p. 54.

[2] *A. N., C., Sér.* C^{13}, vol. vii, fols. 33-34; Le Page du Pratz, vol. ii, p. 259.

[3] *Jes. Rel.*, vol. lix, p. 91; Raynal, vol. v, p. 253; Hennepin, *A New Discovery, etc.*, vol. i, p. 37; *Hist. Colls. of La.*, pt. 4, p. 7.

[4] *Jes. Rel.*, vol. lxvii, pp. 287, 295, 297; Pittman, p. 36.

[5] These conclusions are based on a rough list compiled of all the vessels mentioned in contemporary sources. The references are too numerous for citation.

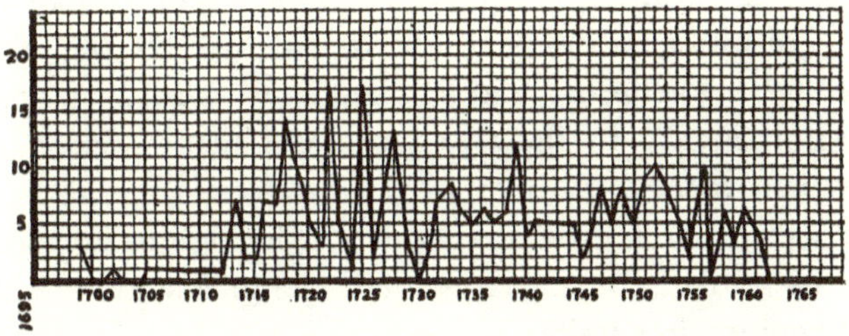

The curve from 1699 to 1712 tells of the time of famine, and from 1712 to 1717 of Crozat's erratic management of the province. Then followed the period when Louisiana was under the rule of the Companies which sent out many vessels with settlers and merchandise. On resuming control of the colony in 1731, the crown was unable to despatch a sufficient number of vessels and hence endeavored to attract merchants to the colonial trade by offering them "gratifications", or bounties, on the shipment of certain classes of merchandise, amounting for a while to as much as forty livres a ton, but eventually reduced to twenty.[1] The curve gives some indication of the success of the effort. From 1744 to about 1752 a change of conditions in the French West Indies sent many merchant vessels to Louisiana.[2] From 1754 to the end of the French régime the curve indicates great irregularity, due to the misfortunes of war and to English interference.

The French vessels coming to Louisiana sailed from the ports of La Rochelle,[3] Rochefort,[4] Bordeaux,[5] St. Malo,[6]

[1] *A. N., C., Sér. B*, vol. lxi, fol. 629; vol. lxii, fol. 235.

[2] *A., B. N., Joly Coll.*, vol. 1726, fols. 145-146.

[3] *A. N., C., Sér. C*^{13}, vol. xiv, fol. 36.

[4] *Ibid.*, vol. i, fols. 514-569.

[5] *Ibid.*, vol. xvi, fols. 38-39; vol. xxxiv, fol. 361.

[6] *Ibid.*, vol. xxiv, fol. 256.

Marseilles,[1] Nantes,[2] Havre,[3] Bayonne,[4] and Dunkerque.[5] The greater number of those despatched by the crown sailed from Rochefort, and by merchants, from La Rochelle and Bordeaux. In the two ports last named there were cases where the same merchant kept vessels in the Louisiana service from the third decade of the eighteenth century onward until the final war with England made trade with the province impossible.

The ships at first were quite small, ranging from thirty-five to sixty tons burden. None seems to have reached one hundred tons or more before the time of the Company of the Indies, when the boats were anywhere from 110 to 500 tons capacity. Those sent out by the crown and by merchants for several years after 1731 were for the most part of small tonnage. Not until 1736 is there a record of a vessel of as much as 250 tons. Some were as small as fifty[6] or sixty[7] tons, whereas the majority were between 100 and 200. After 1736 the size of the vessels was considerably increased. Many of them were between 400 and 500 tons, and a few reached 700 tons.[8] The smaller ones, however, still held their own and in 1759 a boat of fifty tons started on a voyage to Louisiana, but was seized by the British three weeks after it left Havre.[9]

These French ships engaged in the Louisiana service were not essentially different from those despatched to

[1] *A. N., C., Sér. C*[13], vol. xxxiv, fol. 359.

[2] *Ibid.*, vol. iii, fol. 16; vol. xxiv, fols. 254-256.

[3] *A., B. N., Fr.*, vol. 11334, fol. 171.

[4] *A. N., C., Sér. C*[13], vol. xxxiv, fol. 297.

[5] *Ibid., Sér. B*, vol. xcviii, fol. 96.

[6] *Ibid.*, vol. lxii, fol. 91.

[7] *Ibid.*, vol. lxi, fols. 647-648.

[8] *Ibid., Sér. C*[13], vol. xl, fols. 62-63.

[9] *A., B. N., Fr.*, vol. 11334, fols. 186-187.

other French colonies. Nor were they smaller than boats similarly employed by other nations. In fact the French vessels of the time were usually larger than those of other countries. None of the Spanish or English vessels, for example, resorting to Louisiana, was above fifty or sixty tons.[1]

The vessels were known by the various designations of frigate,[2] "paquetbot",[3] "brigantin",[4] "flute",[5] "courrier" or "dogre",[6] "galère",[7] "navire",[8] "gabare",[9] "goèlette",[10] "parlementaire",[11] and "balandre" or "bélandre".[12] Like the names applied to the colonial boats, some are general terms; others refer to boats of a special construction. Regardless of name, each of the ships was some sort of sailing craft, and most of them were merchant vessels carrying both freight and passengers. As a rule the frigate was a warship, yet it also at times was used to carry both freight and passengers.[13]

The passengers were divided into different classes: those "à la table du capitaine", "à l'office du capitaine" "ration munitionnaire", "ration simple", and those who provided

[1] *A. N., C., Sér. B*, vol. xlv, fols. 232-233; *Sloane Coll.*, vol. 32854, fol. 252, British Museum Lib.

[2] *A. N., C., Sér.* C^{13}, vol. iii, fols. 791-792.

[3] *Ibid.*, vol. ii, fol. 544.

[4] *Ibid.*, vol. iii, fol. 186.

[5] *Ibid., Sér. B*, vol. xlix, fol. 119.

[6] *Ibid., Sér.* C^{13}, vol. xi, fols. 31; *A., B. N., Fr.*, vol. 11335, fol. 151.

[7] *A. N., C., Sér.* C^{13}, vol. vii, fol. 40; vol. xi, fol. 31.

[8] *Ibid.*, vol. xv, fol. 54.

[9] *Ibid.*, vol. xxxiii, fol. 28.

[10] *Ibid.*, vol. xxxix, fol. 74.

[11] *Ibid.*, vol. xxxii, fols. 20-22.

[12] *Ibid.*, vol. vii, fol. 40; La Harpe, p. 104.

[13] *A. N., C., Sér. B*, vol. lix, fols. 106-107.

their own food. The "ration simple" was one ration, while that of "ration munitionnaire" was one and a half a day, per person.[1] In 1731 it cost the crown sixty livres, each, plus the price of their food, to send soldiers to Louisiana.[2] Two years later the price of a passage at the captain's table was 150 livres, while at "ration munitionnaire" the fare was only eighty livres.[3] In 1739 the passage of individuals sent out by the crown on merchant ships amounted to 400 livres each. This was an exorbitant charge, however, one of many of the sort in cases where the government paid the bill.[4] By 1756 the price of a single passage to Louisiana without food had arisen to 158 livres, while at the captain's table the price was 500.[5] In 1761 it cost the crown a little more than 172 livres for each passenger it sent to the province.[6]

Many of the vessels came singly from France to Louisiana, but as a rule two or three of the ships made the journey across the sea together. During war times France sent vessels out in convoys at certain fixed periods, in order to give the combined number sufficient protection against seizure and to enable it the more easily and quickly to ascertain its losses at sea.[7]

The vessels were supplied with a captain, under-officers and a crew. Sometimes the captain and owner were one and the same person, who sold the cargo and bought another for the return voyage.[8] The ships had their own

[1] *A. N., C., Sér. B,* vol. lxxxii, fol. 330; vol. lxxv, fol. 379; *Sér. C*[13], vol. xvi, fols. 38-39; vol. xxx, fols. 67-70.

[2] *Ibid., Sér. B,* vol. lv, fol. 148.

[3] *Ibid.,* vol. lviii, fol. 14; *Sér. C*[13], vol. xvi, fols. 33-39.

[4] *Ibid., Sér. C*[13], vol. xxiv, fols. 136-138.

[5] *A., B. N., Fr.,* vol. 11336, fols. 106, 171.

[6] *Ibid.,* fols. 193-194.

[7] *A. N., C., Sér. C*[13], vol. xl, fols. 62-63.

[8] *Ibid., Sér. B,* vol. lx, fol. 106.

pilots. Where there was more than one, the first received fifty livres a month and the second forty.[1] There were also special pilots kept by the crown at the Balise.[2] A pilot of this sort received from the captain of the ship ten livres a hundred tons to bring the vessel in and take it out.[3] Three years later, owing to a scarcity at the Balise, the crown was asked to send out two smart young men as pilots for the post. An officer on one of the royal ships was found to answer the qualifications, and he was secured at 800 livres a year. Later another pilot who had been commander of a "bateau" on the coast of St. Domingue, was obtained for 600 livres.[4]

The number of the crew varied necessarily with the size of the boat and the nature of the cargo. The "flute", for example, carried a crew of from 120 to 140 men and a food supply sufficient for seven or eight months.[5]

Regarding the time required for a voyage from France to Louisiana, forty-six days was considered a quick trip to Cape Français [6] and another forty-six days to reach New Orleans.[7] It was not uncommon, however, for a passage to take three to four months.[8] When in Louisiana the vessels remained for a length of time varying anywhere from a few weeks to a year or more.

[1] *A. N., C., Sér.* C^{13}, vol. iii, fols. 287-309.

[2] *Supra*, p. 27.

[3] *A. N., C., Sér.* C^{13}, vol. xiv, fols. 142-143.

[4] *Ibid.*, vol. xx, fols. 57-60.

[5] *Ibid., Sér. B*, vol. xlix, fol. 119.

[6] *Ibid., Sér.* C^{13}, vol. xiii, fols. 104-105, 204.

[7] *Ibid.*, vol. iv, fol. 847.

[8] *A., B. A. E., Am.*, vol. i, fol. 84.

CHAPTER VI

HIGHWAYS

WHEN the French entered the Mississippi valley they found two sorts of highways fairly well marked out. One was the great migratory and local routes of the buffalo, the other the Indian trails. When these highways were called into existence by different causes the former were distinct from the latter, but when created by a desire to satisfy similar needs they were sometimes, in whole or in part, identical.[1] For example, the buffaloes and Indians entered the Mississippi valley through Cumberland Gap and continued for some distance into the interior over the same road. The highway then divided, the Indian trail leading on to the falls of the Ohio, and the buffalo path to Otter Creek, past the place where later Booneborough was located.[2] In places where the paths were in no way connected they were at times indifferently used by both the Indians and buffaloes. In 1750, when passing over an Indian thoroughfare, a traveler writes, "we met so impudent a Bull Buffalo that we were obliged to shoot him or he would have been among us".[3]

The buffalo paths were the routes the animals took in

[1] *Filson Club Publications,* vol. xiii, pp. 44-51; *Jes. Rel.,* vol. lix, p. 115.

[2] *Filson Club Pub.,* vol. ii, map; vol. xiii. pp. 47, 50; Hulbert, *Historic Highways of America,* vol. i, p. 113; *Boone's Autobiography,* in Hartley, *Life of Daniel Boone,* App.

[3] *Filson Club Pub.,* vol. xiii, p. 70.

going from one to another of the great prairies, or in going from the pastures to the drinking places or salt-licks. Year after year the herds passed over the same path, which was always an astonishingly direct line between the two places. En route they followed one another mile after mile and at night lay down close together to rest. As would be expected, the paths were worn deep, and the earth was packed so hard that no vegetation ever grew upon them. Even upon the resting places only purslain grew.[1] The buffalo "trace", as it was called by the pioneer, was spacious enough for two wagons to go abreast[2] and where the buffaloes "had thundered over it for a thousand years in their journey to the Salt Licks" it was in places five or six feet deep. Even the cross-country roads made by these animals were wider than ordinary public highways are today.[3] The Illinois prairies were covered with a tall, rank grass which made it difficult to go across country without being constantly in danger of losing the way. The multitude of beaten buffalo paths made over it, however, in whole or part, eliminated this danger. Moreover, they took the traveler across the prairies "and through dense forests, impenetrable from heavy canes, pea vines and other undergrowth", over a much more direct route than he could possibly map out for himself.[4]

The buffalo paths in the eastern part of the Mississippi valley, like the rivers in that area, served as English rather than French roads. Here they not only pointed out to the

[1] Hennepin, *A New Discovery, etc.*, vol. i, p. 148; Hall, p. 110; Hulbert, vol. i, pp. 101-120.

[2] Butler, *A History of the Commonwealth of Kentucky*, App., p. 462.

[3] *Filson Club Pub.*, vol. xii, p. 75; vol. xiii, p. 170.

[4] *Ibid.*, vol. xiii, pp. 184-185; Zeisberger, *Diary of David Zeisberger etc.*, in *Hist. and Phil. Soc. of Ohio, New Ser.*, vol. i, pp. 17-19; Jefferys, pt. i, *Louisiana*, p. 136.

English trader the way over the mountains but also directed his course across the country. One of these men writes: "We traveled to Rocky Ridge (Clinch Mountain). I went up to the top to look for a Pass. . . . To the Eastward were many small Mountains and a Buffalo Road between them and the Ridges . . . a large Buffalo Road goes from the Forks to the Creek over the West Ridge, which we took and found the Ascent and Descent tolerably easie".[1] In all probability, other passes through the mountains were discovered in similar fashion.[2] The buffalo roads to the west of the Mississippi, too, aided the pioneer in his advance westward. Thomas Benton at a later date says the "buffalo blazed the way for the railways to the Pacific".[3]

Indian trails, though much less well-defined, were far more numerous than the paths of the buffalo. The Indians had paths for trade, hunting and war, and others that led only from the camp down to the river. Marquette and his companions, at sixty leagues from the mouth of the Wisconsin river, saw the footprints of men, and on further search they found a well-beaten path. This they followed and came to a beautiful prairie and an Indian village two leagues inland.[4] There were still other trails that followed the general course of the streams. When the path lay near the water it often passed through marshes, swamps and thickets where it was almost obliterated by weeds, briars and bushes. In other places, because of the meanderings of the river, the "trace" near the water's edge was abandoned as is shown in the following quotation: "We kept down the Creek to the River along the Indian Road to

[1] *Filson Club Pub.*, vol. xiii, pp. 44-47.

[2] Hulbert, vol. i, pp. 133, 138.

[3] *Ibid.*, p. 137.

[4] *Jes. Rel.*, vol. lix, p. 115.

where it crosses. . . . After riding five miles, . . . we left the River, it being very crooked. In riding three miles we came on it again. . . . We left the River but in four miles we came on it again at the Mouth of Licking Creek, which we went up and down another ".[1] In flood times the path near the water had to be given up entirely. The trail over the hills lying along, but at some distance from the river, necessitated some hard climbing; an instance is given where a horse " stumbled and rolled down the hill like a wheel ".[2]

Leading out from the Indian villages and passing around them through the surrounding country there were well-beaten hunting paths.[3] Where the hunting grounds were remote from the camp the journey thither more frequently was made by the water routes. Many of the shorter trails as well as the longer ones led from one Indian nation to another. The longer were variously used according to the relations existing between the peoples concerned. Trails between the Illinois and Fox in the Illinois country, and the Chickasaw and Choctax in lower Louisiana, were for the most part war paths, and for that reason of use to the French also.[4]

In the Illinois country, as in other parts of the valley, there were places where, from time to time, the Indians congregated for the purpose of securing food or for trading with one another; the most important of these being at what are now Shawneetown, Peoria and Danville, at Fort St. Louis on the upper Illinois, at the present Rock Island, and at the mouth of the Chicago river. The

[1] *Filson Club Pub.*, vol. xiii, pp. 50-51; Zeisberger, vol. i, pp. 17-19.

[2] Journal of Captain Post, in *The Olden Times*, vol. i, pp. 150, 152.

[3] *Jes. Rel.*, vol. lxiii, p. 169.

[4] Adair, *The History of the American Indians*, pp. 295, 298, 302, 305, 310, 326, 338, 356, 357; *A. N., C., Sér. C*[13], vol. i, fol. 159.

Indians, as they went single file in every direction to and from these centers, wore deep narrow paths that were easily discernible and therefore were utilized by Europeans who, by uniting them, in some cases formed inter-colonial trails. From 1706 onward there was such a path between Kaskaskia and Detroit. It ran almost directly northeast from the former village across the present state of Illinois to Danville, avoiding on the way all the larger streams. On this part of the route the French followed such highways as were available through the high prairie land, while for the remainder of the distance they more frequently made use of the Indian river paths. Another of these "traces", known as the "Old Sauk Trail", passed from the mouth of the Rock river almost directly east across Illinois where it turned northeast and finally terminated at Malden, Canada.[1]

Other Indian trails passed from the French settlements on the Kaskaskia and Mississippi rivers to other points in the Illinois country. One extended from Kaskaskia by a somewhat indirect route to Fort Massac on the Ohio. This trail, before the end of French control in the Mississippi valley, was converted into a military road and each mile marked on a tree by the side of the path, the numbers being cut in with an iron and then painted red.[2] Another path went from the same French villages north of east to a point on the Wabash river near the place where Fort Vincennes was afterwards located. Later it was extended to the Falls of the Ohio where it joined the "Wilderness Trail". From Kaskaskia to the Wabash, a

[1] Parrish, *Historic Illinois, etc.*, pp. 121, 123; Bossu, vol. i, p. 159; *Jour. Ill. St. Hist. Soc.*, vol. iv, No. 2, pp. 157-163, 212-222.

[2] *Trans. Ill. St. Hist. Soc.*, No. 8, p. 39.

distance of 105 miles, a horseman could pass in five days. Not during the French period, nor for many years afterward, was it possible to traverse this route with a cart.[1] Still another of these trails passed from Kaskaskia. This one, by way of Cahokia, led to Peoria and from there to the lead regions near the present city of Galena, Illinois. Along this route pack-horses carried lead from the Fever river mines to Kaskaskia, a distance of "thirty leagues." There was also a road fit for horses and carts from the mines to a small river where the lead could be loaded on pirogues of light draught and sent to Kaskaskia by water.[2]

The Indians to the south of the Ohio river also had trade, hunting and war paths. Iberville, in 1702, found some good bridle trails, that he said could easily be made into roads fit for carts, between the different Indian villages around Mobile.[3] The Creek Indians were provided similarly. Their villages were favorably located for trade with the English, and on this account trails led out from the Creek country both to the Indian villages farther into the interior and to the English at Fort Moore and Augusta. The "High Town Path" began at High Shoals on the Oconee river and passed westward to the Chattahoochee river, which it crossed at Shallow Ford north of the present city of Atlanta. It then turned to the northeast and went to High Town in the Cherokee country, and from there almost west to the Chickasaw villages near the source of the Tombigbee river. Another trail began on the same river near the modern city of Milledgeville, ran southwest to the Chattahoochee, which it crossed near Cussets and from there

[1] Parrish, p. 124; *Early Western Travels,* vol. i, pp. 143-153; Collot, vol. i, p. 337.

[2] Parrish, pp. 121, 124; Bossu, vol. i, p. 187; *Reps. and Colls. St. Hist. Soc. Wis.*, vol. xiii, p. 277; *A. N., C., Sér.* C^{13}, vol. xxvi, fols. 11-12.

[3] Margry, vol. iv, p. 514.

the path led north of west to the Coosa river. This river it crossed and followed along its left bank to the Coosa Towns. There was also a Creek trail into the interior between these two, and another from the lower Creeks farther to the south.[1] This latter path extended south of west to the Alabama and Tombigbee rivers to the Choctaw, with a southern branch which in turn divided, one trail going to Mobile, the other to Pensacola. From Fort Toulouse the path followed the high lands at some distance from the river.[2] From St. Louis Bay on the Gulf there was an Indian path that zigzagged from one of the Indian villages to another and terminated at the village of the Choctaw chieftain.[3] The Choctaw also had three trails, western, middle and eastern, that led to Mobile.[4] Between the friendly Natchez and Chickasaw there was a well-defined "trace" which was used in 1742 by Déverges, "ingenieur" for the colony of Louisiana, who that year made a journey to the Chickasaw.[5]

Trips of this sort usually were not made by land because of the danger from Indian attacks and the morasses and thick forests that had to be traveled. There was always more or less difficulty, also, in procuring food. The trail had to be passed over on foot, and even if game were found, it was not of much service when a man could carry only a small supply of ammunition. The Indians, on the other hand, were much better walkers than the French, and

[1] Winsor, *The Miss. Basin*, pp. 20-21, 47, 383; Bartram, *Travels through North and South Carolina, etc.*, pp. 346, 374, 419; *Trans. Ala. Hist. Soc.*, vol. ii, pp. 40-46.

[2] *Trans. Ala. Hist. Soc.*, vol. ii, pp. 40-47; *Catholic Death Register*, MS., Mobile, Ala.

[3] *D'Anville's Map*, 1752, N. Y. P. Lib.

[4] Adair, p. 298.

[5] *A. N., C., Sér. C*[13], vol. xxvii, fols. 145-146.

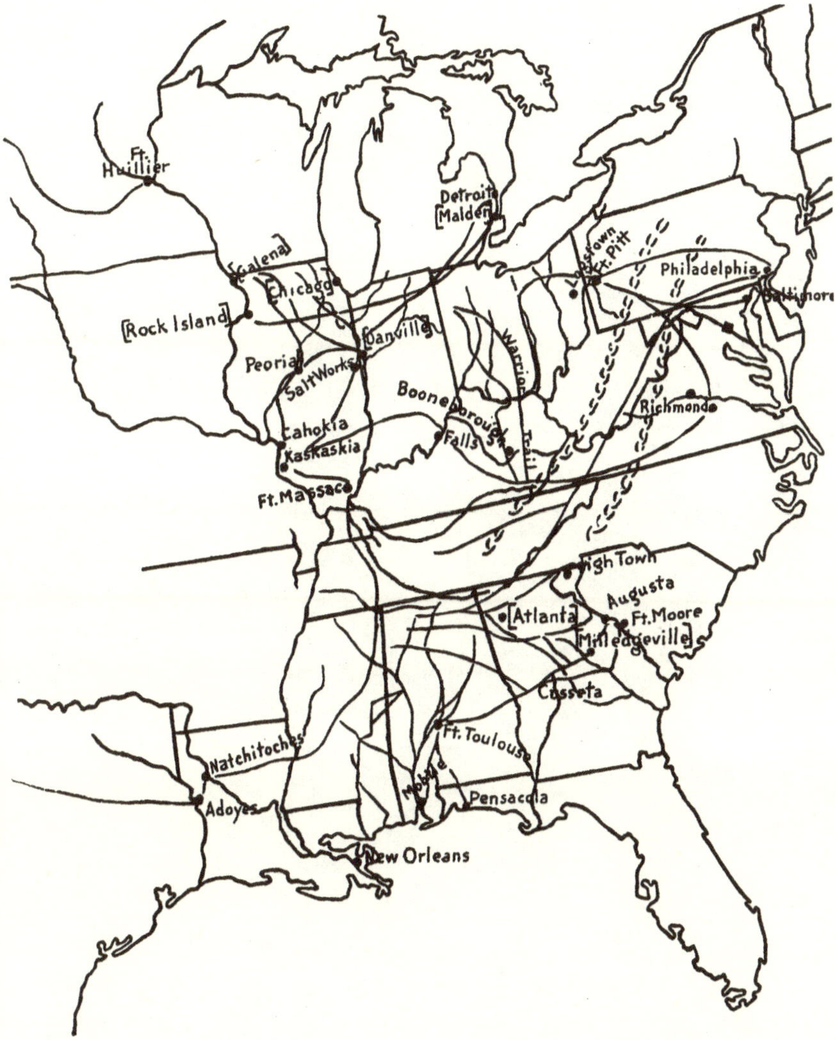
Ft. Huillier
Detroit
[Malden]
[Galena]
[Chicago]
[Rock Island]
[Danville]
Peoria
Salt Works
Cahokia
Kaskaskia
Ft. Massac
Booneborough
Falls
Warrior
Ft. Pitt
Philadelphia
Baltimore
Richmond
High Town
Augusta
Ft. Moore
[Atlanta]
[Milledgeville]
Cusseta
Ft. Toulouse
Natchitoches
Adoyes
Mobile
Pensacola
New Orleans

thought little of going for a considerable length of time without food.[1]

During the French control of the Mississippi valley many of the Indian and buffalo "traces" became trade trails. Along these paths long trains of pack-horses were driven in regular Indian file, the veterans in the van, the free horses, driven along to relieve the worn-out ones, in the rear. After the order of march for the day was arranged, the chief driver cracked his tough cowhide whip and gave an Indian whoop, both of which were repeated by the other drivers, and at once the train set off at a brisk trot which was not slackened as long as the horses were able to move forward. Each animal wore a bell which, at the start, was muffled by means of a twist of grass or leaves. It soon shook out. Nothing further being done to stop the noise which was increased by the Indian whoops and curses of the drivers, the day was filled with a continuous uproar. When two of the horse-trains met on the trail they saluted each other several times with a general whoop and other shouts of friendship; then they struck camp near each other. Due to their well-known preference for waterways, Frenchmen seldom made use of such pack-trains. They were in the main an English device for carrying on illicit trade in Louisiana east of the Mississippi.[2]

Many of the Indians carried on their backs over these trails packs of skins to the English or French markets, and, as was the case in most things, the Europeans followed the example set them by the natives. Two or three of such English pack-peddlers at a time would skulk "Arab like" about an Indian village, while in the winter season they carried their packs of "spirituous liquor and cheating trifles

[1] *The Present State of the Country*, 1744, p. 8.

[2] Bartram, p. 442; Collot, vol. ii, p. 299.

after the Indian hunting camp ".[1] The methods of the French pack-peddlers were not different, except that they carried their packs on their backs where they were held in place by a strap resting against the forehead.[2]

In crossing the streams the travelers attempted, with more or less success, to imitate the methods of the Indians. A tree was cut down so as to fall across a river and thus be used as a bridge; in crossing smaller streams saplings were employed in the same way. An Indian could pass easily and quickly over a " raccoon bridge ", as it was called, with a hundred pounds of skins on his shoulder, while Europeans sometimes found it hard, even without luggage, to shuffle along over it astride.[3] When possible they forded the streams with horses, but when this could not be done with safety to the packs, the horses were unloaded and driven across. The men then stripped themselves and waded the river, breast deep, carrying on their shoulders their belongings in order to keep them dry. One man says it took four crossings to transfer their baggage to the opposite bank. If the stream was too deep and wide for any of these methods, a bark canoe or raft was hastily constructed for the purpose. If the raft was used, when completed, a strong grape vine the length of the width of the river was tied to each end of the raft. A man took the end of one of the vines in his mouth and swam to the opposite shore. By means of the vine he then pulled the loaded raft across the river while a man on the other bank steadied it by means of the other vine, and when it was unloaded pulled it back to be reloaded.[4] Notwith-

[1] Adair, p, 367.

[2] Pittman, p. 102; *A., B. N., Fr.*, vol. 12224, fols. 142-145.

[3] Bartram, p. 445.

[4] *Ibid.*, pp. 444-445; *Filson Club Pub.*, vol. xiii, pp. 47, 52, 73.

standing the difficulties to be encountered in traveling, some of these European wayfarers, as early as 1715, were courageous enough to go across country unaided by either paths or Indian guides.[1]

Later when the Mississippi valley fell under the control of the English some of the Indian trails became well-known roads. For example, the trail through Cumberland Gap to the Falls of the Ohio came to be known as the " Wilderness Road ". Over this route and numerous by-paths pack-horses and travelers passed to all parts of the territory along the Ohio, Tennessee and Cumberland rivers.[2] To the west of the Mississippi the route followed by the Mallet brothers and their companions (1739-1740) in going from the Illinois country to Santa Fé, although not used as a highway by the French, later became the famous " Santa Fé Trail ".[3]

In the settled areas of the Mississippi valley the French made some efforts in the direction of road building. At first they worked in accord with a French law of 1669 that regulated such matters in the mother country, and as settlements were made along the Mississippi, levees and roads were built.[4] For a time each year the Mississippi floods interrupted the communication between the Illinois country and the Gulf settlements. In 1720 the Company of the Indies advised the " ordonnateur " and the commandant to work together to obviate this difficulty. It was proposed, therefore, to establish and keep in good order a series of post-roads between the two areas which would make it possible to forward letters and messages without delay. Two messengers were to leave Biloxi monthly for the Illinois and

[1] *Year Book, City of Charleston,* 1894, pp. 350-351.

[2] Speed, *The Wilderness Road,* in *Filson Club Pub.,* vol. ii, pp. 1-74.

[3] Margry, vol. vi, pp. 455-492.

[4] *American State Papers, Public Lands,* vol. ii, pp. 42-65.

vice versa. The proposal was not acted upon and no such route was ever established.[1] Later in the period of French rule, however, there appears to have been a path without posts, along which the men towing boats traveled up and down the Mississippi.[2]

In 1732 Governor Périer and the "ordonnateur" issued an ordinance which changed the old road law to make it fit conditions in Louisiana. To this end they decreed that men owing land along the Mississippi river must make a clearing along the river front to the depth of three arpents (sixty-six feet). At eight toise (forty-eight feet) from the water and an arpent apart (twenty-two feet) they were to plant a twelve-foot green oak or cypress post, eight feet under ground, with the part above ground not less than four feet in circumference. These posts were for the convenience of vessels that might make landings there. The owners of the land also were to build and keep in repair a levee six feet wide and not less than two feet high near the water's edge. Upon the levee there was to be a foot and bridle path and on the land side of the levee from the capital to Gentilly and Bayou St. Jean a wagon-road eight toise (forty-eight feet) wide. The men owning land contiguous to the road were to keep it and its bridges in repair. Each was to have his part of the work completed within six months after the publication of the ordinance, or be liable to a fine of fifty livres. The burden to the land owners was not great since only the part referring to the levees was enforced.[3]

In 1735 an ordinance was enacted making it illegal for any one to place obstructions upon these highways.[4] Nature,

[1] Margry, vol. v, pp. 624-625.

[2] Hall, p. 221; *Early Western Travels,* vol. xxiv, pp. 60-61.

[3] *A. N., C., Sér. A,* vol. xxiii, October 4, 1732.

[4] *Ibid.,* April 3, 1735.

however, was not included under this ordinance, and during the rainy season all burdens had to be carried over the roads on the heads of negroes.[1] In 1743 it again became necessary to pass an ordinance for the building of new and the repairing of old roads. In the main it differed little from those already enacted.[2] In 1749 still another ordinance was issued. This bade the colonists keep the levees, bridges and roads throughout the province in repair.[3] With the growth of settlements above and below New Orleans the levee was extended and by the end of French control there was a good coach road along the river fifty miles in length, eighteen miles of which was below New Orleans. When the vessels were detained for a considerable length of time at the " English Turn " waiting a change of wind, passengers wishing to hasten their arrival at New Orleans disembarked here and finished the journey by land.[4] By this time, furthermore, many semi-public roads had been built. These highways ran back from the river and lay between the different allotments of land. They were laid out, constructed and kept up at the expense of the men whose land lay on either side and by such persons who derived benefit from them. They were narrower than the public highways, though built in the same way with a ditch on either side of the road itself.[5]

In the village of New Orleans the streets were laid out in much the same way as the highways outside. On either side there was a ditch two feet wide and one to one and a half feet in depth, so as to render the streets passable for

[1] *Ibid., Sér.* C^{13}, vol. xxii, fols. 11-16.

[2] *Ibid., Sér. A,* vol. xxiii, October 13, 1743.

[3] *Ibid., Sér.* F^3, vol. ccxliii, M. S. S. M., October 13, 1749.

[4] Pittman, p. 41; Hutchins, p. 412; Le Page du Pratz, vol. ii, p. 259.

[5] *A., B. N., Joly Coll.,* vol. 1726, fol. 230.

carriages or even for foot passengers. Up to 1732 the bridges over these ditches had been made of wood. As they had always entailed a considerable annual expense for repairs, it was proposed that, for the health and convenience of the people, all such bridges within the villages should be built of brick, since no lumber, in contact with the ground and subjected to the damp climate of New Orleans, would last above a year or two at most. Many of the inhabitants were too poor to bear this expense, if it were to be borne by the householders alone; therefore it was planned to secure a part of the money, at least, from a tax of five sols a head on all negroes. One hundred and sixteen bridges, at an expense for two at each corner of 105 livres and nineteen sols, would be needed. If the water were made to run in such a way as to require but one bridge, this could be built at a cost of fifty-eight livres, twelve sols. The commissioner of public works, Dubreuil, offered to furnish the brick necessary, at nine livres a thousand, taking in payment a note payable in three years.[1] The home government seems to have approved the plan, for on July 4, 1735, an ordinance was passed making it obligatory for the inhabitants of New Orleans to build bridges or suffer a penalty of ten livres for disobedience. The ordinance, however, was not faithfully executed.[2]

Roads were constructed in the Illinois country also. In 1743 Governor Vaudreuil ordered roads at the so-called "square lines" to be built and kept up for carts and cattle to pass over to the "common". The highways to the Kaskaskia river and thence to the Mississippi were maintained at the expense of the community, whereas those to the

[1] *A. N., C., Sér. C^{13}*, vol. xiv, fol. 136.

[2] *Ibid., Sér. A,* vol. xxiii, July 4, 1735.

CARTE DES ENVIRONS DE LA NOUVELLE-ORLÉANS, 1760 [1]

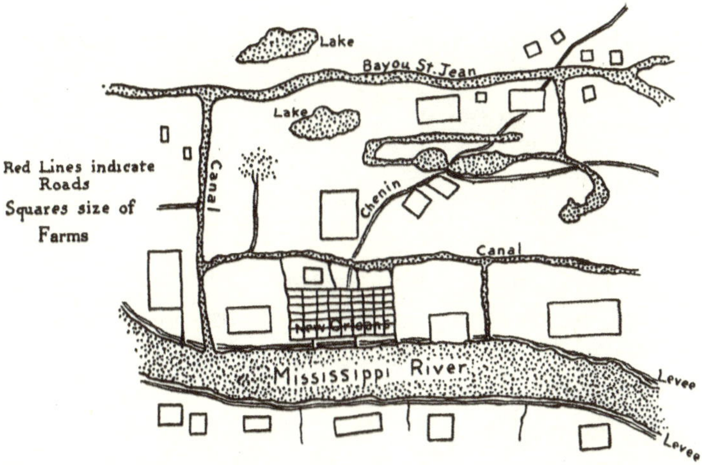

CARTE DES ENVIRONS DE LA FORTE ROSALIE [2]

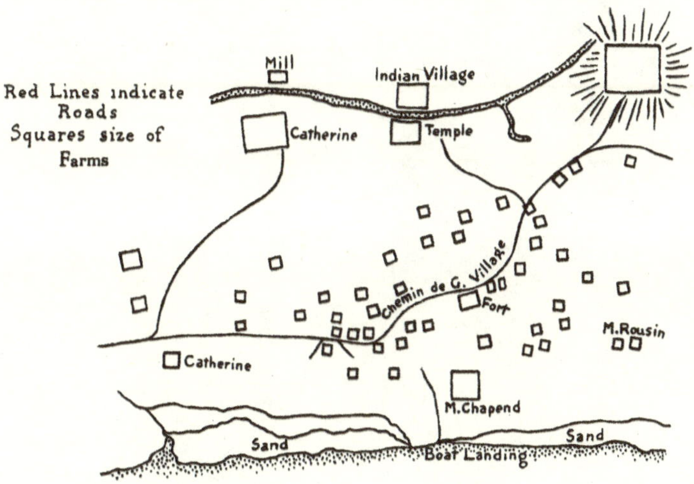

[1] Villiers du Terrage, p. 129.

[2] Dumont, vol. ii, p. 96.

"common" were to be looked after by the owners of the land through which they passed.[1] A road led from Kaskaskia to the other French settlements of the Illinois country. It extended over a distance of fourteen leagues to the village of Prairie du Rocher, passed through it and ran twelve miles farther on to Fort Chartres. From here to St. Philippe it was eight miles, and a day's journey to Cahokia.[2] West of the Mississippi, in the St. Geneviève district, pack-horse roads stretched from the mines to the nearest river, or to St. Geneviève. These trails varied in length from six miles to a hundred.[3] A much-frequented road led from St. Geneviève to the salt-licks one league from the village.[4] In the Natchitoches district also there was a road seven leagues in length and extending to the Spanish settlement of Adayes. This highway and a portage around the falls below the village constituted the only roads in this area during the period of French occupation.[5]

In the Illinois country small native horses drew over the road a two-wheeled "bare-footed" cart (*i. e.*, without tires). To these carts by means of harness neatly made from strong pieces of rawhide, the horses were hitched tandem. Although small, they were strong and willing workers, and consequently pulled fairly large burdens. For the heavier loads oxen, yoked by the horns, were hitched to the carts.[6]

On the lower Mississippi horses were used chiefly for rid-

[1] *A. N., C., Sér. A*, vol. xxiii, Aug. 14, 1743; Breese, App., p. 295.

[2] Bossu, vol. i, p. 159; Collot, vol. i, pp. 325-333.

[3] Austin, *A Summary Description of the Lead Mines in Upper Louisiana, etc.*, pp. 3-17; Pittman, p. 95.

[4] Pittman, p. 95; *Early Western Travels*, vol. xxvi, p. 97.

[5] *D'Anville's Map*, N. Y. Pub. Lib.

[6] Reynolds, *The Pioneer History of Illinois*, pp. 49-50; Moses, vol. i, p. 105.

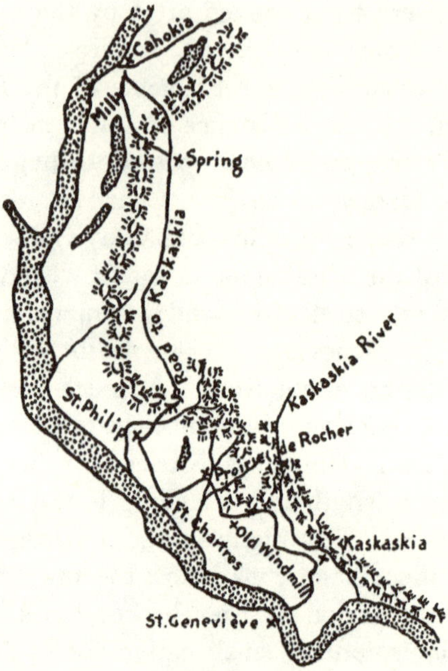

HUTCHINS' MAP[1]

ing and for carriages, and even for those purposes they were too small to be greatly esteemed. The two-wheeled carts were usually drawn by oxen. Before the end of the French régime a large majority of the well-to-do persons in this part of the province owned some sort of conveyance and horses or oxen or both. In New Orleans there were carriages and coaches. The first of the former type was brought from Havana in 1730 and the second, three years later by Bienville, after which the number increased more rapidly. In 1753 almost all men of means at the capital owned a chaise and two horses and there were some who had berlins and coaches drawn by four horses.[2]

[1] *Hutchins' Map;* Winsor, *The Miss. Basin*, p. 460.

[2] *The Present State of the Country, etc.*, 1744, p. 18; Villiers du Terrage, p. 46.

CHAPTER VII

Barter

Turning from this study of the facilities of transportation to an examination of the various commercial processes, it may be remarked that when the French came to the Mississippi valley they found the Indians carrying on trade by means of barter, as might naturally be expected among primitive peoples. Captives taken in war were disposed of in this way. The Illinois Indians warred on tribes to the south and west of them for the sole purpose of securing captives whom they "bartered, selling at a high price to other nations for muskets, powder, kettles, hatchets and knives",[1] and to the Iroquois for peace.[2] To the south of the Ohio were the Chickasaw who in their numerous encounters with weaker tribes, secured captives for whom they, too, bartered with other Indians.[3] Slaves and many objects thus passed from tribe to tribe. It was not uncommon to find bartered goods miles away from the place of their origin. Marquette, for example, found the Arkansas Indians in possession of commodities that had been obtained from the Illinois and other Indians still more remote.[4]

Moreover the Indians along the Mississippi, before the French arrived, had had some experience in trading with Europeans. The Illinois and other tribes met at Michilimackinac traders from New France with whom they ex-

[1] *Jes. Rel.*, vol. liv, p. 191; vol. lix, p. 127.

[2] *Hist. Colls. of La.*, pt. 1, p. 56.

[3] La Harpe, pp. 89-90, 186.

[4] *Jes. Rel.*, vol. lix, p. 155.

changed skins for French merchandise,[1] while the southern Indians made similar exchanges with the Spanish of Pensacola and New Mexico and the English of Carolina.[2] It is, therefore, not surprising to read that Marquette found the Illinois Indians would give " hardly any more than do the French ". They acted so much like skilled traders, in fact, that, after he had traded a cubit of tobacco with them for three fine ox skins, he felt impelled to say mass immediately on being rid of them.[3]

Throughout the period of French control trade with the Indians continued to be carried on by means of barter. Father Gravier, on his way to the Illinois, in 1700, gave " a little lead and powder, a box of vermillion wherewith to daub his young men, and some other trifles " to the chief of the Arkansas tribes for a quantity of " dried peaches, of Piachimina " (persimmons), and squashes.[4] Several years later Father Poisson, in passing over the same route, observed that the Indian "gives nothing for nothing" and declared that the French must follow the same practice or expose themselves to the contempt of the Indians.[5] The French traders made no error of that sort. They carried their merchandise to the Indians and exchanged it for bear's oil, corn, beans, horses, furs, slaves and other Indian commodities. In such transfers each party forced upon the other the hardest possible bargain.[6]

Where the French traders held practically a monopoly of

[1] *Jes. Rel.*, vol. lix, p. 91; Shea, *Disc. and Exp. etc.*, p. liv.

[2] Margry, vol. iv, pp. 516-519; *The Present State of the Country, etc.*, 1744, pp. 9-11.

[3] *Jes. Rel.*, vol. lix, p. 175.

[4] *Ibid.*, vol. lxv, pp. 121-123.

[5] *Ibid.*, vol. lxvii, p. 257.

[6] Margry, vol. vi, pp. 230, 246, 280; *Kerlérec's Report*, 1758, p. 67; Charlevoix, *Hist. and Gen. Description of New France*, vol. vi, p. 32; *The Present State of the Country, etc.*, 1744, p. 11; *Doc. Rel. Col. Hist. of N. Y.*, vol. ix, p. 409.

control in any region they were able to secure fabulous profits from their dealings. Sometimes they carried their extortions to the extent of offending the Indians by the ridiculously low prices they offered. One such trader had the temerity to offer an Indian one charge of powder and a bullet for a beaver skin, whereupon the Indian replied by burying a hatchet in the head of the trader.[1] The possibility of such unfair exchange, however, came to an end when the English traders entered the field as competitors. The newcomers studied the tastes of the Indians with more care than the French did, and hence were able to offer a more attractive, diversified and richer stock of merchandise.[2] With these two sets of traders in the field, each trying to gain the whole of the trade, the Indians henceforth were able to secure for themselves better returns in trading operations with Europeans.

Since the Indians looked upon good opportunities for traffic as a clear evidence of friendship, the competitor who offered the better commodities at a lower rate was always able to attract them and to keep them friendly and obedient, so long at least as the advantage lasted.[3] For the most part the attitude of the Indians toward the whites was based on economic considerations alone. During the time of the French and Indian War the Creeks were accused of playing off the French and English against each other in order to secure better bargains in trade. When forced out of this neutrality they went over to the side that seemed to them the stronger.[4]

[1] *Penn. Col. Rec.*, vol. v, p. 87.

[2] *Public Records of South Carolina*, vol. v, p. 196; vol. viii, p. 227. Transcripts, Columbia, S. C.

[3] *Ibid.*, vol. v, p. 196; *Board of Trade Papers*, pt. 2, vol. x, 1718-1720, *Penn. Hist. Soc. Trans.*

[4] *Bancroft Papers, Col. Doc.*, 1755-1757, Dec. 25, 1756; 1758-1760, Oct. 20, 1758, N. Y. Pub. Lib.

Barter was not confined to exchanges made between the Indians themselves, as has been shown, nor was it used only when the Indian was a party. In the French settlements of the interior, barter was always the way in which by far the larger number of exchanges were effected. Almost from the beginning of French occupation, also, produce from the Arkansas, Natchitoches, Wabash and Illinois districts found its way to the Gulf region there to be exchanged for other merchandise. Wheat, flour, hams, bees-wax, lead, salt, furs, tobacco, bear's oil and other products were traded for spirituous liquors, groceries, dry goods and articles especially needful in the Indian trade.[1] In none of these transactions was there a fixed standard of value. They were carried on purely by barter. Undoubtedly peltry and lead passed freely in exchange;[2] but there is no evidence of any standard of value among the French of the interior settlements or elsewhere in Louisiana comparable with the "made beaver",[3] or wampum of the English.[4] The article last named was not used by the French in the Mississippi valley except by traders from New France when they were dealing with Indians who were allies of the English.[5]

In the French settlements of lower Louisiana, as in those to the northward, barter was always used in exchanges with the Indians. This method of action, however, did not persist among the French themselves in that area.

[1] *Jes. Rel.*, vol. lxix, p. 213; Le Page du Pratz, vol. i, p. 331; Pittman, pp. 62, 82, 98; Dumont, vol. ii, pp. 56-57.

[2] *Early Western Travels*, vol. xxvii, p. 54.

[3] *New England Magazine*, vol. xxxiii, p. 260; "Made beaver" was a full-grown, perfect beaver skin taken from the animal killed in season, properly cured and weighing from a pound to a pound and a quarter.

[4] Dumont, vol. ii, p. 56; *Early Western Travels*, vol. xxvii, p. 54.

[5] *Early Western Travels*, vol. i, p. 59.

Almost from the foundation of the colony the French here made use of some form of money. There were, nevertheless, many transactions in which merchandise was given for service rendered, and for colonial products. Those who had labor or produce to sell for the most part preferred to exchange it for French foodstuffs and other goods.[1] In 1723 the carpenters at work for the Company of the Indies received in merchandise the amount of the wages they were to use in Louisiana, whereas the part that was to go to the support of their families in France was paid in silver.[2]

[1] Charlevoix, *Hist. and Gen. Desc. of New France*, vol. vi, pp. 32-33; Margry, vol. v, pp. 653, 661; *A. N., C., Sér.* C^{13}, vol. viii, fol. 123.

[2] Margry, vol. v, pp. 652-653, 661.

CHAPTER VIII

Silver Coins

The only coins in circulation in Louisiana during the earlier years of its existence were those brought over by the colonists themselves or received by them from sailors for provisions.[1] Efforts were soon made, however, to secure piastres from the Spanish settlements near by.[2] Trade sprang up between the inhabitants of Biloxi and the soldiers of Pensacola, which put a small amount of silver into circulation. It did not remain long, because on the arrival of the first vessel it was exchanged for European merchandise and carried to France on the return voyage.[3] From this source, nevertheless, a little silver continued to flow into the colony until the arrival, in 1712, of the Crozat officials who ordered the Pensacola trade stopped. The enforcement of the order greatly distressed trade and practically deprived the province of its only medium of exchange.[4]

With the transfer of Louisiana to the Company of the West another channel through which a little Spanish money might enter was opened by the planting of the outpost of Natchitoches on the frontier of Texas, not far from the Spanish station of Adayes. The former supplied the latter with food in exchange for Spanish money. This trade lasted only about two years when the Spanish of that

[1] Dumont, vol. ii, p. 53. [2] Margry, vol. vi,, p. 180.

[3] *A. N., C., Sér.* C^{13}, vol. iii, fols. 212-213; Charlevoix, *Hist. and Gen. Desc. of New France*, vol. vi, pp. 32-33.

[4] *A. N., C., Sér.* C^{13}, vol. v, pp. 48-49.

post began to cultivate the soil and thus provide themselves with a food supply. For some time longer the trade in French merchandise continued, and amounted annually to about two hundred piastres. Later this sum was considerably reduced by the introduction into Adayes of cheaper and more desirable English merchandise.[1] Some Spanish coins also came into Louisiana by way of the Illinois country. These the French obtained in trade with the western Indians who secured them directly or indirectly from New Mexico.[2] With the entrance of the Company of the Indies into control, the Mobile-Pensacola trade was revived, and by 1720 Mobile had become a flourishing village with an abundance of Spanish money.[3]

The Spanish, like the French, specie flowed out of the province too freely, thereby leaving a serious shortage. This drain, due, it was believed, to the fact that the piastre was received in trade in Louisiana for but four livres, while by royal decree it was given a higher value in Martinique and St. Domingue, could be checked only by making the value of the Spanish piece uniform in all the French colonies in America. Accordingly the home government by an edict, January 12, 1723, raised the piastre to the value (seven livres ten sols) it had in the French West Indies.[4] As this action did not improve conditions, a series of reductions, February 26, May 2, and October 30, 1724, were made, which brought the value of the piastre down to four livres ten sols, almost the value it had had before the first change was made, though without greatly affecting the outflow.[5]

[1] Margry, vol. vi, p. 231.

[2] *A. N., C., Sér.* C^{13}, vol. vi, fol. 297.

[3] *Ibid.*, p. 363; La Harpe, p. 327.

[4] *A. N., C., Sér. A*, vol. xxiii, January 12, 1723; *French MSS. Miss. Valley*, 1679-1796, La. Hist. Soc. Lib.

[5] *A. N., C., Sér. A*, vol. xxiii; *Sér.* C^{13}, vol. xi, fols. 51-62.

For about two years the Spanish money retained the value given it by the edict of October 30, 1724. On June 15, 1725, the crown increased the rate for the coinage of gold and silver bullion received at the mint of France. To meet this situation, on September 13, 1726, it raised the value of the piastre from four livres to five, and the change should go into effect when the royal edict was published in Louisiana.[1] As specie continued to be scarce, in 1727 the Company of the Indies made five-sol silver pieces of the same value as the Spanish piastre and the French écu. Since local necessities required something like 20,000 livres in circulation, the Company was requested by its agents in the colony to send over not less than 50,000 or 60,000 livres' worth of these five-sol pieces, so as to offset somewhat the risk that, on the arrival of the first vessel, most of the hard money would be carried back to France. The next year the silver asked for had not yet reached Louisiana, where it was greatly needed to pay the troops and meet other expenses of the government.[2] Any assurances on this point in fact, seem never to have been fulfilled, for both gold and silver to the end of the Company's control continued to be rare, and what was received quickly passed back to France.[3]

From 1731 to 1735 the crown met the expenses of government in Louisiana partly with French money, and partly with merchandise.[4] As was the case during the time of the Company, the silver speedily found its way to France, leaving the colony without a metallic currency, except a small amount of copper and a few Spanish coins gotten

[1] *A. N., C., Sér. F*[3], vol. ccxlii, M. S. S. M., June 15, 1725.

[2] *Ibid., Sér. C*[13], vol. xi, fols. 54-56, 86; vol. x, fols. 193-194.

[3] *Ibid.*, vol. xvi, fols. 166-171.

[4] *Ibid.*, vol. xiv, fols. 142-143; vol. xvi, fol. 271.

in trade with Pensacola.[1] The use of these two kinds of money caused difficulty in Louisiana, since some of the Spanish coins had no equivalent in the French money. On January 26, 1732, in order to facilitate commerce, Governor Périer, in conjunction with the "ordonnateur", issued a decree fixing the value of the Spanish silver in terms of French money. Beginning with the highest, each of the Spanish coins was to have a value double that of the next lower denomination. Even the smallest of these pieces, the "quarter real," though unknown in the other French colonies, was used in Louisiana, because of the shortage of small money there.[2]

The estimation of values of the different coins in use in the province no doubt was a benefit to domestic trade, but gave no aid to the keeping of the silver in the colony, which was the problem baffling the provincial officials. On April 12, 1734, there were about 140,000 livres in specie in the treasury. On April 15, 1735, this amount had dwindled to 51,000; on October 12 there were but 32,290 livres, and by February 20, 1737, the silver had entirely disappeared. Consequently, even though required by royal order so to do, the officials were unable, for the next two years, to pay the troops in specie.[3] To meet this emergency the gov-

[1] *A. N., C., Sér. F*[3], vol. ccxlii, M. S. S. M.

[2] *Ibid., Sér. A*, vol. xxiii, January 26, 1732; Baudry des Lozières, *Second Voyage à la Louisiane*, p. 89.

Value of the coins as stated in the decree:

Piastre, equal to 5 *livres*, to pass for......100 *sols*.
Half *piastre*, equal to 50 *sols*, to pass for.. 50 *sols*.
"Double real," equal to 20 *sols*, to pass for 25 *sols*.
"Real," equal to 10 *sols*, to pass for...... 12 *sols* 6 *deniers*.
"Half real," equal to 5 *sols*, to pass for... 6 *sols* 3 *deniers*.
"Quarter real," equal to 3 sols. to pass for. 3 *sols* 1 *denier* and a half.

[3] *A. N., C., Sér. C*[13], vol. xix, fols. 32-33; vol. xxi, fols. 230-232; vol. xx, fols. 15-16, 213-215.

ernor and "ordonnateur" requested the home government to issue a special money for Louisiana. The crown in its replies, March 24 and April 9, 1738, complained that the colonial officials had proposed first one and then another kind of money, but that it seemed they preferred an issue of silver because it could not be counterfeited easily. Since the whole proposition was so vague and indefinite that it was impossible to determine just what was desired, the request was denied.[1]

The scarcity of silver in Louisiana continued until about 1740 when the vessels from France on their way thither began to make stops at the Spanish-American colonies, where they exchanged merchandise for Spanish silver. The latter was carried to the province and there paid over for colonial products and bills of exchange, thus assuring a considerable increase in the silver in circulation.[2] Although the war with England (1744-1748) disturbed this trade, it brought about a condition that made it possible to augment the supply of Spanish money in Louisiana so much that from 1745 to 1748 the expenses of the colony were paid entirely in this medium. The first year of the war business took an official of the French West Indies to Havana where he learned that a number of French merchants there had Spanish silver which they wished to ship to France. This could be done directly only at very great risk of capture by the English. The island officials proposed to the merchants in question that they send their silver to Louisiana and there exchange it for bills of exchange on the French treasury. The plan was adopted and carried out without an appreciable increase in the amount of bills of exchange. Throughout the period the rate of exchange remained five livres for each

[1] *A. N., C., Sér. B,* vol. lxvi, fols. 8-10.

[2] *Ibid., Sér. C*[13], vol. xxxi, fol. 111.

piastre. The English believing Louisiana of small consequence had left it unguarded.[1] During each year of the war a million piastres found their way to the province, and in 1749 a squadron of six vessels, carrying 80,000,000 piastres brought from Havana, left for France.[2]

In 1750 the French merchants in the West Indies were able to send their shipments of silver directly to France, therefore the old-time scarcity was again felt in Louisiana. The next year there was not enough specie in the province to pay the troops,[3] and by 1752 practically all the Spanish money in circulation at New Orleans was the little that had found its way thither from the settlement at Natchitoches.[4] Silver money became rarer each year, and after 1759 there was virtually none of it available.[5]

[1] *A., B. N., Joly Coll.*, vol. 1726, fols. 136-147.

[2] Villiers du Terrage, p. 79; *The Present State of the Country, etc.*, pp. 26-34; *A. N., C., Sér.* C^{13}, vol. xxiii, pp. 6-8.

[3] *A. N., C., Sér.* F^3, vol. ccxliii, M. S. S. M., May 18, 1751.

[4] *Records of the American Catholic Historical Society of Philadelphia*, vol. x, p. 206.

[5] *A. N., C., Sér.* C^{13}, vol. xli, pp. 318-322; Pittman, p. 48; Ker, *The Memoirs of John Ker of Kersland in North Britain, Relating to Politicks, Trade and History*, pt. 3, ii, 19.

CHAPTER IX

Copper Coins

With the growth of the colony the necessity for small currency soon began to be felt, especially in the settlements on the Gulf coast. To meet this demand in some measure, a royal edict was issued, in December, 1716, providing for the coinage of 150,000 marcs (eight ounces) of copper money in twelve and six denier pieces, to be used exclusively in the American colonies. By a second decree, March 9, 1717, authorization was given for the new money to circulate in Louisiana. The process of coinage was soon stopped, however, because of the inferior quality of the copper received at the mints.[1]

Nothing further was done in the matter until June, 1721, when, by a further edict the mints were again ordered to coin 150,000 marc of copper money, as follows: at Bordeaux, 30,000; at La Rochelle, 50,000; at Nantes, 40,000; and at Rouen, 30,000. The coins were to be used in paying the troops and for meeting other public expenses. They were to circulate with the following fixed values: those of twenty marcs to the silver marc, at eighteen deniers; those of forty, at nine deniers; and those of eighty, at four deniers. The colonists were assured, moreover, that they need have no fear to receive this money from the troops or other persons in payment for the products they had to sell, since it would be received by the Company in payment for

[1] *A., B. N., Fr.*, vol. 14273, fol. 108; *A. N., C., Sér. B*, vol. xxxix, fol, 341; Zay, *Histoire Monétaire des Colonies Françaises*, pp. 48-51; *Pro. St. Hist. Soc. Wis.*, vol. xli, p. 169.

all sorts of European merchandise without discrimination between it and gold or silver.[1] The mints at Bordeaux and Nantes struck no coins under this edict and the other two, only the nine-denier pieces. The coins issued at La Rochelle, 1721-1722, were marked by the letter "H", those at Rouen, 1721, by the letter "B".[2]

Before the colonial copper had been twelve months in circulation in Louisiana it had fallen into the hands of speculators. In September, 1723, complaints were made to the officials at New Orleans that twenty-five livres of copper money was demanded for a piastre. Thereupon the authorities made an unsuccessful attempt to fix the rate of exchange for the piastres at seven livres, ten sols. The officials went still further and instituted a search for the men who were carrying on the business of speculation. In this, however, they had no better results than in their efforts at rate-fixing. Consequently copper money gradually fell into greater and greater disfavor until it came to be looked upon as entirely worthless, and no one wished to receive it in exchange for even the most trifling article.[3] For example, Father Raphael de Luxembourge, of New Orleans, September 7, 1723, declared: " there are few offerings for masses, some (fees for) parochial functions in copper coin, which is valued so low that during our sickness I sent everywhere to get a couple of eggs, offering as much as — sous apiece, but could not find them. Those who sold them replied that they could do nothing with our copper, and that if we had white money to give them, they had eggs to sell us ".[4]

[1] *A. N., C., Sér. A,* vol. xxiii, Sept. 27, 1721; *Sér.* C^{13}, vol. vi, fol. 421; Zay, pp. 52-53; La Harpe, p. 295.

[2] Zay, p. 54.

[3] *A. N., C., Sér.* C^{13}, vol. vii, fols. 15-17.

[4] *Proc. St. Hist. Soc. Wis.*, vol. xli, p. 172.

The colonial agents of the Company of the Indies at the time informed the home government that, if the copper coins in circulation in Louisiana were made legal money in France, they would be received in the province at the proper rate of exchange. The suggestion, should it be followed, would entail only the added expense of carrying the copper, with other shipments of money, back to the mother country. If this plan were not feasible, it was further proposed that the copper pieces be received at a ratio of one to five with silver at the posts in the interior where the vessels from the province landed, the deduction being made in order to put as little as possible of this money into use there. The Company could well afford this rate since, under the arrangement then in force in the province, it was obliged to receive some piastres at twenty-five livres each in copper money, a loss of 300 livres on every forty thus secured and sent to France. Moreover, the royal government was informed that the prevailing system of copper currency was most detrimental to the development of Louisiana, and that even the poor quality of laborers whom the crown succeeded in sending over were so dissatisfied with their pay that they were planning to return to France.[1]

By a decree of May 2, 1724, applicable both to France and to the colonial dominions, the copper coinage was made to suffer a reduction in value. That circulating in Louisiana was henceforth to have the following values: coins of eighteen deniers to pass for twelve; those of nine, for six; and those of four and a half, for three. Moreover, the colonial officials were given explicit orders for the enforcement of the decree.[2]

As a result of this act, bringing the face value of copper

[1] *A. N., C., Sér. C^13*, vol. vii, fols. 15-17.

[2] *Ibid., Sér. A*, vol. xxiii, May 2, 1724; Zay, pp. 56-57.

nearer to its current rate, an impetus was given to its circulation. On August 17, 1724, the superior council of the province made a loan to one of the inhabitants of 10,000 livres in copper money, payable in six months in different kinds of lumber. The next day it made a similar loan to the captain of the troops at Mobile for 3,600 livres, returnable in six months in the same medium.[1] On February 27,[2] and again on July 27, 1725,[3] it was officially stated that the copper money had at no time been refused in payment for all sorts of merchandise at the Company's storehouses. At the same time, nevertheless, the Capuchin father, on the plea of insufficient knowledge in money matters, was demanding that offerings and gifts, as well as money for the services, should be paid in silver.[4]

In view of the fact that many persons who had contracted debts were being made to meet their obligations with Spanish silver, the crown issued a decree, October 31, 1726, ordering the copper coins to be received at their fixed value, without discrimination between them and silver, bills of exchange or notes, in payment of all debts whatsoever. Persons violating this law were to be whipped and branded on the hand by the executioner. The piastres were to be confiscated and a fine of 3,000 livres also was to be imposed, one-half to be given to the informer, the other half to the hospital.[5]

No sooner was copper made a legal tender for all debts than it began to leave the colony. On April 23, 1727, there was not a sol of it in the colonial treasury, despite the efforts

[1] *A. N., C., Sér. C*[13], vol. viii, fol. 126.

[2] *Ibid.*, vol. ix, fol. 26.

[3] *Ibid.*, fols. 51-52.

[4] *Ibid.*, fol. 150.

[5] *Ibid., Sér. F*[3], vol. ccxlii, M. S. S. M., Oct. 31, 1726.

of the officials to prevent it. The pay of the laborers, sailors and other men employed by the Company was two months in arrears.[1] Therefore even though the vessel "Dromadaire" brought to Louisiana, October 2, 1727, 13,000 livres in copper money, the sum was insufficient to meet immediate needs. It was officially stated, in fact, if the coins had been distributed before the departure of the vessel, not a sol would have remained in circulation. The coins were kept, therefore, and notes given out instead. In order to prevent the copper from leaving the colony, Governor Périer and the "ordonnateur" asked the crown to legalize the issuance of notes or bills of exchange in favor of any one willing to leave in the province the copper money he possessed. For this purpose the crown gave permission to draw 6,000 livres in treasury notes annually, stipulating, however, that the notes were to be discounted at ten per cent and the "ordonnateur" was to make no loans whatsoever in copper.[2]

The metal still continued to leave the province. On July 31, 1728, there was no copper left in the colonial treasury, the drawing of the 6,000 livres allowed by the royal government being insufficient to hold it.[3] By October of the same year there was almost no copper in circulation anywhere in Louisiana,[4] and the governor accordingly requested the home government, March 25, 1729, to instruct him how it wished him to provide a medium of exchange, since under the present arrangement it was not possible to keep specie in the colony.[5] There was no reply, and nothing further was done

[1] *A. N., C., Sér.* C^{13}, vol. x, fol. 174.

[2] *Ibid.*, fols. 193-194; vol. xi, fols. 86-87.

[3] *Ibid.*, vol. xi, fols. 54-56.

[4] *Ibid.*, fol. 125.

[5] *Ibid.*, fols. 322-336.

in the matter during the rule of the Company of the Indies.[1]

For a time after Louisiana became a royal province the crown attempted to make use of copper as a medium of exchange. In order to meet the deficiency in small coins, Governor Périer and the "ordonnateur" were allowed to issue an ordinance, January 26, 1732, giving to the copper money in circulation a value of six deniers.[2] On April 10, 1735, Bienville, who was now governor, requested the home government to increase the amount by sending to Louisiana yearly, for three years, about 6,000 livres of the copper currency issued under the Company of the Indies, or some other having equivalent value. Such pieces of money, he declared, were especially needed at the treasury where everyone demanded the last denier due him, and in commercial transactions where very small amounts were purchased.[3] On October 12, 1735, there were but eighty livres of copper in the colonial treasury, and by February 18th of the next year the amount had been reduced to twenty-five.[4]

The copper money used by the Company of the Indies while in control of Louisiana was not available, but the home government relieved the shortage in small currency by ordering, October 11, 1735, 6,000 livres in "sols marqués" to be sent to the province.[5] The following year, October 15, 1736, a similar order was issued.[6] Bienville at once took measures to retain the money in circulation. To this end he asked to have its value in Louisiana increased by one-fifth of its value in France, and to have dispatched

[1] *A. N., C., Sér.* C^{13}, vol. xi, fol. 125.
[2] *Ibid., Sér. A,* vol. xxiii, Jan. 26, 1732.
[3] *Ibid., Sér.* C^{13}, vol. xx, fols. 16-17, 18-20.
[4] *Ibid.,* vol. xxi, fols. 230-232.
[5] *Ibid., Sér. B,* vol. lxiii, fol. 622.
[6] *Ibid.,* vol. lxiv, fols. 276-277.

in 1738, not less than 12,000 or 15,000 livres instead of the yearly allowance of 6,000.[1] Though French copper money was not afterwards brought to Louisiana in large quantities, some of it was seen in circulation there as late as 1769.[2]

[1] *A. N., C., Sér.* C^{13}, vol. xxii, fols. 5-6.

[2] *Museum Building, New Orleans*, No. 40, Oct. 31, 1769.

CHAPTER X

Paper Money and Credit, 1699-1739

The rapidity with which specie of all kinds left Louisiana made it necessary for the colonial officials to resort to various expedients in order to retain it in the province. To this end before 1739 a number of forms of paper to serve as currency were made use of, such as bills of exchange, treasury notes, orders on the treasury, orders on the storehouse, contracts between individuals and with the Company of the Indies, royal notes and card money.

As early as 1703 Iberville received furs from the Canadian traders and gave in return bills of exchange.[1] These were called a " designated " or " named " money and were negotiable only when indorsed. As stated at the time, a bill of exchange was drawn to the order of a certain person without affording any details as to the nature of the transaction, or indicating the kind of money in which it was to be paid. Otherwise, it was stated, much disorder in trade would have been caused through merchants being forced to make public the secrets of their business, thereby violating the freedom and security of commerce.[2] At the time of the founding of Louisiana, and for some years afterward, bills of exchange, in all the French colonies, were drawn by the treasurer general of the particular province on the treasurer general in France and were signed by the intendant or a corresponding officer.

[1] *A. N., C., Sér.* C^{13}, fol. 29; Margry, vol. iv, p. 628.

[2] *A., B. N., Fr.*, vol. 11342, fols. 95-102.

The home government, on the other hand, held that it had not pledged itself to pay such drafts without first making an examination of their validity. The law of trade, " a law so dangerous to break ", it was asserted, furnished the crown a " simple procedure " in the matter. Any one who drew bills of exchange might forge them on the person on whom they were drawn. If the latter accepted them when presented, the implication was that he recognized the indebtedness and obligated himself to pay them when they fell due. If he refused so to do, naturally they were protested. But in either case the bills ought to be paid, since in the hands of the holder of the last endorsement they were current money, the circulation of which should not be interrupted. The question then arose as to how this payment was to be effected.[1] The payment, it was further declared, was to be made only after the holder had applied to the last endorser for reimbursement. He in turn was to go back to the preceding signer who was likewise pledged to redeem them, and thus by a retrograde movement the bills could be traced to their source, that is, to the original drawer who must prove the crown to be his debtor. Such was the " simple procedure " by which the home government was to secure justice in the payment of bills of exchange without thereby disturbing trade. Thus also the officials in France were to be given the legal means to ascertain and destroy abuses in the drawing of such bills, and at the same time to punish the offenders.[2] By 1720 these irregularities had become so excessive that the government itself was much embarrassed and only with great difficulty could meet its indebtedness. Louisiana, however, when compared with other French provinces was only a mild offender.[2]

[1] *A., B. N., Fr.*, vol. 11342, fols. 95-102.

[2] *Ibid.*

Other kinds of paper were early made use of. One of them took the form of orders on the treasury. On February 25, 1708, for example, the inhabitants of Louisiana were encountering much difficulty in securing domestic animals because they could find no one willing to accept such orders in payment.[1] Another form of paper that was suggested, June 15, 1715, but apparently not utilized, consisted of royal notes of fifty and one hundred livres to be received in payment for half of every debt.[2] On March 9, 1717, the home government announced that a new sort of paper money would be sent to New France, Martinique and Louisiana with an injunction that the decree providing for it should be registered with the respective superior councils. Almost two years later the Company of the Indies, under this ordinance, was supplied with 25,000,000 livres in numbered bank notes bearing the corporate seal, for which a receipt was given, the purpose being " to enable the inhabitants of Louisiana to trade amongst themselves and bring to France the fruits of their labor ". In order that such notes should be paid to no one but himself, the holder, on receipt, was to sign them, and in case of loss immediately to notify the Company. If not recovered by the end of five years the Company pledged itself to pay to the holder the full value.[3]

Along with the royal notes a local currency established itself naturally. When a person employed by the Company required merchandise from the storehouse, he made a memorandum or statement of the things he desired and

[1] *A. N., C., Sér. C*[13], vol. ii, fols. 89-117.

[2] *Ibid.*, vol. iii, fol. 860.

[3] *La Revue Canadienne*, 1893, vol. xxix, p. 31; *The Am. Weekly Mercury*, vol. i, No. 8, p. 15, Feb. 9, 1719; Anderson, *Hist. and Chron. Deduct. of the Origin of Commerce, etc.*, vol. iii, p. 312; MacPherson, *Annals of Commerce, etc.*, vol. iii, p. 68.

presented it to the local director who deleted the articles that seemed to him unnecessary and signed for the remainder. The commodities were to be furnished on presentation of the statement thus approved. The holder could carry it directly to the storehouse and have it cashed, or could exchange it for whatever he saw fit. In other cases, by some form of endorsement, it became negotiable paper and served as currency. Either directly or indirectly, in the course of time, the order found its way to the storehouse and was duly honored.[1]

By the end of 1719 the ratio of paper money to silver stood at five to one or two. The Company was in a fair way to be ruined. It was obliged to receive its notes on a par with silver, but could not discharge its own debts with them unless the creditor saw fit to accept them. From the settlers who were not in the colony when the orders on the storehouse were put into circulation, or from other persons who could not be legitimate possessors, the Company refused to receive them at such a parity. Accordingly to persons who presented the orders in exchange for supplies, and who could not prove rightful ownership of them, the price of merchandise was advanced a hundred per cent.[2] Conditions were not improved by this procedure; therefore, it was decided, October 26, 1721, to receive old orders on the storehouse at an advance of thirty per cent on the face value. Three months later this was cut to ten per cent, because it was believed the new rate would be just to all concerned, inasmuch as merchandise was then cheaper than when the original orders were put into circulation.[3]

An ordinance of May 20, 1722, decreed that no more

[1] *A., B. N., Joly Coll.*, vol. 1726, fols. 126-127; Dumont, vol. ii, pp. 53-57.

[2] *A. N., C., Sér.* C^{13}, vol. v, fol. 353.

[3] *Ibid.*, vol. vi, fols. 148-151.

orders on the storehouse were either to be issued or received by the Company. Instead, the first of January, 1723, the old paper in circulation was to be replaced by a species of card money having an equivalent value. This new currency was to be drawn by one official but signed, registered and numbered by another, and was to be received by the storekeeper in payment for merchandise and then retired. Public employees, on the other hand, were to be paid by the treasurer in copper money by means of orders supplied by the comptroller.[1] Despite this ordinance, the practice of drawing orders on the storehouse went on much as before; hence, on August 30, 1722, a second decree was issued prohibiting the practice absolutely. Instead, public employees should be paid in copper money by means of orders issued on the colonial treasury.[2]

At the interior post the older forms of paper money were still in use, and for a while the Company continued to redeem them.[3] Eventually, in order to relieve the treasury of this drain, an ordinance was issued, December 4, 1722, calling in the outstanding notes drawn on the Company by the local commandants. These notes, too, were to be converted into cards.[4]

Since the several changes in question had led to speculation, on September 6, 1723, an ordinance was passed making it illegal to buy and sell the Company's notes. Confiscation and a fine of 3,000 livres were to follow conviction for the offense.[5] The paper in circulation, however, continued to depreciate. In the Illinois country, for example,

[1] *A. N., C., Sér.* C^{13}, vol. vi, fols. 422-425.

[2] *Ibid.*

[3] *Ibid.*, vol. vii, fols. 16-17; vol. viii, fols. 286-289; *A., B. N., Joly Coll.*, vol. 1726, fols. 131-132.

[4] *A. N., C., Sér. A*, vol. xxiii, Dec. 4, 1722.

[5] *Ibid., Sér.* C^{13}, vol. vii, fols. 15-16.

it required 5,000 livres in bills of exchange to buy a "quart" (16 gallons) of brandy.[1]

In the latter part of 1724, therefore, the Company's officials in France ordered the retirement of the 81,243 livres, 4 sols, 9 deniers of cards issued under the ordinance of 1722. The instructions sent in this connection made no mention of other forms of paper in circulation, because by the decree, in theory at least, they became valueless on January 1, 1723. This omission brought protests from many persons who held older forms of paper, including 120,000 livres in bills of exchange drawn by the commandant in the Illinois country on the local directors and on Paris before the date last-named. The reasons given to the " ordonnateur " by the holders for not having converted the paper into cards at the proper time were as follows: they had had no knowledge of the ordinance before its expiration in 1723; the Illinois country was too far from New Orleans for them to make the journey to the capital in the period allotted; it was the general supposition that the first ordinance was simply a warning, and that no action would be taken until a third had been issued. The case, together with these protests, was placed before the superior council, by which, May 13, 1725, it was decided that all forms of paper money then in circulation should be redeemed, the same reduction being observed as under the decree of 1722. The comptroller, thereupon, was instructed to receive all forms of paper money presented, but to keep a separate record for each kind.[2] As late as April, 1728, some of this old paper was sent to New Orleans to be redeemed. It was refused on the ground that ample time for redemption had been given in 1725.[3]

[1] *A. N., C., Sér.* C^{13}, vol. vii, fol. 15.

[2] *Ibid.*, vol. viii, fols. 286-289; vol. ix, fols. 110-113, 133.

[3] *Ibid.*, vol. xi, fols. 46-47.

Tampering with the paper still in circulation followed; it was subjected to all sorts of alterations and some of it was forged outright. In order to put an end to these illegal practices, the superior council, October 11, 1725, issued a decree that forgers should be arrested and punished. Any one caught altering, falsifying, counterfeiting, scraping or interlining any of the paper money was to be flogged and then prosecuted criminally by the attorney general.[1]

Scarcity of coin had forced the use of paper as a currency and fraudulent practices had caused it, from 1723 to 1726, to stand at a ratio of from thirty to thirty-five livres with silver.[2] On October 27, 1727, the colonial officials informed the home government that 26,800 livres in treasury notes (billets de la caisse) had been put into circulation by the "ordonnateur" in order to keep specie in the treasury, and asked to be allowed to draw bills of exchange for a similar purpose. Permission was granted so to do on condition that the amount should not exceed 6,000 livres a year.[3] This sum was far too small. A single merchant sometimes carried away as much. Indeed the "ordonnateur" declared that 20,000 francs a year were needed to keep specie in the province.[4]

The shortage in bills of exchange and copper money made it necessary for the agents, in order to meet the obligations of the Company, to put into circulation 50,000 livres in treasury notes for each of the years 1728 and 1729. The paper was scarcely in circulation when it began to be falsified and soon 1,000 livres in fraudulent notes were abroad. In the former year a treasury clerk and two accomplices were arrested on suspicion. One of the con-

[1] *A. N., C., Sér. A*, vol. xxiii, Oct. 11, 1725.

[2] *Ibid., Sér.* C^{13}, vol. xvi, fols. 166-177.

[3] *Ibid.*, vol. xi, fols. 51-52, 86-87.

[4] *Ibid.*, fols. 51-62, 125, 329.

federates turned state's evidence and thereby escaped punishment; the other, because of his extreme youth, was dismissed. The originator of the fraud was convicted and sentenced to the galleys for life. The whole of the issue of notes was retired, and in its place others for the same denominations were given out. This second emission was signed by all the members of the council because it was believed the added signatures would make them difficult to forge.[1]

From 1729 to 1731 the Company sent merchandise to the colony and managed through its sale to retire a great many of the notes at a reduction of fifty per cent on the face value. This action forced the piastres down to ten or twelve livres. Consequently when on July 1, 1731, the crown took control of affairs in Louisiana there was not a great deal of the Company's paper in circulation there.[2]

During the last year of its control contracts involving the use of notes for payment were made by the Company, and between private individuals, which later gave rise to litigation. Circulating as money, these notes were sometimes offered at a reduction of half their nominal value; in other cases the full face value was demanded. On October 15, 1731, the governor and "ordonnateur" issued jointly an ordinance to the effect that the notes were disarranging the values of royal money, hence would be considered only as contracts between private individuals and were no longer to pass current. In order to give some ease to the holders, a time limit of fifteen days was allowed for adjusting the matter.[3] A similar ordinance was issued, October 30th, giving to persons holding such notes, and residing at the remote

[1] *A. N., C., Sér.* C^{13}, vol. xi, fols. 51-62, 125, 329.

[2] *Ibid.*, vol. xvi, fols. 166-177.

[3] *Ibid., Sér. A,* vol. xxiii, Oct. 15, 1731.

posts, an additional fifteen days for the purpose.[1] By May 15, 1732, the notes still in the colony had lost half their value.[2] The matter dragged on until September 30, 1733, when it was decreed by the superior council that all paper of the old type should be reduced in value by one-half and then redeemed in such currency as the treasury saw fit to give. This loss fell in large measure upon the Company, which was not in a position to protest since it had paid its own notes on practically the same basis.[3]

After the retrocession the crown sought to place the finances of Louisiana on a specie basis by sending over silver and merchandise to meet the yearly expenses.[4] The royal government next tried to meet local obligations with merchandise alone.[5] To this end it made several unsuccessful attempts to ascertain in advance the approximate yearly expense for Louisiana, but the estimate was always too inaccurate to be of any use in devising plans in advance for the financing of the province. These methods at all events did not keep the silver money in circulation, but it did hold the piastres at five livres.[6] The crown soon fell back on the use of bills of exchange as a means of retaining specie in the province, and by the end of the fiscal year, July, 1732, 46,629 livres, 16 sols, 5 deniers had been drawn.[7]

On February 16, 1733, there was scarcely enough metallic currency in the treasury to meet the government's obligations for the ensuing six months. In order to preserve what

[1] *A. N., C., Sér. A*, vol. xxiii, Oct. 30, 1731.

[2] *Ibid., Sér. C[13]*, vol. xv, fols. 133-136.

[3] *Ibid.*, vol. xvi, fols. 166-177; Margry, vol. v, pp. 654-655.

[4] *Supra*, p. 104.

[5] *A. N., C., Sér. C[13]*, vol. xxxiv, fols. 376-378; *A., B. N., Joly Coll.*, vol. 1726, fols. 132.

[6] *A., B. N., Joly Coll.*, vol. 1726, fols. 132-133.

[7] *A. N., C., Sér. C[13]*, vol. xv, fols. 174; vol. xvii, fols. 178-180.

there was, orders were issued on the local treasurer to the amount of 55,090 livres, one sol, eight deniers.[1] On May 12, 1733, the governor and "ordonnateur" recommended the employment of bills of exchange in moving the tobacco crop.[2] Accordingly the end of the fiscal year, in July, 108,-933 livres, thirteen sols, eight deniers were utilized in this form, and the amounts due for general expenses paid in merchandise.[3]

So serious indeed was the shortage of specie in Louisiana that the crown deemed it advisable, September 15, 1733, to issue card money for the province similar to the kind used in New France. Unlike the old notes, the cards were to be received at the royal storehouse on a par with silver and bills of exchange, the supposition being that the new currency would cause no increase in the price of merchandise and other supplies.[4] Before putting the cards into circulation the home government ordered the governor and "ordonnateur" to ascertain how the money was likely to be received by the people of the province.[5]

On April 3, 1734, the colonial officials reported that they had examined conditions in Louisiana with the greatest possible care, but could discover nothing that would make an issue of cards dangerous. Metallic currency was not much needed at the interior posts where everything was purchased largely by means of barter. Practically all the actual money required in Louisiana was for the settlements on or near the coast. There a certain amount of silver was

[1] *A. N., C., Sér.* C^{13}, vol. xvii, fols. 55-56; vol. xxxi, fols. 108-113; *A., B. N., Joly Coll.*, vol. 1726, fols. 132-133.

[2] *A. N., C., Sér.* C^{13}, vol. xvi, fols. 80-82.

[3] *Ibid.*, vol. xvii, fols. 178-180.

[4] *Ibid., Sér. B*, vol. lix, fols. 578-588.

[5] *Ibid., Sér.* C^{13}, vol. xviii, fols. 45-50.

needed, part of which would come from Pensacola by way of Mobile. It would be well, however, to delay the issue two or three years, in order to let time efface any remembrance of the Company's paper which had fallen into great discredit, and also to allow some of the settlers to become more prosperous. But, if the royal government were determined to make the issue at once, it probably would be received by the people of the province without objection. In that case the officials proposed that, in order to accustom the settlers gradually to the new money, the crown issue no more than 300,000 livres, half of which, together with an equal amount of silver, should be put into circulation in 1735 and the remainder in the following year.[1] To this communication the home government replied, August 17, 1734, stating that since 1729 card money had been in use in New France and had given the greatest satisfaction there. Hence no doubt was felt that a similar issue for Louisiana would produce a like effect.[2]

Meanwhile the officials continued to encounter great difficulty in keeping specie in the colony. By the close of the fiscal year of 1734 the "ordonnateur" had drawn in favor of the merchants 118,476 livres, sixteen sols, ten deniers in bills of exchange and had issued notes also on the colonial treasury. Moreover he had drawn 104,410 livres, eleven sols, four deniers in bills of exchange payable in 1735, and 2,210 livres, in 1736.[3] To this amount were added 12,349 livres, two sols, four deniers drawn on New Orleans by the commissary at Mobile.[4] For the two years beginning

[1] *A. N., C., Sér.* C^{13}, vol. xviii, fols. 45-50.

[2] *Ibid., Sér. B*, vol. lxi, fol. 696.

[3] *Ibid., Sér.* C^{13}, vol. xix, fols. 32-33, 86-87, 104-105, 106-107; vol. xxi, fols. 245-249.

[4] *Ibid.*, vol. xix, fols. 151-157.

April 1, 1732, the "ordonnateur" had drawn in bills of exchange 361,671 livres, fourteen sols, eight deniers.[1]

Since the reception of the communication from the crown the governor and "ordonnateur" had been working to create a sentiment in the province in favor of the card money. It seemed that their efforts met with some success, for in a dispatch, April 10, 1735, they stated that the people were awaiting the introduction of the new currency on the arrival of the first vessel. As at this time the piastre was still valued at five livres, they suggested that it be used as a unit of value for the cards.[2]

On August 29, 1735, the royal government informed the officials that it had been put to great trouble to redeem the large quantities of bills of exchange they had drawn and ordered that in future the amount be lessened. This command seems not to have been heeded.[3] Before the end of the year the amount of bills of exchange drawn was 327,384 livres, six sols, nine deniers, whereupon the crown proceeded to fix the yearly allowance at 150,000 livres.[4]

On September 14, 1735, the home government finally issued an ordinance creating a card money for Louisiana to the amount of 200,000 livres in denominations of twenty, fifteen, ten, five and two livres ten sols, and in still smaller ones of twenty-five sols, twelve sols six deniers, and six sols three deniers each. The money was to bear the royal arms and was to be written and signed by the comptroller in Louisiana. Cards of the first five values were also to bear the signatures of the governor and the "ordonnateur", while the lower denominations required only the initials of these offi-

[1] *A. N., C., Sér. C13*, vol. xix, fols. 32-33.

[2] *Ibid.*, vol. xx, fols. 16-17; see note 15, p. 105.

[3] *Ibid., Sér. B*, vol. lxiii, fol. 584.

[4] *Ibid., Sér. C13*, vol. xxi, fols. 245-249, 311-316.

cers. In order to detect counterfeits when presented for redemption, four duplicates were to be made and deposited with the officials in charge of the finances of the province; three in Louisiana and one in France. Moreover, in order not to flood the colony with the new issue, the crown decreed that at first only part of it was to be put into circulation.[1] So much for a project, the realization of which was to take place some years later.

The year 1736 opened with the finances of the province in a bad condition. Only 53,074 livres, sixteen sols, three deniers of the 150,000 allowance remained unused; there was a debt of 105,385 livres, nine sols, five deniers for the war against the Natchez and Chickasaw; the foreign merchants were making heavy demands upon the colonial treasury for bills of exchange. To meet these obligations, the "ordonnateur" resorted to the use of large quantities of treasury notes, and drew on the allowance of the current year 69,878 livres, fourteen sols, seven deniers; 80,122 livres, two sols on that of 1737 and 31,202 livres, two sols, three deniers on 1738.[2] On October 10, 1736, the crown saw fit to increase the amount of bills of exchange permitted for that year to 230,122 livres, which amount was to include the 80,122 livres, two sols that had been drawn in advance on 1737.[3] At the close of the year it was estimated that there were 350,000 livres in paper circulating in the province.[4]

The disorder in the finances of Louisiana grew gradually worse. In the early part of 1737 the merchants

[1] *A. N., C., Sér. A,* vol. xxii, fol. 146; vol. xxiii, Sept. 14, 1735; *Sér.* C^{13}, vol. xxxiv, fols. 376-378.

[2] *Ibid., Sér.* C^{13}, vol. xxi, fols. 245-249, 301-302, 319-323; vol. xxii, fols. 268-269.

[3] *Ibid.,* vol. xxii, fols. 134-135, 190-191.

[4] *Ibid.,* vol. xxi, fols. 328-329.

took from the province 72,891 livres, six sols, eight deniers in bills of exchange, and by June there remained only 15,058 livres, twelve sols, six deniers of the allowance which the "ordonnateur" had reserved for current expenses. Therefore he informed the crown that, if it were not for the extraordinary expense of the war and the debt of 42,000 livres due merchants who would reach the province toward the end of the year, he would be able to keep the amount expended within the annual allowance of 150,000 livres.[1] Under existing circumstances, however, it was impossible. The ordinary expenses for the year were 156,000 livres and the war debt was 42,803 livres, nine sols, seven deniers. It therefore became necessary to increase the paper in circulation by 150,000 livres, thus bringing the quantity at the end of 1737 up to 500,000 livres.[2]

The crown refused to sanction an increase in bills of exchange. Accordingly, in 1738, after deducting 31,202 livres, two sols, three deniers that had been drawn in advance, the "ordonnateur" had but 118,797 livres on hand. This was not enough to satisfy the claims of the French merchants, to say nothing of the obligations of the war which amounted to 90,000 livres, not including the supplies that had been drawn from the royal storehouses.[3] The colonial officials were unable longer to keep the paper in the province from depreciating. Each year since the retrocession public expenses had increased without provision being made to meet them.

[1] *A. N., C., Sér. C*[13], vol. xxii, fols. 134-135, 190-191.

[2] *Ibid.*, vol. xxxi, fols. 108-113.

[3] *Ibid.*, vol. xxii, fol. 216; vol. xxiii, fols. 134-137; vol. xxxi, fols. 108-113.

CHAPTER XI

PAPER MONEY AND CREDIT, 1739-1763

EXCEPTING the years 1742-1750, the period under consideration was one in which paper money was practically the only form of currency in use in Louisiana. During these years there were no entirely new kinds of paper introduced, yet the variations in the forms and the irregularities and excesses in the use of this currency make the period distinctive.

At the beginning of 1739 only 45,389 livres, eleven sols, five deniers were left of the annual allowance in bills of exchange.[1] Before the end of the year the war debt had risen to 530,353 livres, eleven sols, three deniers, not including the bills of exchange drawn by the commandants at l'Assomption. Moreover the demands of the merchants for bills of exchange were increasing.[2] The "ordonnateur", therefore, found it necessary to make use of large quantities of treasury notes, 200,000 livres being in circulation at the close of the year; to exceed the amount of bills of exchange permitted by the crown by 50,000 livres and also to draw on the grant for 1740, in order to meet current expenses.[3] Under the circumstances the officials were unable to redeem the paper with either silver or bills of exchange, and as a result the piastre which had been equivalent to eight or nine, soon equaled eighteen livres of

[1] *A. N., C., Sér.* C^{13}, vol. xxiv, fols. 121-122.

[2] *Ibia.*, vol. xxv, fol. 136.

[3] *Ibid.*, vol. xxiv, fols. 31-32; vol. xxv, fol. 137.

treasury notes and other paper currency.[1] As a remedy, the "ordonnateur" proposed to the crown an issue of 200,000 livres more in cards for the purpose of retiring all the treasury notes which he was continually being forced to redeem in bills of exchange.[2] The people of the province, in fact, regarded the cards with so much favor that they had withdrawn them almost entirely from circulation.[3]

Each year the finances of Louisiana became more and more entangled. In 1740 the "ordonnateur" was confronted with a war debt of 830,137 livres, fifteen sols, ten deniers,[4] with no funds supplied by the home government to meet it. He was forced to make a generous use of treasury notes and to draw 244,236 livres, sixteen sols, one denier in bills of exchange. At the end of the year there were 900,000 livres in all kinds of paper passing current in the province.[5]

The finances in 1741, therefore, were in even greater confusion than in the previous year. To make matters worse, the governor and "ordonnateur" were not on friendly terms. It was not until the former returned from his last campaign against the Chickasaw that he learned of "the unwise distribution of bills of exchange which had made it possible to buy and sell them the same as silver". For some time, in fact, many of the speculators had been using their entire credit in order to obtain bills of exchange for the purpose of trafficking in them with the merchants for paper at an advance of fifty per cent and, in two instances, sixty per cent. The abuse was followed by the

[1] *A. N., C., Sér.* C^{13}, vol. xxiv, fols. 31-32, 133-135.

[2] *Ibid.*, vol. xxiv, fols. 31-32; vol. xxv, fols. 9-16.

[3] *Ibid.*, vol. xxv, fols. 9-16.

[4] *Ibid.*, vol. xxxi, fols. 108-113.

[5] *Ibid.*, vol. xxv, fols. 350-362; vol. xxxi, fols. 108-113.

usual consequences. Cards and treasury notes (bons de la caisse), equally, lost half their face value and every one in the province, except a few jobbers who were able to establish themselves on well-equipped plantations, was greatly injured by the trade.[1]

Foreseeing this decline as soon as he heard of the liberal use of the treasury notes, Count de Maurepas, minister of marine, declared it would be wise to retire all the paper at once. He further asserted that every increase in the amount would cause it only to fall into still greater discredit. His suggestion, however, was acted upon only to the extent of sending an order to Louisiana to find out how much paper was actually in use. There the colonial office allowed the matter to rest, since the procuring of information on this point was next to impossible owing to the irregularity in the way the currency had been issued at the interior posts. On his own account, however, and without waiting for orders from the crown, the "ordonnateur", May 15, 1741, issued an ordinance calling in all notes which, on penalty of invalidation for non-compliance, were to be signed and registered at his office. Through neglect of enforcement or other reasons the ordinance did not bring in the paper or remedy the financial distress.[2]

This decline in the value of paper caused a demand to be made by the colonial officials for bills of exchange on France in payment of their services, they being unable to live on their salaries if paid in any other way.[3] On October 13, 1741 the crown informed Salmon his letter was most unsatisfactory. His silence on some points concerning the finances it disapproved; in other cases the action

[1] *A. N., C., Sér.* C^{13}, vol. xxvi, fols. 61-65.

[2] *Ibid.*, vol. xxviii, fols. 334-340; *Sér.* F^{3}, vol. ccxlii, M. S. S. M., April 30, 1744.

[3] *Ibid., Sér.* C^{13}, vol. xxvi. fol. 182.

he had taken it strongly condemned. The home government had been informed that the great quantities of paper money issued thus far caused a depreciation in value. It commanded the " ordonnateur ", therefore, to ascertain the amount outstanding, to call in the paper and redeem it with bills of exchange. It further ordered him when distributing such bills, always to give preference to the merchants from France.[1]

Before receiving this communication from the crown, Salmon had drawn 176,682 livres, eight sols in advance on the year's allowance of bills of exchange, which had been raised to 200,000 livres annually. The home government gave him permission to draw 60,000 livres more, which sum he exceeded by 1,245 livres, nineteen sols, six deniers, bringing the total for the year to 237,928 livres, seven sols, six deniers. In addition to this amount he drew 119,112 livres, ten sols, six deniers on the allowance for 1742. This last act greatly disturbed the French government, because it was unable to determine how it could meet its bills in the following May.[2]

By 1742 the officials and men who were living on salaries or wages paid in colonial paper were almost destitute. They could not buy themselves shoes and other necessities. The money received was scarcely enough to enable them to pay even their laundry bills. The European traders, moreover, made so great a distinction between colonial paper and piastres that there were few persons in the province with means sufficient to engage in the Spanish trade, which was in a fair way to be ruined. In fact the merchants would receive only silver or bills of exchange for their goods. As a means of relieving the situation, therefore, the governor

[1] *A. N., C., Sér. B, Louisiane,* vol. lxxiii, fol. 309.

[2] *Ibid.,* vol. lxxii, fols. 30-31.

asked the crown to pay half of the salaries or wages of employees in bills of exchange. This plan, he claimed, would have two beneficial results. In the first place, it would improve the condition of men who had nothing to sell and every thing to buy; secondly, it would prevent the constant increase in the number of treasury notes which led to a proportionate depreciation in all forms of paper.[1] The crown seems to have taken no action in the matter, hence the amount in bills of exchange drawn, though beyond the limit of 200,000 livres which the home government had instructed Salmon under no circumstances to exceed, was 236,620 livres,—only a little less than the amount for the previous year.[2]

The depreciation of paper money that had begun somewhat gradually in 1730 went on more rapidly later, and in 1743 silver and bills of exchange stood at a ratio of two to five and even in some instances reached three to one in terms of paper.[3] The ordinance of May 15, 1741, failed in its purpose; a second was issued January 15, 1743, giving the settlers a month in which to bring to the capital their treasury notes in order to have them converted into new money. Failure to present them in time made them valueless. This ordinance seems to have been better enforced. It is stated by the colonial officials that in a short time the greater part of 454,620 livres then outstanding had been turned in and converted into "bons de la caisse", thereby fulfilling the object of the law.[4]

Some persons in the colony and others in the mother

[1] *A. N., C., Sér.* C^{13}, vol. xxvii, fols. 48-49, 127-128.

[2] *Ibid.*, fols. 190-191.

[3] *Ibid.*, vol. xxviii, fols. 334-340; vol. xxxii, fols. 151-158; *Sér. B*, vol. lxxviii, fol. 40; *Sér.* F^3, vol. cclxii, M. S. S. M., April, 30, 1744.

[4] *Ibid., Sér.* F^3, vol. cclxii, M. S. S. M., April 30, 1744; *Sér.* C^{13}, vol. xxviii, fols. 334-340; vol. xxxi, fols. 106-113; *Sér. B*, vol. lxxviii, fol. 47.

country asserted that one of the chief causes of the financial disorder in Louisiana was the maladministration of Salmon, the "ordonnateur", who was accordingly recalled and Normant, a man who had rendered intelligent, accurate and valuable service at Cape Français, was named as his successor.[1] The charges against Salmon were at once investigated by the governor who sent a report to the crown stating that the accusations were not borne out by the evidence presented. In fact he could not find the slightest ground for any of the charges adduced, and gave it as his opinion that no one under the same circumstances could have managed the finances better or more profitably than Salmon had done.[2] Moreover, this opinion is reinforced by the fact that the new "ordonnateur", in his communication to the royal government on the finances of the province at the time he entered office, criticised few of the methods employed by his predecessor. Instead, he traced the chief causes for the disorder to the fact that the crown since the retrocession had annually supplied inadequate funds to meet the colonial expenses, and to the method in which European merchants carried on trade in the province.[3]

Normant entered upon his duties in October, 1744. He found 1,050,000 livres of paper money in circulation made up as follows: 454,620 livres in "bons de la caisse", issued in 1743 to retire the existing treasury notes; 200,000 livres in cards; 395,380 livres in "simples récépissés", and orders on the treasury (ordonnances). The "ordonnateur" began his administration of the finances of Louisiana by collecting royal debts and using the money thus secured in

[1] *A. N., C., Sér. C*[13], vol. xxviii, fol. 333.

[2] *Ibid.*, vol. xxix, fols. 27-31; vol. xxxi, fols. 108-113.

[3] *Ibid.*, vol. xxxi, fol. 110; vol. xxix, fols. 184-186.

redeeming the "simples récépissés" and orders on the treasury. By the close of the year the paper in circulation had been reduced to 847,435 livres, twelve sols, six deniers.[1]

Experimenting with these forms of currency having brought no relief, there was general agreement in favor of their retirement. There was, however, no such unanimity of opinion as to the method of withdrawal. The governor and "ordonnateur" proposed the sending to the colony of merchandise or cargoes of negroes to be exchanged for paper at a fixed ratio with silver. Currency thus drawn into the hands of the home government could be readily retired. The suggestion was rejected because its fulfillment was considered too slow in accomplishing the results desired, and also because a large part of the paper was in the hands of speculators and traders who would get the merchandise or negroes and sell them to the settlers at such high prices as to injure rather than benefit the colony.[2]

Another point under discussion at the time was whether all forms of paper should be retired on the same basis. Since cards had always been preferred to other kinds of colonial currency, some were inclined to give them an advantage in the rate of exchange, at least over the treasury notes which had contributed most to the course of depreciation. This method of adjustment received small support because it would create a new zest for speculation, and thus would be lucrative only to the persons who had been so instrumental in discrediting paper money. As far as the crown was concerned, one kind of colonial paper was

[1] *A. N., C., Sér.* C^{13}, vol. xxviii, fols. 334-340; *Sér. B,* vol. lxxviii, fols. 46-47. According to another of the "ordonnateur's" reports: 455,000 livres, "bons de la caisse"; 167,799 livres in old paper of the Company of the Indies, 110,000 in "simples récépissés"; 200,000 livres in cards, total 932,799 livres.

[2] *Ibid., Sér.* C^{13}, vol. xxviii, fols. 334-340.

as good as another, and from its point of view all deserved the same treatment. It was thereupon decided to fix the ratio of withdrawal at five to two, the degree of depreciation in terms of silver in August, 1743. The retirement was to be effected by means of silver and bills of exchange, part in 1745 and the remainder in 1746.[1] In compliance with the royal command the "ordonnateur" proceeded to call in the paper money, then verify, check and burn it. By October 24, 1745, 838,148 livres, eight sols, nine deniers of the sort had been canceled.[2]

This done, it at once became necessary to determine the nature and form of a new issue. The "ordonnateur" was opposed to paper currency of any kind. It was impossible, he declared, for him or the governor to limit the amount drawn on the colonial treasury by the post commandants whose bills were not received for a year or eighteen months after their date. Moreover he could not know in advance how much would be needed for Indian affairs. The great distance between the mother country and the province often delayed the royal ships and made it necessary for him to buy supplies at the private shops where he was obliged to pay high prices. Then, too, when these vessels reached the colony in considerable numbers it was often impossible for him to dispose of the merchandise advantageously. It was consequently out of the question to estimate even approximately the amount of paper money required for the fiscal year, and the bills of exchange needed to redeem it. This state of affairs made the paper subject to depreciation and led to a complete disarrangement of the local finances. Even a small depreciation was dangerous, since there was a strong tendency among the people of the province to en-

[1] *A. N., C., Sér. C*[13], vol. xxviii, fols. 334-340.

[2] *Ibid.*, vol. xxix, fols. 184-186; vol. xxxi, fols. 110-111.

gage in speculation with anything susceptible of it. In fact the "ordonnateur" claimed it was the only occupation to which the inhabitants were really attached. Normant admitted that a card money would give temporary relief, which might last perhaps a year, but asserted that this advantage would in no way counteract the trouble that would be caused by attempting to maintain it longer. He proposed instead: first, the use of Spanish money, assigning it a value greater than its intrinsic worth in order to keep it in circulation in the province; secondly, the making of the prices of colonial products so attractive that the people would be induced to take up substantial local industries and thereby raise products that could be exchanged for foreign goods, thus eliminating the need of other forms for foreign trade.[1]

By this time it seems to have been demonstrated that silver, under ordinary circumstances, could not be kept in the province. The experience of New France with card money, on the other hand, indicated that there was no better form of currency available for Louisiana, even if its issue might bring on a repetition of the old troubles. Those who upheld this viewpoint argued that the cards formerly in use had maintained their value for two years and had lost credit only on account of the extraordinary expense of the war then in existence, and the action of the "ordonnateur" in giving preference over them to the treasury notes. Therefore it was asserted that, with merchandise in the royal storehouses and bills of exchange drawn on the treasury of France as security, card money would put the finances of the provinces on a substantial basis.[2] The opinion at all events won the approval of the home government,

[1] *A. N., C., Sér.* C^{13}, vol. xxxi, fols. 112-113; vol. xxxiv, fols. 376-378.

[2] *Ibid.*, vol. xxxi, fols. 112, 113; *Sér. B*, vol. lxxviii, fols. 40, 42-51.

which, April 30, 1744, ordered a card money to be issued for Louisiana on the five to two basis, and put into circulation two months from the day that the decree should be made public there.[1]

Because of a change in the situation in the French West Indies,[2] and the continuance of the war, it was deemed advisable to take no action in the matter as yet. Silver in considerable amounts was brought to the colony causing some difficulty in the drawing of bills of exchange. In order to insure a safe arrival, much against his better judgment, Normant was forced to make as many as five separate issues of the same bills of exchange, sent by different routes, via Havana, Canada, *etc.*, to France.[3]

In 1746 the entire allowance of 200,000 livres was used up in return for Spanish silver expended on strengthening the fortifications at the "English Turn" and at Mobile.[4] On December 9, 1748, the colonial officials informed the home government that they had to meet local expenses by means of bills of exchange and a small amount of silver obtained from sales of merchandise from the royal warehouses.[5]

The new "ordonnateur", Michel de la Rouvillière was convinced very soon after entering office that there was an absolute need for more money. Without consulting Governor Vaudreuil, he drew up an ordinance on the subject and presented it to that officer for his signature. Because of the irregularity of this procedure, and because of his doubt as to its legality, the governor hesitated to attach his name,

[1] *A. N., C., Sér. B.* vol. lxxviii, fols. 42-51.

[2] *Supra*, p. 106.

[3] *A. N., C., Sér. C*[13], vol. xxix, fols. 184-186.

[4] *Ibid.*, vol. xxxi, fol. 139.

[5] *Ibid.*, *Sér. B*, vol. lxxxvii, fols. 30-31.

whereupon the " ordonnateur " informed him, that if he refused to sign, the issue would be made without his approval. On further reflection the governor signed the ordinance, believing that since there would be an issue anyhow, the joint sanction of governor and "ordonnateur" would give the people greater confidence in the paper money provided for, and make its circulation more acceptable. The notes were to be drawn in denominations of from twenty-five sols to thirty livres; larger values, if needed, were to be numbered, registered, signed and placed in the colonial treasury to be there used in paying public expenses. The ordinance, without stating the amount to be issued, went into effect February 1, 1750, along with an assurance from the " ordonnateur " that there need be no fear to accept the new money in payment for all debts. About 108,000 livres were put into circulation at this time, which amount was soon so considerably augmented as to create public uneasiness. The " ordonnateur ", however, assured the governor that there was no cause for anxiety but gave him no information regarding his confidence, nor did he explain the increase in the quantity of notes.[1]

On October 23, the home government reprimanded the governor and " ordonnateur " for their action in the matter, since no one but the crown, the commanders of besieged cities or blockaded colonies during times of actual investment had the right to issue money. Creating or altering the money of the kingdom, it declared, was a sovereign right to be shared with no one. Therefore, the " ordonnateur " had exceeded his power and had broken a most important law for which act there was not the slightest justification. If the treasury was without money, the " ordonnateur " could have recourse to bills of exchange

[1] *A. N., C., Sér.* C^{13}, vol. xxxiv, fols. 259-260; vol. xxxv, fols. 99-101.

and the sale of merchandise from the royal storehouses. For the last two years the records of receipts had shown large quantities of supplies there. The home government stated further that there were still other expedients that might have been tried. Even if there were none, the colonial situation did not warrant Michel in adopting the course he had followed, especially since the province was only just recovering from the disorders occasioned by an excessive amount of paper. The "ordonnateur", thereupon was ordered to withdraw, by means of bills of exchange on the allowance for succeeding years, all the notes he had put into circulation. It was further stated that the shortage in the silver drawn from the Spanish trade could be made up either by sending over French money, by a new issue of cards or by some other method not yet undertaken.[1]

Before it was possible to make the ordered retirement, counterfeits began to be found in circulation. Public uneasiness through distrust in the paper was thereby greatly augmented.[2] In order to increase public confidence in the paper money, some effort was made to bring the counterfeiters to justice. Too many important personages, however, were implicated in the transaction. The prosecution ended disgracefully in the trial and conviction of but one culprit, a mulatto slave belonging to the crown. The negro was whipped, branded on the hand with the *fleur-de-lis* and sold into slavery in St. Domingue.[3]

The "ordonnateur", January 30, 1752, sent to the royal government a report of the finances during his term of

[1] *A. N., C., Sér. B,* vol. xci, fol. 31.

[2] *Ibid., Sér.* C^{13}, vol. xxxv, fols. 99-101; *Sér.* F^{3}, vol. ccxliii, M. S. S. M., May 18, 1751.

[3] *Ibid., Sér.* C^{13}, vol. xxxv, fol. 205; *Sér.* F^{3}, vol. ccxliii, M. S. S. M., May 18, 1751.

office. It is evident from this statement that the Spanish trade still made it necessary each year to draw large sums in bills of exchange. In 1749, the amount was 453,408 livres, nine deniers; in 1750, 550,000 livres; in 1751, 700,000 livres; and in 1752, but 535,000 livres. The sum for 1752 indicates a recovery from the conditions in the Spanish trade brought on by the war (1744-1748), and the whole statement brings out the further fact that during these years the home government had made much more liberal provision for meeting the expenses of the province. The 200,000 limit of bills of exchange was disregarded and during the years in question the provision in money made exceeded the amount of bills of exchange used by the colonial officials. Therefore in 1752 there remained 532,023 livres, nine sols, eleven deniers in unused funds, which shows that for these years there was no need of an issue of paper money.[1]

This same year Michel was recalled and his place taken by d'Auberville as "ordonnateur". Governor Vaudreuil was transferred to New France and Kerlérec sent over in his stead. Nevertheless Michel's example in issuing notes redeemable with bills of exchange was followed by all his

[1] *A. N., C., Sér.* C^{13}, vol. xxxvi, fols. 299, 243.

	"Fonds ordonnés et à ordonner"			"Fonds remis à la colonie les lettres de change"			"Fonds remis à la colonie par les procès verbaux"		
Year	Livres	Sols	Den.	Livres	Sols	Den.	Livres	Sols	Den.
1749..	529,537	19	11	453,408	..	9	62,137	6	..
1750..	601,264	3	6	550,000	..	..	19,481	1	1
1751..	889,957	16	..	790,000	..	..	7,268	1	8
1752..	928,567	..	..	535,000	..	..	.....	..	..
	2,949,326	19	5	2,328,408	..	9	88,886	8	9

Unused funds—532,023 livres, 9 sols, 11 deniers.

successors.[1] The war begun with England in 1756 made the risk of sending silver to the province too great; accordingly the governor and "ordonnateur" were instructed to issue certain special notes, also called "bons", and deriving their name, it was said, from the first word of the inscription. Drawn on the colonial treasury in denominations ranging from ten sols to 100 livres, they were to be payable in three months and redeemable at New Orleans in bills of exchange on France if presented to the amounts of 300 or 400 livres at a time. During the progress of the war, also, the governor and "ordonnateur" gave the commandants at the interior posts the power to issue similar "bons" for provisions, public works and Indian affairs. These debts, contracted with merchants and settlers by the officials, grew to enormous sums and the abuses accompanying the privilege rendered the expense excessive.[2] For the years in which the annual outlay exceeded the amount in bills of exchange, treasury notes, instead of being redeemed in the regular manner, were exchanged for "bons" payable in colonial currency twelve months after date,—an arrangement termed "making the reduction".[3]

In order to expedite matters, the officials of Louisiana occasionally drew bills of exchange on the treasury of other French colonies. In 1755, for example, the "ordonnateur" took such action in the case of Cape Français, sending receipts of the bills to the home government, so that it might make no mistake in effecting payment.[4]

In 1754, both card money and notes were redeemable on equal terms by means of bills of exchange payable in part

[1] *A. N., C., Sér. F*[3], vol. xxv, fols. 201-205.

[2] *Ibid.;* Pittman, pp. 46-47.

[3] *Trans. Lit. and Hist. Soc. of Quebec,* 1871-1877, p. 101.

[4] *A. N., C., Sér. C*[13], vol. xxxix, fols. 76-77.

during 1754, 1755 and 1756, of which 800,000 livres were drawn in the year first named. The "ordonnateurs" from 1752 to 1758, in fact, contributed nothing novel to the administration of colonial finances. Large quantities of paper money of one sort or another continued to be put into circulation.[1]

Rochemore, the new "ordonnateur", on reaching New Orleans, August 17, 1758, reported to the home government that he found a vacancy in the office of comptroller, no records for that office to give him any information concerning the department, and the work being carried on by various persons at different places without any one being directly in charge. The treasury he found without specie, more than 1,800,000 livres in paper money outstanding, and 1,401,800 livres, eight sols, nine deniers in bills of exchange drawn on the allowance for future years. As the royal storehouses were entirely empty, he was obliged to buy at the local shops at high prices.[2] Accordingly he thought it advisable to call in all paper in circulation and make a new emission, similar in form but signed by himself, in order, as he stated, to distinguish his administration from that of his predecessor. The withdrawal and replacement were effected on December 13, by means of bills of exchange to the amount of 1,469,848 livres, seventeen sols, eight deniers, drawn on the allowance for 1758, and also of 525,151 livres, two sols, four deniers on that for 1759, or altogether 1,995,000 livres.[3] For the process of recall only eight days were allowed, a requirement that caused great inconvenience and much discontent. Everything, furthermore, was done without the advice or even the

[1] *A. N., C., Sér.* C^{13}, vol. xxxviii, fol. 265; *Trans. Lit. and Hist. Soc. of Quebec*, 1871-1877, p. 101.

[2] *A. N., C., Sér.* C^{13}, vol. xl, fols. 181-182.

[3] *Ibid.*, fol. 215.

knowledge of the governor, who first learned of the transaction when he read the notice to the people on the public bulletin board.[1]

On January 2, 1759, Rochemore sent to the home government his plans for the adjustment of the colonial finances. In his opinion it would be wise, for the present at least, possibly also for the future, to establish a card money, similar to the one of 1744, with the emission, however, being made entirely in France. Such a money, he affirmed, would put confidence in colonial paper and thereby reduce the price of all sorts of commodities; provided that treasury notes, signed and issued by the "ordonnateur" were prohibited, except in cases of absolute necessity. For the knowledge of the crown, should it act upon his suggestion, Rochemore estimated the value of the card money needed for current expenses at 7,000,000 or 8,000,000 livres, 200,000 livres of which, he stated, should be in small denominations for use in local transactions. Before this communication reached the home government it had learned of the work of the "ordonnateur" during his first months of incumbency, and therefore, made no reply to the proposal.[2]

On the other hand, the crown, January 19, 1759, dispatched to the "ordonnateur" a severe reprimand for the unauthorized emission of paper money of the previous year. He had violated the instructions given him on leaving France. To have introduced a new money into Louisiana was declared a flagrant violation of the law that made such an act exclusively a royal privilege. Not to have consulted the governor in the matter was condemned, and the whole affair pronounced a blunder that in no way could be excused. He was then ordered at once to

[1] *A. N., C., Sér.* C^{13}, vol. xli, fols. 75-76.

[2] *Ibid.*, fol. 154.

call in all of the paper in question and redeem it by means of bills of exchange. In future he was to furnish the governor a report on the conditions of the finances semi-annually, oftener if the latter requested it. Furthermore he was to make his superior a quarterly report on the bills of exchange drawn on the French treasury.[1]

On February 25, and again on June 25, 1759, the governor informed the crown that the finances of Louisiana were in a deplorable state. On the latter date he asserted it was positively known that, of the 1,995,000 livres in bills of exchange drawn the previous year, not more than 200,000 livres were issued in the regular way. Instead they were sold at an advance of from fifteen to eighteen per cent to the merchants who made up the premium by a proportional increase on the selling price of their goods. Moreover it was affirmed that the treasurer, who was also in control of munitions, had permitted supplies to the amount of 200,000 livres to be taken from the storehouses in order to provision royal ships. He then drew on the French treasury a bill of exchange for an equal amount, thus making the merchandise cost the crown 400,000 livres. The bill of exchange he sold to the jobbers at the above-named profit. In order to keep himself better informed and if possible to prevent such practices as enumerated above, the governor proposed to provide the treasury with a safe in which the records and cash were to be kept. The safe was to be provided with a lock having three keys. One was to be held by the treasurer, a second by the comptroller, and the third by someone whom the governor himself would name. Rochemore on his part informed the crown that such allegations were simply incredible.[2]

[1] *A. N., C., Sér. B*, vol. cix, fols. 1-2; *Sér.* F^3, vol. ccxliii, M. S. S. M., Jan. 19, 1759.

[2] *Ibid., Sér.* C^{13}, vol. xli, fols. 30-31, 72-75.

The home government seems to have gotten a different impression from the governor's reports. On August 29, it addressed Rochemore as follows: "your antipathy for Governor Kerlérec and a disregard for all the wise council he gave you on your arrival in the province; your haste, in spite of his advice, to call in all the treasury notes and to draw that year more than 1,800,000 livres in bills of exchange on the French treasury . . . for these reasons and for many more, founded upon your unsociable nature and incompatibility with the colonial service . . . the crown has decided to recall you to France".[1] Because of the political influence of his family in France, however, no order to return immediately, was sent to him at this time. Accordingly for several months more, Rochemore continued to hold the office of "ordonnateur".[2]

Ignorant of the results of his labor upon the home government, and determined that it should know the truth about the administration of the finances of Louisiana by Rochemore, Kerlérec continued to send further information directly to France and also by way of Denmark, Holland and Spain. On October 8, 1759, he despatched a letter to France stating that the "ordonnateur" was selling from the royal storehouses goods intended for Indian presents. This merchandise, at low prices, passed into the hands of members of Rochemore's political clique who sold it at a profit of 500 to 600 per cent. By such a manœuver the "ordonnateur" was able to share the gains and at the same time present to the governor a balanced treasury report. The governor also asserted that the "ordonnateur", contrary to his instructions, was buying up whole cargoes of European merchandise in order to con-

[1] *A. N., C., Sér. B*, vol. cix, *Louisiane*, fol. 13.

[2] *Villiers du Terrage*, pp. 140-144.

trol prices. One instance is cited in which Rochemore gave a bill of exchange amounting to 250,000 livres for a cargo that he was able to dispose of for 400,000. Public clamor against such proceedings, it was affirmed, was increasing daily, and the discontent was augmented by the way in which bills of exchange were distributed. Unless they belonged to the Rochemore faction, it was difficult for persons in the service, who had families in France, to secure bills of exchange to make them remittances. Some of these men were able to send part of the amount they desired, while others, for example, four captains and Macarty, commandant in the Illinois country, could obtain none.[1]

Such methods made speculation in bills of exchange lucrative. A treasury clerk, an appointee of Rochemore, kept a shop in New Orleans where he sold bills of exchange at an advance of fifteen per cent or more.[2] It seems the crown had received, in part at least, the same information. On October 1, it asked for a fuller report on the administration of the finances of the province, and asserted that it was impossible for Rochemore's secretary to amass 40,000 livres in less than a year unless the "ordonnateur" himself had had some part in the intrigue.[3]

On October 12, Rochemore defended his action in regard to the recall of treasury notes the preceding year on the ground that he had simply followed the example set him by Michel and Vaudreuil, but made no mention of the many accusations made against him by colonial officials. He at this time informed the home government that for the past six months his health had been in a wretched state, hence he greatly needed a change of climate—the only point, perhaps, on which he and the governor were ever in ac-

[1] *A. N., C., Sér. C*[13], vol. xli, fols. 120-125. [2] *Ibid.*

[3] *Ibid., Sér. B,* vol. cix, fol. 25.

cord.[1] October 16 he made another report to the crown stating that he had drawn on 1759 for but 869,000 livres.[2] On December 7 he sent the home government a more detailed statement in which he asserted the only money in use in the province was treasury notes, orders on the treasury and a very little silver. The paper of itself depreciated in value by soon becoming so worn and torn that it was difficult to know its value, hence no one wished to receive it except at a very great discount. Speculation in bills of exchange, the " ordonnateur " asserted, had now become a business with the discount on treasury notes so great as to make them almost worthless.[3]

The financial perplexities of Louisiana at this time were augmented greatly by the conditions existing in the royal treasury. So nearly was the home government bankrupt that it was obliged, October 15, 1759, to suspend payment on bills of exchange and was able to send to Louisiana none of the supplies asked for. For the coming year it permitted Kerlérec to draw on the crown in bills of exchange to the amount of 400,000 livres to be used for the most pressing current expenses and to hold, if possible, the confidence of the troops and colonists in the royal government.[4]

The outlook for an improvement in the finances of Louisiana in 1760 could scarcely have been more discouraging, yet the governor kept up his efforts to rid the province of the services of Rochemore. In his report, March 30, he attempted to elucidate the matter to the crown by making a summary of the financial operations of the "ordonnateur" for the past eighteen months, as follows: from the 1,996,-

[1] *A. N., C., Sér.* C^{13}, vol. xli, fols. 282-287.

[2] *Ibid.*, fol. 310.

[3] *Ibid.*, fols. 318-322.

[4] *Ibid.*, *Sér. B*, vol. cxiv, *Louisiane*, fols. 20-21.

000 [1] of bills of exchange issued in October, 1758, he deducted 1,400,000 livres for the administration of Descloslaux, "ordonnateur" *ad interim,* which subtracted, left charged to Rochemore 596,000 livres. The last issue of October, 1759, amounted to 1,050,000 livres. The records since that date, he asserted, showed 4,000,000 livres more were issued, which made the entire amount 5,646,000 livres. Before the governor was able to despatch the report to France he learned of 1,041,850 additional, drawn in October, 1759, which brought the amount for the period in question to 6,687,850 livres. The governor affirmed that this last issue had been announced in Louisiana to be 500-000 or 600,000 livres.[2] Rochemore's statement to the crown made it 869,000 livres.[3] On June 25, 1760, the "ordonnateur", in making reference to this same issue, apparently, put it at only 150,000 livres, 70,000 livres drawn on 1759 and 80,000 on the allowance of 1760.[4]

During the year the bitter struggle between the governor and "ordonnateur" reached its climax when Kerlérec, amid shouts from the people of "Vive le roi et Monsieur le governeur", and with the physical support of the soldiers, entered a house and seized goods belonging to Rochemore. It had been rumored that the "ordonnateur" was to be assassinated. He undoubtedly believed the time had come. Rochemore, a man of less than mediocre ability, deprived of his best political supporters by this time, fearful of being murdered, was unable, henceforward, to carry on extensively his evil practices in the administration of the finances of the province. Kerlérec was practically in full control.[5]

[1] *Supra*, pp. 143, 145. The governor's error.

[2] *A. N., C., Sér.* C^{13}, vol. xlii, fols. 12-21.

[3] *Supra*, p. 148.

[4] *A. N., C., Sér.* C^{13}, vol. xlii, fols. 126-127.

[5] Villiers du Terrage, p. 94.

The governor now formulated a plan which he believed would improve the colonial currency and communicated it to the crown. He informed the home government that there were more than 3,000,000 livres in different kinds of treasury notes in use. They had been issued from time to time by the "ordonnateurs" because of a lack of funds for current expenses, and at first had been redeemed each year with bills of exchange; but that practice long since had been given up. Since the notes were signed only by the "ordonnateur" and comptroller, it was the general belief in the province, that they were without royal sanction, hence no one had the least confidence in them. He therefore proposed, as his solution of the currency difficulty, the issuing of 4,000,000 livres in parchment or paper money to be used in redeeming the treasury notes. They were to have the form of "bons", six by four inches in size, bearing the king's arms, and ranging in value from six sols up to 5,000 livres.[1] After receipt in New Orleans, they were

[1] *A. N., C., Sér. C*[13], vol. xlii, fol. 198. The values and amounts of each kind of "bons" to be issued:—

Number.	*Denominations in livres.*	*Total in livres.*
100	5,000	500,000
100	4,000	400,000
200	3,000	600,000
300	2,000	600,000
600	1,000	600,000
1,000	500	500,000
1,000	300	300,000
1,000	200	200,000
1,000	100	100,000
1,000	50	50,000
1,000	40	40,000
1,000	20	20,000
2,000	12	24,000
2,000	6	12,000
3,000	3	9,000
10,000	48 sols	24,000
10,000	24 sols	12,000
10,000	12 sols	6,000
10,000	6 sols	3,000
55,300		4,000,000

to be numbered and signed by the comptroller and also by the governor and " ordonnateur ", after which they were to become current money for the sum cut in the corner. This currency was to be accepted on a par with silver and bills of exchange, and was to be legal tender for all debts. Six months, from the date of the publication of the ordinance in Louisiana, were to be allowed in which to bring the old notes to the treasurer at New Orleans, by whom they would be redeemed with " bons "; otherwise they would be null and void.[1] Notwithstanding the fact that the proposal would have gone far toward the solution of the currency problem, nothing was done to enact it into law.

On May 20, 1761, Foucault became acting " ordonnateur ". He found the storehouse entirely empty, hence was obliged to buy supplies for the troops at the private shops at extravagant prices. There were abuses everywhere. Paying the officers in bills of exchange fostered speculation in paper money of which he found 6,783,347 livres in circulation, standing at five to one with silver.[2] On July 7 the governor informed the royal government that the irregularities in the administration of the finances multiplied daily, that there were innumerable petty annoyances and many quarrels of a most indecent sort. He estimated the paper money outstanding at 10,000,000 livres, and added, " France is indeed to be pitied if it can find no one there, nor here, with whom to replace Rochemore. For some time I have forced him to hold the position of a secretary and in so doing I have rendered great service to the crown and to the state ".[3] Before the end of the year the home government appointed d'Abbadie " ordonnateur " of

[1] *A. N., C., Sér.* C^{13}, vol. xlii, fols. 195-200.

[2] Villiers du Terrage, pp. 144-145.

[3] *A. N., C., Sér.* C^{13}, vol. xlii, fols. 221-223.

Louisiana. December 22 it granted him a "gratification" of 6,000 livres to be paid him immediately, and on that day he left France, reaching Louisiana April 29, 1762.[1]

For the administration of the office, the crown gave the new "ordonnateur" very full instructions, perhaps too complete ever to be read. On the subject of the finances, for example, he was permitted to draw 600,000 livres in bills of exchange for current expenses, 250,000 livres of which were to be expended at Vera Cruz and Campeachy in supplying urgent needs, the remaining 350,000 livres in paying for provisions drawn from France. 200,000 livres additional were allowed for the purpose of liquidating the colonial debt. The "ordonnateur" was further instructed to divide the bills of exchange into parts with four, six or eight months to run so that their time of maturity would be equally distributed over the twelve months of the year. Moreover, it was stated, no bills of exchange would be paid unless a report explaining the cause for which drawn either preceded or accompanied the bills. In order to restore confidence in the treasury notes and other paper money issued by Rochemore and those who had held the office before him, d'Abbadie was commanded to redeem the paper with new notes of the same value and form. He was further ordered to make an exact valuation of the paper money in circulation. The statement was to be signed by himself, the governor, the treasurer and the comptroller and then sent to the home government. It was its wish to withdraw as soon as practicable all the paper money in use in the province and to replace it with silver. The "ordonnateur" was finally commanded to carry out the royal instructions in conjunction with the governor and comptroller.[2] Just how well d'Abbadie followed this instruction

[1] *A. N., C., Sér. B,* vol. cxiii, pt. 1, fols. 298, 313.

[2] *Ibid.,* vol. cxiv, *Louisiane,* fols. 10-14; vol. cxvi, *Louisiane,* fol. 1.

belongs to the story of the finances under the Spanish régime. Before the province passed to Spain, however, a bill of exchange for 50,000 livres drawn by Rochemore for supplies furnished the new floating post established just before he left office, reached the royal treasury. This bill astonished the home government, since it had supplied that post with provisions at Havana to the amount of 71,000 livres.[1]

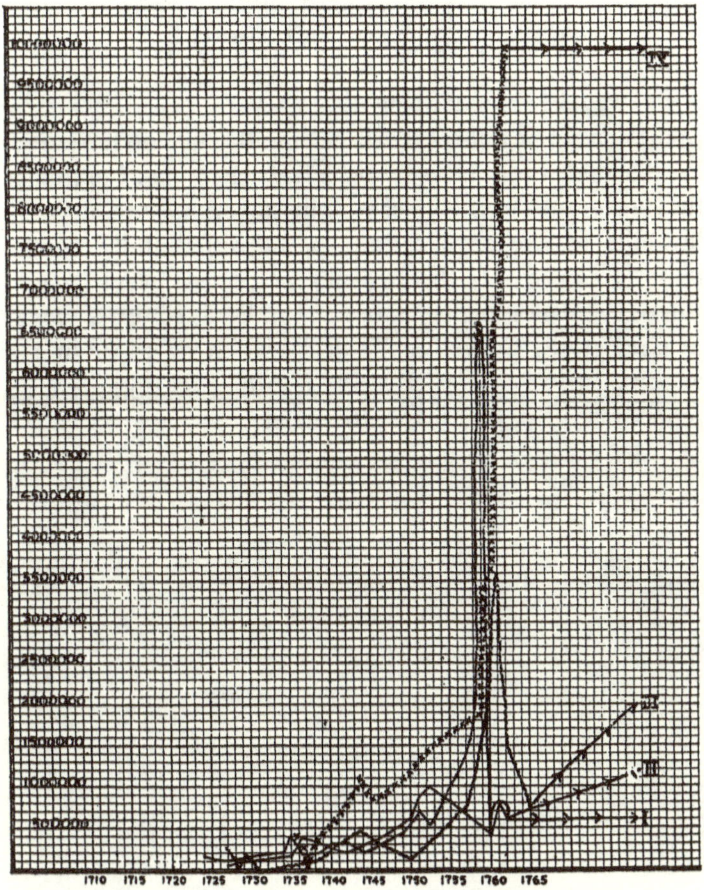

[1] *A. N., C., Sér. B,* vol. cxiv, *Louisiane,* fols. 20-21.

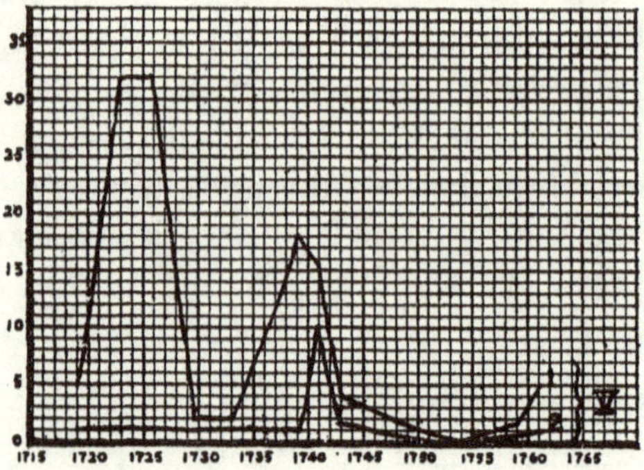

By way of summarizing the story of paper money in Louisiana during the French régime the five above curves have been drawn. Curve I represents the bills of exchange that were authorized by the home government; Curve II, the bills of exchange drawn by the different "ordonnateurs"; Curve III, the treasury notes that were in use; Curve IV, the estimated amount of all kinds of paper money in circulation; Curve V, the depreciation of paper money as compared to that of silver or bills of exchange. Line 1 represents the paper; line 2, the silver.

CHAPTER XII

TRADE BETWEEN FRANCE AND LOUISIANA, 1699-1731

THE men who made up the settlement founded by Iberville on Biloxi Bay in 1699, were interested chiefly in mining and trading, with scarcely even a secondary interest in agriculture. Consequently, for the first years of the settlement's existence the mother country was obliged to send foodstuffs from France in order to keep the colony alive. For the reception of this merchandise a storehouse, 52x 26x14 feet, was built on Dauphin Island at a cost to the crown of 490 livres, and was paid for with royal merchandise at a considerable advance on the cost in France.[1]

On the orders from the home government, commodities from this repository were to be drawn for the support of the settlement and for the purpose of building up trade between France and her infant colony. From 1702 to 1706 the colonial officials, without the royal orders, took out of this warehouse 47,807 livres, eleven sols, eight deniers worth of merchandise, some of which sold at a profit on the cost in France of 600 per cent. Unfortunately for the crown, however, the gains did not find their way into the royal treasury. Instead, the profits passed into the pockets of Iberville and his brothers who often sold the goods to the Spaniards when the colonists of Louisiana, themselves, were actually suffering from lack of food. At the end of the year 1706, the results from this method of administration were that the province had made but little advance-

[1] *A. N., C., Sér. C*[13], vol. 1, fols. 1-20.

ment and as yet no trade with the mother country was established.[1] Scarcity of food could not always be traced to the unwise distribution of the merchandise by the officials. The French government, during the early years of the colony, was too hard pressed for money to send commodities regularly to Louisiana. Moreover, some that were provided were unfit for use when they reached America.[2]

To establish trade with a province having so few products for export as Louisiana during the first years of its life was a difficult undertaking. The crown had instructed Iberville to make pearls and buffalo wool the two chief articles for the trade in question. The pearls found in Louisiana were fine neither in luster nor shape, yet the royal government ordered that a careful search be made for them. It was soon admitted, even by the crown itself, that Louisiana pearls were worthless, but it was some time before the wool project was given up.[3] In 1708 the home government sent out a vessel for the purpose of establishing fisheries in the province where fish could be dried for the export trade. This venture, however, was no more successful than that in pearls and wool.[4]

Iberville had told Count de Pontchartrain that it was his opinion, as well as that of men " most versed in American affairs, that Louisiana would never be settled unless trade was thrown open to all the merchants in the kingdom ".[5] No importance being attached to this opinion, the royal authorities began to look about for some one who, for an

[1] *A. N., C., Sér. B*, vol. xxxii, fol. 47; *Sér. F³*, vol. ccxli, May 13, 1710.

[2] *Ibid., Sér. C¹³*, vol. i, fols. 514-569; vol. ii, fols. 519-527; *Sér. B, IC*, vol. xxix, fol. 1.

[3] Charlevoix, *Hist. and Gen. Desc. of New France*, vol. v, pp. 128-129.

[4] *A. N., C., Sér. C¹³*, vol. v, fols. 257-259.

[5] Charlevoix, *op. cit.*, vol. v, p. 128.

exclusive trading privilege, would be willing to relieve them of the task of supporting the new colony. An offer was made to some merchants of St. Malo, to whom Louisiana was represented as having great possibilities in mines and in a trade in ship lumber with the Spanish-American colonies. The venture, it seems, did not appeal to these men; hence the crown was forced to go on with the work until some one, willing to relieve it of the burden, could be found.[1] During the intervening period the government, to some extent, increased its activities and by 1712 had two ships making trips more or less regularly.[2]

On September 24, 1712, the crown by letters-patent granted to Antoine Crozat, a French merchant, the sole right of trade in Louisiana. This trade monopoly for a period of fifteen years required, among other things, the sending to the colony, yearly, of a fixed number of settlers and a certain amount of merchandise for the support of the garrison. Crozat was to pay the crown a fifth part of all gold, silver and precious stones he secured from the province. He was permitted to buy all kinds of peltry, except beaver skins, and under some limitations his trade between France and the colony was to be free from duties. The plan of giving a province to a merchant or company of merchants was not a new policy. It had been tried elsewhere with very discouraging results, yet the French government was too glad to be rid of this unprofitable possession to consider possible consequences.[3]

At first, trade under Crozat's control was confined to Dauphin Island and Mobile, the only articles of export being peltry and lumber. Scarcity of ships from France

[1] *A. N., C., Sér. B*, vol. xxx, fols. 51-52.

[2] *Ibid.*, vol. xxxi, fol. 513; *Sér. C13*, vol. ii, fols. 193-211, 213.

[3] *Hist. Colls. of La.*, pt. 3, pp. 38-42.

at times made it necessary to keep the pelts so long in the warm, damp climate of the Gulf coast that they were partly destroyed by insects.[1] In April, 1713, a vessel from France came to the colony with a cargo of merchandise and ammunition which was deposited in the royal storehouse.[2] The next year a boat brought to the province a cargo of 80,000 pounds of merchandise, but before it was landed the ship and cargo were lost. So great was the distress caused by this disaster that the officials of Louisiana were obliged to send out a vessel in search of food.[3] From the end of the year 1712 to the beginning of 1716 four ships loaded with merchandise left France for the settlements on the Gulf coast. As yet the province had made little progress, hence with the exception of peltry, it was producing no exports for the mother country.[4]

An exclusive privilege like the one given to Crozat in 1712, stands always in need of protection. In making other grants in the colony the crown was careful not to bestow any that might run counter to the trading interests of Crozat.[5] This merchant, himself, however, took means to protect his Louisiana rights. He first selected colonial officials upon whom he could rely to carry out his instructions, but unfortunately both for him and the province these men were not otherwise fitted for colonial posts. Under no circumstances were foreign traders allowed in the province. Therefore, in 1714 and 1715, when ships with car-

[1] *A. N., C., Sér. C*[13], vol. iii, fols. 212-213, 216-223.

[2] Margry, vol. v, p. 506.

[3] La Harpe, p. 115.

[4] *A. N., C., Sér. C*[13], vol. iv, fols. 67-68; Charlevoix, *op. cit.*, vol. vi, p. 32.

[5] *A. N., C., Sér. B*, vol. xxxiv, fol. 127.

goes of merchandise sorely needed by the colonists reached Louisiana they were not permitted to be sold. At the same time these selfsame agents were buying peltry for what they chose to pay for it and selling European merchandise at a profit of not less than 300 per cent.[1] Such greed on the part of Crozat's officers created much discontent in the colony and caused the inhabitants to trade clandestinely on every possible occasion.[2]

Infringements of this sort were not conducive to the success of Crozat who from the first had found the enjoyment of his patent very expensive. As early as 1714 he informed the crown that the maritime trade had been reduced almost to nothing.[3] He kept control of Louisiana three years more and then surrendered his rights. In the month of August, 1717, the crown ceded the province to the "Company of the West" with substantially the same trading privileges as those bestowed in the patent of 1712. Vessels not belonging to the Company and found trading in Louisiana were, together with their cargoes, to be confiscated.[4] This grant was made for twenty-five years and by the decree of September 27, 1717, the territory within which it should operate was extended so as to include the Illinois country.[5]

The Company of the West began its control of Louisiana by making an attempt to establish trade on a better basis. By means of colonization with settlers who would engage in agriculture the Company planned to secure products for export. Growth of settlement was to be effected on the

[1] *A. N., C., Sér.* C^{13}, vol. iii, fols. 209-310; Charlevoix, *op. cit.*, vol. vi, p. 34.

[2] *A. N., C., Ser.* C^{13}, vol. iii, fols. 245-251.

[3] Charlevoix, *op. cit.*, vol. vi, p. 36.

[4] Le Page du Pratz, vol. i, pp. 47-81.

[5] Margry, vol. v, p. 589; *A. N., C., Sér. B*, vol. xli, fol. 616.

lower Mississippi where there were direct connections both with the Illinois country and the interior settlements of Mexico, with which the Company desired to open trade. Accordingly, about a hundred miles from the mouth of the Mississippi a site for a new capital, New Orleans, as the center of commercial activities, was selected.[1]

During the period of the Company's control vessels came oftener and much more regularly than before, touching always, both on the inward and outward voyages, at the French West Indies.[2] They brought settlers and merchandise, and carried away peltry. Between November 14 and 25, 1718, alone, three ships took from the province 100,000 pounds of tobacco, Campeachy wood and skins. The two first-named articles, however, were not products of the colony, itself, but had been secured from Spanish merchants who had conveyed them to the province in order to exchange them there for French merchandise which had been brought over in large quantities during August and September of that year.[3]

In December, 1718, certain changes were made in the French trading corporations. The Company of the West acquired the rights of the Senegal Company, and after other changes assumed the name of the "Company of the Indies", March 9, 1719.[4] The policy adopted by the reorganized Company was much the same as that of its predecessor; that is, sending out ships with settlers and merchandise so as to secure products for export.[5] This method under the management of the Company of the

[1] Margry, vol. v, pp. 549-550.

[2] *A. N., C., Sér. B*, vol. xxxix, fol. 70; *Sér. C*[13], vol. v, fols. 16, 36-41.

[3] Le Gac, *op. cit.* Newberry Lib., Chicago.

[4] Margry, vol. v, pp. 589-590; *A. N., C., Sér. C*[13], vol. v, fols. 240-241, 267.

[5] *A. N., C., Sér. C*[13], vol. ix, fols. 26-28.

Indies resulted in a substantial increase in the population of the province. In 1719, German settlers willing to engage in agriculture were sent to the colony.[1] In 1720, a ship from Dunkerque brought to Louisiana 300 galley slaves, hardly a valuable contribution to the development of it, since few of them could be induced to take up any kind of work, let alone a laborious occupation like agriculture, in a new country where fields had to be cleared before crops could be planted. Before the end of the year, however, two vessels brought from France 300 men of a much better quality. Many of them took up land from choice and began the cultivation of the soil.[2]

Already the province was exporting peltry, lumber, pitch and tar, with the last-named product selling at eight livres a barrel if paid for with silver, but ten if bills of exchange or merchandise were offered in payment. To this list of exports the Company was attempting to add both rice and tobacco. Furthermore the Company, in 1720, proposed the building at New Orleans, Biloxi and Mobile of large sheds or covered markets for the reception of colonial products, and also agreed to pay at these places twenty-five livres a hundredweight for the best tobacco, twenty for the second, and fifteen for the third grade. In order to increase more rapidly the amount of tobacco put upon the market, it was further proposed to allow the overseer of plantations for the Company, the only person in the province in a position to take up the culture, a bounty of 500 livres annually and an additional one of three per cent on the price of the best grade of tobacco. Under the new rules, furthermore, only one or two cases, taken at random

[1] Margry, vol. v, p. 571.

[2] *A., B. de l'A.*, vol. 4497, fols. 65-66; *A. N., C., Sér.* C^{13}, vol. vi, fol. 23; Chaville, p. 7.

from the lot presented for sale, were to be weighed and these weights taken as the standard for the remainder. The arrangement, however, seems to have been unsatisfactory to the colonists who from lack of laborers were unable to make the regulation cases. They preferred to ship the tobacco in any sort of contrivance they could most easily construct.[1]

The price of rice was at the same time fixed at twelve livres a hundredweight, with the same arrangement with regard to the cases as for tobacco. Foreign merchandise was to be sold in the coast settlements for an advance of 50 per cent on the cost in France and an increase of 100 in the Illinois country, with proportional prices for the posts between. Under this regulation wine sold in lower Louisiana for 120 livres a cask (60 gal.) and brandy at 100 livres a "quart" (15 gals.), a rate that made the former retail at ten and the latter at 20 sols a quart.[2] It was reported to the royal government that the settlers wished to make an agreement whereby they would be allowed to pay for European goods with indigo, tobacco and cotton payable at the close of each harvest.[3]

In 1722, nine ships arrived in Louisiana with 4,200 prospective settlers on board. Among the newcomers were men, with their families of German, French and Jewish origin. Many of these colonists took up land along the Mississippi and at once began to devote themselves to agriculture.[4] The colony was now able to make some progress in producing exports for trade with the mother

[1] Margry, vol. v, pp. 617-621; *A. N., C., Sér. C*[13], vol. vi, fol. 23; vol. xii, fols. 202-207; La Harpe, pp. 290-291.

[2] *A. N., C., Sér. C*[13], vol. vi, fols. 14-24; xii, fol. 204.

[3] *Ibid.*, vol. vi, fol. 23.

[4] Margry, vol. v, pp. 576-583; *A. N., C., Sér. C*[13], vol. vi, fols. 14, 287-289.

country. The Natchez district contained what was regarded as the best tobacco land in the province, yet the exportation there was hampered in two ways: first, by the regulations as to cases, and second, by a shortage of boats to carry the tobacco to market.[1] Other parts of the province were not so restricted and on January 20, 1725, a boat that had been waiting at New Orleans for the coming of the convoys from the Illinois country left the capital for Mobile where it took on a cargo of tobacco and tar. This craft, with its cargo valued at 200,000 livres, was wrecked soon after setting sail and both ship and cargo were lost.[2]

In September a vessel left the colony for France with a cargo consisting in part of indigo and peltry valued at 8,438 livres, six sols. A few days later an incoming ship, through the ignorance of the pilot, was run aground on an island off the Louisiana coast and in order again to put the boat afloat it was necessary to cast overboard between 300 and 400 barrels of flour and many boxes of shoes. The loss of the two cargoes was a great setback to the trade between France and the province.[3] In order to counterbalance these disasters, the colonial council requested the royal government to send over a supply of fish oil, cloth and knives to be used in the making of indigo.[4]

This year the people of Louisiana were granted some liberty in trade. They were to be allowed to sell their tar and pitch either at the colonial market proper, or to ship it directly to France at their own risk. In the latter case freight rates for these commodities were fixed at 100 livres

[1] *A. N., C., Sér.* C^{13}, vol. viii, fol. 227.

[2] *Ibid.*, fol. 234.

[3] *Ibid.*, vol. ix, fols. 241-243.

[4] *Ibid.*, fols. 239, 243.

a ton of not less than eight barrels. One-half of each shipment was to go toward paying the bills due the Company, the remainder could be disposed of as the owner saw fit. In order to stimulate production, the Company agreed to pay for these products, for a year or two, fifteen livres a barrel (200 pounds), after which time the price was to drop to eight or ten livres. The plan was financially beneficial to all concerned. It was calculated that at each shipment the exporter would send not less than 100 barrels, twelve and a half tons. This amount would net the Company 1,250 livres from the freight and leave the manufacturer 250 livres for other expenses and profit.[1] The privilege seems to have brought about no immediate improvement for on October 24, 1725, the colonial council complained that the ordinance had not been put properly into execution.[2]

In 1726 the exports of Louisiana were silk, tobacco, rice, indigo, pitch, tar, lumber, masts, sassafras and quinine of a rather poor quality.[3] The next year the Company's interest was centered chiefly in making tobacco the most important export product. Because of the expense necessary to begin the growing of tobacco, and in order to encourage the settlers who were financially able to enter this industry but were slow in doing so, the Company paid in some particular localities ten sols a pound for this commodity. The farmers at Capitoulas, three leagues above New Orleans, received this special price for some of a very inferior quality because they considered the culture unprofitable and had determined to give it up.[4]

The inhabitants of the Natchez settlement were also paid

[1] *A. N., C., Sér. C*[13], vol. xi, fols. 46-49.

[2] *Ibid.*, vol. viii, fol. 243.

[3] *Ibid.*, vol. x, fols. 151-153.

[4] *Ibid.*, fols. 186-187.

ten sols for what they put upon the market. Many persons in other places in lower Louisiana were already established in the industry. At this time they requested the Company to take for the next ten years what tobacco they had to sell at eight sols a pound, if delivered in bundles, and payable in silver; seven sols, if in bills of exchange and ten, if for cancelling debts they had contracted under the old régime. The Company rejected the proposal on the ground that it was offering farmers already started in this work a fair price for tobacco.[1]

The encouragement the Company gave to the tobacco growers was somewhat fruitful. On April 29, 1728, a ship sailed for France with a load of tobacco and peltry.[2] In July another one set out laden with lumber, tobacco, peltry and 2,382 piastres, and before the end of the month still another with a shipment of tar and lumber.[3]

The tobacco crop of 1728 was very short and much of that put on the market was of inferior quality. Some of the colonists nevertheless were cultivating the plant to the exclusion of all other products, not even excepting their own food supply. Tobacco of the best grade was then selling at three " reaux " (real = twelve sols, six deniers) a pound and, in bundles, two " reaux ". The governor said he had paid as much as eight " reaux " for some of a superior quality.[4] The following year the crop was short because of a season of almost continuous rain, suffering a reduction from 400,000 pounds to about 300,000. In spite of these unfavorable conditions, therefore, the colony put upon the market a considerable amount, and some cotton as well.[5]

[1] *A. N., C., Sér.* C^{13}, vol. x, fols. 169-170, 186-187.

[2] *Ibid.*, vol. xi, fols. 165-167.

[3] *Ibid.*, fols. 52, 56.

[4] *Ibid.*, fol. 65.

[5] *Ibid.*, vol. xii, fols. 138-140.

There were other products that might have been included among the exports if France, like other countries of the time, had not prohibited raising in her dominions commodities that competed with similar articles brought forth in the mother country. Thus hemp, flax and wine were not produced in Louisiana. For a while also there was quite a trade in walking-sticks made from the root of the cane. They were very popular in France and varied in value according to the closeness of the nodes of the root from which the sticks were made.[1]

The endeavors of the Company of the Indies to establish Louisiana on a substantial commercial basis had, therefore, not been a failure from the point of view of the province. A goodly number of new settlements had been made, and the production of commodities for export had undergone a considerable increase. By 1731, pitch, tar, lumber, tobacco, rice, corn, beans, indigo and cotton were produced, and each year, on a whole, showed a gain in quality.

It is now needful to consider the cost to the Company in bringing about this development. Almost from the start it had been hampered by abuses in the trade; hence on October 1, 1722, it issued an ordinance forbidding anyone, without the consent of the commandant, to board a vessel on its arrival in the province for the purpose of buying up the cargoes and thereby of controlling the price. Because of this practice the colonists were often forced to purchase European goods at unnecessarily high rates. Violations of the ordinance were to be punished with a fine of 100 livres and confiscation of the merchandise.[2] Since the law did not put an end to the trouble, on May 26, 1723,

[1] Dumont, vol. i, p. 28.

[2] *A. N., C., Sér. A*, vol. xxiii, Oct. 1, 1722.

the council issued a decree making it illegal for any one to board such ships without a permit from that body itself.[1]

In the following September the "ordonnateur" complained to the home government that the boats coming to the province brought prodigious quantities of trumpery owned by the officials and crew. The commander of one craft sold in Louisiana what belonged to his private account for more than 3,000 piastres. There were others, also, on board owning goods which they disposed of on arrival. A galley slave, in fact, had smuggled on board 100 piastres worth of such wares, enough to buy his freedom and passage money for his return to France. This ship, the colonial officials claimed, was only a fair example of the enormous quantity of "pacotille" carried by all boats coming to the province.[2] The master of a slave vessel in 1723, for another example, touched at Cape Français, where, under the pretext of buying supplies for his craft, he purchased instead, wine, soap and other kinds of merchandise which he sold to advantage in Louisiana.[3] Two years later these private sales were still going on. One ship captain in particular disposed of a cargo of wine, flour, cheese and beer on a plea that the Company had not sent merchandise enough to supply the needs of the colonists. This private trade was injurious to the Company in two ways; its vessels were being used to carry freight from which it received no profit, while at the same time the crews were being rendered wholly indifferent to their employer's interests, and the development of Louisiana was being made to suffer by the excessive prices demanded for the goods. These private merchants paid no attention to the official rates of sale, but disposed of their goods for whatever the needs

[1] *A. N., C., Sér. A,* vol. xxiii, May 26, 1723.

[2] *Ibid., Sér.* C^{13}, vol. vii, fol. 27.

[3] *Ibid.,* fol. 61.

of the people would allow them to charge; thereby, to a considerable extent, defeating the Company's desire to advance the industries of the province.[1]

In April, 1728, other irregularities in the trade were brought to the attention of the crown. It was discovered that on the five ships that reached the province this year, there was a marked leakage in brandy, wines and all kinds of drugs on board. This shortage entailed great loss to the Company and indirectly was detrimental to the province as a whole, in that there were not enough drugs with which properly to treat the sick. This in turn led to a considerable increase in the death rate, a further obstacle to a realization of the Company's plans.[2] To these losses arising from dishonesty of employees must be added those produced by the inefficiency of these persons and by actual misfortunes.[3]

Aside from the obstacles above described, the Company of the Indies as early as 1722 began to realize the enormity of the undertaking of making Louisiana a lucrative commercial province. The principles adopted to develop trade between the province and France were sound, but they entailed large investments on which the profits were most precarious. Moreover it was soon evident that the large expenditure must go on for many years. The Company, therefore, transferred its interest to the building up of a trade with the Spanish colonies by making Louisiana the base for the necessary merchandise. Therefore, at the end of thirty-two years of the existence of the province, and after having been under several different controls, the trade with the mother country was still not yet well started.

[1] *A. N., C., Sér.* C^{13}, vol. ix, fols. 17-19.

[2] *Ibid.*, vol. xi, fols. 30-32.

[3] *Supra*, p. 161.

CHAPTER XIII

Trade between France and Louisiana, 1731-1763

France, in 1731, stood at a considerable disadvantage in the commercial world when compared with the Dutch and English who had on the seas a hundred merchant vessels to her one.[1] There seems to be no justification for this difference. At this time France, like all other European states having foreign possessions, permitted its colonies to trade with no one but the mother country. In America, where its provinces were far greater in extent than those of England, France employed but 300 ships. By providing a sufficient number of white settlers and black laborers whereby commerce might be augmented, it was claimed that in a few years, and at no expense to the home government, 1,000 vessels would be needed to carry on the American trade.[2] Such was the spirit of France when Louisiana, for a second time, became a crown colony.

From the commencement of the royal control, this spirit is reflected in the administration of Louisiana. An earnest endeavor was made to interest French merchants in the commerce of the province. Soon an agreement was reached with a trader of La Rochelle to send a vessel of 200 tons with a cargo of food and other merchandise to the province toward the end of August, 1731. This pledge, however, was made only on the condition that the crown should get a merchant of Bordeaux to make a similar promise. To

[1] *A. B., A. É., Fr.*, vol. 1990, fol. 79.

[2] *Ibid.*, fols. 109, 113; Margry, vol. v, p. 590.

this end, on July 31, the men there engaged in maritime activities were appealed to by the royal government and urged to send ships to Louisiana.[1] A further attempt was made to draw the merchants of the kingdom into the trade when, August 4, the crown exempted for six years all merchant vessels from carrying soldiers and arms and declared the commerce of the province open alike to all its subjects. The fare for each soldier sent out by the home government was in future to cost it sixty livres plus the food necessary for the voyage.[2]

The goods of the Company of the Indies at the time of the retrocession consisted for the most part of articles suited only to the Spanish trade and in amount about 180 tons.[3] As early as June 24, 1731, the supply of flour, wine, brandy and salt was inadequate.[4] The governor and "ordonnateur" estimated that the colony would require annually, exclusive of the flour for the troops, 3,000 quintals of flour, 200 casks of wine and 3,650 gallons of brandy.[5] At the time bread for the soldiers was made of a flour composed of equal parts of rice and wheat—a practice the "ordonnateur" proposed to continue since the former was one-fourth cheaper than the latter, and because there was always, when the supply of wheat flour from France for any reason was shortened, the danger of being forced to give the troops a bread made entirely from rice, a diet that never failed to create discontent among the men.[6]

[1] *A. N., C., Sér. B*, vol. lv, fols. 55-56.

[2] *Ibid.*, fol. 148; *Sér. A*, vol. xxiii, Aug. 4, 1731.

[3] *Ibid., Sér. C*[13], vol. xiv, fol. 3.

[4] *Ibid.*, vol. xiii, fol. 146.

[5] *Ibid.*, fol. 17.

[6] *Ibid.*, vol. xv, fol. 11.

Supplies from France reached the province in December, 1731, when a royal ship brought to the colony merchandise, and carried back between 40,000 and 50,000 pounds of Louisiana tobacco. The "ordonnateur" advised the settlers to send to France only that of the best grade since there was transportation for but part of what was then ready for the market.[1] Heretofore the exporters had been allowed to send this commodity to France on the Company's vessels at a freight charge of fifty livres a ton for cotton, tobacco and rice. The settlers at this time asked the crown to continue the practice and also to exempt Louisiana imports from all duties, as was the custom in all French colonies not well established. They further begged the royal government not to reduce the price of six sols a pound that the Company was paying them for their tobacco.[2] The crown, therefore, September 30, 1732, for a period of ten years, permitted the exemption asked for.[3]

Before the end of the year 1731 the vessel promised by the La Rochelle merchant reached the province with a cargo valued at 37,000 livres, cost in France, and consisting of some good wine, 875 quintals of flour and other merchandise. The captain began selling the day after his arrival at New Orleans and in the first few days the receipts were 9,000 livres, after which the merchandise was disposed of much less rapidly. In order to hasten the return to France, it was decided to sell at 50 per cent advance on the cost in France what was left of the cargo. A prominent settler who represented a colonial association took the remainder of the goods and gave in exchange something more than 100,000 pounds of tobacco, also rice and cotton in consid-

[1] *A. N., C., Sér.* C^{13}, vol. xiii, fols. 79, 132-133; vol. xiv, fol. 4.

[2] *Ibid.*, vol. xiv, fol. 4.

[3] *Ibid., Sér. A*, vol. xxiii, Sept. 30, 1732.

erable quantities and the balance in cash. This money the captain invested partly in peltry, brick and logwood to complete the cargo, and for 15,157 livres, the remainder, received from the "ordonnateur" a bill of exchange on France.[1] The supplies of the province were still further augmented by the arrival, December 22, of a vessel belonging to the Company. The captain of the ship spent ten days in disposing of the cargo and in buying up tobacco, peltry and cotton for another for the return voyage.[2]

During the year 1732 trade in Louisiana was good. In March a royal vessel brought to the province 100,000 livres in French money, 1,200 quintals of flour, 20,000 pounds of powder, and clothing for the troops, all of which, excepting the dry-goods, was in good condition when it reached the province.[3] Early in the next month a ship belonging to a Bordeaux merchant arrived. The merchandise on board did not sell readily because during the last month of the previous and the early months of the current year there had been landed in the colony an abundance of European goods. In most things, therefore, the supply was already adequate. In order that the merchandise from Bordeaux should be disposed of as advantageously as that from La Rochelle, the governor proposed to the captain of the former ship to sell enough goods for cash to buy a cargo of brick which he should carry to the French West Indies and there exchange it for sugar and syrup, meanwhile leaving the remainder of the merchandise in Louisiana. Bricks were selling for fifteen livres a thousand, on which it was claimed a profit of nine livres, ten sols could be made. On the return from the islands the tobacco crop

[1] *A. N., C., Sér. C*[13], vol. xiv, fols. 139-141; vol. xv, fol. 5.

[2] *Ibid.*, vol. xiv, fols. 37, 44-45.

[3] *Ibid.*, vol. xiv, fols. 5-6; vol. xv, fols. 57, 117-118.

which was then estimated as worth between 3,000 and 4,000 livres would be ready for shipment. He could then sell his merchandise well and at the same time secure a cargo for the return to France. The proposal was not accepted. It, however, seemed impossible to glut the market with liquor. The inordinate demand for this commodity made it possible, at this time, to sell wine at thirty sols a pot, and at wholesale at from 150 to 200 livres a cask. Brandy from the ship was sold at from forty to fifty sols a pot. The colonial officials desiring supplies for the hospital bought part of the cargo in question, worth 5,160 livres, sixteen sols, six deniers. They gave in exchange deerskins at twenty-five sols a pound. The officials considered this transaction advantageous to the crown, since the peltry had already begun to decay and all would have been lost if allowed to remain longer in the storehouse. When the products of the province suited to the French trade were exhausted, the remainder of the merchandise was sold for 30,472 livres in silver. This amount, however, was left in the colonial treasury and the captain took instead a bill of exchange on France.[1]

In August, 1732, Louisiana was visited by a violent storm that swept over the province, destroying crops and property of all kinds. Many worthy settlers were ruined and would have died of starvation but for a daily distribution of rice from the royal storehouse. There were still in the province many lazy and shiftless men who spent at cards on Sunday all they could earn in the following week, and at this time such persons were reduced to extreme want, since the government gave support only to deserving persons who showed a willingness to work.[2]

[1] *A. N., C., Sér.* C^{13}, vol. xiv, fol. 63; vol. xv, fols. 173-174.

[2] *Ibid.*, vol. xvi, fols. 3-6, 7-8.

The vessels reaching Louisiana in the latter part of the year were, therefore, most opportune in the time of arrival. Every thing in the way of foodstuffs was very scarce and prices correspondingly high. The first ship to reach the province was unable to furnish enough supplies even to remove the existing distress, consequently when a ship from St. Malo arrived at New Orleans on December 6, it found brandy and wine selling at twenty-four and fifteen livres a pot, respectively.[1] The men in charge of this vessel, however, were not satisfied with these prices and endeavored to push them up by circulating a rumor that the royal ship, then overdue, had been lost at sea. This report, the captain of the merchant craft believed, would destroy all hope there was left of securing aid from the crown and thus enable him to put upon his merchandise any price his fancy might dictate. Whatever the influence of the story upon prices, the cargo, valued at between 10,000 and 12,000 livres, was disposed of for 100,000 livres; some very poor wine that cost in France only fifteen to twenty livres a cask sold for 300, while brandy brought seven livres, and " guildive ", a kind of rum, four to five livres a pot.[2]

In order to develop the trade on the colonial side the settlers on their part were urged to grow tobacco and cotton, since with a small labor supply a greater amount of exports could be produced from these two than from any other of the staples. In tobacco, it was claimed, a good worker could easily harvest a thousand pounds, while a very industrious man in the same season could produce double that amount and be able to find time to raise his own foodstuffs.[3]

[1] *A. N., C., Sér. C*[13], vol. xvi, fols. 3-6, 7-8.

[2] *Ibid.*, fols. 5-6.

[3] *Ibid.*, vol. xiv, fols. 148-150.

Louisiana cotton was marvelously beautiful and could be produced quite as easily and as abundantly as tobacco, but its culture was hampered by the difficulty the planters found in separating the fiber from the seed. This obstacle was formidable and resulted in greatly reducing the value of cotton as an export, since it took as much as three pounds in the grain to make one without the seed. The freight to France at fifty livres a ton for unseeded cotton was too expensive, while a rate of twenty-five livres for it separated from the seed was quite out of the question, since there were no laborers in the province to remove the seed before exportation.[1]

The inhabitants of Mobile themselves took the initiative in the matter of adopting measures whereby they could increase their exports. On May 12, 1732, one of the men at that post proposed to make an experiment in order, if possible, to increase the output of tar. He asked for and was granted free transportation on a royal ship for 250 barrels of tar which he proposed to send to France. It was to go to New Orleans and there to be placed on the first of the government's boats bound for France, where it was to be offered for sale on the open market at Rochefort at twelve livres a hundredweight for the tar and eight or nine for the pitch. Such prices would insure a good profit on the venture, it was claimed, and would result in increasing the output by stimulating many persons to enter the industry.[2]

For several years the province had been producing indigo for the export trade, yet nothing at this time was done to increase the yearly amount put upon the market. Silk culture received some attention, but no definite plans were laid for the development of the article.[3] Lumber, however,

[1] *A. N., C., Sér.* C^{13}, vol. xiv, fols. 3-4, 148-149.

[2] *Ibid.*, vol. xv, fols. 113-114.

[3] *Ibid.*, vol. xiv, fols. 44-46.

came in for a share of the consideration for an increase in the colonial exports, and the same year a cargo of cypress lumber was sent to France in order to ascertain whether further shipments would be advisable.[1]

The European side of the Louisiana trade was also investigated with the hope of improving conditions. The crown on its part advised the merchants engaged in the commerce of the province not to send too many vessels to the colony at one time, because the merchandise thus carried would glut the market and therefore would not sell well, and because there would not be enough products there to supply all the ships with cargoes for the return voyage.[2] The home government, however, virtually had control of this matter since a merchant must, before sending out his ship, first secure for the venture a royal permit which fixed the time of departure of the vessel from France, the destination and to some extent the nature of the cargo carried.[3] The royal government, therefore, during the year 1732, had taken much interest in the province and had expended considerable energy in promoting its development.

The crown's activities among the French merchants was fruitful, and by the beginning of 1733 merchants from La Rochelle, Bordeaux and St. Malo had vessels in the Louisiana trade. The successful disposition of the first cargo sent to the colony perhaps spoke more eloquently than any urging on the part of the French government. Be that as it may, the port from which the first ship set sail had two vessels in the traffic while the others represented had only one each. The home government, moreover, appreciated this fact and did what it could to make the ventures of the merchants bring back good returns, yet, at the same time,

[1] *A. N., C., Sér. C*[12], vol. xiv, fol. 142.

[2] *Ibid., Sér. B*, lvi, fol. 95.

[3] *Ibid.*, vol. lxii, fols. 7, 62, 83.

it did not lose sight of the development of Louisiana. Accordingly for the transportation of goods to and from the province the merchants, by making special petitions to the crown, could secure a "gratification", or subsidy, at this time amounting to forty livres a ton, on such merchandise. After the subsidy had been granted, the merchant in order to secure the money must present to the home government a certificate of sales of the cargo and also a statement showing the amount of colonial products carried on the return trip. No statement of certificates, however, would be honored by the crown unless made out and signed by the "ordonnateur" of Louisiana.[1]

During the year 1733 the hopes for a rapid increase in the amount of cotton put upon the market was raised by the introduction into the province of a species of cotton gin which, it was believed, would make the separation of the seed from the fiber easy and rapid.[2] The merchants in France interested in the tobacco trade, however, obscured this rosy outlook for Louisiana cotton through a possible lessening of the prospects for colonial tobacco, by refusing to pay anything like reasonable prices for that commodity unless shipped in rolls. The supply of laborers in the province often made this work impossible; therefore the planters were obliged to take any price the traders saw fit to offer them, or make the shipment of tobacco to France at their own risk, paying freight for transportation either on the royal or private vessels. Most of the settlers were in no condition to wait for the sale of their tobacco and the return from France, which occupied as much as eighteen months. During this period they were apt to be without

[1] *A. N., C., Sér. B*, vol. lxi, fols. 629, 641; *Sér.* C^{13}, vol. xix, fols. 22-24.

[2] *Ibid., Sér.* C^{13}, vol. xvii, fols. 47-48.

means of support for their families and negroes. Moreover, the price of twenty-five livres a quintal for tobacco was not enough when they were forced to pay for merchandise at double and even treble its cost in France.[1] At this time the home government added to the difficulties of the tobacco growers by fixing the freight rate on tobacco at fifty livres a ton, a rate that before had been as low as twenty-five livres.[2]

The royal ship reported lost[3] and others reached Louisiana early in 1733. Although they had on board a considerable amount of supplies for the colony there was not enough, under the extraordinary circumstances then existing in the province, to have any appreciable effect upon prices, since these combined cargoes did not exceed 400 tons. This supply, moreover, was scarcely enough to dissuade the discouraged settlers from their intention of returning to France. The discontent was great among the "bourgeoisie" and planters in and around New Orleans. The settlers who, just at this time, were beginning their establishments were also much discouraged.[4] One of these vessels later took on a cargo of 150 "boucauts" (hogsheads) of tobacco, all that was left of the storm-ridden crop, and some peltry at Mobile.[5] Further discouragement just now was heaped upon the people of Louisiana by the rejection of their brick and lumber in the markets of France, where they had been pronounced of inferior quality and sold at a price too low to warrant further shipment.[6]

[1] *A. N., C., Sér.* C^{13}, vol. xvi, fols. 80-82.

[2] *Ibid., Sér. B.*, vol. lviii, fol. 182; vol. lix, fol. 580.

[3] *Supra*, p. 174.

[4] *A. N., C., Sér.* C^{13}, vol. xvi, fols. 110, 140-141.

[5] *Ibid.*, vol. xvii, fols. 89-90, 163.

[6] *Ibid.*, fols. 204-207.

On February 17, 1733, a boat left Bordeaux for Louisiana, where it arrived on May 27, with a cargo of 100 tons. Of this consignment there were sixty tons of wine, nine tons of brandy, ten of flour and the remainder dry merchandise (merchandise sèche). The whole of the cargo was of good quality and sold readily. Therefore the vessel was able to leave for France on July 25.[1] A second merchant ship arriving about this time also sold its cargo to advantage.[2] No more vessels set out from France for Louisiana until August, when three left for the province almost at the same time, one each from the ports of St. Malo, Bordeaux and La Rochelle.[3]

The first of these crafts to reach Louisiana was the one from St. Malo. It carried only a trade permit for Mobile. Lack of such a privilege for New Orleans, however, was of small consequence to the captain. On reaching the Gulf of Mexico he sailed to the capital under the pretext that he was forced to do so in order to prevent his boat being seized by the English. The colonial officials, however, were not misled by this statement, and asserted that, had this story not been a satisfactory reason for the appearance of the boat at New Orleans, another would have been immediately forthcoming. The captain disposed of some of the merchandise on board, then went to Mobile where he sold wine at 120 livres a cask, brandy at thirty-five sols a pot, and flour at thirty livres a barrel. The dry-goods of the cargo he disposed of at five times the cost, and the other merchandise at a profit of from 60 to 80 per cent. For the return trip he took on tar, deerskins and logwood. He paid for the tar thirteen livres a barrel of 200 quintals,

[1] *A. N., C., Sér.* C^{13}, vol. xvi, fols. 116, 266; vol. xvii, fols. 89-90.

[2] *Ibid.*, vol. xvi, fols. 38-39.

[3] *Ibid., Sér. B*, vol. lxi, fols. 629-631.

the whole of the purchase amounting to 18,440 livres.[1] For the remainder of the sales he received a bill of exchange on New Orleans for the sum of 12,349 livres, two sols, four deniers, thus making the amount disposed of 30,789 livres, two sols, four deniers. The vessel then returned to New Orleans where the captain finished buying his cargo for France. Here he sold what was left of the European merchandise and purchased 383 "quarts" of tar.[2]

The governor and "ordonnateur" requested the home government to send other ships directly to Mobile. They asserted that in so doing it would save the people there from paying a second profit and also many trips to New Orleans for supplies. Moreover, it would stimulate the pitch and tar industry which, it was thought, could be increased to one hundred or one hundred and fifty tons annually. These products the inhabitants of Mobile wished to exchange for wine, brandy, flour and other European goods.[3]

The vessel from La Rochelle was the second of the three merchant ships to reach the colony. Its cargo was disposed of much to the advantage of the owner. The captain, however, declared the venture unprofitable and asserted he had no desire to bring his boat again to Louisiana while the situation in the cotton and tobacco trade remained unchanged. These products were selling at prices which, he further claimed, robbed him of legitimate gains.

[1] *A. N., C., Sér. C*[13], vol. xviii, fols. 8-12. Governor's report gives wine at 500 livres, the number of skins as 10,000 to 12,000.

[2] *Ibid.*, vol. xviii, fols. 8-12; vol. xix, fols. 3-5, 22-24, 151-157; *Sér. B*, vol. lviii, fol. 60; vol. lxi, fols. 629-631.

[3] *Ibid., Sér. C*[13], vol. xvii, fols. 89-90; vol. xviii, fols. 8-12; vol. xix, fols. 3-5, 22-24.

The "ordonnateur" nevertheless informed the home government that every trader coming to the province indulged in such talk, and that it was wholly unwarranted by the facts in the case. The sales of the merchandise of the vessel in question certainly seem to bear out the statement of the colonial official, since the captain sold wine at 480 livres a cask, brandy at thirty to thirty-five sols a pot, flour at from eighteen to twenty livres a barrel and the remainder of the goods brought over was also disposed of profitably. The captain took in exchange lumber of all kinds, brick, pitch, tar (eighty "quarts"), and some other colonial products suited to the St. Domingue trade and the balance in a bill of exchange on France. Before leaving the province he bought also some tobacco which he secured permission from the "ordonnateur" to send to France on one of the royal ships.[1]

The vessel from Bordeaux was the last of the three crafts to reach Louisiana. The colony was comfortably supplied with a better quality of wine than that coming from Bordeaux, hence it did not sell well. The captain thereupon decided not to attempt immediately to dispose of what he had brought to the province. Instead he rented a room in New Orleans where he stored the wine, in order to hold it until that of a better quality had been consumed when, he believed, he would be able to sell more advantageously. This procedure necessitated a stay in the province of many months. Just at the time that he was able to command 200 livres a cask for the inferior wine the untimely arrival of another vessel from Bordeaux with a better grade on board, put an end to his scheme and he was obliged to sell the 100 casks still remaining, in lot, at 57 livres each. Had

[1] *A. N., C., Sér.* C^{13}, vol. xvii, fols. 89-90; vol. xviii, fols. 8-12; vol. xix, fols. 3-5, 22-24.

he sold all the wine on his arrival, he would have received from 140 to 150 livres a cask and not consumed his profits by a long stay in Louisiana where the cost of living was very high. In the meantime, however, he had bought up 100 "quarts" of tar which he sent to France on a royal ship and he finally left the province with a cargo of pitch and tar for the West Indies trade and 30,000 livres in bills of exchange on France.[1]

It seems there were no more merchant boats in Louisiana until August, 1734, when one from La Rochelle and two from Bordeaux arrived with a supply of wine, brandy and quantities of other merchandise for which the captains were willing to receive only bills of exchange on France; their vessels were too small to make a cargo of bulky colonial products worth while. This demand on the part of the traders disarranged the finances of the province and gave displeasure to the officials who requested the crown to grant no more subsidies to boats under 200 tons.[2] The request the home government seems to have granted, for, December 14, 1734, it gave a ship of seventy-five tons permission to carry a cargo to Louisiana, but no subsidy was promised.[3]

The red wine from the cargoes of two of the vessels was sold in Louisiana at 480 livres a cask, the white at 320 livres, and the brandy at thirty sols a pot, and all sorts of merchandise brought equally good prices. The captain of one of the ships received from the "ordonnateur" a certificate of sales for ninety-six tons and bills of exchange amounting to 47,053 livres, six sols, while another got one for sixty tons and bills of exchange for 92,251 livres, one sol, four

[1] *A. N., C., Sér.* C^{13}, vol. xviii, fols. 8-12; vol. xix, fols. 22-24, 69-70.

[2] *Ibid.*, vol. xix, fols. 82-83; *Sér. B.*, vol. lxi, fol. 629.

[3] *Ibid., Sér. B*, vol. lx, fol. 106.

deniers.[1] The supplies from these two vessels brought colonial prices down, therefore the third captain could command but 150 livres a cask for wine. Before the end of his sojourn in the province, however, he was able to advance that price to 200 livres; brandy he sold at thirty, thirty-five and forty livres an "ancre" (sixteen pots). On leaving Louisiana he took with him a certificate of sales for 131 tons and bills of exchange on France drawn on the allowance of 1735 for 16,100 livres, thirteen sols. Another bill of exchange on the same year was drawn for 7,615 livres, two sols, four deniers in favor of a trader who brought merchandise to the province on this vessel.[2]

During the year 1734 there were three royal ships in Louisiana. These crafts carried merchandise for the support of the province and one brought to it a shipment of lead. On the return voyage they took to France tobacco, cotton, tar and some other products, much of which was shipped by settlers or by men owning vessels in the Louisiana trade occupied in carrying other cargoes to the French West Indies where they received a cargo for the return to France.[3]

The "ordonnateur" in making an inventory of the supplies brought to Louisiana from France by the eleven merchant ships during the years 1732-1734, inclusive, asserted that it showed an astonishingly large amount of wine and brandy imported into a province where there were so few people. For these years there were but fifty tons of flour, a shortage explained by the large supplies of flour sent to New Orleans from the Illinois country and by the fact that many persons in the province used rice flour entirely for making bread.[4]

[1] *A. N., C., Sér.* C^{13} vol. xix, fols. 106-107.

[2] *Ibid.*, fols. 104-107; *Sér. B*, vol. lxi, fol. 641.

[3] *Ibid., Sér.* C^{13}, vol. xix, fols. 22-24, 37-40.

[4] *Ibid.*, vol. xx, fols. 31-32.

Since 1731 the crops of Louisiana had been light and the prospects for 1735 were not promising. This year the lumber output was greatly decreased by the floods that began in December, 1734, and continued well into April. For four months much of the land was under water, thus preventing the men from working in the forests.[1] The cotton gin introduced in 1733 [2] had not been a success, and although some attempts had been made to improve the machine, nothing as yet had been accomplished.[3] The quality of the cotton was fine and sold for fifteen livres a quintal in France. In March, 1735, in the grain, cotton brought four sols a pound, while at the same time the seeded was received at the royal storehouse at eighteen sols a pound.[4]

The tar experiment made at Mobile in 1732 had borne fruit. It was estimated in 1735 that there would be marketed that year between 12,000 and 15,000 barrels of pitch and tar at Mobile; and at Lake Pontchartrain, where the work had been taken up later, between 10,000 and 12,000 barrels. In the French market the price stood at six and eight livres a quintal, respectively. The price seems to have been satisfactory since the men engaged in the industry complained only of a shortage of negro labor for manufacturing, and a lack of vessels in which to send the commodity to France. The crown was asked at this time to do what it could to remove these two obstacles to the production of tar and pitch.[5] The home government had in some instances allowed the settlers to send their tar to

[1] *A. N., C., Sér. C*[13], vol. xix, fols. 37-40; vol. xx, fols. 52-56.

[2] *Supra*, p. 177.

[3] *A. N., C., Sér. C*[13], vol. xviii, fols. 14-19, 41-44; vol. xix, fols. 8-10.

[4] *Ibid.*, vol. xvii, fols. 89-90; *Sér. A*, vol. xxiii, March 30, 1735.

[5] *Ibid., Sér. C*[13], vol. xviii, fols. 14-19, 41-44, 51-53; *Sér. B*, vol. lxi, fol. 653.

France on its vessels free of freight charges. Moreover it had ordered the colonial officials always to give preference on its ships to the tar thus owned. Many of the producers as in the case of tobacco [1] were unable to take advantage of the privilege because it was out of the question for them to have so much of their year's earnings tied up for so long. To relieve this condition the "ordonnateur", in worthy cases, made advances of money to the shippers.[2]

The tobacco output for the year 1735 was very short. Only the cultivators at Pointe Coupée were able to raise a crop, hence the shipment for the year consisted of what they produced, in all about 100,000 pounds.[3] The royal government fixed freight rates on tobacco at fifty livres a ton, with the order that tobacco belonging to settlers, as in the case of tar just cited, should be preferred to that offered by the merchants in making up cargoes on its vessels.[4] The rice crop too was light, and many of the farmers were now turning to indigo as their staple, the production of which was encouraged by an increase in price from three livres, four sols to three livres ten sols a pound.[5] On March 30, the prices of colonial products at the royal storehouse were as follows: rice, not hulled, three livres a barrel; indigo, three livres, ten sols a pound; raw pitch and tar, seven livres, ten sols a quintal, in France nine livres; peltry, one livre, ten sols a pound; cotton, grained, eighteen sols a pound; and tobacco, six sols a pound.[6]

The home government, it seems, sent but one boat to

[1] *Supra*, p. 177.

[2] *A. N.*, *Sér.* C^{13}, vol. xix, fols. 22-24, 58-59.

[3] *Ibid.*, vol. xx, fols. 52-56.

[4] *Ibid.*, vol. xx, fols. 31-32; *Sér. B*, vol. lxiii, fol. 593.

[5] *Ibid.*, *Sér.* C^{13}, vol. xx, fols. 52-56, 208-212.

[6] *Ibid.*, fols. 208-212; *Sér. A*, vol. xxiii, March 30, 1735.

Louisiana during 1735. It had on board ten tons of wine of a very poor quality, of which a considerable part had soured during the voyage over; a quantity of flour which sold at from thirty to thirty-five livres a barrel, and 200 quintals of lard. For the return voyage the vessel took on sixty-five hogsheads of tobacco, and thirty-three of peltry, about 346 barrels of pitch and 273 of tar, and seven bales of cotton.[1]

In the same year, however, French merchants sent a number of ships to Louisiana. In December, 1734, it appears that the crown had granted to a captain, who was also the owner, permission to carry a cargo of merchandise to the province. The vessel of seventy-five tons left France in that month. About the same time a second such ship set out from St. Malo carrying a trade permit for Mobile only, and a third from La Rochelle for New Orleans.[2] On March 29, the crown granted another boat a trade permit for Louisiana.[3] April 30, a vessel reached the province from Bordeaux with a cargo of wine, brandy and flour, the sales of which amounted to 1,860 livres. For its return voyage the ship took brick, lumber, laths and joists which it carried to the French West Indies.[4] On July 25, a ship landed at the capital a cargo of 200 tons, most of which consisted of foodstuffs which the royal officials had told the merchants were most needed and always sold best.[5] The "Comte de Maurepas", a vessel that had been in the Louisiana service almost from the time the colony was taken over by the royal government, at this time carried to

[1] *A. N., C., Sér. C*[13], vol. xx, fols. 31-32, 210, 229-230.

[2] *Ibid.*, fols. 208-212; *Sér. A*, vol. xxiii, March 30, 1735.

[3] *Ibid., Sér. B*, vol. lxii, fol. 153.

[4] *Ibid., Sér. C*[13], vol. xx, fols. 85-91, 101-104.

[5] *Ibid.*, fols. 267-272; *Sér. B*, vol. lx, fol. 106.

the province a cargo of a little more than 209 tons of which seven were salt.[1] From the colony it took 4,629 pounds of beaver skins and between 2,000 and 3,000 pounds of indigo for which three livres, ten sols a pound was paid, and some pitch and tar. The last two articles were received at the royal storehouse at Rochefort at the rate fixed by the government, but the request of the trader that he be allowed to sell the skins in Holland was denied, the crown explaining that the trade in peltry belonged exclusively to the Company of the Indies.[2] On October 25, the home government granted a merchant of Bordeaux permission to put his boat of fifty tons in the Louisiana trade. He was, however, not to set sail until December, since there were at the time already three such ships in the province.[3] Another grant, October 29, was made to a merchant to send a vessel to Mobile with a supply of foodstuffs on which he was allowed a " gratification " of twenty livres (reduced from forty livres in 1734) a ton on both the outgoing and incoming cargo. As there were no other ships at Mobile no restrictions were placed upon the time of departure.[4]

The next year, 1736, the home government had one ship[5] in Louisiana and the merchants five. Three of the latter carried to the colony 226 tons of wine and 450 casks of brandy; sixty tons, 250 barrels, 111 " quarts " and 3,600 quintals of flour; 200 barrels of powder of fifty pounds each, and large quantities of dry merchandise (marchan-

[1] *A. N., C., Sér. B,* vol. lxii, fol. 83.

[2] *Ibid.,* fols. 83, 241; *Sér. C¹³,* vol. xx, fols. 105-109, 257-259.

[3] *Ibid., Sér. B,* vol. lxii, fol. 91.

[4] *Ibid.,* fol. 233.

[5] *Ibid., Sér. C¹³,* vol. xxi, fols. 256-260.

dise sèche). Of this amount ninety tons of wine, 3,600 quintals, 111 "quarts" of flour and the powder were sent over by the royal government. For fifteen casks (114¾ pots each) of wine the crown paid 2,321 livres, fourteen sols, four deniers, and for fourteen casks more it paid 2,100 livres.[1] In exchange the merchants took colonial products, in which tar and pitch were included, and the balance in bills of exchange on France, the boats not being large enough to carry on the return voyage cargoes equal in value to the European goods they had brought to the province.[2] As in the previous years the traders received for each such shipment a subsidy of twenty livres a ton on the foodstuffs carried to, and the products of the province taken from, the colony.[3] In June of the same year a request was sent to the crown from the "entrepreneur of public works" for twenty tons of coal and a supply of salt. If, however, the crown should be unable to provide both, it was requested, by all means, to send the coal which was needed far more. The royal government was further informed that many blunders, due to the absence of this commodity, had been made in large as well as small undertakings where effective heat was required quickly and could not be gotten from the burning of wood.[4]

As early as January, 1737, a scarcity of flour made itself felt in Louisiana notwithstanding the fact that quantities of it had been sent over the year before.[5] There were five vessels in the province in 1737, two of which belonged to the crown, but no description of the cargoes they carried

[1] *A. N., C., Sér. C*[13], vol. xxi, fols. 243-244, 245-249, 263.

[2] *Ibid.*, fols. 273-277, 328-329.

[3] *Ibid., Sér. B*, vol. lxiv, fol. 271.

[4] *Ibid., Sér. C*[13], vol. xxi, fol. 287.

[5] *Ibid.*, vol. xxii, fols. 121-123, 132-133.

either to or from the colony is given.[1] As Louisiana was now entering upon a war with the Chickasaw an increase in both munitions and soldiers was necessary. In order to furnish such supplies with the least possible expense, the crown, July 15, 1738, took away, for six years, the exemption accorded the merchants in 1731.[2] Free transportation thus obtained seems to have aroused too much opposition to make its continuance advisable; therefore on November 25, the royal government withdrew the ordinance and issued another renewing the former exemption.[3]

Notwithstanding the discouraging elements that from time to time entered into the trade between France and Louisiana, it gradually increased, and in 1738 there were seven vessels in the province, six merchant ships and one belonging to the home government.[4] With the exception of three cases of medicaments sent from the province to France, the cargoes for these boats are not described. As in the previous years, the merchants while in the colony bought up tobacco, tar, pitch and peltry which they sent to France on ships belonging to the crown, while on their own they took cargoes of colonial products to the West Indies.[5] The royal officials were still receiving requests from merchants to be allowed to enter the Louisiana trade. This year it granted a permit to a trader of Nantes, up to the time a port having no vessels engaged in this commerce. Accompanying the permit was the allowance of a "gratification" of twenty livres a ton.[6]

[1] *A. N., C., Sér.* C^{13}, vol. xxii, fols. 46-50, 128-129, 182, 216.

[2] *Supra*, p. 171.

[3] *A. N., C., Sér. A*, vol. xxiii, July 15, 1738.

[4] Ordonnance du Roi du Novembre 25, 1738, N. Y. Pub. Lib.

[5] *A. N., C., Sér.* C^{13}, vol. xxiii, fols. 123-124, 127-128.

[6] *Ibid.*, vol. xxiv, fols. 167, 202-203; *Sér. B*, vol. lxvii, fol. 49.

Due in part at least to the Indian war then in progress, trade between France and the province in 1739 was very active. During the year eleven vessels, six by the merchants and five by the crown, were despatched to Louisiana. The cargoes carried were made up of liquor, large supplies of lard for the troops, and quantities of other merchandise, also with two of the royal boats bringing to the province many soldiers and 50,000 pounds of powder.[1] One of these ships had a capacity of 500 tons;[2] that of the remainder was much less, therefore, they could carry from the colony only a limited amount of tobacco, pitch, tar and cotton to France, and brick and lumber to the French West Indies.

An abuse[3] that had been practiced while the Company of the Indies was in control of the province was renewed at this time though in a somewhat different form. Then the wine in the casks on reaching Louisiana was found to be short of the amount stated in the invoice; now there was a shortage in the number of casks. One vessel on its arrival in the colony was short sixty-one and a half casks out of a consignment of 170. Nothing, however, was done to remedy the evil.[4]

In the province itself bad harvests followed hard upon one another. The excessively rainy year of 1737 was succeeded by one, the first part of which was very wet, whereas during the remainder there was a drought, and in 1739 there was too much moisture for the crops.[5]

[1] *A. N., C., Sér.* C^{13}, vol. xxiv, fols. 8-9, 25, 85-87, 166-169, 173, 207, 221, 243, 250-251; *Sér. B,* vol. lxix, fols. 250, 251, 334.

[2] *A., B. de, l'A.*, vol. 4817, fol. 186.

[3] *Supra*, p. 168.

[4] *A. N., C., Sér.* C^{13}, vol. xxiv, fols. 26-28.

[5] *Ibid.*, vol. xxii, fols. 37-41, 51-54, 121-123; vol. xxiii, fols. 134-137; vol. xxiv, fol. 207.

In 1737 the greater part of the tobacco was grown at Pointe Coupée,—the entire output being estimated at 350,-000 pounds—and was put upon the market the next year, one-third in rolls and the remainder in the leaf. For the former the growers demanded from twelve to fifteen sols a pound,[1] but for the latter the merchants could be induced to pay only three sols, six deniers. As the last price was too low, the colonial officials requested the crown to fix the price at seven livres a quintal in order to prevent the settlers from abandoning the culture altogether.[2] In 1739, the planters of Pointe Coupée put only 130,000 pounds of tobacco on the market, of which 100,000 were in "manoques" and sold at four sols, six deniers a pound, and 30,000 in rolls which brought from ten to twelve sols.[3] The output of tobacco as well as of other products, furthermore, was lessened in 1739 by the withdrawal of 300 negroes from agricultural work for use in the Chickasaw War.[4] The home government was asked to repair this loss by sending a supply of negroes from Africa. Since the crown was known to be much interested in the Louisiana tobacco trade, this fact was put forth as the reason for the petition. In order to impress it with the importance of such action, the colonial officials called its attention to the circumstances that France was, at the time, drawing almost its whole supply of tobacco from the English who had 200 vessels engaged in the traffic which amounted annually to 70,000 " boucauts " (hogsheads). The whole of the French side of this trade, it was claimed, would fall to Louisiana if only enough laborers were furnished to produce the tobacco, since the quality and flavor of the article

[1] *A. N., C., Sér. C13* vol. xxiii, fols. 134-137.

[2] *Ibid.*, vol. xxii, fols. 37-41.

[3] *Ibid.*, vol. xxiv, fol. 154.

[4] *Ibid.*, fols. 10-13.

grown in that province were quite as good as those of Maryland and Virginia.[1]

The rice crops for 1737-1739, inclusive, were light and as a result prices were most unstable. In 1737 rice that in the previous year had been selling at three livres a quintal had advanced to seven livres, ten sols,[2] and the next year went to twenty livres.[3] Since no improvement had been made in the methods of separating the seed from the fiber of the cotton,[4] the number of bales put upon the market during the three years in question had not increased much. The decrease of interest in cotton was extended to that in indigo, which also had suffered much from the stress of bad weather. In 1737, an effort was made to enable the small farmer to enter upon the cultivation of the dyestuff. A merchant was granted a permit to establish in Louisiana a factory where the raw product could be brought directly from the fields and converted into indigo. The small farmers, it seems, had not been able to enter this business because they had not a sufficiency of capital and labor to establish and maintain factories. The scheme, however, was never realized.[5] In 1737, indigo sold at four livres a pound, which the buyers declared was more than it was worth. The next year, however, both crops were light and, although there were fourteen or fifteen men around New Orleans engaged in the growing of indigo, they were able to put upon the market only about 70,000 pounds of it, which sold at five livres a pound.[6] In 1739 it was pre-

[1] *A. N., C., Sér.* C13, vol. xxiv, fols. 259-278.

[2] *Ibid.*, vol. xxii, fols. 121-123.

[3] *Ibid.*, vol. xxiii, fols. 134-137.

[4] *Supra*, pp. 177, 184.

[5] *A. N., C., Sér.* C13, xxiii, fols. 134-137.

[6] *Ibid.*

dicted in the early part of the season that the indigo crop of these same producers would be 150,000 pounds. The dry weather that set in before the plants were matured cut the harvest to between 16,000 and 17,000 pounds. This decrease, however, did not dampen the enthusiasm of the men engaged in the culture. At this time they sent to the home government for its approval and support a plan whereby the amount of indigo put upon the market could be increased.[1]

While weather conditions had less effect upon the output of pitch and tar, there were other and quite as formidable obstacles in the way of a rapid increase in the annual production. First there was, as there always had been, a shortage in the supply of vessels to carry the commodities to France.[2] Then again the Choctaw in 1739 became unfriendly to the French and it was rumored that they intended to carry away the negroes engaged in these industries. Thereupon work slackened at Mobile, and at Lake Pontchartrain was abandoned entirely and the negroes were taken to a place of safety.[3] The price of pitch and tar during these years, however, was most encouraging for a large output; the former was selling at sixteen, the latter at twelve livres, a barrel.[4] Just before the close of the year 1739 the crown reduced the price of tar to six livres a quintal and pitch to six livres, five sols.[5] Before the cut in the price was known in the province two French merchants contracted with some of the settlers to take, at the old rates of twelve and sixteen livres, respectively, all the tar and pitch they could put on the market for the next

[1] *A. N., C., Sér. C*[13], vol. xxiv, fol. 154.

[2] *Ibid.*, vol. xxiii, fols. 195-196.

[3] *Ibid.*, fols. 134-137, 169-174.

[4] *Ibid., Sér. B*, vol. lxviii, fol. 11.

[5] *Ibid., Sér. C*[13], vol. xxiii, fols. 134-137.

year beginning March 1, 1739. The colonists proposed to hold the merchants to their contract, but upon an appeal to the home government the case was decided against them.[1]

Although lumber had by this time practically ceased to form directly a part of the commerce with France, it was indirectly very helpful to the advancement of trade with the mother country, by offering an inducement to French merchants to bring shiploads of European goods to Louisiana where they could get a cargo with which to buy another for the return to France. From 1737 to 1739, lumber for building purposes had doubled in value. Planks that had brought only forty livres a hundred at the beginning of the years in question, at the end were selling at 120 livres, thus trebling in value.[2] Peltry, however, greatly decreased in quantity due to the war between the French and Chickasaw and to the English traders among the Choctaw.[3]

The crown and the merchants on their part also encountered obstacles in the way of increasing the trade with Louisiana. In 1738 two of the royal ships, and two belonging to the merchants were wrecked by storms during their stay in the province. In some cases everything was lost, while in others, only the boat and part of the cargo were destroyed.[4] The crews, however, easily found places on other vessels bound for France, because of the loss of men from yellow fever which at the time was raging in the province. The great swarms of mosquitoes, it was claimed, were responsible for the spread of the disease. On one of the ships belonging to the royal government forty-eight, and on another twenty-two, of the sailors died of the malady and many of the others were too ill for further service.[5]

[1] *A. N., C., Sér. B,* vol. lxviii, fol. 11.

[2] *Ibid., Sér. C*[13], vol. xxxiii, fols. 127, 134-137.

[3] *Ibid.*

[4] *Ibid.*, vol. xxiv, fols. 202-203, 221.

[5] *Ibid.*, fols. 166, 207, 243; *A., B. de l'A.*, vol. 4817, fol. 186.

CHAPTER XIV

TRADE BETWEEN FRANCE AND LOUISIANA, 1731-1763 (CONTINUED)

EARLY in 1740 commerce between Louisiana and the mother country was impeded somewhat by the English who the previous year had declared war upon Spain and were seizing French merchant ships and holding them for search in order to prevent a contraband trade with the enemy. For example, a French vessel bound for the province was seized and taken to Jamaica where it was held pending the investigation.[1] Except for an increase from forty to ninety livres a ton [2] in the freight rate on royal merchandise sent to the province on private vessels, the commerce with France was the same as in previous years. On the return voyages the cargoes were still being carried to the French West Indies where they were exchanged for others better suited to the European market.[3]

During the year there were in Louisiana seven merchant ships and two belonging to the royal government.[4] One of the latter, May 9, was the first to arrive, but before the end of the month two of the former also had reached New Orleans. One of these had sprung a leak that had caused the

[1] *A. N., C., Sér. C*[13], vol. xxvi, fol. 128.

[2] *A. N., C., Sér. B*, vol. lxxi, fols. 104-105.

[3] Le Page du Pratz, vol. iii, p. 388.

[4] *A. N., C., Sér. C*[13], vol. xxv, fols. 3-4, 21, 25, 27, 42, 141-143, 165-166, 178, 229-231, 238-239; vol. xxvi, fol. 128.

loss of the greater part of the half-cargo of salt on board.[1] Two of these three boats brought to the province twenty tons of wine which sold at 200 and 230 livres a cask, and even when to this amount was added what the third supplied, there was a shortage for the troops of eighteen tons.[2] Large consignments of flour had also been despatched; but even with the 6,000 quintals additional from the Illinois country the amount was inadequate. Therefore it was sold in New Orleans at seventy livres a " quart " [3] and in smaller quantities at nine sols a pound. 885 quintals, ninety-five pounds of very poor flour that a trader had been holding for five or six months, hoping to secure a better price, was at this time put upon the market where it brought ten livres a quintal. Officials with salaries of as much as 1,800 livres were by such prices reduced to a diet of bread and water.[4] The royal ships carried on the return to France cotton, tobacco, indigo, peltry, and as an experiment 33,000 brick worth between fourteen and fifteen livres a thousand.[5]

From September 11 to 18, 1740, Louisiana was again swept by storms that destroyed crops and property to the amount of 20,000 livres. Rice that had been selling for six livres a barrel by the end of the year advanced to twelve livres.[6] The men engaged in the production of tar and pitch received some encouragement as a partial offset to the losses from the storm by having their tar in the French markets pronounced of very good quality. They were told, however, that the trade would be much improved if the tar were refined a little more before shipment.[7]

[1] *A. N., C., Sér. C*[13], vol. xxv, fols. 3-4. [2] *Ibid.*, fols. 21-24, 230, 264.

[3] When applied to flour it was 160 to 200 pounds.

[4] *A. N., C., Sér. C*[13], vol. xxv, fols. 21-24, 230, 264.

[5] *Ibid.*, fol. 177; Le Page du Pratz, vol. iii, p. 387.

[6] *A. N., C., Sér. C*[13], vol. xxiv, fols. 66-67, 97, 130.

[7] Le Page du Pratz, vol. iii, p. 370; *A. N., C., Sér. B*, vol. lxx, Louisiane, fol. 7.

Had the trade in tobacco been free from fraudulent practices, that article would have sold readily at ten sols, six deniers a pound. It was shipped in hogsheads of which the weight and quality of the contents were taken from the shippers' statements, many of which were found to be false. The "ordonnateur" had already pointed out that such dishonesty would only ruin the trade, yet the practice continued. This official, accordingly, issued an ordinance against it. Henceforth tobacco was to be received only in "monoques" or hogsheads, the packing of which was performed in the presence of an inspector. On casks thus filled and closed for shipment, this official placed stamps, provided him by the superior council, showing the weight and quality of the contents.[1] This legislation caused men of a better type to begin cultivating tobacco. In 1740, five or six men gave up growing indigo around New Orleans and went to Pointe Coupée to engage in raising tobacco. The output, it was believed, would soon be considerably augmented.[2] In anticipation of this enlarged production, the "ordonnateur" asked the crown to make some provision for an increase in the number of boats to be used in transporting the tobacco from the province. At the same time he suggested that the simplest and most effective way of solving the freight problem would be to throw the trade open to the Spaniards, who would then come to Louisiana to buy French merchandise for which they would pay cash, thus leaving the French ships free to carry to the mother country cargoes of tobacco.[3]

The frequent use of inferior tobacco in making up the rolls led the next year to the issuing of a somewhat different ordinance, which provided for payment in accordance

[1] Le Page du Pratz, vol. iii, p. 390; *A. N., C., Sér. B*, vol. lxxii, fol. 14.

[2] *A. N., C., Sér. C*[13], vol. xxvi, fols. 15-16. [3] *Ibid.*, fols. 150-151.

with actual values. It was decreed that henceforth leaf tobacco only should be shipped to France, but in order to give the colonists a market for inferior grades the crown was to take a third of the shipment from the first crop, a half from the second, and a sixth or more from the third. The three different sorts of tobacco were to be separated, placed in piles and weighed, in order to ascertain whether the above proportions were strictly adhered to. In cases where they were not, the inspector was instructed to take the whole amount offered at the price of third-grade tobacco and to impose upon the offender any fine he thought best. When the consignments were made in conformity with the law, the inspector placed upon the tobacco stamps issued by the council, and it was paid for according to the grade to which it belonged as shown by the stamps.[1] The regulation seems to have satisfied the buyers in France; at least no further complaints appear.

The crown, in 1741, had two vessels in Louisiana. One brought a cargo of guns and other war material, and carried back to France a heavy cargo of colonial products, without exhausting by any means the stock ready for export.[2] During the year the merchants sent three vessels to the province. The cargoes consisted of royal merchandise for which the crown paid high freight rates and allowed a " gratification " of twenty livres a ton on similar goods carried at their own risk.[3] Among the items were dry goods, sufficient in quantity to enable the officials to supply themselves with at least the most needed articles of clothing,[4] and wine which sold at 350, 400 and even 500 livres a cask in European money and for 800 when paid for in

[1] *A. N., C., Sér.* C^{13}, vol. xxvii, fols. 24-25.

[2] *Ibid.*, vol. xxvi, fols. 9-10, 145-146, 178; *Sér. B*, vol. lxxii, fol. 4.

[3] *Ibid., Sér.* C^{13}, vol. xxiv, fols. 91, 107-109. [4] *Ibid.*, fol. 91.

colonial paper. All foodstuffs were equally expensive and wheat flour was such a rarity as to have no really fixed price, bread being made from a mixture of corn and rice.[1] The "ordonnateur", in fact, informed the crown that there was no other French colony in which merchants disposed of their merchandise so advantageously, selling as they did at 100 per cent profit and in some cases even at 400 and 500 per cent. He stated further that one captain had brought to the colony a cargo valued in France at 30,000 livres and had left with one worth 100,000, and a considerable sum of piastres and bills of exchange for the remainder of his profits. He asserted, moreover, that the above example was not an isolated case but that a second such trader effected an equally advantageous exchange of cargoes.[2]

Yet the owners of the ships pretended not to be satisfied with the Louisiana trade, from which they attempted, even by dishonest methods, to augment their already large profits. Some of the boats on reaching the province had wine on board belonging to the crown that showed a leakage of as much as one-sixth of the amount (120 pots each) the casks were supposed to contain, and flour in which the weight of the "quarts" varied from 155 to 170 pounds, which difference the trader attempted to account for under the head of tare. Another captain sold wine and flour at Cape Francais that the crown had given him permission to carry only to Louisiana and had replaced those commodities with "guildive", meanwhile collecting from the home government a subsidy of twenty livres a ton on the cargo put on in France.[3] On examination of the bills of exchange taken back to France by these persons the "ordonnateur"

[1] *A. N., C., Sér.* C^{13}, vol. xxiv, fols. 128, 165-166, 185.

[2] *Ibid.*, fols. 107-109.

[3] *Ibid.*, fols. 165-166.

recommended to the royal government to suspend the exemption on imports and exports granted to the merchants on September 30, 1732, for a period of ten years. Acting upon this advice the crown, December 6, 1741, discontinued the exemption.[1]

The French merchants in 1742 had four vessels trading in Louisiana, one at Mobile and three at New Orleans; but no description of the cargoes is given. The boats carried lumber and other products to Cape Français where these commodities were exchanged for others better suited to the home market.[2] The crown sent two ships. The first reached Louisiana on February 2, but nothing is told of its cargo except that 100 tons were for the "entrepreneur of public works" and were transported free of freight charges.[3] The other was seized by the English and taken to Jamaica whence its cargo of merchandise, minus contraband of war, after almost two months delay was allowed to proceed to Louisiana where it arrived in August.[4]

Five merchant ships visited the province in 1743, bringing supplies of flour and wine, one cargo alone amounting to 200 tons. In the sale of their own merchandise they were most avaricious, or as the "ordonnateur" remarked: "the merchants seem desirous of making a fortune out of a single venture; they wish to receive only bills of exchange or silver for their merchandise for which they demand extravagant prices".[5]

On the other hand, the home government seems to have sent but one vessel to the colony, carrying thither, flour, wine and other merchandise. It left New Orleans in August with

[1] *A. N., C., Sér. B*, vol. lxxii, fol. 35.

[2] *Ibid.*, vol. lxxv, fol. 107; *Sér.* C^{13}, vol. xxvii, fols. 38, 109, 142.

[3] *Ibid., Sér.* C^{13}, vol. xxvii, fols. 5, 38, 109.

[4] *Ibid.*, fols. 78, 122.

[5] *Ibid.*, vol. xxviii, fols. 24, 31, 103, 114-115, 145.

400 "quarts" of tar costing twenty-five livres a "quart", some indigo at nine livres a pound, 40,000 pounds of tobacco at nine sols a pound and 30,000 pounds of lead from the Illinois country. These commodities were sold in France as follows: tobacco, five sols a pound; indigo, four; and tar for about half the cost in Louisiana. The difference to be sure was lessened somewhat by the price for European goods. In any event the crown felt that the development of the province justified the prices paid.[1]

The home government, however, had not neglected Louisiana as much as the sending there but one boat during the year might indicate. It had sent supplies to the province on the merchant ships, yet the amount was only about half of what the colony needed. The shortage was in some measure due to the dishonesty of the merchants who had been granted permits to carry supplies to the province. The captains of these ships made stops at the Spanish West Indies and coast settlements on their way over. There they sold to the Spaniards what they could of the merchandise and carried the remainder to Louisiana, where they offered it at high prices, even securing from the "ordonnateur" a certificate that entitled them to a subsidy on the entire cargo as shipped from France. Before the end of the year, however, the home government learned of this abuse and sent word to the officials in question to be more careful in making out such documents, which were to be granted only in cases where the goods were actually sold in that province.[2] The crown had also received word from the colony that the casks still showed considerable leakage, a circumstance which made it hard for the home government to provide what was needed for the coming year, 1744.[3]

[1] *A. N., C., Sér.* C^{13}, vol. xxviii, fols. 20-21, 24, 44; *Sér. B*, vol. lxxviii, fol. 16.

[2] *Ibid., Sér. B*, vol. lxxvi, fol. 2.

[3] *Ibid.*, vol. lxxvii, fol. 131.

War between France and England which for some time had been imminent broke out in 1744. At the commencement of the struggle France had 600 vessels employed in colonial trade which brought in 150,000,000 livres annually. By the end of the first year of the war about one-half of the ships, estimated to be worth 90,000,000 livres, had been taken as prizes by the English. The mother country's commerce with Louisiana, therefore, was greatly retarded while that with New France had to be suspended entirely.[1] The vessels bound for the former province were obliged for safety to cross the ocean with ships going to the West Indies. During the year 1744 only two boats found their way thither from Europe, of which one belonged to the crown while the other was owned by a merchant of Nantes. Louisiana, therefore, by October was in need of all kinds of supplies.[2]

Considering the difficult circumstances under which it was carried on, the home government's share in the Louisiana trade from the end of 1744 to the beginning of 1750 was comparatively stable. In each of these years, except 1748 and 1749, it sent out two vessels.[3] In the former three [4] of its ships were in the province and in the latter but one.[5] Even this showing cost the crown heavily, for in spite of the precaution taken of sending the boats in squadrons under commanding officers,[6] several of them were seized by the English.[7] In order to keep itself informed

[1] *A., B. A. É., Fr.*, vol. 2006, fols. 7-12.

[2] *A. N., C., Sér. C*[13], vol. xxviii, fols. 241, 276-277, 279, 293.

[3] *Ibid.*, vol. xxix, fols. 109-111, 255; vol. xxx, fols. 93, 159; vol. xxxi, fols. 52, 118.

[4] *Ibid.*, vol. xxxii, fols. 4-5, 24-25, 52, 222.

[5] *Ibid.*, vol. xxxiii, fols. 66, 79, 115.

[6] *Ibid.*, vol. xxxi, fol. 13.

[7] *Ibid.*, vol. xxxii, fols. 33, 88-90.

concerning conditions in Louisiana and the number of vessels still flying the French flag, the crown instructed the captains of its ships to sail directly to and from the province without stops at either the French or Spanish West Indies. Moreover, the colonial officials were commanded to delay the departure of the royal ships only for the most pressing need. Therefore, the greater number of these boats, during the war, remained only long enough to take off and put on the cargoes.[1] In many cases the instructions were not followed, yet in 1748 a " wise and prudent " captain of one of the royal ships made two quick trips across the ocean without stops, and remained in the province only a very short time.[2]

The merchandise consigned was not different in kind from that sent out in previous years. There was, however, a change in the quantity; guns, ammunition, Indian goods, lard and flour bulked much larger.[3] In 1745, a single vessel brought to the province 400 quintals of flour valued at twenty-seven livres a quintal;[4] the next year another carried over a fraction over 2,695 quintals.[5] In 1747, a royal boat and two merchant vessels when they reached the province had on board 3,600 quintals, a sufficiency for the colony for the ensuing year.[6] As usual the royal craft took from Louisiana tobacco, peltry, indigo, tar, pitch, piastres, logwood, lead, and a few other products in small amounts. The two government vessels that left the province for France in 1745 carried such cargoes sent over at the risk of the owners of whom in one case there were fifteen local consignors and in the other nineteen, made up as follows: the local agents of the Company of the Indies,

[1] *A. N., C., Sér. B*, vol. lxxxvii, fol. 8.

[2] *Ibid., Sér.* C^{13}, vol. xxxii, fol. 51.

[3] *Ibid.*, fols. 4-5, 40.

[4] *Ibid.*, vol. xxix, fol. 255.

[5] *Ibid.*, vol. xxx, fol. 144.

[6] *Ibid.*, vol. xxxi, fol. 116.

traders, planters, small farmers, the "entrepreneur of public works", a major, a lieutenant, and a doctor. Only the agent of the Company of the Indies, Rochemore, Major Macarty, and Dr. Prat had shipments on both boats. The amounts paid the crown for transportation of the former cargo was 9,620 livres, five sols,[1] and of the latter 5,401 livres, ten sols.[2]

[1] *A. N., C., Sér.* C^{13}, vol. xxix, fols. 109-111.

Freight bill for "L'Elephant," 1745:

		Liv.	*Sols.*
976	packs, deerskins, 4 liv. a pack	3904	
56	hhds., tobacco, 25 liv. a hhd	1400	
8	packs, buffalo skins, 4 liv. a pack	32	
29	"barriques," buffalo skins, 10 liv. a "barrique"	290	
303	"plaques" (bars), lead	free	
52	"barriques" indigo, 15 liv. a "barrique"	780	
18	"quarts" indigo, 7 liv. 10 cols a "quart"	135	
65500	lbs. logwood, 2254 logs, 1 liv. 10 sols a quintal	982	10
6	cases indigo, 3 liv. a case	18	
30	sacks tobacco, Spanish, 4 liv. a sack	120	
3	"ancres" (10 gals. each) indigo, 3 liv. 10 sols each	11	5
2	hhd. of trees, 1 case seed for royal garden	free	
25968	piastres	1947	10
	Totals	9620	5

[2] *Ibid.*, vol. xxx, fols. 67-70.

Freight bill for the "Chameau," 1745:

		Liv.	*Sols.*
65	"barriques" indigo, 15 liv. a "barrique"	975	
11	"quarts" indigo, 7 liv. 10 sols a "quart"	82	10
1	"tierçon" (42 gals.) indigo, 3 liv. a "tierçon"	3	
3	bbls. indigo, 7 liv. 10 sols	22	10
476	packs, deerskins, 4 liv. a pack	1904	
92	hhd. tobacco, 25 liv. a hhd.	2300	
219	bars lead	free	
76594	lbs. logwood	free	
45	buffalo skins, 1 liv. 10 sols each	67	10
8	packs, deerskins, 4 liv. a pack	32	
1	case, tobacco (carottes), 15 liv. a case	15	
	Totals	5401	10

On the way to France the above vessels and cargoes were seized and confiscated by the English. The loss of their part of these cargoes was too great for the local shippers to engage in further ventures of the sort during the continuance of the war.[1] Therefore in 1748 there were quantities of tobacco and peltry in the province, but no one was willing to take the risk of exporting such commodities to France.[2] The next year, however, a vessel belonging to the crown carried on the return voyage colonial products at the hazard of the European merchants who paid the royal government 2,440 livres, three sols, three deniers in freight charges.[3]

During the same years, 1745-1749, inclusive, the merchants also sent boats to the province: one each in 1745 and 1746,[4] four in 1747,[5] one in 1748,[6] and five in 1749.[7] These craft sailed from the same ports as before the war, except that Marseilles had been added to the list.[8] For the most part they were sent out by the same merchants, yet the royal officials from time to time were able to persuade a merchant or commercial company to enter the trade.[9] The boats were still small and unable, therefore, to carry any considerable amount of colonial products. Moreover, the merchants preferred cargoes made up of logwood, sugar and Spanish silver of which there was a great deal in

[1] *A. N., C., Sér.* C^{13}, vol. xxxii, fol. 33.

[2] *Ibid.*, fol. 52.

[3] *Ibid.*, vol. xxxiv, fol. 207.

[4] *Ibid.*, vol. xxx, fols. 34-35, 169.

[5] *Ibid.*, vol. xxxi, fols. 98, 116-118, 212, 252; *Sér. B*, vol. lxxxvi, fol. 128.

[6] *Ibid., Sér.* C^{13}, vol. xxxi, fol. 253; vol. xxxii, fols. 4-5, 41, 190.

[7] *Ibid.*, vol. xxxiii, fols. 4, 49-50, 73, 79, 115.

[8] *Ibid.*, vol. xxxiv, fols. 49-50.

[9] *Ibid.*

Louisiana during the war. In some instances if such cargoes could not be secured, bills of exchange were demanded in payment. Otherwise, the ships carried back rice, cotton, indigo, peltry, tar, pitch, pine, cedar, cypress and oak lumber,[1]

The goods imported by the merchants were very similar to those brought thither before the war broke out. One of these vessels, in 1747, carried over one hundred and thirty-one and nine-sixteenths tons on which the crown agreed to pay a " gratification ", which in this case amounted to 2,631 livres, five sols. The bill, however, it was understood, would be paid only on the presentation to the royal officials of an itemized[2] statement of the merchandise actually sold

[1] *The Present State of the Country, etc.*, p. 10.

[2] *A. N., C., Sér.* C^{13}, vol. xxxi, fol. 252.

The required statement:

	Tons.	*"Bar."*	½ *"Bar."*	⅛ *"Bar."*
352 " barriques," wine, 4 to ton	88	0	0	0
5 " ancres " (10 gals. each) brandy 16 to ton	00	1	0	2
200 bbls., flour, 8 to ton	25	0	0	0
60 cases, soap, 40 to ton	1	2	0	0
110 cases, molded candles, 40 to ton.	2	3	0	0
12 cases, brandied fruit	0	3	1	0
25 cases, capers, olives, anchovy....	1	2	0	0
50 " ancres " salt pork, 28 to ton...	1	3	0	0
50 firkins, butter, 32 to ton	1	2	0	0
39 cases, olive oil	1	1	0	0
22 bbls., goose thighs	00	2	0	0
10 packs, paper, linen	1	2	0	0
5 large packs, woolen cloth	2	1	0	0
2 hhds., hams	00	3	0	0
10 bbls., salt beef	1	1	0	0
2 hhds., trumpery, glass beads, etc.	00	2	0	0
20 sacks, salt	00	0	2	0
Totals	131	2	0 (*sic*)	2

in Louisiana, which statement had to be signed by the "ordonnateur" of that province.[1] Another boat in the same year bore a cargo of a little more than 164 tons of merchandise even more diversified. It comprised wine, brandy, vinegar, lard, flour, butter, hams, salt, beef, prunes, limes, rope, nails, soap, candlesticks, glass goblets, cork, hoopwood, long saws, cloth, handkerchiefs, stockings, caps, shoes, Brittany linen, white cloth, wooled cloth, laces, and 150 pairs of silk stockings.[2] For the transportation and delivery in Louisiana of about sixty-one tons of flour, munitions and other merchandise owned by itself the crown, the next year, paid a merchant of La Rochelle, at a freight rate of 140 livres a ton, 8,618 livres, fifteen sols.[3] In March the "ordonnateur" informed the home government that the captain of the serviceable "Comte de Maurepas"[4] had delivered the supplies in question.[5] In 1749, a merchant vessel brought to Louisiana for the home government 1,499 quintals, sixty-five pounds of flour, guns, flints, rope, and all sorts of wine and brandy.[6]

By 1750, more than 100 vessels had come to the province from different ports. This influx, however, was not altogether satisfactory. The colony was glutted with all kinds of merchandise except goods suited for building up the Indian trade. Because of this over supply the boats were forced to make long stays in order to have their cargoes sold, or were obliged to leave the goods in the hands of an agent. Some of the captains of the ships pre-

[1] *A. N., C., Sér.* C^{13}, vol. xxxi, fol. 252.

[2] *Ibid.*, fol. 212.

[3] *Ibid.*, fol. 252-253.

[4] *Supra*, p. 185.

[5] *A. N., C., Sér.* C^{13}, vol. xxxii, fols. 4-5.

[6] *Ibid.*, vol. xxxiii, fol. 4.

ferred to carry the stuff away with them rather than to employ either of these alternatives.[1]

From 1743 to 1750 the seasons were the most favorable for agriculture that the province had experienced, therefore the harvests were large. Indigo had improved in both quantity and quality, and at the same time the price had advanced from four livres in 1741 to nine livres in 1743,[2] hence it was a profitable crop and much of the commodity was put upon the market.[3] Throughout the period in question the producers spared neither time nor labor in their attempts to improve further the quality and to increase the size of the harvests of this staple.[4] In 1749, however, the trade was believed to be in danger. The English parliament had placed a bounty of six shillings on indigo produced in its American colonies and it was feared smuggling operations would spring up to the injury of the French article.[5]

The production of tobacco was easier and much less expensive than that of indigo, therefore, during these favorable seasons much of the former commodity was gotten ready for exportation.[6] By 1747 quantities of it had accumulated at Pointe Coupée and New Orleans because of a shortage of vessels in which to transport it to France. Being unable to dispose of the two previous years' crops, the farmers, because of need, low prices, and discriminations against tobacco at the port of shipment, were contemplating abandoning the culture. The governor, however,

[1] *A. N., C., Sér.* C^{13}, vol. xxxiv, fols. 269, 297-300.

[2] *Ibid.*, vol. xxviii, fols. 17-19, 21-22; vol. xxxi, fol. 103; vol. xxx, fol. 71.

[3] *Supra*, p. 204.

[4] *A. N., C., Sér.* C^{13}, vol. xxviii, fols. 271-272; vol. xxx, fol. 112.

[5] *Ibid.*, vol. xxxiv, fols. 5-7.

[6] *Ibid.*, vol. xxx, fol. 274.

succeeded in having them continue the work by assuring them he would do what he could to have the home government adjust the matter satisfactorily. Vaudreuil, thereupon, informed the crown of the grievances of the farmers engaged in this industry and of the fact that the captains on royal ships had taken on cargoes of sugar and logwood when at the time there were 400 hogsheads of Pointe Coupée tobacco on the wharf ready for shipment. He then requested the crown to uphold him in his promises to the tobacco growers, by instructing the commanders of its vessels coming to the province to give this staple preference over other commodities in making up cargoes for France and by issuing an ordinance commanding the "fermier général of tobacco" to take this import from Louisiana at six sols a pound, a price which the governor asserted would satisfy the producers and advance greatly the colony as a whole. Tobacco was the sole export, excepting cotton, as the crown had previously been informed, which the small farmer with one, or at most two, slaves was able to produce.[1]

The crown, it seems, instructed its captains bound for Louisiana in accordance with the wishes of Governor Vaudreuil and also took up the matter with the French merchants who agreed to send vessels to the province.[2] It informed them how to proceed so as to make such ventures profitable.[3] By way of encouragement, November 25, 1748, it renewed for six years the exemption granted such ships from carrying to Louisiana men and guns.[4] The lack of boats from France to the province during the war was due in part to the fact that the merchants had found it

[1] *A. N., C., Sér.* C^{13}, vol. xxxi, fols. 74-75.

[2] *Ibid., Sér. B*, vol. lxxxvii, fol. 10.

[3] *Ibid.*, fols. 29-30. [4] *Ibid.*

quite as profitable, and the risk from seizure much reduced, if they arranged to have the cargoes carried to the French West Indies, where it was comparatively easy to form convoys for the voyage to and from France large enough to afford some protection from the English, whereas to ship them to Louisiana direct was much more difficult.[1] In 1749 the governor reported to the home government that there was at the time no tobacco in the province. This commodity, together with much indigo, he asserted, had been carried to France by three merchant ships and one belonging to the crown.[2]

Cotton, the other staple of the farmer of small means, was not increased much during the period under discussion. As already observed, a gin had not yet been invented that would with rapidity separate the seed from the fiber; therefore since the farmer could seed only a limited amount he grew only what he could treat in that fashion. In 1848, however, the report of a satisfactory gin operating in France[3] led some of the growers of Louisiana to send over a quantity of raw cotton to test the new machine. At the end of the war the results of this experiment were not known and nothing further appears to have been done in the matter.[4] The exports of peltry and pitch and tar had during the war been disturbed by Choctaw hostility.

The exports of Louisiana to France from 1743 to 1746, inclusive, were estimated as follows; 55,000 pounds of peltry at thirty sols a pound, 82,500 livres; 200,000 quintals of indigo at three livres a quintal, 600,000 livres; 170,000 pounds of tobacco at three sols, six deniers a pound, 29,750

[1] Pownal, App., p. 20.

[2] *A. N., C., Sér.* C^{13}, vol. xxxiii, fol. 66.

[3] *Ibid.*, vol. xxxi, fol. 191; vol. xxxii, fol. 165.

[4] *Ibid., Sér. B*, vol. lxxxi, Louisiane, fol. 7.

livres. To these exports must also be added what the colonists sent annually on the royal ships at their own risk, amounting in value to approximately 100,000 livres. The combined exports, therefore, were worth about 812,250 livres.[1] Two other writers of the time each estimated the peltry exported at about 200,000 pounds, one placing the tobacco and indigo at 300,000 and the other the tobacco at 450,000, and the indigo at 240,000 pounds. These exports the latter claimed made only two or three good cargoes.[2] However conscientiously such statements may have been made, there were complaints of a shortage of vessels for the exportation of tobacco.[3] Moreover, in order to relieve the congestion in pitch and tar at Mobile, the crown was requested in 1749 to send thither two ships of 200 tons annually with foodstuffs and other merchandise to exchange for the lumber, tar, pitch, and silver accumulating at the port.[4]

During the period beginning 1750 and ending 1754 the home government annually despatched vessels to Louisiana. One such boat reached the province in 1750,[5] three in 1751,[6] two each in 1752, 1753 and 1754.[7] They carried food supplies, ammunition and merchandise and in most cases officers and recruits for the colonial army.[8] At the

[1] *A., B. N., Joly Coll.*, vol. 1726, fol. 242.

[2] *A., B. A. É., Am.*, vol. ii, fol. 108; *A., B. N., Fr.*, vol. 12224, fol. 113.

[3] *Supra*, p. 208.

[4] *A. N., C., Sér.* C^{13}, vol. xxxii, fols. 222-227.

[5] *Ibid.*, vol. xxxiv, fols. 297, 310.

[6] *Ibid.*, vol. xxxv, fols. 7, 24, 73, 194, 342.

[7] *Ibid.*, vol. xxxvi, fols. 3-4, 121; vol. xxxvii, fols. 34, 57, 137-138, 151; vol. xxxviii, fols. 6, 90, 141-142.

[8] *Ibid.*, vol. xxxiv, fol. 310; vol. xxxv, fols. 24, 73, 194; vol. xxxvi, fol. 27; vol. xxxvii, fol. 277; *Sér. B*, vol. xcviii, fols. 310; vol. xcix, fol. 3.

beginning of hostilities with England voyages to the colony became hazardous; hence the captains of royal ships bound for Louisiana were instructed to make no calls at the West Indies, except for an absolute need for water or in case the vessel were badly disabled. The commanders were further instructed to set sail from the province as soon as the cargo was taken off and another put on, unless orders from Governor Kerlérec should be received to remain longer. The colonial officials on their part were ordered to hold vessels in the province only when they were sure they could give a satisfactory reason for doing so.[1]

In May, 1754, one of the royal ships left Louisiana with a cargo made up in part of logwood belonging to a French merchant. As the wood was not on the certified inventory made by the "ordonnateur" for the royal officials, it was believed to have been put on board clandestinely and fraudulently, hence should be confiscated. The crown, however, waived the right and allowed the merchant, on payment of freight charges at a rate previously fixed by the "ordonnateur" on that commodity, to receive the logwood.[2]

During the same years twenty-eight merchant ships came to Louisiana: five in 1750,[3] then six,[4] four,[5] ten,[6] and three,[7] respectively, in the years following. They sailed from La Rochelle, Bordeaux, Marseilles, Dunkerque, St. Malo and Bayonne. Besides the cargoes of troops, ammunitions and supplies carried for

[1] *A. N., C., Sér. B*, vol. xcviii, fols. 308-309.

[2] *Ibid.*, vol. c, fol. 53.

[3] *Ibid.*, vol. xci, fol. 2; *Sér. C13*, vol. xxxiv, fols. 310, 346, 359, 361, 365.

[4] *Ibid., Sér. C13*, vol. xxxv, fols. 4, 24, 56, 73, 164, 194, 340.

[5] *Ibid.*, vol. xxxiv, fols. 10, 64, 84, 177, 277.

[6] *Ibid.*, vol. xxxvii, fols. 25, 28, 34, 57, 60, 71, 157; *Sér. B*, vol. xcviii, fols. 96, 230.

[7] *Ibid., Sér. C13*, vol. xxxviii, fols. 26, 27, 53, 88.

the royal government, as before,[1] the merchant vessels brought to the colony merchandise on their own account. One such cargo in 1751 consisted of 750 barrels of flour, 100 barrels of lard and 50 plowshares.[2] In order to increase the amount of freight taken on board, the owners and possibly captain, with the connivance of the port inspector at Rochefort, had caused the boat to be loaded in a most unprofitable way. In the bottom of the hold was placed a consignment of coal upon which without dunnage were packed barrels of flour belonging to the crown. During the voyage the rolling of the ship caused the first layer of barrels to work down into the leakage soaked coal. As a result eighty-three "quarts" of flour were totally destroyed.[3]

The following year the ships were late in reaching Louisiana, a circumstance that made European supplies scarce and increased their price. Not a single vessel came before July; though a little later fifteen arrived almost at the same time. Since several of them were not from France, the amount of merchandise in the province was too scanty to meet all demands and yet leave in Louisiana a sufficiency of European goods to bring down prices.[4] At the end of the year wine was selling for 400 livres a cask and flour at twenty livres a hundredweight.[5] In the preceding year the crown had issued for the province a new set of regulations, one of which, though simply a restatement of an old law,[6]

[1] *A. N., C., Sér.* C^{13}, vol. xxxiv, fol. 310; vol. xxxv, fols. 24, 164, 194; vol. xxxvi, fols. 62-63, 177.

[2] *Ibid.*, vol. xxxv, fol. 340.

[3] *Ibid.*, vol. xxxvi, fol. 177.

[4] *Ibid.*, fols. 229, 269.

[5] *Ibid.*, fol. 334.

[6] *Supra*, p. 166.

was of value at this time in keeping the trade in European merchandise out of the hands of speculators. Punishment to the offender and confiscation of the merchandise were made the penalty for a person to go on board the vessel before landing at New Orleans. It was desired to give everyone in the village, at least, an equal chance to buy goods at first hand.[1]

For the most part the French merchants disposed of their wares to advantage, exchanging them for lumber, Spanish smoking tobacco, logwood, sugar, cotton, indigo, myrtle-wax, and native tobacco and an unusually large supply of peltry.[2] Cargoes made up of a diversified stock like this, were a decided advantage to the colony as a whole over one made up entirely of tobacco. In the latter case a vessel bringing imports valued at 100,000 to 300,000 livres could carry away only 20,000 livres worth of tobacco, thereby, as has been shown, causing difficult financial problems.[3]

From the beginning of 1750 to the opening of hostilities with England in 1754, Louisiana was comparatively fortunate in its productions for export. The season of 1750, while unfavorable to the corn crop, was most admirably suited to the culture of rice; consequently there was plenty of it as food for the slaves and some to put upon the market.[4] In 1752 the season was variable. The province was visited by numerous and very severe storms that did much damage to the harvests, yet without affecting greatly the supply of corn and rice, because of the large number of farmers that had this year planted them.[5] In 1753 the crops

[1] *A. N., C., Sér. C¹³*, vol. xxxv, fol. 46.

[2] *Ibid.*, vol. xxxvi, fol. 270.

[3] *Ibid.*, fols. 327-328; *A., B. A. É., Am.*, vol. ii, fol. 198. *Supra*, pp. 181, 204.

[4] *A. N., C., Sér. C¹³*, vol. xxxiv, fol. 297-298, 307.

[5] *Ibid.*, vol. xxxvi, fols. 228, 271.

were again light.[1] They were followed in 1754 by a year in which there was a splendid yield.[2] In 1750 the amount of indigo raised was very large, though much of it was destroyed by a storm that occurred just at the harvest time. The supply in 1752 was again lessened by a storm and too great an amount of rainfall. This diminution, however, was in part balanced by an increase in the quantity planted. The shortage also was compensated for by excellent prices; the rate being from 100 to 105 sols a pound.[3] Such prices increased the number of producers. On September 21, 1754, the "ordonnateur" estimated the amount for the year at 50,000 pounds. At the time the first crop was already on the market, where it brought the farmer five livres, ten sols and in some cases six livres a pound.[4] Another writer at this time states that there were in the province forty-seven planters, each owning an indigo factory, and estimates the total output for the year at 82,000 pounds, which he asserted was then selling at the price above quoted.[5]

In 1750 the quality of the tobacco grown in the province was good but the yield light.[6] The home government, thereupon, attempted to advance the trade in this commodity and at the same time to further the development of the colony as a whole by providing an easy and advantageous market for it in France. Such an outlet, it was claimed, would cause much more land to be cleared each year and hence a considerable increase in the acreage devoted to the indus-

[1] *A. N., C., Sér.* C^{13}, vol. xxxvii, fols. 70-71.

[2] *Ibid.*, xxxviii, fols. 26, 176-177.

[3] *Ibid.*, vol. xxxiv, fols. 297-298, 349; vol. xxxvi, fols. 228, 271.

[4] *Ibid.*, vol. xxxviii, fols. 176-177.

[5] *Ibid.*, vol. xxxviii, fol. 262.

[6] *Ibid.*, vol. xxxiv, fols. 297-300.

try. To this end the crown for a certain consideration granted a license to Jean Girardin whose duty was to find buyers for Louisiana tobacco. The time of the permit was to begin October 1, 1750, and to terminate September 30, 1756. For each quintal of such tobacco sold and delivered the royal government agreed to deduct fifty sols from the sum paid for the privilege. In addition he was to receive four per cent on the selling price from the owner of the commodity. Since 1738 the "fermier général" of tobacco in France had been obliged to pay twenty-five livres a quintal, net weight, for Louisiana tobacco, which was more than that paid for the foreign article, therefore, the former often remained some time in the warehouses before it was used. Notwithstanding the amount paid for tobacco in the past, the crown at this time fixed it at thirty livres a quintal, net weight; twenty-seven livres, ten sols of which was to be paid by the "fermier général", and by the royal government two livres, ten sols, so as to cover the expense incurred in handling the article at the French ports where it was to be received and placed in the warehouses of the "fermier général" and locked up until it was sold. What was not disposed of by Girardin, if of good quality, was to be taken by the "fermier général", at the rate stipulated above. To guard against any irregularities that might enter the trade, the crown still further stipulated conditions under which it should be carried on, by ordering that the tobacco from the province should be shipped either in leaf or "monoque". Moreover it was to be landed only at the ports of Calais, Dieppe, Havre, Honfleur, St. Malo, Morlaix, Brest, Nantes, La Rochelle, Bordeaux, Bayonne, Cette, Marseilles, Dunkerque and Vannes. If shipped to any other port the owner was not to be allowed the exemption of thirty sols a pound, the duty charged on foreign tobacco since May 4, 1749. Violations of the above rules were to be punished by confiscation of the tobacco and by a fine of 1,000 livres.[1]

The next year the tobacco crop at Pointe Coupée was large and of good quality. The "ordonnateur" informed the crown that there was a vessel there ready to transport it to France and that the outlook for the future of that trade was promising.[2]

The fine quality of Louisiana cotton alone kept alive among the planters the hope that eventually it would be made a paying export. Each year a little was sent to France and continued effort was exerted to find some sort of device whereby the seed could be separated from the fiber. In 1752 the "entrepreneur of public works" of the province invented such a machine and was trying it out on his plantation near New Orleans.[3] This same year the farmers around the capital were making another experiment. They had begun the myrtle-wax industry and already there were a great number of small fields planted and most of these were to be enlarged the following year. It was believed by them that the wax would soon be exported to France and elsewhere, and already small amounts had been shipped.[4]

During the period under consideration the trade with France and other ports was estimated at 2,056,000 livres, made up as follows: indigo, 82,000 pounds, at five livres a pound, 410,000 livres; 200 hogsheads of tobacco, 800 pounds each, 160,000 pounds, at twenty-two livres, ten sols a quintal, 36,000 livres; piastres, 300,000 livres; peltry,

[1] *Arrest du Conseil d'etat du Roy, Octobre* 13, 1750, Newberry Lib., Chicago.

[2] *A. N., C., Sér.* C^{13}, vol. xxxvi, fol. 229.

[3] *Ibid.*, fol. 272.

[4] *Ibid.*, fol. 229.

250,000 livres; myrtle-wax, 25,000 livres; bear's oil, 25,000 livres; pitch and tar, 30,000 livres; lumber, 180,000 livres; and bills of exchange amounting to 800,000 livres.[1] For the year 1754 the value of the tobacco shipment to France was stated to have been 50,000 livres, of indigo 120,000 livres, and that of peltry 30,000 livres, making a total for the year of 200,000 livres in these three exports.[2]

As early as 1755, the war was showing its effects upon Louisiana trade. During the year there came from France to the province no royal boats and but one belonging to the merchants, and that one escaped the ravages of war only to be destroyed by a storm as it was entering the Mississippi river. The greater part of the merchandise on board, some of which was owned by the crown, was saved.[3] The next year six vessels left France for the colony loaded with royal consignments of ammunition, foodstuffs and troops.[4] The freight bill for one of these shipments was 3,415 livres, sixteen sols.[5] For two other bills, one, at 158 livres a ton, was 5,689 livres, fifteen sols, three deniers and the second, at 180 livres a ton, amounted to 15,692 livres, two sols, ten deniers. When these two particular bills were presented for payment the royal government saw no reason for such a difference in rates when the voyages were made only two months apart, and proceeded forthwith to equalize them on the basis, naturally, of the lower rate.[6]

In 1757 there seem to have been no vessels from France in Louisiana. In March of the following year a merchant

[1] *A. N., C., Sér. C*[13], vol. xxxviii, fol. 262, 265.

[2] *Ibid.*, vol. xl, fols. 6-7; *A., B. A. É., Am.*, vol. ii, fol. 233.

[3] *A. N., C., Sér. C*[13], vol. xxxix, fol. 74.

[4] *Ibid.*, fols. 140, 213, 223; *A., B. N., Fr.*, vol. 11335, fols. 97-141; vol. 11336, fol. 106.

[5] *A. N., C., Sér. C*[13], vol. xxxix, fol. 213.

[6] *A., B. N., Fr.*, vol. 11335, fols. 141, 142.

ship from Bordeaux reached the province.[1] There were no further arrivals until August, when two frigates belonging to the crown and a merchant boat reached New Orleans. On leaving France the convoy had comprised two more freighters, but they had been lost en route. The empty colonial storehouses and ammunition supply, therefore, were not fully replenished, for besides the disaster at sea, the vessels had left in the warehouses at Rochefort 700 tons of royal merchandise put there for shipment by the home government on the request of the governor of the province.[2]

By 1759 the trade with France was greatly diminished. As early as February the troops were put on half rations. At the time flour was selling at 250 livres a " quart ", wine, 900 livres a cask, with all other supplies equally as expensive.[3] In June a vessel from Bayonne reached New Orleans with a cargo of 150 tons so varied in its make-up as to meet, in part, the needs of persons in every class of society. The governor, observing the fact, at once secured from the captain of the ship a promise to sell the entire stock at retail, thereby giving everyone in the village an equal chance to make purchases without paying the middleman's profit. Coming under the corrupting influence of the " ordonnateur " the commander broke his promise and sold the whole cargo for 250,000 livres to Rochemore,[4] who in turn disposed of it at retail at 400,000 livres.[5]

Such prices as were thus demanded for merchandise, the governor claimed, threatened the very life of the colony

[1] *A. N., C., Sér.* C^{13}, vol. xl, fols. 31, 32.

[2] *Ibid.*, fols. 34, 37, 62, 63, 182; *Sér. B*, pt. 2, cviii, fol. 3.

[3] *Ibid., Sér.* C^{13}, vol. xli, fols. 30, 76.

[4] *Supra*, p. 147.

[5] *A. N., C., Sér.* C^{13}, vol. xli, fols. 120, 122.

and justified him in buying supplies from whomsoever he could, even from the English enemy. The "ordonnateur" and his faction, naturally, since they had practically all there was to sell, stood strongly for the confiscation of all vessels and cargoes found in Louisiana belonging to foreigners.[1] The conduct of that officer in this, as well as in most of his other acts, had made him thoroughly hated by the greater part of the population.[2] In response to many protests against his maladministration, as already observed,[3] the crown finally recalled the "ordonnateur" who, however, did not leave the province until some time later. The war beyond the borders of the province was even less distracting to trade than the one waged at New Orleans between the two factions among the colonial officials.[4] Soon after the arrival of Rochemore at New Orleans, it seems, he and the governor had formed a plan whereby they believed the home government could save annually at least 10,419 livres and at the same time have the trade between France and the province better administered. This scheme provided for a commercial company to be formed and put into control of the trade of the province. This project was not adopted by the royal government and there is no evidence that the governor and "ordonnateur" ever came to another agreement upon that or any other matter during the latter's term of office. As a result of this situation trade conditions in Louisiana went from bad to worse.[5]

Disputes over trading matters were frequent and of a violent and disgraceful character. Such disagreements

[1] *A. N., C., Sér. C¹³*, fol. 30; *Sér. F³*, vol. xxv, fol. 35.

[2] *Ibid., Sér. C¹³*, vol. xli, fol. 32; *Sér. F³*, vol. xxv, fols. 101, 105.

[3] *Supra*, p. 146.

[4] *Supra*, pp. 146-149.

[5] *A. N., C., Sér. C¹³*, vol. xli, fol. 8.

were adjusted by the "ordonnateur's" secretary who decided in favor of the contestant who agreed to pay him the larger sum of money. The "ordonnateur", in direct disobedience to the royal instructions, began to discriminate against the French merchants in drawing bills of exchange.[1] In violation of law also he bought up further entire cargoes of European goods which he placed in his own private warehouse and retailed to the people of the colony, pocketing the receipts. For example, he purchased a cargo of "guildive" for the royal account which he disposed of on his own account at a very high price. In another instance a cargo of salt was sold to a merchant of New Orleans. The "ordonnateur" on learning of the transaction ordered the whole consignment to be sold to him, presumably for a supply for the troops. The salt instead found its way to the people through the private warehouse of that official who put the receipts, at the price of three sols, six deniers a pound, into his own coffers.[2] When there were no cargoes to buy for the crown and sell as private goods the "ordonnateur" took merchandise out of the royal storehouses and similarly disposed of it, always at very excessive rates.[3]

Three other vessels before the end of the year left France for Louisiana, two owned by the crown, the other by a merchant, all carrying ammunition and recruits for the army. The latter ship and cargo, on which the royal government paid freight charges at the rate of 167 livres a ton, was seized by the English on the outward voyage.[4]

Early in January, 1760, a royal ship and a merchant

[1] *Supra*, pp. 146-147.

[2] *A. N., C., Sér. F*[3], vol. xxv, fols. 101, 105.

[3] *Ibid., Sér. C*[13], vol. xli, fols. 147-149.

[4] *Ibid.*, fol. 323; *Sér. B*, vol. cxii, pt. 2, fol. 109; *A., B. N., Fr.*, vol. 11334, fols. 187-188.

boat reached New Orleans with enough supplies to meet the most pressing needs.[1] The following month the crown ordered sent out under convoy from Bordeaux a number of vessels with cargoes of merchandise for New France and Louisiana. Navigation on the Gulf of Mexico at the time was most uncertain, but that on the St. Lawrence river was far more hazardous. Therefore the commander in charge of the convoy, and the captains of the other ships bound for the former province, were instructed to sail for the southern colony if they could not reach the northern, the merchandise on board being selected to make such a change of destination possible.[2] Whether sent out under this command or not, at least a number of boats left France during the year for both Quebec and New Orleans. There seems to be no evidence that any of those bound for Louisiana ever reached that port.[3] The ships that arrived in the province at the end of the previous and at the beginning of the present year were ready to sail for France by the end of April. They were detained longer because of the arrival just at that time of a report that Quebec had fallen. The next month Governor Kerlérec held two war councils in which it was decided to arm these crafts, two royal frigates and a merchant boat, and supply them with food for five weeks, for the purpose of ousting an English man-of-war stationed at the mouth of the Mississippi which had been shutting off communication with the mother country. In the encounter the French were victorious and the English were driven out.[4] With the entrance to the Mississippi open once more, trade between France and Louisiana was resumed. On December 19,

[1] *A. N., C., Sér.* C^{13}, vol. xlii, fols. 56-57, 93.

[2] *Ibid., Sér. B*, vol. cxi, fol. 1.

[3] *A., B. N., Fr.*, vol. 11336, fols. 106, 171, 193-194.

[4] *A. N., C., Sér.* C^{13}, vol. xlii, fols. 56-57, 93-96.

1760, a vessel belonging to the crown set sail for France with two "quarts" of sugar and 400 pounds of coffee on board.[1]

In 1761 conditions in the province were not greatly improved; the warring factions were still present, though one of them was leaderless. The English being now more formidable at sea than ever, it was with great difficulty that the mother country supplied the province with necessary food and war materials. The crown urged the merchants to go on with the work. In June it succeeded in securing a ship belonging to a merchant of La Rochelle, to whom it paid 167 livres a ton for the transportation, to carry a cargo to Louisiana. Other merchants were solicited, but this year no others were secured.[2] In December the royal government obtained the services of a Dutch merchant at Amsterdam to take supplies to the province. The ship left early the next year, carrying with it instructions for the colonial officials to receive the boat and its cargo.[3]

Unable to find French merchants willing to undertake such ventures, the home government, in 1762, despatched from Bordeaux five ships, each of about 300 tons burden. Each vessel had on board soldiers and much merchandise. The royal warehouse by this time was entirely empty and the prices were high.[4] Wine was selling at 3,500 livres a cask and flour at 600 livres a "quart", 160 pounds.[5] The new "ordonnateur" found return cargoes for all but one of the vessels, which finally took 62¾ tons of logwood and two small cases of tobacco, commodities belonging to the

[1] *A. N., C., Sér. B*, vol. cxii, pt. 2, fol. 150.

[2] *Ibid.*, vol. cxiii, pt. 1, fols. 240, pt. 2, fol. 30; *A., B. N., Fr.*, vol. 11336, fols. 193-194.

[3] *Ibid.*, vol. cxi, fol. 3.

[4] *Ibid.*, vol. cxiv, Louisiane, fol. 15; *Sér. C[13]*, vol. xliii, fol. 5.

[5] *Ibid., Sér. C[13]*, vol. xliii, fol. 122.

preceding " ordonnateur ", on which the crown was asked to fix the freight charges.[1]

During the war the exports from Louisiana had increased somewhat in spite of the obstacles that had arisen. This was especially the case with tobacco, indigo and peltry.[2] In 1762 the receipts from exports were stated to be over 6,000,000 livres.[3] When Governor Kerlérec left the province in the following year he bore with him letters from the superior council and from private persons appreciative of his efficient administration in such trying times.[4]

Except in the case of indigo, peltry and tobacco just cited, there seems to be no way to ascertain, even approximately, the proportions of the trade between Louisiana and the mother country during the time the former was a French province. There are, as has been shown in the account of this commerce, records of prices for both the exports and imports. Those paid at different times for indigo and tobacco, on the one side, and wine and flour on the other have been summarized in the following diagrams.

[1] *A. N., C., Sér. C¹³*, vol. xliii, fol. 149.

[2] Villiers du Terrage, pp. 147-148.

Years.	*Indigo. Livres.*	*Tobacco. Livres.*	*Peltry. Livres.*
1756	270,000	90,000	120,000
1757	475,000	135,000	150,000
1758	540,000	210,000	180,000
1759	891,000	288,000	240,080
1760	1,350,000	480,000	240,000
1761	....	480,000	......
1762	410,000	3,600,000	250,000

[3] *Ibid.*, p. 148.

Years.	*Livres.*
1755	672,000
1756	850,900
1757	1,258,000
1758	1,868,600
1759	2,886,200
1760	4,440,100
1761	5,611,000
1762	6,662,200

[4] *A. N., C., Sér. F³*, vol. xxv, fol. 54.

Diagram III shows that the variation in these two imports was not due to freight charges.

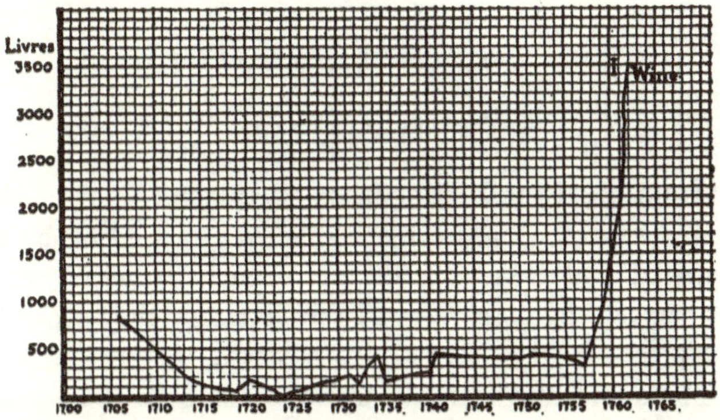

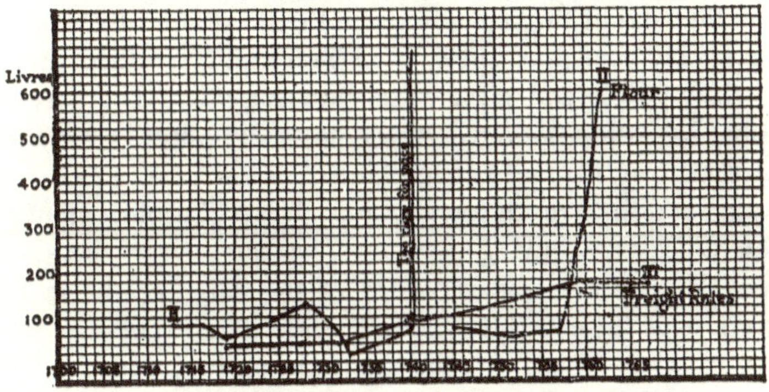

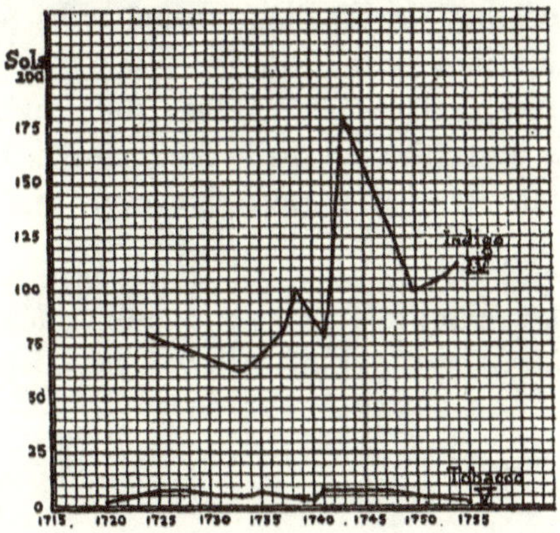

CHAPTER XV

The Slave Trade

Before the French established themselves in the Mississippi valley there was a trade in slaves carried on by the Indians of that area.[1] When the French by actual settlement became the possessors of this territory they soon discovered that it was necessary to buy war captives in order to deal successfully with the natives. La Salle at once saw a way whereby he could make of this traffic a lucrative business and at the same time win the good-will of the savages. His plan was to buy the slaves and carry them back to their people and there offer them for sale. The parent tribe, La Salle discovered, would pay more liberally for one of their own than of foreign blood.[2]

In 1700 the French found the English of Carolina among the Chickasaw buying slaves. The same year Iberville sent Tonty to sell beaver skins to the English; the main purpose of the expedition being to ascertain, if possible, the nature and extent of the English slave trade in the valley. From this time onward the French asserted and reasserted that the English created wars between different Indian tribes in the interior solely for the purpose of securing the captives.[3] Whether the English actually did originate hostilities for such a purpose is not relevant to this account. It is of concern, however, that the French

[1] *Supra*, p. 97.

[2] Margry, vol. ii, p. 79; *A. N., C., Sér.* C^{13}, vol. i, fols. 315-322, 522.

[3] Margry, vol. iv, p. 406; *A. N., C., Sér.* C^{13}, vol. i, fol. 429.

implicitly believed they did, and in order to thwart the English, formed a peace policy.

As early as 1702, Bienville began exhorting the Choctaw and Chickasaw to abandon the English and become friends. He tried to show them that the English aimed only at making them slaves. Moreover, he pointed out that such wars had caused the death of over 1,800 Choctaw and the taking of more than 500 prisoners who had been sold as slaves. He drew the attention of the Chickasaw, on their part, to the fact that they had lost over 800 of their warriors. Bienville told the latter tribes that if they would unite with the former Indians and drive the English from the Mississippi valley, that he would have the Illinois cease their wars upon them. This argument was convincing. The Indians entered into a general peace that lasted for nearly three years, at the end of which time the two nations resumed hostilities and the English came among them to buy up the captives.[1] The French peace policy for the time being, therefore, broke down because the English knew how to "have their slaves". Under the circumstances it became necessary for the French to adopt the English methods.[2]

The French traders even went so far as to imitate the English in the matter of creating wars for the sole purpose of securing the prisoners.[3] In 1720 the French "voyageurs" on the Arkansas and Missouri rivers were said to have brought about tribal differences for that purpose. In order to put an end to such behavior the crown issued a decree that offenders of this sort were to be seized and their merchandise confiscated. Furthermore, all the officials

[1] Margry, vol. iv, pp. 516-518.

[2] La Harpe, pp. 89-91.

[3] *A. N., C., Sér.* C[13], vol. ii, fols. 395-403.

were directed to do what they could to suppress the disorder.[1] These Frenchmen, however, were clever enough to carry on the traffic secretly and thus escape punishment.[2] The Indians at times, it seems, themselves entered the slave trade of their own volition. In May, 1709, the Alibamon fell upon the Mobile Indians, killed the men and carried some twenty-seven or twenty-eight women and children as slaves to the French at Mobile.[3]

The officials of Louisiana desired to follow still further the English methods of dealing with Indian slaves. To this end they requested the home government in 1706, 1707 and 1708 to allow them to exchange, in the French West Indies, Indians for negro slaves, the rate being fixed at two of the former for three of the latter. Bienville informed the crown that the reason for such an arrangement was to put the Indians where they would be unfamiliar with the country and, therefore, could not run away. On the other hand, he asserted, "negroes in Louisiana would not dare to, because the Indians would kill them". Another colonial official in his request to the royal government for such a traffic gave as a reason that the English were making profit out of a similar trade. The home government, however, was not convinced by the argument of its agents in Louisiana, and accordingly rejected the proposal.[4]

On October 12, 1708, a merchant coming to the province from St. Domingue bought fifteen Indian slaves. Notwithstanding the home government disapproved of such transactions, an agreement was made with him to bring

[1] Margry, vol. vi, p. 316.

[2] Charlevoix, *Hist. and Gen. Desc. of New France*, vol. vi, pp. 32-33; Carver, p. 348.

[3] *A. N., C., Sér. C*[13], vol. ii, fol. 398.

[4] *Ibid.*, vol. i, fols. 514-519; vol. ii, fols. 57-69, 359-362.

negroes, for each of whom he was to receive in exchange two Indians.[1] About the same time a similar trade was proposed to the merchants of Cape Francais.[2] The Louisiana officials, it seems, preferred to carry on such exchanges with royal sanction, therefore in 1713 they again requested the crown to allow them to carry on the traffic, which proposal was again rejected.[3]

In buying from the Indians, and in their clandestine slave dealings with islanders, the French were never able to make as good bargains as did the English in a similar trade. Governor Cadillac acknowledged he was not able to understand the genius of an Englishman who could buy a slave from a native for fifty pistoles (forty-two livres, six sols, ten deniers), for which a Frenchman would be obliged to pay as much as 100 to 105 livres.[4] These differences in price sometimes led French traders to attempt to secure Indian slaves from the English. In 1716, for example, a nephew of Bienville lost his life while engaged in such a traffic in Carolina. The work, however, was too hazardous to become widespread.[5]

The unprofitableness of the trade in natives together with the inability of the owners to keep them from running away when forced to work, and the royal opposition to it caused the French of Louisiana gradually to abandon this form of servitude.[6] In 1728 Governor Périer pronounced it to be detrimental to the advancement of the province.[7]

[1] *A. N., C., Sér.* C^{13}, vol. ii, fols. 178, 471-480.

[2] *Ibid.*, vol. iii, fol. 120.

[3] *Ibid.*, fol. 110.

[4] *Ibid.*, fols. 65, 511-533.

[5] *Ibid.*, fols. 511-533; vol. iv, fols. 241-242.

[6] *Ibid.*, vol. v, fols. 53-54.

[7] *Ibid.*, vol. xi, fol. 7.

The number of Indians held as slaves in Louisiana, therefore, was never large. In 1708 there were eighty of both sexes in the Mobile valley, 110 in 1721, and thirty-seven in 1725. Along the Mississippi, in and around New Orleans, there were, in 1721, 118; in 1727, seventy-three; and in 1731, forty-seven. There appears but one census, each, for the Illinois country and Natchitoches. In it, 1731, 117 for the former district and seven for the latter are recorded. The only inventory of the property of the entire province was made in 1726 and in it there are 229 Indian slaves recorded.[1] By 1744 the number had fallen to 122. It was, at this time, asserted that there were very few in Louisiana because the French were at peace with all the Indian nations. The savages still in bondage, it was further claimed, had been taken in former wars and had as yet not been given their freedom.[2]

As might be expected the price of Indian slaves in Louisiana was not high. From time to time a few savages were sold to merchants coming from the French West Indies, but no details of the transactions are given. As late as 1752 a trader from Cape Français bought at New Orleans three Indian men and two women, but no figures are quoted.[3] In 1755 an Indian slave in the Illinois country sold for 733 livres, perhaps as large a sum as was given for a native slave during the French régime.[4]

Since the French were not permitted by the home government to exchange Indians for island negroes, they early began to make requests for a supply from Africa.[5] In one

[1] *A., M. des C., Sér. G*^{1}, vol. 464.

[2] *The Present State of the Country, etc.*, p. 26.

[3] *A. N., C., Sér. C*^{13}, vol. xxxvi, fols. 62-63.

[4] Register 1755, Courthouse, Belleville, Illinois.

[5] *A. N., C., Sér. C*^{13}, vol. i, fol. 50; vol. ii, fol. 57-69; vol. iii, fol. 120; *Sér. F*^{3}, vol. xxiv, fols. 236-237.

way or another a black from time to time was procured and in 1712 the number in the whole province was ten.[1] Crozat's patent, issued this year, gave him the exclusive right to bring annually to the province from the Guinea coast one cargo of negroes.[2] The patentee, himself, made but little use of the privilege; nevertheless he guarded it carefully. On July 27, 1717, an English ship anchored at Dauphin Island. The captain asked for a supply of wood and water which was given on the condition that he agree, among other things, to refrain from a trade in slaves.[3]

The Company of the West in 1717 agreed to take over all negroes belonging to Crozat and to pay for them with their notes or with merchandise. Moreover, it arranged to receive the colonists' unpaid slave contracts and to allow them to finish payment in accordance with the old arrangement or to return the negroes to the Company.[4] The slave-trading privilege accorded to Crozat in his patent was not incorporated in the one issued to the Company of the West. Through a readjustment[5] that took place in 1719, Louisiana passed under the control of the Company of the Indies which owned the right to a trade in slaves.[6] Its privileges in regard to the slave traffic was extended to include also Louisiana.[7]

At this juncture the representative of a small trading company in France requested the home government to allow it, while preparations were being made to secure them

[1] *A. N., C., Sér. C*[13], vol. ii, fol. 178; vol. iii, fol. 65.

[2] *Hist. Colls. of La.*, pt. 3, p. 42.

[3] *A. N., C., Sér. F*[3], vol. 241, M. S. S. M.

[4] *Ibid., Sér. C*[13], vol. v, fol. 333.

[5] *Supra*, p. 31.

[6] Margry, vol. v, p. 590.

[7] *Hist. Colls. of La.*, pt. 3, p. 52.

from the Guinea coast, to procure 1,500 blacks from the English for the province.[1] The permission was not granted and no importations of negroes were made until 1721, when the Company landed in Louisiana 1,312, the largest number brought over in any single year.[2] For some time afterward slave ships reached the province from Africa almost every year with cargoes of negroes, and by the end of its control of the province the Company had transported thither more than 6,000 negroes, bringing the whole number landed since colored laborers were first employed, close to 7,000.[3] The colonial officials were required by the home government to make a certified statement of every slave ship, which report contained the number and conditions of the negroes on board. In some cases the number that had died during the voyage was also stated.[3]

The negroes were drawn from Caye, Gorée, Juida, Angola and Senegal, though by far the greater number was obtained from the coast last named.[4] The mortality while on the journey across the ocean was high.[5] In one instance, however, due to a very quick trip of only four months from the time the slave ship left France until it arrived in Louisiana, together with especially good treatment of the blacks during the voyage, only nine died. On reaching Louisiana they were fat, spirited and apparently healthy. A few days later, however, many fell sick with flux and scurvy, and 200 out of 341 had to be sent to the

[1] *A. N., C., Sér.* C[13], vol. v, fols. 299-302.

[2] *Infra*, p. 249.

[3] *Ibid.*

[4] *A. N., C., Sér.* C[13], vol. xi, fols. 27-29, 51, 131, 315.

[5] *Infra*, p. 249.

hospital for treatment, while others were given medical aid on the plantations to which they were assigned.[1]

Scurvy, measles, dysentery, flux, and sore eyes, that sometimes caused blindness, were the most common diseases while on shipboard. When large numbers of negroes were landed at one time, the Company was unable to provide for them warm woolen clothing, therefore, the strong as well as the weak at times found the temperature of the Gulf coast too low for them. Such climatic conditions caused other maladies and aggravated the more common complaints, which resulted in the death of many of the blacks soon after their arrival.[2]

The procuring of enough food often was a very great obstacle in the way of expanding the slave trade. In 1723, when 574 were disembarked in Louisiana, there were provisions available for feeding so large a number only for a short time. A boat, therefore, was immediately despatched to Cape Français for a supply of food.[3]

In the distribution of negroes the Company was very practical. It advanced them only to such colonists as were able to provide them with food and clothing and under anything like favorable conditions would meet the payments as they fell due. In order to make the reimbursements for everyone as easy as possible, the Company divided those desiring to receive slaves into two classes, namely, old and new comers. To the former it allowed a credit of one year on half the price of the negro, and to the latter two years. For the execution of the order all persons who had lived in the province two years or more were to be placed under the heading "old".[4] In order to

[1] *A. N., C., Sér.* C^{13}, vol. xi, fols. 52-53.

[2] *Ibid.*, vol. x, fol. 189; vol. xi, fols. 27-29, 315.

[3] La Harpe, p. 287.

[4] Dumont, vol. ii, p. 240; *A., B. A. É., Am.*, vol. ii, fols. 203-225.

make no mistakes in the placing of the slaves the Company sent out each year an agent whose duty it was to visit all farms and plantations for the purpose of observing conditions there. He was to report to the director what he saw and to name the men who, in his judgment, should receive slaves.[1] At the expiration of their term of service, if they wished to become civilians and would agree to take up agriculture, the Company made such advances to soldiers, on reasonable terms, payable, as was always its custom, entirely in farm products.[2] Augmentation in the number of land owners brought about a corresponding increase in the requests for laborers. In one year alone there were as many as 1,862. The number of negroes asked for in these various petitions ranged from one to fifty.[3] Such applications were made to the "ordonnateur" who made up the list of names and the number of blacks to be allowed from the recommendations of the Company's agent mentioned above.[4]

On the arrival of a slave ship the health inspector was at first the only person permitted to go on board. He examined the negroes, separated the sick from the well and put the former under treatment. The latter were allotted to persons whose names appeared on the official list. The distribution was accomplished by placing a string, to which was attached a card bearing a number, around the neck of each of the blacks. Duplicate cards were made and put in a bag from which the men at random each drew out one or more according to his authorized assignment, and took possession of the negroes bearing the corresponding

[1] Margry, vol. v, p. 625; *A., M. des C., Sér.* G^1, vol. 464.

[2] Margry, vol. v, p. 625.

[3] *A., M. des C., Sér.* G^1, vol. 464.

[4] Dumont, vol. ii, pp. 240-241.

numbers. The sick were sold at auction. Since the supply never was adequate, the bidding was usually brisk, sick negroes often bringing quite as much as healthy ones. There were some persons in the province who made a business of buying them, taking the chance of being able to cure them and when well of selling them at a considerable advance on the cost. These doctors, it was said, were careful " to put their curative secrets in practice only for themselves ".[1]

The buying of a negro was not easy. The best way, it was asserted, was to strip both " men and women as naked as the hand ", and then to have an " honest doctor " examine them, from the bottom of the foot to the top of the head, looking carefully between the toes and fingers, in the mouth, ears, eyes and other places where disease might lodge. The physician, it was further affirmed, should be especially requested to look for the malady called "pians " (yaws). Its detection, however, did not require an expert, since it caused deep black spots on the skin that were as smooth as glass. It was desirable that the slave buyer, himself, should be able to discover this as well as other defects, since the doctors very frequently were interested in buying slaves and hence did not make a correct diagnosis.[2]

The Company found it necessary to regulate the slave trade by special legislation. On March 12, 1722, a law was passed for the purpose of keeping negroes in the province. The act prohibited, on penalty of a fine of 1,000 livres and confiscation of the slaves, the selling of negroes to persons who would take them from the province.[3] The sale of slaves was put under still further legal restrictions

[1] Le Page du Pratz, vol. i, pp. 335-340; Dumont, vol. ii, pp. 240-241.

[2] Le Page du Pratz, vol. i, pp. 335-340.

[3] *A. N., C., Sér. A*, vol. xxiii, March 12, 1722.

on July 25, 1724. Henceforward it was to be unlawful for captains of slave ships to sell negroes, as had been done sometimes, before the health inspector had examined the cargo. Violations of the law were to be punished by a fine of 100 livres payable to the person who proved the guilt of the offender.[1] By 1725 many of the slaves, received from the Company on credit, had been resold before payment was completed. It was believed the transfer would make it impossible for the officials to seize and sell the negroes at auction in order to obtain the balance due. On December 11, by royal decree, such seizures and sales were made legal. Out of the money thus received, the Company's claims took precedence over all others, next the second buyer or present owner of the slave, and if there was a remainder, it passed to the man who made the attempt to defraud the Company.[2]

In 1727 the local director believed it possible to open up a lucrative trade in slaves with the interior provinces of Mexico and communicated the fact to the authorities in France. Nothing came of the proposal, due perhaps to the fact that the Company was about convinced that it was impossible to put trade of any kind on a paying basis in Louisiana.[3]

The crown appreciating the importance of negro labor for the development of the province began, in 1731, to look about for ways and means to augment it.[4] Before the end of 1732, the officials in France were informed that the colonists, themselves, could not carry on a trade in African slaves but that they could pay for them in cotton

[1] *A. N., C., Sér. A*, vol. xxiii, July 25, 1724.

[2] *Ibid.*, Dec. 11, 1725; *A., B. N., Fr.*, vol. 11332, fols. 321-323.

[3] *A., B. A. É., Am.*, vol. vii, fol. 246.

[4] *Ibid., Fr.*, vol. 1990, fol. 113; *A. N., C., Sér. C*[13], vol. xiv, fols. 36-37.

and tobacco, if only the royal government would bring them to the province. If it could not carry on such a trade, itself, it was the wish of the settlers that it interest the merchants of France to take up the work of transporting blacks from the Guinea coast to Louisiana.[1] There seems to have been no response to this communication. By 1734, the colonists from both New Orleans and Mobile were making urgent appeals for slaves, offering for them as much as 1,400 livres apiece.[2] The governor and "ordonnateur", thereupon, informed the crown of the need of negro labor for the development of the province.[3]

A chance to increase the slave trade seems to have presented itself in December, 1733, when there arrived from St. Domingue a merchant boat of sixty tons. During the stay of the proprietors, captain, and two merchants in the province they sold the cargo they brought and bought another to be carried to Martinique, meanwhile formulating with the Louisiana officials a plan for bringing negroes from Africa to the colony. En route to Martinique they stopped at St. Domingue in order to land one of the merchants who was there to take passage on a royal ship bound for France for the purpose of presenting the project to the home government. From the former island the captain was to take the vessel to the coast of Guinea where he was to procure a cargo of negroes for Louisiana. According to the plan formulated before leaving the province the royal government was to be requested to allow these men to buy in France a ship of 150 tons to be used in carrying slaves from Guinea to New Orleans. If the crown granted the permit without remuneration and allowed a "gratifica-

[1] *A. N., C., Sér.* C^{13}, vol. xiv, fols. 36-37.

[2] *Ibid.*, vol. xviii, fols. 51-53; vol. xix, fols. 25-29.

[3] *Ibid.*, vol. xviii, fols. 14-19, 41-44.

tion" of forty livres a head on all negroes imported, they were to be sold in the province for 450 livres each. On reaching St. Domingue a letter was despatched to the colonial officials soliciting them to recommend to the home government that a boat of 800 tons be purchased in Holland instead of the one of 150 tons in the original scheme; a subsidy of forty livres a ton be granted on cargoes of colonial products carried from Louisiana, as accorded to French merchants for similar service; and that the selling price of the negroes be raised to 600 livres. The governor and "ordonnateur" jointly sent a letter to the royal officials strongly recommending the proposal, together with the changes. The crown, it seems, took no action in the matter.[1]

On the failure of the above project the Louisiana agents urged upon the home government the necessity of sending negroes to the province, informing it that a cargo of 200 slaves could easily be paid for in two years, since they would be sold only to planters in comfortable circumstances.[2] The enthusiasm of the royal officials for such a trade perhaps was dampened somewhat by the fact that the sales for the negroes they already had furnished were still 63,200 livres in arrears, which they were assured would be paid at the coming harvest.[3] This year the "ordonnateur" issued an ordinance that was meant to protect owners from loss of slaves through escape and drunkenness. The law, however, was enforced poorly, hence brought little relief.[4]

Three years now passed before another proposal was presented for the building up of the slave trade of the province. In 1737, a merchant of La Rochelle made an offer to

[1] *A. N., C., Sér. C¹³*, vol. xix, fols. 88-89, 90-91, 198-199.

[2] *Ibid.*, vol. xx, fols. 105-109; vol. xxi, fols. 25-30.

[3] *Ibid.*, vol. xxi, fols. 284-286.

[4] *Ibid., Sér. A*, vol. xxiii, Dec. 7, 1736.

carry negroes from Africa to Louisiana for from 550 to 850 livres a head, according to the age and quality of the blacks. He pointed out the fact that at this time slaves in St. Domingue were selling for from 1,200 to 1,300 livres each. He made the offer, therefore, only on the condition that the colonists would agree to buy all the slaves he landed. According to the proposal the negroes were to be paid for in tobacco, indigo, peltry or other products suited to the French market. The first payment was to be made from the harvest nearest the date of sale of the negro. The merchant on his part agreed to pay three livres a pound for indigo, three sols, six deniers a pound for tobacco, and one livre and a half for deerskins.[1]

Since nothing came of this proposal the home government was again informed of the great need there was in the province for colored laborers for the production of indigo and other commodities.[2] No negroes being provided, a settler living near Mobile, in December, made a bargain with the captain of an English vessel to open a slave market on the "Isle of Vessels", situated near the mouth of the Mobile river, where the commander of the ship at this time disposed of five blacks.[3]

The next year, 1738, the governor and "ordonnateur" jointly informed the crown that it had been eight years since the province had received slaves from it and that the need for a new supply was most pressing, since those in the service were growing old. Therefore for the advancement of the colony as a whole, and for the indigo industry in particular, the proposal of Bienville and Salmon was recommended as being worthy of approval. For a num-

[1] *A. N., C., Sér. F*[3], vol. 242, M. S. S. M., Feb. 22, 1737.

[2] *Ibid., Sér. C*[13], vol. xxii, fols. 37-41, 51-54.

[3] *Ibid.*, fols. 198-203.

ber of years, fixed by itself, the crown was petitioned by these two officials to permit them, jointly, to form a company for the exclusive trade in slaves between the Guinea coast and Louisiana. The formation of the company was to be made as follows: the crown was to advance it 150,000 livres; to provide a ship and crew secured in France; to exempt it from paying a duty to the Company of the Indies. If it was impossible to supply the vessel, a "gratification" of 200 livres a head was proposed as an acceptable substitute. Under these conditions the blacks were to be sold in the province for 800 livres apiece. As in the case of the various proposals above cited the crown took no action regarding the matter.[1]

The next year the royal government was requested to grant large tracts of land for the establishing of tobacco plantations, and to make to the planters an advance of 600,000 livres to be held for fourteen years without interest. Of this sum 500,000 livres was to be used in buying negroes and the remainder in fitting up the farms. For the fourteen years the crown was to permit blacks to be procured for the province wherever they could be purchased most advantageously. The settlers were to be paid five sols a pound for tobacco, with its transportation to France made as easy as possible. This scheme being less attractive, from the point of view of the home government, no consideration was given it.[2]

In April the "ordonnateur" informed the crown that the planters were chagrined because their negroes were all old, due to the fact that for twelve years there had been no importations from Africa.[3] Of the 4,000 blacks then

[1] *A. N., C., Sér. C*[13], vol. xxiii, fols. 120-131.

[2] *Ibid.*, vol. xxiv, 268, 274.

[3] *Supra*, p. 239.

in the province, it was asserted that two-thirds were creoles, a condition that did not exist even in the Antilles, a province where there was a much smaller quantity of exports produced. Salmon was positive that a cargo of 250 adult negroes brought annually to Louisiana would go far toward removing the shortage in slave labor.[1] In the latter part of the year Governor Bienville informed the royal government of an opportunity to secure slaves. Two planters from Martinique had come to the colony, secured land, and one of them with ten negroes had begun work on it, while the other had returned to bring over the remainder of their blacks. Through these men the governor had learned that there were many more slave owners in that island who wished to migrate to Louisiana and requested the crown to allow them to do so.[2] Bienville further informed the home government that a La Rochelle merchant who, during the year, had a vessel trading in the province, had promised to carry over a cargo of negroes in 1742. These he had agreed to sell in Louisiana for 1,500 livres each, one-third payable on delivery in colonial currency, and one-third at each of two succeeding harvests in native products.[3] The activities of the officials of the province, therefore, had brought to the colony this year no acquisitions of slaves.

There seems to have been no end to the schemes intended to bring about such results. In 1742, d'Alcour and Dubreuil worked out a plan of the sort with the full approval and coöperation of the governor and "ordonnateur", d'Alour making a journey to France in order to bring the project to a successful termination. In July, 1743, a re-

[1] *A. N., C., Sér.* C^{13}, vol. xxvi, fols. 138-139.

[2] *Ibid.*, fols. 108-109.

[3] *Ibid.*, fol. 109.

port reached the province that there would soon be a cargo of 200 negroes brought to Louisiana from Senegal, where they had been purchased from the Company of the Indies. In order to help the venture along, the "ordonnateur" made to the promoters an advance in bills of exchange and permitted them ship 100 tons of freight on royal boats bound for France. The first payment to the Company, 30,000 livres, was due July, 1742; in July of the following year 30,000 pounds of tobacco and 400 barrels of tar were placed on board a vessel to be sent to France to meet the obligation. On the same boat there also were despatched 40,000 pounds of tobacco, 400 barrels of tar and some indigo for the second 30,000-livre instalment.[1]

In August, 1743, d'Alcour with his vessel reached Louisiana with 190 full-grown negroes on board, what was left of about 250 taken on in Africa.[2] The venture evidently was profitable, since the crown was at once petitioned to allow a second cargo, this time one of 220 blacks.[3] About the same time Governor Vaudreuil suggested to the royal government that it was advisable to send to the province the next year 600 negroes, or 300, each, for two or three years. The cost to it, the governor claimed, would be 600 livres and the selling price in the province 1,800 livres a head. The venture, therefore, would bring about two beneficial results, namely, the retiring of colonial paper,[4] and the providing of the settlers with an adequate number of laborers.[5] The home government not being convinced of these inherent probabilities rejected the proposal.

[1] *A. N., C., Sér.* C^{13}, vol. xxvii, fols. 5-8; vol. xxviii, fols. 20-21.

[2] *Ibid.*, vol. xxviii, fols. 84-85.

[3] *Ibid., Sér. B*, vol. lxxix, fol. 38.

[4] *Supra*, p. 135.

[5] *A. N., C., Sér.* C^{13}, vol. xxviii, fols. 83-84.

Vaudreuil, having given up hope of securing negroes through the crown or the French merchants, in 1746, engaged a Dutch trader to import them. He then informed the royal authorities of the action he had taken and proceeded to justify it on the ground, first, that France was not at war with Holland, and secondly, that the advancement of the province absolutely depended upon an augmentation of slave labor.[1] The Hollander seems to have made no use of the privilege accorded him, therefore another of the schemes for increasing the number of negroes ended in failure.

The struggle between France and England, 1744-1748, diverted the attention of the colonial officials somewhat from the slave trade. As soon as peace was restored many persons in the province began to establish new plantations on the Mississippi above New Orleans. Therefore an urgent need of importation of negroes was soon manifested. In 1752, the "ordonnateur" informed the crown the demand was so great for blacks to clear the land on these farms that some of the planters had deposited money with him to be used in buying slaves for them at Cape Français. At the same time he asserted there were a number of men in the French West Indies, especially Martinique,[2] who wished to establish themselves in Louisiana. He requested the crown to permit the migration.[3] Its sanction, however, was not given.

From time to time the merchants from St. Domingue and Martinique brought to the province what blacks they could procure at the slave markets of those two islands. Some of these traders paid willingly the duty customary

[1] *A. N., C., Sér. C*[13], vol. xxx, fols. 110-112; vol. xxxii, fol. 32.

[2] *Supra*, p. 241.

[3] *A. N., C., Sér. C*[13], vol. xxxvi, fols. 273, 275.

in other French provinces on such importations, while others refused. Not deeming it wise to force such payments without direct instructions from the crown, the governor, in 1754, asked to be informed as to its wishes in the matter.[1] To this communication there was no reply. In the advancement of such a commerce it seems the royal government was somewhat interested, for in January it was willing to allow a merchant of Bordeaux to enter the trade but refused to aid him in carrying out his project.[2] In the following April it was considering the granting of a permit to this same merchant to transport negroes from the Guinea coast to Louisiana. Moreover it was inclined to allow him a "gratification" on each negro thus imported.[3] Since the close of the war the slave owners of the province evidently had prospered. At any rate the "ordonnateur", in September, informed the royal government they were now financially able to pay the capitation tax of five livres that some time before it had proposed to put on negroes.[4] Just at this juncture war again broke out between France and England, and the placing of the tax was for the time being deferred.

From 1754 to the end of the French control of the province there was very little interest taken in the slave trade. In 1756, an old complaint against Dubreuil was again up for adjustment. In 1739, he had bought some negroes, agreeing to pay for them 30,000 livres in three equal annual instalments. In 1742, but 16,000 livres had been paid and the case was taken to the superior council for settlement. Enough of the planter's property to pay the debt

[1] *A. N., C., Sér.* C^{13}, vol. xxviii, fol. 51.

[2] *Ibid., Sér. B*, vol. c, fol. 8.

[3] *Ibid.*, fol. 52.

[4] *Ibid., Sér.* C^{13}, vol. xxxviii, fols. 176, 177.

was ordered to be seized and sold. For some reason the order was not carried out. Although the Count de Maurepas had written the "ordonnateur" a number of times concerning the matter, except for 4,000 livres in 1752, no remittances had been made.[1]

Three French frigates in 1759 seized an English vessel that had on board 414 negroes. Two-thirds of the number were left at Grenada and the remainder carried to Louisiana. The governor of the latter province did not know how to deal with importations of blacks, since no reply had been given him in regard to his request concerning the duty to be levied on negroes brought to the colony.[2] They were therefore held from January to May in order to receive instructions.[3] With this sale the slave trade of Louisiana as a French province practically came to an end. However, such a commerce with the French West Indies to some extent must have gone on after 1759. At any rate on July 9, 1763, an act was passed by the superior council forbidding the importation of negroes from St. Domingue because so many deaths of whites of that island had occurred, due to poison administered by the blacks.[4]

At the time of the retrocession of Louisiana in 1731 there were 3,395 negro slaves in the province.[5] Through the great industry of the colonial officials, described in the preceding pages of this chapter, and through natural increase, the number in 1746 was 4,730,[6] and at the end of the French period there were in the entire province about

[1] *A. N., C., Sér. B*, vol. ciii, fol. 4.

[2] *Supra*, p. 244.

[3] *A. N., C., Sér. C¹⁸*, vol. xli, fol. 173.

[4] *Hist. Colls. of La.*, pt. 2, p. 63.

[5] *A., M. des C., Sér. G¹*, vol. 464.

[6] *A. N., C., Sér. C¹⁸*, vol. xxx, fol. 256.

6,000 black slaves.[1] In the Illinois country where such laborers were not thought to be desirable there were, in 1750, 300, and by 1763, 900.[2]

For the first decade and a half there seems to be no information available as to the prices the French of Louisiana paid for negro slaves. The Company of the Indies fixed them at 660 livres for a black between the ages of seventeen and forty, and 440 for those from eight to ten. Payments were to be made in three equal parts, either in rice and tobacco or notes of the Company. At the end of the first year if the obligation was not met the slave became again the property of the Company. If the negro on being resold did not bring enough to satisfy the debt, the person who bought the black in the first instance was to pay the balance.[3] In 1723, a dispute arose between the settlers and the Company over the price of rice used in paying for negroes. The former were contending for twenty livres for a barrel that weighed only a little more than 100 pounds, while the latter demanded one of 130, the ordinary weight for such commodities.[4]

The selling price of slaves did not remain at 660 livres long after it was legalized. In 1722, it advanced to 1,000 livres and for a full-grown, healthy negro did not go below that during the time of the control of the province by the Company.[5] In 1724, however, 800 livres would be received by it if lead were given in payment.[6] There seem

[1] Dubroca, *L'Itinéraire des Français dans la Louisiane*, p. 84.

[2] *Jes. Rel.*, vol. lxix, p. 145.

[3] La Harpe, pp. 289, 291; *A. N., C., Sér.* C^{13}, vol. vi, fol. 239; *Sér. A*, vol. xxiii, Sept. 27, 1721.

[4] *A. N., C., Sér.* C^{13}, vol. vii, fol. 45.

[5] *Infra*, p. 249.

[6] *A. N., Sér.* C^{13}, vol. viii, fols. 103-104.

to have been no sales under this arrangement. In 1727, a priest tried to secure a slave from a dying man for 800 livres but no mention is made of the lead. The matter went to the superior council for settlement, where it was decided the negro was still a part of the estate which was later sold at public sale where the slave brought 1,330 livres.[1] Blacks sometimes sold collectively [2] for less than 1,000 livres.[3] Nevertheless the Company, in 1732, was able to secure from 25,000 to 30,000 livres for lots of ten and twelve, all skilled laborers, therefore not an extravagant price.[4] What quotations are available for the different sexes all show that males usually brought more than females,[5] and children much less than adults; [6] and in 1732 a cash payment of 600 livres was equivalent to 900 on a credit of three years.[7] The next year the price was low, blacks bringing at auction only 400, 500 and 700 livres

[1] *A. N., Sér.* C[13], vol. x, fols. 249, 250.

[2]

Dates.	*Number.*	*Livres.*
1721	500	150,000
1724	7	4,500
1731	9	2,700
1731	80	99,327
1731	87	87,000
1732	12	30,000
1732	260	182,000
1733	50	42,000
1735	54	42,500
1736	8	10,000
1738	5	3,000
1739	225	157,500

[3] *A. N., C., Sér.* C[13], vol. viii, fol. 104.

[4] *Ibid.*, vol. xv, fols. 13, 14.

[5] *Ibid., Sér.* F[3], vol. ccxlii, M. S. S. M. Women, 750 livres; men, 850; girls, 550; boys, 650.

[6] *Ibid.*

[7] *A. N., C., Sér.* C[13], vol. xv, fol. 22.

apiece.[1] In 1734, it was doubled, adults selling for 1,400 livres.[2] A decrease in the importation from Africa caused it, by 1743, to advance to 1,800 livres a head; at this time a lot of twenty-nine men, fourteen women and eleven children brought 42,500 livres.[3] At a public sale in New Orleans, in 1763, there was a wide range of prices when the slaves were sold either singly or in families.[4]

[1] *A. N., C., Sér.C*[13], vol. xvi, fols. 96, 97; vol. xvii, fols. 167, 169.

[2] *Ibid.*, vol. xix, fols. 25-29.

[3] *Ibid.*, vol. xx, fols. 205-207; vol. xxii, fols. 196-197.

[4] *Ibid.*, vol. xliii, fols. 315-351.

Value in livres of negroes sold singly and in groups.

Man	Man and wife	Man, wife son	Man, wife daughters son	Man, wife daughter, 2 sons	Man, wife 3 sons daughter
420	2050	5690	11500	10100	24000
2900	4000	6850	13200	20050	
3050	5500	7000	14125		
3800	6500	7500		Man, wife, son, 2 daughters	
4610	7260	7500			
5400	7800	12200			
5550	8150	12200		10150	
6000	8400				
6020	8400	Man, son, daughter			
6200	8450				
6260	8550	9900			
7000	10200 (indgt.)	11550			
7050	10650	12050			
7100	11000	17500			
7500	11200	18500			
8000	11450				
10700 (Bl. S)	12600	Man, wife, mother			
12250 mason					
13000		13100			
Women	Man and son				
6700	6550				
10700	Woman and son				
	7350				
Boy (16 yrs.)					
5100					
145310	156060	141540	38825	40300	24000

Totals: 132 negroes brought 546,035 livres.

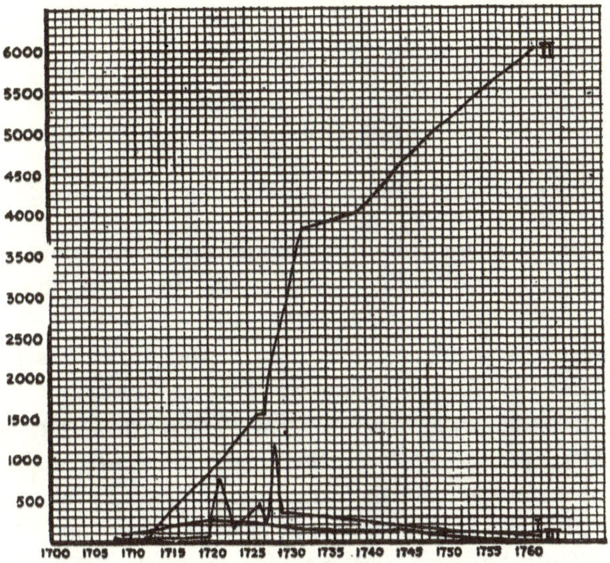

Diagram I, the number of negroes landed.
Diagram II, the entire number of negroes in the province.
Diagram III, the entire number of Indian slaves in the province.

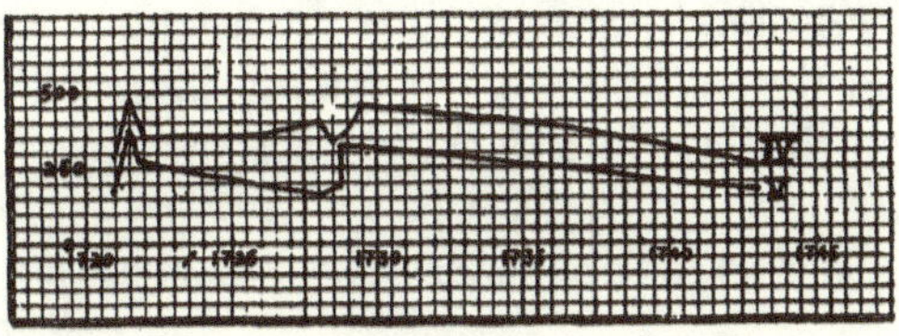

Diagram IV, number of negroes taken on board in Africa.
Diagram V, the number landed in Louisiana.
Variations of the two, mortality during the voyage.

CHAPTER XVI

The Domestic Trade of Lower Louisiana

Trade in Louisiana, like the colony itself, developed slowly, due for the most part to the fact that the first settlers were either fortune-seekers or exiles from France because of their crimes; therefore neither class was fitted for pioneer work. Absolute want, however, forced some of them to take up agriculture. By 1710 there were settlers who were producing more than they consumed and this year sold to the officials 8,140 livres, 18 sols worth of native products for the maintenance of the garrison.[1]

The Crozat régime was most detrimental to trade. In the first place the price offered for colonial products was entirely out of proportion to that demanded for French merchandise. This condition created discord between the settlers and the officials and discouraged the former from attempting to produce in excess of consumption. Secondly, the local agents, following their instructions, persistently encouraged the settlers, even at the sacrifice of their farms, to spend their time in a futile search for mines that were

[1] *A. N., C., Sér. C*[13], fols. 529-530. Products supplied:

	Liv.	*Sols.*
180 quintals, 99 pounds of fresh lard		
34 quintals, 79 pounds of fresh beef	6,470	10
116 barrels corn, 14 liv., 8 sols bbl. of 150 lbs.	1,670	08
Total	8,140	18

believed to be located somewhere in the interior of the province.[1] The unfair dealings the colonists received from the resident officials caused many irregularities in trade. The " ordonnateur ", writing on June 3, 1716, asserts there were at Mobile not more than forty settlers; that there were so few domestic animals in the province that beef was selling at nine sols a pound, moreover the colonists were finding it hard to provide themselves with food of any kind.[2] On August 23 of this year, in order to eliminate some of the abuses, the governor and " ordonnateur " issued an ordinance making it a crime punishable with a fine of 50 pistoles for any person to kill domestic animals belonging to another, without first securing the consent of the owner; at the same time the price of beef was fixed at four sols, six deniers a pound; veal, two months old, at six sols a pound. To sell at a higher rate was to be punished by a fine of 30 livres.[3]

The Company of the West recognizing that its predecessor's failure was due in part, at least, to a too great restriction of the trade of the province, inaugurated a system that allowed the settlers much liberty in domestic exchanges.[4] Notwithstanding the unfavorable conditions in which the province had been placed, it had grown. At this time there were in lower Louisiana garrisons at Mobile, Alibamon, Yazou and on Dauphin Island.[5] Life in the province, however, was still hard to maintain.[6] Meat was very expensive, notwithstanding the fact the price had been fixed by law.

[1] *A. N., C., Sér.* C^{13}, vol. iii, fols. 197-207, 210-217, 216-223, 251-253.

[2] *Ibid.*, vol. iv, fols. 391-392.

[3] *Ibid., Sér. A*, vol. xxiii, Aug. 23, 1716.

[4] *Lettres Patentes*, Aug., 1717, N. Y. Pub. Lib.

[5] *A. N., C., Sér.* C^{13}, vol. v, fol. 86.

[6] *Ibid.*, fols. 44-45, 46.

Fowl at the time were selling at three livres, 12 sols, each, and all other provisions at equally high prices.[1]

By 1720 Mobile, though still the capital, was no longer the only market place in the province. New Orleans already had become one for the planters nearby, and those all along the Mississippi.[2] The trade, to be sure was small. The Company, however, was doing all that it could to augment it.[3] To this end the colony was divided into nine military districts [4] as follows: New Orleans, Biloxi, Mobile, Alibamon, Natchez, Yazou, Natchitoches, Arkansas and the Illinois country, each district being provided with a garrisoned post.[5] In order to regulate prices of merchandise in the different parts of the province, the Company fixed them for Mobile, Dauphin Island and Biloxi at 50 per cent advance on the coast in France. To these prices five per cent was to be added if sold at New Orleans, 10 per cent at Natchez, 15 per cent at Yazou, 20 per cent at Natchitoches and 50 per cent on the Illinois and Missouri.[6] On September 20, 1721 there was another adjustment of prices, the Company of the Indies fixing them at 50 per cent on the cost in France for the posts of Alibamon, Biloxi, Mobile and New Orleans; at 70 per cent for Natchez and Yazou; at 80 per cent for Natchitoches and on the Arkansas, and at 100 per cent in the Illinois country.[7]

[1] *A. N., C., Sér. C*[13], fol. 48.

[2] *A., M. des C., Sér. G*[1], vol. 464; Le Page du Pratz, vol. i, p. 166; vol. ii, pp. 253-255.

[3] *A. N., C., Sér. C*[13], vol. vi, fols. 14, 20, 21.

[4] *Supra*, p. 26.

[5] *A. N., C., Sér. C*[13], vol. vi, fols. 218, 219.

[6] *Ordonnance de la Compagnie d'Occident*, April 25, 1719, N. Y. Pub. Lib.

[7] *A. N., C., Sér. C*[13], vol. xii, fol. 204; La Harpe, p. 293.

Biloxi was at this time supplying the new settlers with cattle, hogs and fowls, as well as fresh meat to the crews on the ocean-going vessels.[1] Every year the hunters went to the St. François river for a supply of salt buffalo meat for the New Orleans market.[2] On July 17, 1722 the superior council fixed the maximum price for fowls at three livres, each, for Biloxi; at 40 sols for New Orleans and Mobile; spring chickens at 30 sols for the former and 20 sols for the two latter villages. Everywhere in lower Louisiana fresh beef was to sell for not more than ten sols a pound, buffalo meat, fresh or salted, at eight sols, venison at four livres a quarter.[3] A fine of 200 livres was to be imposed upon persons who violated the law. The day after its publication a settler sold beef at 15 sols a pound and was promptly arrested and fined. Other similar offenses were dealt with in the same fashion.[4] This year part of the salt meat for New Orleans was provided by the hunters of Pointe Coupée who supplied 5,000 pounds of it, cured from 80 buffaloes.[5]

In 1723 it was claimed by the "ordonnateur" that if every vessel that stopped at Cape Français on the way to Louisiana would bring six or seven cows, the number of cattle in the province soon would make it possible for the butchers at New Orleans to kill two animals a week. The price at the Cape was only 40 livres a head and each one in Louisiana would sell for 600, thereby making such transactions very profitable to the shipper. Beef at this time was selling at ten sols a pound, the highest price allowable

[1] *A., B. de l'A.*, vol. 4497, fol. 64.

[2] Le Page du Pratz, vol. i, p. 150.

[3] *A. N., C., Sér.* C^{13}, vol. vi, fols. 417-418, 421-422.

[4] *Ibid.*, fol. 329.

[5] La Harpe, p. 309.

by the law.[1] It seems to have been impossible to keep it longer at that rate, therefore, in 1725, the superior council advanced it to 12 sols for fresh beef, and made the punishment for violations 50 livres, payable to the person bringing about the conviction.[2] In October of the following year the "ordonnateur" asserted that for some months it had been possible to procure fresh meat daily at the markets of New Orleans, due to importation of cattle from St. Domingue.[3] Two Canadian hunters, in 1727, carried to the capital 480 buffalo tongues from the animals they had killed during the winter. The usual method was to sun dry the flanks and salt the remainder.[4]

By 1728 there was in Louisiana a great need for standardizing the weights and measures used in trade and May 7, the superior council fixed the standards for many articles. In the case of beef 360 pounds, henceforward, were to be considered a hogshead, 240 pounds a cask, 180 a "quart" and 90 pounds an "ancre."[5] During the last years of the control of the province by the Company buffalo meat and venison sold at six sols and beef at eight sols a pound, paid in paper money. The suppression of this currency,[6] however, brought the former to four and the latter to six sols a pound. During this period the soldiers, in winter, were given but two sols a day for meat in order to force them to forage for the remainder of such food. In summer they were allowed a slightly larger amount, since game at that season was not made use of.[7]

[1] *A. N., C., Sér. C13*, vol. vii, fol. 19.

[2] *Ibid., Sér. A*, vol. xxiii, July 24, 1725.

[3] *Ibid., Sér. C13*, vol. xi, fols. 117-118.

[4] *Jes. Rel.*, vol. lxvii, p. 285.

[5] *A. N., C., Sér. F3*, vol. ccxli, M. S. S. M., May 7, 1728.

[6] *Supra*, p. 122.

[7] *A. N., C., Sér. C13*, vol. xix, fols. 18-20.

By 1732 the German settlers ten leagues above New Orleans consisted of more than 60 families all very industrious and prosperous. These men supplied the New Orleans markets with large quantities of fowls.[1] The "ordonnateur" in 1733, bought meat coming from the Illinois country at four sols a pound. The salt used in curing it was of inferior quality and 6,000 pounds of the amount purchased spoiled before it could be consumed. Early in the following year Salmon thereby was put to the trouble of procuring more with which to feed the troops until the end of November when game would be fit for use again.[2] In March 1734 one of the settlers petitioned the "ordonnateur" to give him the entire contract for supplying New Orleans with meat at four sols a pound for the soldiers and at five to the general public. The exclusive privilege was granted, perhaps, because it was recommended by Bienville who believed it would be a decided advantage to the province. The cattle for the supply were to be drawn from Mobile, Dauphin Island and Natchitoches where they were raised in excess of local consumption, instead of exclusively from the vicinity of the capital as heretofore.[3]

An ordinance was issued in 1735 requiring all persons to have game inspected before it could be sold upon the streets of New Orleans. Any one violating the law was to be punished by confiscation of the merchandise and a fine of 50 livres.[4] In 1737 two butchers were supplying the capital with beef at six sols a pound for the best cuts and five for the poor grades. Cattle continued to be drawn from Natchitoches for this market. In May the supply

[1] *A. N., C., Sér.* C^{13}, vol. xiv, fol. 138.

[2] *Ibid.*, vol. xix, fols. 18-20.

[3] *Ibid.*

[4] *Ibid., Sér. A*, vol. xxiii, Jan. 2, 1735.

from that post had not reached the lower Mississippi, due to the bad condition of navigation of the Red river. Commandant St. Denis, at this time, informed the officials that from 60 to 80 head were on the way and could be expected to reach New Orleans some time during the following month. As a protection to the herds in this part of the province veal was not now permitted to be sold.[1]

On May 18, 1737 the "ordonnateur" issued an ordinance which fixed the price of meat and made it illegal to kill any domestic animal without first having it inspected by an official. The slaughter of suckling calves was forbidden and also of cows, bulls, oxen, sheep and hogs, unless a declaration of such a procedure had been made in advance at the office of the "ordonnateur".[2] On July 27 Salmon issued another, making it illegal to sell fish that had not been passed upon by a government inspector.[3]

The disorder in the finances of the colony in 1739[4] brought about a disarrangement in the price of many commodities, for example turkeys that had sold at from 50 sols to three livres, each, advanced to ten livres.[5] Because of the Indian war, nevertheless, it was thought advisable to provide meat to the troops at four, that cost the government six sols a pound, the legal price. Moreover the army officers were, in addition, to be supplied with hams and salted tongues.[6] Some of the stock-raisers of the province now had quite large herds. Anticipating a greater demand for beef due to the increase in the number of soldiers for

[1] *A. N., C., Sér.* C^{13}, vol. xxii, fols. 148-151.

[2] *Ibid., Sér. A*, vol. xxiii, May 18, 1737.

[3] *Ibid.*, July 27, 1737.

[4] *Supra*, pp. 129-130.

[5] *A. N., C., Sér.* C^{13}, vol. xxiv, fol. 133.

[6] *Ibid.*, fols. 8-9, 139-140.

the war against the Chickasaw, they advanced the price of cattle. The " ordonnateur " believed the rise unwarranted and on August 29, 1739 issued an ordinance fixing the price to the butchers at the same amount as before the arrival of the troops.[1]

After the close of the Indian war the price of meat became more stable. In 1744 there were " every day at the shambles beef, veal and mutton." In winter the shops had buffalo meat and all sorts of game which, even at that season of the year, did not prevent the killing daily of domestic animals. Pork was common food for all. Much of it was slaughtered by the colonists themselves, therefore did not pass through the shops. The slaves, even, were able to provide themselves with pork and fowls. Domestic beef, at this time, sold at six sols a pound, suckling pigs at 100 sols, each, turkeys at from three to four livres apiece, geese at 50 sols, ducks at 25 sols and teal at 12 sols each.[2]

By 1745 the butchers of New Orleans were placing such high prices on veal that on March 22 Governor Vaudreuil issued an ordinance making it illegal for them to charge more than three livres, 15 sols a quarter. This ruling, intended to protect the general public, was also beneficial in that it tended to prevent a too great slaughter of young animals, that in a short time would yield a much larger supply.[3] By another ordinance, July 12, the planters along the Mississippi were each week to bring to the New Orleans market two beeves to be used in supplying the troops with meat.[4]

For some time stock-raising in all parts of the province,

[1] *A. N., C., Sér. A*, vol. xxiii, Aug. 29, 1739.

[2] *The Present State of the Country, etc.*, pp. 14, 19.

[3] *A. N., C., Sér. A*, vol. xxiii, March 22, 1745.

[4] *Ibid.*, July 12, 1745.

and especially at Mobile and Natchitoches, had been greatly stimulated by the excellent prices of meat. In 1746 it was estimated that there were 10,000 head of cattle in the colony and also many good-sized flocks of sheep and large droves of hogs. It was the belief, at the time, that in future such foods would be adequate to the needs of the province. This conviction, moreover, was strengthened by the fact that salt fish was now being put upon the market in considerable amounts. The by-products, such as cowhides, sheepskins and wool, were selling at good prices, all of which tended to make the trade profitable to those engaged in it.[1]

When Normant came as " ordonnateur " to New Orleans in 1747 he found the old rule for the sale of merchandise at the different posts of the province not being observed; in some cases the goods sold for more, while in others for less than the legal rate. Moreover the trade contained many abuses which he at once set about to eliminate, at least, some of the more flagrant of them. Since the plan of having different prices for the same kind of merchandise at the various posts of the province had not worked well, he proposed to make them the same throughout the province. Rate fixing heretofore had not worked well. For the most part all commodities went on selling for just the same as before the change. Under the arrangement in question the " ordonnateur " did not propose to include foodstuffs; therefore, he believed it would be observed.[2]

A contagion among animals in lower Louisiana appeared in 1748 and continued to manifest itself for about three years, during which time the herds were greatly reduced in size. By 1749 there were frequent shortages in the meat supply for New Orleans. In winter beef, veal, mutton,

[1] *A. N., C., Sér.* C^{13}, vol. xxx, fols. 242-282.

[2] *Ibid.*, vol. xxxi, fols. 125-127.

buffalo meat, venison, turkeys and ducks usually could be procured. Nevertheless it was pointed out that game was becoming less abundant each succeeding year and no longer could be relied upon for sustenance when other food failed. This fact no doubt was impressed upon the minds of the officials just at this time by the presentation for payment of a bill of between 1,000 and 1,200 livres for game that during the year had been provided for the table of a commander of a convoy during his voyage from New Orleans to the Illinois country. Therefore in order to make the colony self-supporting in meat it was proposed that the killing of heifers and cows, for the present, should be prohibited absolutely. Moreover it was to be made obligatory for each farmer in that part of the province to keep as many domestic animals as his land would maintain.[1] The mortality among beasts had been so high that the above provision was not adequate. In 1751, therefore, the scarcity of domestic animals had become so great that the "ordonnateur" was obliged to finance an enterprise for procuring them from the Spanish colonies. He found it equally necessary, also, to advance money for the establishment of fisheries on Lake Pontchartrain for the purpose of supplying fish at reasonable rates daily to the markets of New Orleans and to the troops.[2] Before the end of the year he made such an arrangement with one of the colonists.

In 1752 fowls were selling in New Orleans at from 30 to 35 sols each, spring chickens at 25 sols, and turkeys at from 7 livres, ten sols to ten livres. In season much game was to be had at very low prices. Throughout the year it was possible to procure fish which sold at the same rate per pound as beef.[3]

[1] *A. N., C., Sér. C*^{13}, vol. xxxiii, fols. 153-156, 167-168; vol. xxxiv, fol. 294.

[2] *Ibid.*, vol. xxxv fols. 26, 330-331.

[3] *Ibid.*, vol. xxxvi, fol. 334.

By 1762 the prices of meat in New Orleans had advanced considerably. Turkeys, weighing from 40 to 50 pounds, were selling for 45 livres; capons, for 17 livres, ten sols; fowls, weighing ten pounds, 12 livres, ten sols; spring chickens, 7 livres, ten sols, each; ducks the same as fowls; a pair of pigeons, five livres; a quarter of venison, 50 livres; mutton, weighing 80 to 100 pounds, 90 livres; and beef two livres, ten sols a pound.[1] After 1762 there are no further reports made concerning the meat trade of Louisiana while under French control.

Lard, tallow, olive oil, bear's oil, butter, eggs, cheese and milk at an early date were bought and sold in Louisiana. The first named article was brought from France as well as made in the province itself. In spite of these two sources there was often a great shortage.[2] In 1708 the settlers on the Gulf coast agreed to supply the garrison with this commodity at nine sols a pound, half payable in cash, the remainder in merchandise.[3] Up to 1710 the amount thus supplied was 180 quintals, 99 pounds.[4] In 1714 it was selling for 15 livres a quintal,[5] with the domestic product bringing at the same time, six sols a pound.[6] In 1725 the retail price for fresh lard was fixed by the superior council at 12 sols a pound.[7] The same body, in 1728, adjusted the weights for this product at 360 pounds for a hogshead, 240 pounds for a barrel, 180 pounds for a quintal and 90 pounds for an "ancre."[8] By 1735 the price of both French and

[1] *A. N., C., Sér.* C^{13}, vol. xliii, fol. 122.

[2] *Ibid.*, vol. iii, fols. 245-248; vol. xix, fol. 19.

[3] *Ibid.*, vol. ii, fols. 237-248.

[4] *Supra*, p. 250.

[5] *A. N., C., Sér.* C^{13}, vol. iii, fols. 287-309.

[6] *Ibid.*, vol. xx, fols. 250, 251.

[7] *Ibid.*, *Sér. A*, vol. xxiii, July 24, 1725.

[8] *Ibid.*, *Sér.* F^3, vol. ccxli, M. S. S. M., May 7, 1728.

domestic lard had fallen to six sols a pound,[1] but in 1747 it advanced to ten sols.[2] The stress of war by 1762 made it retail at New Orleans at seven livres, ten sols a pound.[3]

Tallow had been put upon the market as early as 1720 by the hunters from the Arkansas district.[4] It was widely used by both the French and Indians for illuminating purposes and by the former was sometimes mixed with myrtle-wax in making candles.[5] In some measure the myrtle-wax supplanted tallow because its harvest came at a time when there was little to be done on the plantations. It was firmer also in a warm climate like that of Louisiana. Moreover it gave a clearer light. In 1747, the wax sold at the capital at fifteen sols a pound and it was believed that the best grade would soon bring from eighteen to twenty sols. The amount put upon the market increased each year and in 1752 one planter alone produced 6,000 pounds. A number of other persons was producing it also but in smaller amounts.[6] In 1754 the entire output of this commodity and that of bear's oil was valued at 25,000 livres annually.[7]

Before 1719 olive oil had had some sale in the province. On April 25, 1719, the Company fixed the price at which it should be sold at twelve reaux, one livre, ten sols a pot, payable in silver.[8] Notwithstanding the adjustment of the rate, olive oil advanced and in 1726 was reduced from

[1] *A. N., C., Sér.* C^{13}, vol. xx, fol. 250; vol. xxi, fol. 273; *Sér. B*, vol. lxiv, fol. 518.

[2] *Ibid., Sér.* C^{13}, vol. xxxi, fol. 127.

[3] *Ibid.*, vol. xliii, fol. 122.

[4] Le Page du Pratz, vol. i, p. 150.

[5] *A. N., C., Sér.* C^{13}, vol. xv, fol. 35.

[6] *Ibid.*, vol. xxxiii, fol. 169.

[7] *Ibid.*, vol. xxxviii, fols. 265.

[8] *Ibid.*, vol. v, fol. 332.

forty to twenty-five sols a pot.[1] When weights and measures were standardized in 1728 a hogshead of olive oil was henceforth to contain 100 pots; a " quart ", forty-five pots; and an " ancre ", twenty-two pots.[2] Information about the sales of olive oil during the royal régime in Louisiana is very scanty. In 1735 it was again selling for forty sols a pot,[3] and in 1762 advanced to thirty-three and a third livres a pint.[4]

The French of Louisiana learned from the natives to use bear's oil and soon began to substitute it for olive oil.[5] It was claimed by some to be quite as good for salads as the best grades of the latter.[6] By 1719 the settlers of Natchitoches were carrying it to New Orleans.[7] This supply was augmented by hunters who left the capital each winter to go to the St. François river to hunt bear. In 1721 it was plentiful and sold at twenty sols a pint.[8] There was a shortage the next year due to the fact that the Arkansas Indians who usually furnished New Orleans with something like 2,500 or 3,000 pots of oil annually this year had none to sell.[9] The amount thus reduced, the prices rose to ten and twelve livres a pot;[10] by 1735 it was down to forty sols.[11] From this time onward the hunters and In-

[1] *A. N., C., Sér.* C^{13}, vol. ix, fol. 254.

[2] *Ibid., Sér.* F^{3}, vol. ccxli, M. S. S. M., May 7, 1728.

[3] *Ibid., Sér.* C^{13}, vol. xx, fols. 250, 251.

[4] *Ibid.*, vol. xliii, fol. 122.

[5] *Ibid.*, vol. vi, fol. 51; Le Page du Pratz, vol. ii, pp. 88-90.

[6] Margry, vol. vi, p. 230.

[7] Le Page du Pratz, vol. i, p. 150.

[8] *Ibid.*, p. 207.

[9] Margry, vol. vi, p. 382.

[10] *A. N., C., Sér.* C^{13}, vol. vii, fols. 23, 24.

[11] *Ibid.*, vol. xx, fols. 250, 251.

dians continued to bring bear's oil in constantly increasing quantities to the markets of both Mobile and New Orleans, and by 1754 the sales of it and tallow together were 25,000 livres each year.[1] Six years later the oil was selling in New Orleans at twenty livres a pot.[2]

As early as 1731, New Orleans became the butter and cheese market for the German settlements and continued as such to the end of the French control.[3] From the large herds in the Mobile valley a supply of butter and cheese was carried both to Mobile and New Orleans. Ten farmers at Bayagoulas, midway between those two villages, likewise provided both markets with these commodities.[4] The price of butter like all foods was advanced by the war, and in 1762 was selling at ten livres a pound.[5]

Eggs were market products in 1717 and sold at fifty sols a dozen,[6] which price was maintained at both Mobile and New Orleans until 1723,[7] when it dropped to sixteen and eighteen a dozen.[8] By 1727, however, the price of eggs at New Orleans was at forty-five and fifty sols a dozen.[9] A decline followed and in 1752 they were eighteen, twenty, thirty-two sols, six deniers, and thirty-five sols a dozen.[10] In 1762 eggs had advanced to three livres, fifteen sols a dozen.[11]

[1] *Supra*, p. 261.

[2] *A. N., C., Sér.* C^{13}, vol. xliii, fol. 122.

[3] *Ibid.*, vol. xiv, fol. 138; vol. xxxiii, fol. 167.

[4] *Ibid.*, vol. xxx, fol. 253.

[5] *Ibid.*, vol. xliii, fol. 122.

[6] *Ibid.*, vol. v, fol. 48.

[7] *Ibid.*, vol. vi, fols. 417-418, 422.

[8] *Ibid.*, vol. vii, fols. 23, 24.

[9] Gravier, p. 30.

[10] *A. N., C., Sér.* C^{13}, vol. xxxvi, fol. 334.

[11] *Ibid.*, vol. xliii, fol. 122.

Although the greater part of the people of the province no doubt owned a cow or two and provided themselves with milk, there was a market for it as early as 1713.[1] In 1716 the inhabitants at Biloxi were selling it to the newcomers and to the crews of vessels that at times touched there at forty sols a pot.[2] At New Orleans, in 1723, there was a dairy carrying on a trade.[3] In order to protect the sick from the extortionate prices of the dealers, the superior council issued an ordinance, July 24, 1725, fixing the maximum price of milk at fifteen sols a pot and making the punishment for violations a fine of fifty livres, one-half of which was to go to the informer, the remainder to the hospital.[4] For a time the law seems to have been enforced, for in 1727 milk was selling in New Orleans at fourteen sols a pot, half of the ordinary measure used in France by milk dealers.[5] In 1751, there was a new dairy established at Bayagoulas, the cows for which being procured at Natchitoches. At the time it was the opinion of the officials that the development of this industry would be an advantage to the province.[6] The next year milk sold at New Orleans at two sols, six deniers a pot.[7] Trade in this commodity was carried on at the different posts of the province. In 1762, the bill from one of these alone cost the royal government 20,000 francs for the amount consumed in a single year. The chronicler remarked that " the garrison of that post must have been suckled all that year ".[8]

[1] *A. N., C., Sér. C*[13], vol. iii, fols. 209-310; vol. vii, fol. 73.

[2] *Dumont*, vol. ii, p. 53.

[3] *A. N., C., Sér. C*[13], vol. vii, fol. 73.

[4] *Ibid., Sér. A*, vol. xxiii, July 24, 1725.

[5] Gravier, p. 30.

[6] *A. N., C., Sér. C*[13], vol. xxxv, fols. 97-98.

[7] *Ibid.*, vol. xxxvi, fol. 334.

[8] *Hist. Colls. of La.*, pt. v, p. 136.

The supply of flour for lower Louisiana came both from France and from the Illinois country, the climate of the Gulf region being unsuited to the growing of wheat. The amount secured from these two sources, however, was never constant, therefore the prices were most variable. From 1713 to 1719, flour from France sold at Mobile at twenty piasters (eighty livres) a barrel of 180 pounds.[1] When rates were fixed by the Company of the Indies, in 1719, flour was placed at fifteen livres a hundredweight.[2] In 1725, the Company again adjusted prices; this time the commodity was to sell at sixty livres a "quart", 160 pounds, an amount double what it brought in 1719.[3] The legal measure for flour, in 1728, was made 180 pounds for a "quart".[4] At this time rice flour was selling at three sols, six deniers a pound; 118 to 120 pounds of unhulled rice sold at seven to eight livres and made about fifty-nine pounds of flour.[5] In 1734, the price of flour from France reached at New Orleans thirty livres a barrel.[6] Three years later it advanced to forty livres a quintal or eight sols a pound,[7] but dropped the following year to twenty-two livres a quintal for both the domestic and French articles.[8]

In 1740, a "quart" of flour brought seventy livres and at the time both corn and rice were mixed with it in making bread. In 1741, it became so scarce that it could be given no price.[9] As the war approached, one source of supply

[1] *A. N., C., Sér.* C^{13}, vol. iii, fols. 216-223; vol. iv, fols. 391-392.

[2] La Harpe, p. 176.

[3] *A. N., C., Sér.* C^{13}, vol. viii, fol. 181.

[4] *Ibid., Sér.* F^{3}, vol. ccxli, M. S. S. M., May 7, 1728.

[5] *Ibid., Sér.* C^{13}, vol. xi, fol. 119.

[6] *Ibid.*, vol. xviii, fols. 8-12; vol. xix, fols. 151-157.

[7] *Ibid.*, vol. xxii, fols. 140-147.

[8] *Ibid.*, vol. xxiv, fol. 127.

[9] *Ibid.*, vol. xxvi, fol. 185.

was cut off; therefore, an increase in the price followed, and in 1747 it was selling in New Orleans at seven livres, ten sols a pound.[1] The war over, the price again became normal; in 1752, it was twenty livres a hundredweight.[2] The second war with England coming so soon after the close of the first threw trade into more disorder than ever; in 1757, flour was selling at 280 livres[3] and in 1762 at 600 livres a "quart" of 160 pounds.[4]

To the cost of flour must be added the profit of the baker and the shop-keeper in order to get at the price of bread. In 1723, the officials found it necessary to put it at forty sols a pound. This year some very poor black bread was sold by a woman at three livres a pound, whereupon she was arrested and brought before a magistrate who demanded that she tell from whom she had received it. She at first refused to answer, but upon being lodged in jail, she reconsidered and named a woman as the person from whom she had purchased it. This second woman was forthwith arrested and likewise questioned. She declined, at first, to state from whom she had received the bread, saying she could not remember the name, but that it was a soldier, whereupon she was sent to jail to spend the night and refreshen her memory on a diet of water and some of the bread she had sold. The next morning she still asserted that she could not recall the name of the soldier. On hearing the order that the incarceration and diet be continued she burst into tears, giving the name of the baker who was responsible for the making of such a quality of bread. She further informed the magistrate that she had been carrying on the trade secretly for some months but declared that

[1] *A. N., C., Sér.* C^{13}, vol. xxxi, fol. 127.

[2] *Ibid.*, vol. xxxvi, fol. 334.

[3] Villiers du Terrage, p. 80.

[4] *A. N., C., Sér.* C^{13}, vol. xliii, fol. 122.

during that time she had never sold it at more than twenty sols a pound. Here the examination ended. The woman was fined 500 livres and commanded at once to return to her last customer the thirteen livres she had received from her for the bread.[1] A similar complaint was made in 1725 against a baker in New Orleans who sold it to a Spanish captain at three reaux a pound, which price it was claimed was detrimental to the building-up of a trade with Spain's colonies.[2] Still, much of the bread used by the colonists was made in whole or part of corn meal or rice flour. In 1727 it sold at the capital for ten sols a pound.[3] For some time before the crown took over the province in 1731 the bread for the troops had been made half rice; it was proposed to continue the practice since it made it about a fourth cheaper, even if it did fall short of making the same amount as wheat flour by about twenty pounds a hundredweight.[4]

The storm that visited the province in 1732 completely destroyed the bakery at New Orleans that had been engaged to provide bread for the troops.[5] The royal government's bakers at New Orleans and Mobile were receiving 400 livres a month for their services, while a negro at the Balise was doing the same work quite as well for his clothes and a soldier's rations. It was the belief that the cost of bread for the troops could be reduced at the first two places named.[6] In 1744 bread sold in New Orleans at twelve sols a pound, if paid for in silver, but at sixteen sols, eight deniers, if colonial money were given in exchange.[7]

[1] *A. N., C., Sér.* C^{13}, vol. vii, fols. 49-50.

[2] *Ibid.*, vol. ix, fol. 137.

[3] *Ibid.*, vol. x, fol. 198; vol. xii, fol. 135; Gravier, p. 30.

[4] *A. N., C., Sér.* C^{13}, vol. xiv, fol. 16; vol. xviii, fols. 24-27.

[5] *Ibid.*, vol. xvii, fols. 192-195.

[6] *Ibid.*, vol. xvi, fol. 58.

[7] *The Present State of the Country, etc.*, pp. 14, 27.

By 1720 rice was grown all along the Mississippi and could be procured in great abundance. Its price the next year was fixed by the Company at twelve livres a quintal.[1] Soon, however, it began to fluctuate, and in 1726 was twenty livres a barrel, of 200 pounds.[2] Only two years later unhulled rice was as low as seven or eight livres a barrel, of 118 and 120 pounds.[3] The last year of the Company's control of the province it paid three livres a "quart", and in some instances not above forty-five sols for that quantity of rice. When the transfer was made, the crown took over 8,000 barrels of it that was then in the storehouse at the Company's rate of three livres a barrel.[4] Almost the entire crop of the commodity was lost in the storm of 1732. Rice became scarce and the price advanced. Some of the planters, in order to keep their slaves from starving, were obliged to pay for it as much as fifty-two livres a " quart ". For the purpose of protecting these men from such extortion an ordinance was issued making the further practice of it illegal.[5] Before the end of the year rice had dropped to twenty livres for a barrel of 200 pounds.[6] In 1735 the price was three livres a " quart ", but a bad harvest in 1736 advanced it to seven livres, and in a few instances it was seven livres, ten sols.[7] In 1737 it sold at six and seven livres a quintal.[8] In 1738 the shortage of the crops was

[1] *A. N., C., Sér.* C^{13}, vol. vi, fol. 20; vol. vii, fols. 168-169; *Sér. B*, vol. xliii, fol. 88.

[2] *Ibid., Sér.* C^{13}, vol. x, fol. 152.

[3] *Ibid.*, vol. xi, fols. 112-113.

[4] *Ibid.*, vol. xvi, fol. 97; vol. xvii, fols. 78-84.

[5] *Ibid.*, vol. xvi, fol. 97; vol. xvii, fols. 78-84.

[6] Le Page du Pratz, vol. iii, p. 387.

[7] *A. N., C., Sér.* C^{13}, vol. xx, fols. 105-109, 123-125; vol. xxi, fols. 256-260.

[8] *Ibid.*, vol. xxii, fols. 121-123, 140-147.

somewhat offset by an abundant harvest in the Illinois country. The products from that part of the province not only held prices at normal level but were able to reduce rice to seven and eight livres a quintal.[1] Floods in 1741 swept away the greater part of the rice produced that year and caused the price to advance from six to twelve livres a barrel,[2] the next year hulled rice sold at twenty-five livres a quintal.[3]

Corn for lower Louisiana was secured both from the natives and Europeans, therefore should have been plentiful and cheap. As early as 1710 the settlers provided the government with 116 barrels of 150 pounds each, at fourteen livres, eight sols a barrel, to be used as food for the troops.[4] In 1716 it sold at three piastres a barrel of 200 pounds.[5] La Harpe on his journey up the Mississippi in 1719 met at the mouth of the Red river some Natchitoches farmers who were carrying their products to New Orleans. He bought from them five barrels of corn, for which he paid five piastres each.[6] The next year corn at the same post was selling at sixteen livres a barrel.[7] In 1735 it brought two livres a "minot." The bad harvest the following year caused the price to advance to seven livres in 1736[8] and to nine in 1738.[9] The floods mentioned above destroyed large quantities of corn, which became so scant that it sold

[1] *A. N., C., Sér. C*[13], vol. xxiv, fol. 153; vol. xxiii, 134-137.

[2] *Ibid.*, vol. xxvi, fols. 67, 130.

[3] *Ibid.*, vol. xxvii, fols. 5-8.

[4] *Supra*, p. 250.

[5] *A. N., C., Sér. C*[13], vol. iv, fol. 624.

[6] Margry, vol. vi, p. 251.

[7] *Ibid.*, p. 231.

[8] *A. N., C., Sér. C*[13], vol. xxi, fol. 256; vol. xxii, fols. 121-123.

[9] *Ibid.*, vol. xxiii, fol. 120.

at fifteen and sixteen livres a barrel.[1] In 1750 the price was still high, due to a great scarcity.[2] In 1754 there was a large yield in this commodity.[3] It sold in 1760 at ten livres a "quart". At this time it was necessary to buy a supply for the royal storehouse. Rochemore received an offer of the entire amount needed, delivered at the storehouse at ten livres. The "ordonnateur", being unfriendly to the grain dealer, refused to take it. Instead he bought what was wanted, 2,312 "quarts", at Pointe Coupée, paying also ten livres. An additional expense was incurred in transporting it to New Orleans and placing it in the storehouse; a cost to the government of 18,099 livres, nine sols and three deniers.[4] In 1763 corn sold at four livres, five sols, three livres, ten sols and three livres, five sols a "quart".[5] Of the trade in other kinds of grain grown in Louisiana there are few records. On April 25, 1719, however, the Company fixed the price of rye at seven, wheat at ten and oats and barley at four livres a hundredweight, which perhaps would indicate some trade in these commodities.[6]

The first products put upon the market by the French settlers on the Gulf coast were vegetables which were offered to the soldiers of the garrison.[7] The amount of such foodstuffs increased as the province developed, and in 1719 one planter alone sent to market 200 livres worth of corn, beans, potatoes, other vegetables and fruit; while a second

[1] *A. N., C., Sér.* C[13], vol. xxvi, fols. 67, 130.

[2] *Ibid.*, vol. xxxiv, fol. 298.

[3] *Ibid.*, vol. xxxviii, fol. 176.

[4] *Ibid.*, vol. xlii, fol. 78.

[5] *Ibid.*, vol. xliii, fols. 315-351.

[6] La Harpe, p. 176.

[7] *A. N., C., Sér.* C[13], vol. iii, fols. 213-214.

sent a similar assortment which brought 100 livres.[1] This year La Harpe bought five barrels of so-called "Apalaches" beans from the Toniac Indians at the mouth of the Red river, which was all that tribe had to sell.[2] In 1720 these beans brought from Nachitoches sold in New Orleans at sixteen livres a barrel.[3] At the same time the colonists on the Mississippi were supplying that market with beans, potatoes and vegetables.[4] The farmers in the vicinity of the village in 1722 were selling beans to the soldiers at twenty-five sols a pound, a price so exorbitant that the "ordonnateur" requested Bienville to fix the maximum for the retail price at four sols a pound, thirty livres a barrel. It was claimed the petition was just, since eighteen livres a barrel made the producer a good profit.[5] By 1723 there was an abundance of all kinds of vegetables, most of which brought good prices at New Orleans where, for example, watermelons in season sold for three livres each; and a "handful" of peas at fifty and sixty sols.[6] The next year the harvest of corn, rice and beans for the New Orleans district alone was 5,093 barrels, and the potato crop 2,900 barrels.[7] On June 27, 1725, a list of legal prices for the different domestic products to be found in the markets was published. Like many similar laws during the French régime it was not well enforced. The next year the great abundance of vegetables of all kinds forced the farmers to take what they could get for them.[8] In 1728 the legal weight of a

[1] *A., B. de l'A.*, vol. 4497, fol. 55.

[2] Margry, vol. vi, p. 249.

[3] *Ibid.*, p. 231.

[4] *A., M. des C., Sér. G*[1], vol. 464.

[5] *A. N., C., Sér. C*[13], vol. vi, fol. 330.

[6] *Ibid.*, vol. vii, fols. 23-24.

[7] *A., M. des C., Sér. G*[1], vol. 464.

[8] *A. N., C., Sér. C*[13], vol. ix, fol. 246.

barrel of French beans was fixed at 360 pounds and for the smaller weights the same as those for flour,[1] while for domestic beans 150 pounds were to be considered a barrel. The price of "Apalaches" beans at this time was ten livres a barrel.[2]

Nothing more is to be learned of the market-gardening trade of Louisiana until 1744, when it is asserted that both Mobile and New Orleans had markets containing quantities of fruit, almonds, oranges and lemons, also many kinds of vegetables, such as pumpkins, water melons, melons of other sorts, cabbages, herbs, beans, peas, rice and potatoes. On ordinary market days and on fête days a great many German farmers came to the capital bringing with them fine apples, peaches, pears, figs, sweet potatoes, melons of all kinds, artichokes, large cabbages, salad plants, herbs, all of which were finer than those grown in France.[3] For the most part the prices received are not given. For a salad plant they often got as much as thirty sols;[4] for a quintal of red beans twelve to thirteen livres.[5] At this time all, especially fine, domestic products were labeled in the shops with the word "creole".[6] In 1754 the output of pitch, tar and vegetables amounted to 30,000 livres annually. There seems to be no way of ascertaining how much of the sum was gotten from the sale of vegetables alone.[7]

The liquor business of Louisiana, as is the case in most

[1] *Supra*, p. 265.

[2] *A. N., C., Sér. F³*, vol. ccxli, M. S. S. M., May 7, 1728; Le Page du Pratz, vol. iii, p. 387.

[3] *A. N., C., Sér. C¹³*, vol. xxx, fols. 254-255; vol. xxxiii, fols. 167-168.

[4] *The Present State of the Country, etc.*, p. 14.

[5] Le Page du Pratz, vol. iii, p. 387.

[6] *German-American Annals*, vol. vii, p. 186.

[7] *A. N., C., Sér. C¹³*, vol. xxxviii, fol. 265.

frontier communities, had many representatives, most of whom were doing well. As early as 1706 there was a liquor shop in the province, said to have been owned by Bienville but administered under the name of another person. At this place wine was sold at 200 piastres a cask, the price remaining constant until 1712.[1] Governor Cadillac assured the crown such profits would not be made under the new régime.[2] Before the end of 1713 the Crozat agents themselves, however, were selling wine in the province at 320 livres a cask; in small quantities four reaux for red, and three for white wine; brandy four livres, and vinegar four reaux a pot.[3] The next year the retail price for brandy, red and white wine was three livres, thirty sols and twenty sols a pot, respectively.[4]

On May 24, 1717, because of the disorder in the province caused by the selling of brandy to the Indians and slaves, an ordinance was issued making it an offense punishable by a fine of fifty livres to make such sales; half of the money thus derived to go to the church, the remainder to the hospital.[5] In 1719 the Company made the rates just quoted the legal prices for the province.[6] The act, however, did little to bring stability to the trade in such commodities. The Company, itself, made a change in 1721, when it made the selling price of wine and brandy at Mobile 120 livres a cask.[7] At New Orleans, the next year, brandy was retailed at fifty sols a pot and in 1724 at one piastre, and

[1] *A. N., C., Sér.* C^{13}, vol. i, fols. 500-501.

[2] *Ibid., Sér.* F^{3}, vol. ccxli, May 13, 1713.

[3] *Ibid., Sér.* C^{13}, vol. iii, fols. 216-223; vol. v, fols. 332, 336.

[4] *Ibid.,* vol. vi, fol. 421.

[5] *Ibid., Sér.* F^{3}, vol. ccxli, May 24, 1717.

[6] *Ibid., Sér.* C^{13}, vol. v, fols. 332, 336.

[7] *Ibid.,* vol. viii, fols. 88, 90.

wine at the same price.[1] By the end of 1726 wine was down to twenty sols a pot and brandy to three livres, five sols.[2] On October 5th, the superior council enacted the first of a series of laws aimed at the regulation of the liquor traffic. This act provided for the closing of all dram-shops on Sunday while church was in progress.[3] On March 29, 1727, another was passed making the selling of intoxicants to slaves illegal. Moreover they were not to be given it to carry to their masters unless they presented to the innkeeper a written order from their masters so to do. The law was not well enforced.[4] The council on May 7, 1728, fixed the legal measures as follows: 110 pots for a hogshead of red wine, "guildive" and vinegar; 100 pots of white wine for a hogshead; 150 pots for a hogshead of brandy; and fifty pots for a "quart" of brandy, and red and white wine; twenty-three pots for an "ancre" of brandy.[5]

The transfer of the province to the crown had no beneficial effects upon the liquor traffic. In May, 1732, wine sold in New Orleans at 120 livres a cask, and by July had advanced to 150 and even 200 livres. At the same time it was retailed at thirty sols a pot and brandy at from forty to fifty sols.[6] At the beginning of the next year wine sold at ten livres, brandy at twenty-seven livres and "guildive" at four and five livres a pot. These excellent prices brought about a considerable increase in the number of dram-shops and taverns in New Orleans, where the consumption of liquor of all kinds was large. On December

[1] *A. N., C., Sér.* C^{13}, vol. viii, pp. 90-91,, 290-291, 336-337.

[2] *Ibid.*, vol. ix, fol. 253.

[3] *Ibid., Sér. A*, vol. xxiii, Oct. 5, 1726.

[4] *Ibid.*, March 29, 1727.

[5] *Ibid., Sér.* F^3, vol. ccxli, May 7, 1728.

[6] *Ibid., Sér.* C^{13}, vol. xv, fols. 115, 173.

19, 1733, the "ordonnateur" put forth an ordinance aiming at the suppression of the disorder arising from drunkenness, by making it illegal for any one, under penalty of a fine of fifty livres and confiscation of the liquor in his possession, to sell either wine, brandy or other liquors by the pint, pot or cup without first having secured from his office a license permitting such sales. The ordinance was to go into effect three days after its publication.[1] Moreover, the governor and "ordonnateur" were both of the opinion that the prices for liquors should be reduced one-half, thereby bringing them about to the same as they were at the time of the retrocession. Whether the decrease was made officially is not evident. At any rate wine, in 1734, sold at 120 and 200 livres a cask and brandy at thirty-five, forty and fifty sols a pot. By October good white wine at the capital had advanced to 320 livres a cask, red to 480 livres and brandy at the same time had dropped to thirty sols.[2] In December a further shifting of prices took place. Wine now sold at 150 and 200 livres a cask and brandy at thirty, thirty-five and forty livres an "ancre" (sixteen pots).[3] This year the "ordonnateur" took another step toward placing the liquor business under some restraint. His ordinance made it an offense for any one to sell liquor to the Indians. The law was so poorly enforced that it was practically of no value.[4] In 1735 wine at New Orleans brought 600 livres a cask and brandy thirty-five livres a pot.[5] The "ordonnateur", December 7, 1736, made a further attempt to prevent liquor from being sold to the slaves. To this

[1] *A. N., C., Sér. A*, vol. xxiii, Dec. 19, 1733.

[2] *Ibid., Sér.* C^{13}, vol. xviii, fols. 95-97; vol. xix, fols. 104-105, 151.

[3] *Ibid.*, vol. xix, fols. 106-107.

[4] *Ibid., Sér. A*, vol. xxiii, Oct. 14, 1734.

[5] *Ibid., Sér.* C^{13}, vol. xx, fols. 106-107.

end he issued an ordinance making it illegal to sell it to them without direct permission from their masters.[1] Again the lack of its enforcement defeated the purpose of the law.

Wine, in 1740, was selling at 200 [2] livres, but the next year the price advanced to 500 if paid in Spanish silver, and 800 livres if in colonial paper.[3] In September it was down to 350 and 400 livres a cask. Notwithstanding the law of 1733,[4] prices so attractive caused much secret selling by unlicensed shops. In such places, in 1744, whiskey was sold at a pistole, brandy at three livres, ten sols, and rum and wine at fifty sols a bottle. Public disorder in New Orleans increased in direct proportion to the amount of liquor used.[5]

Governor Vaudreuil and the " ordonnateur ", August 19, 1746, made another attempt to do away with some of the drunkenness at the capital by suppressing all unlicensed drinking places. In the hope of accomplishing this work they demanded all keepers of dram-shops to have from the " ordonnateur " a permit to sell liquor.[6] The police of the village, however, found great difficulty in enforcing the law. In 1751 only six shops in New Orleans were licensed by the government. These proprietors were permitted to sell drinks only in moderation to " voyageurs ", sick persons, settlers and sailors. They were forbidden absolutely to sell it to the soldiers and negroes. For the privilege they were each to pay 200 livres yearly to the government and an additional 100 livres to be used in taking care of the

[1] *A. N., C., Sér. A*, vol. xxiii, Dec. 7, 1736.

[2] *Ibid., Sér. C*[13], vol. xxv, fol. 264.

[3] *Ibid.*, vol. xxvi, fols. 165-166, 185.

[4] *Supra*, pp. 274-275.

[5] *The Present State of the Country, etc.*, p. 14.

[6] *A. N., C., Sér. A*, vol. xxiii, Aug. 19, 1746.

poor of the village. These drinking places were to close daily at nine in the evening, after which hour no one was to be allowed to enter. Moreover, on penalty of a fine and annulment of the license for any violation of this part of the law, they were to close the shops on fête days and on Sundays during divine services.[1]

The soldiers were to receive liquor at two canteens, provided especially for them by the officials. At these places no civilians were to be allowed to buy. Violations were to be punished by a fine of ten écus and confiscation of all liquor and a stay in the pillory, the length of time being fixed by the officials; the second by a life sentence to the galleys.[2] Had the law been rigorously enforced it seems that the punishment was severe enough to do away with the illicit trade entirely. Such, however, was not the case. At this time some farmers of the province left their farms in order to engage in an illicit business in and about New Orleans. Here they dispensed liquor secretly, selling it even to slaves. The officials called upon the better class of settlers to help them in the suppression of the evil. The offenders were given eight days, counting from the date of the publication of the ordinance, in which to return to their farms, after which time if they were still in New Orleans they were to be treated as vagabonds and driven from the village.[3]

In 1752 the quantity of "guildive" that was disposed of at the canteens had become so excessive that it was ruining many of the soldiers by making them dangerous maniacs.[4] Wine at this time was selling at 400 livres a cask.[5] During

[1] *A. N., C., Sér. C*[13], vol. xxxv, fols. 41-43.

[2] *Ibid.*

[3] *Ibid.*

[4] *Ibid.*, vol. xxxvi, fols. 228, 267.

[5] *Ibid.*, vol. xxxvi, fol. 334.

the war it seems to have advanced in price gradually until in 1762 it was 3,500 livres a cask.[1]

As early as 1722 both New Orleans and Mobile had large wooden shops that would not "ornament a village of France".[2] In 1726 Governor Périer established in the former a general merchandise store and placed d'Anville in charge. The latter's commission was fixed at six deniers a livre on all sales. He was to keep in this shop all sorts of goods, excepting, however, flour, wine, brandy, coffee, shirts, shoes, soap, limbourg and other articles that usually were scarce. The project had the approval of the people who believed it would be a decided advantage to the community.[3] By 1729 the capital had shops not under government control, in which was carried merchandise similar to that just mentioned. The proprietors of these stores proposed to the director of the Company to give them annually a larger supply of merchandise and to agree to allow them to return the part they could not dispose of. They further requested the Company to advance them at once merchandise to the amount of 20,000 livres. The proposition was accepted because, it was declared, it involved small risk and the possibility of bringing to the Company very large profits.[4] Little is to be learned of the manner in which the private shops carried on business, except that they charged excessive prices for everything. The next year they were pronounced by the "ordonnateur" as detrimental to the province because of the high rate they demanded for their goods.[5]

[1] *A. N., C., Sér.* C^{13}, vol. xliii, fol. 122.

[2] Charlevoix, *A Voyage to North America,* vol. ii, p. 207.

[3] *A. N., C., Sér.* C^{13}, vol. ix, fol. 252.

[4] *Ibid.*, vol. ix, fol. 361.

[5] *Ibid.*, vol. vii, fol. 49.

On April 25, 1719, the Company fixed the price of powder at fifteen sols a horn, copper candlesticks at four livres a pound and bullets at eight sols a pound.[1] At quite an early date there were some shoemakers in the province who made "galoshes", but nothing is given as to the price they brought when sold.[2] In 1723 imported shoes cost in New Orleans forty livres,[3] in 1733, thirty and thirty-five,[4] and 1762, forty-five livres a pair.[5] Gold trimmings and velvet, by 1727, were commonly used at the capital where, it was asserted, they cost three times as much as at Rouen.[6] All kinds of wearing apparel were always expensive in Louisiana.[7] In 1762 they sold at New Orleans as follows: an ell of cloth for a man's coat, 250 livres; with a lining of silk, 150 livres additional; a beaver hat 400 livres, with a band of gold 250 livres extra; a hat half beaver, 250 livres; a pair of silk stockings, 150 livres; a purse, twenty-five livres; an ell of cloth for a shirt, sixty livres; the same amount of batiste, 120 livres; and of muslin, 200 livres; powder for the face and hair, fifteen livres a pound.[8] Imported soap, in 1762, sold at twenty-five livres a pound, while at the same time the domestic article brought from two to six livres a brick.[9]

Lower Louisiana received salt from France and also from the Illinois country. It was sold at the private shops and by the government officials; for example, Crozat's

[1] *Ordonnance de la Compagnie d'Occident*, 1719, N. Y. Pub. Lib.

[2] *A., M. des C., Sér. G*^{1}, vol. 464.

[3] *A. N., C., Sér. C*^{13}, vol. vii, fol. 16.

[4] *Ibid.*, vol. xvi, fols. 166-177.

[5] *Ibid.*, vol. xliii, fol. 122.

[6] Gravier, p. 30.

[7] *A. N., C., Sér. C*^{13}, vol. xxxvi, fols. 229, 269-270.

[8] *Ibid.*, vol. xliii, fol. 121.

[9] *Ibid.*

agents demanded two sols a pound for it from civilians and eighteen deniers from the soldiers.[1] There was often a shortage in the supply for this part of the province, due to some extent to the fact that much of it deliquesced before it could be consumed because of the excessive amount of moisture in the air. In 1719 the Cadodaquian Indians provided the French with 200 pounds.[2] The commodity, in 1723, sold at New Orleans at sixty sols a pound.[3] When the superior council in 1728 standardized the weights and measures of the province, it fixed that of salt at 500 pounds to the hogshead.[4] In 1731 the settlers on the Gulf coast were entirely without salt;[5] in 1759 a cargo of 250 hogsheads arrived at the capital where it brought twenty deniers a pound.[6] Rochemore, seeing in this transaction a chance for big profits for himself, demanded the whole amount of the supply for the government. Later, however, all but fifty hogsheads of it was retailed at six sols, three deniers a pound to the civilian population.[7] Of the trade in other groceries very little is said. In 1728 the weight for sugar was made 500 pounds to a hogshead, 200 to a "quart", and for molasses at 110 pots to a case.[8] In 1762 sugar was selling for five livres, and coffee at seven livres, ten sols a pound.[9]

A banquet given in honor of Governor Kerlérec on his arrival in 1752 affords some idea of what the shops and

[1] *A. N., C., Sér.* C^{13}, vol. v, fol. 33.

[2] *Ibid.*, vol. ii, fol. 248; vol. xxv, fol. 4; Margry, vol. vi, p. 272.

[3] *A. N., C., Sér.* C^{13}, vol. vii, fol. 20.

[4] *Ibid., Sér.* F^3, vol. ccxli, M. S. S. M., May 7, 1728.

[5] *Ibid., Sér.* C^{13}, vol. xiii, fol. 145.

[6] *Ibid., Sér.* F^3, vol. xxv, fols. 101-105.

[7] *Ibid.*

[8] *Ibid.*, vol. ccxli, M. S. S. M., May 7, 1728.

[9] *Ibid., Sér.* C^{13}, vol. xliii, fol. 122.

markets of the capital had to sell. The governor asserts there were 200 persons present, of whom half were most richly dressed women. The hall and tables were elaborately decorated; and from the latter he partook of delicious meats, vegetables and fruits. The whole affair, it was claimed, would have done honor to such an entertainment in the wealthiest cities of Europe.[1]

The drug supply for the province came from France and at first was given out from the government storehouse. In July, 1732, the "ordonnateur" made a bargain with the apothecary at the hospital in New Orleans to supply medicine to the sick at two sols, six deniers a person. The hospital physician was authorized to send to the home government a report of the drugs given out, with the price according to the list it had furnished.[2] Up to 1734 the amount thus furnished cost the crown annually 2,400 livres.[3] In 1738 drugs were very scarce at New Orleans and therefore expensive, due in part to the fact that in some instances the supply asked for had been reduced more than half; for example, quinine was cut from sixty-five to thirty pounds, while from the same list sal ammoniac, antimony and diaphragmatic was omitted entirely. Quinine, rhubarb and spirits of wine sold at nine livres, ten sols a pound, fifty livres a pound, and three livres a pint, respectively. These prices were declared to be a third higher than they should be. Sarsaparilla was thirteen to fifteen sols a pound.[4] Governor Vaudreuil, during his term of office, had a third interest in all the trade that was carried on between New Orleans and other posts of

[1] Villiers du Terrage, p. 46.

[2] *A. N., C., Sér.* C^{13}, vol. xv, fols. 164-165.

[3] *Ibid.*, vol. xix, fols. 25-29.

[4] *Ibid.*, vol. xxiii, fols. 119-120; Le Page du Pratz, vol. iii, p. 391.

the province. At the capital he converted one room of his dwelling into a store where every sort of drug was sold. The house steward usually attended to the trade but in his absence Madame Vaudreuil, herself, did the selling. She, it was declared, was a very clever business woman, being able to force other merchants to buy goods from her husband at prices fixed by herself. The governor made no objection to the trade since it brought handsome profits into his coffers.[1]

Trade in live stock in lower Louisiana was sporadic. Horses were bought either from the Spaniards or from the Indians and were paid for in merchandise.[2] In 1733 the crown gave 800 livres for fourteen horses that belonged to the Company.[3] Fine geldings sold at New Orleans in 1737 for thirty livres each, 250 being brought hither from Natchitoches.[4] Horses owned by the Jesuits sold in 1763 at from ninety livres for a single animal to 455 for a mare and gray colt.[5]

The cattle that Iberville brought with him to the Gulf coast in 1699 cost him in the French islands eighty livres a

[1] Gayarré, *Histoire de la Louisiane*, vol. ii, p. 54.

[2] Margry, vol. vi, p. 280.

[3] *A. N., C., Sér.* C^{13}, vol. xvi, fol. 100.

[4] Dumont, vol. i, p. 81.

[5] *A. N., C., Sér.* C^{13}, vol. xliii, fols. 315-351.

Value of horses in livres:

Young	Old	Drove of 10
90 (bay)	135	2400
90 (bay mare)	205	
100 (gray)	480 (wheeler)	
225 (colt)		
435 (gray mare and colt)		
455 (mare and gray colt)		
1395	820	2400

Totals, 21 head brought 4,615 livres.

head.[1] Such animals, in 1713, sold at Mobile at thirty and forty piastres each.[2] By 1725 the price of cattle had advanced to 500 and 600 livres a head.[3] A pair of oxen with their harness sold in lower Louisiana in 1749 at 300 livres, while at the same time cows brought only sixty livres each.[4] No further sales seem to have been recorded until 1763, when the Jesuits' herd was sold at public auction.[5]

[1] *A. N., C., Sér.* C^{13}, vol. i, fols. 185-195.

[2] *Ibid.*, vol. iii, fols. 245-248.

[3] *Ibid.*, vol. vii, fol. 19.

[4] *Ibid.*, vol. xxxiii, fols. 196-200.

[5] *Ibid.*, vol. xliii, fols. 315-351.

Value of cattle in livres are as follows:

Cow and calf	Heifers	Cows	Young bulls	Oxen in pairs	Heifer and bull	Pair oxen yoked to cart	Pair oxen yoked to plow
240	70	80	100	730	205	530	570
245	115	80	115	800	275	885	
250	145	130	120	900	280	930	
250	150	180	130	900			
255	170	230	135	960		Pair oxen and	
260	175	240	135	980		two carts	
265	180	250	150			900	
265	195	250	230				
280	200	250	270				
315	210	280					
315	250	285	Big bull				
350	260	290	200				
350	305						
355	305						
355	340						
365							
370							
375							
375							
375							
375							
375							
375							
380							
390							
8105	3070	2545	1585	5270	760	3245	570

Bunch of 27 oxen, 1200 livres; 51 cows, 12500 livres; 24 calves, 2400 livres.

Totals: 217 head of cattle brought 52,050 livres.

Iberville also brought to Louisiana, in 1699, some hogs for which he paid forty livres each.[1] In 1713 they were selling in the province at twelve reaux each, and sheep at four reaux a head.[2] At the Jesuit sale, in 1763, the former sold as follows: barrows, fifty-six livres each; a sow 130 livres; a sow and barrow, 150 livres.[3] Sheep sold at the same sale in lots of six at from 150 to 245 livres and a flock of seventy for 3,000 livres.[4]

Trade in lumber was considerable. In lower Louisiana, in 1716, there were two saw mills. Cedar boards, 20 ft. by 1 ft. by 2 in., sold at six livres each; those 10 ft. by 10 in. by 1 in., at 100 livres a hundred feet; and other varieties at sixty livres; oak boards, 15 to 20 feet long by 3 ft. by 1 in., at two sols, six deniers a foot; large pieces of building lumber at three livres a cubic foot; and that suited to boat building at two sols, six deniers a foot.[5] 1,010 feet of cypress building material sold in 1723 at five sols a foot; 408 planks at twenty sols each; 1,150 feet of bark for covering houses at thirteen livres, thirteen sols, eleven deniers a hundred feet; shingles at 100 sols a thousand; and laths, hand turned, at the same price.[6] Siding was selling at New Orleans, in 1726, at twenty livres a thousand; planks at fifty livres; and oars, five sols each. The Company considered these prices very exorbitant.[7] The next year the manager of a mill located on Bienville's land

[1] *A. N., C., Sér.* C^{13}, vol. i, fols. 185-195.

[2] *Ibid.*, vol. iii, fols. 245-248.

[3] *Ibid.*, vol. xliii, fols. 315-351.

[4] *Ibid.*

Value in livres of nine different bunches of six each: 150, 160, 200, 205, 210, 210, 220, 230, 245. Totals: 124 head brought 4,830 livres.

[5] *Ibid.*, vol. iv, fols. 389-398.

[6] *Ibid.*, vol. vii, fols. 178-181.

[7] *Ibid.*, vol. ix, fol. 242.

contracted to saw 2,500 pieces of lumber, 10 ft. by 8 or 10 in. by 1½ in., for a church at fifty livres a hundred.[1] The producing of lumber went on much the same after as before Louisiana became a royal province. In 1736 joists were selling at the capital at three livres a foot; planks at one sol, six deniers.[2] By 1739 lumber for building purposes had trebled in price since 1731. What had sold at forty livres a hundred at the earlier date at the latter brought 120 livres.[3] The higher prices did not continue, however, for in 1747 lumber was down to six sols a foot.[4] Above New Orleans, in 1752, large quantities of it were sawed and floated down stream to that market.[5] The output for 1754 was worth 180,000 livres.[6] In a community where wood for fuel was so plentiful as in Louisiana one would not expect to find a large trade in cord wood, yet there was some sale for it. In 1757 it sold on the wharf at New Orleans at fifteen livres a cord.[7] In 1763 twenty cords brought at a public sale 200 livres and ten more, seventy-five livres; that is, ten livres and seven livres, ten sols a cord, respectively.[8]

Very soon the people of lower Louisiana began making brick, because, for certain purposes, due to the dampness of the climate, lumber was not serviceable. Brick 12 by 8 by 2 sold at New Orleans, in 1729, at thirty and thirty-five livres a thousand for the export trade and to the settlers at twenty livres. At the brick yards, pottery, floor and roof

[1] *A. N., C., Sér.* C^{13}, vol. xi, fol. 37.

[2] *Ibid.*, vol. xxi, fol. 115.

[3] *Ibid.*, vol. xxiv, fol. 178.

[4] *Ibid.*, vol. xxxi, fol. 189.

[5] Bossu, vol. i, p. 35.

[6] *A. N., C., Sér.* C^{13}, vol. xxxviii, fol. 265.

[7] Villiers du Terrage, p. 80.

[8] *A. N., C., Sér.* C^{13}, vol. xliii, fols. 315-351.

tiles also were made, the latter selling at sixty livres a thousand.[1] In 1732 the price for brick was fifteen livres a thousand, but the cost of delivery brought it down to about nine livres, ten sols for the producer.[2] 20,720 brick for two chimneys and the foundation of a house in New Orleans cost the purchaser, in 1733, ten livres a thousand.[3] In 1746 the price was from seven livres, ten sols to ten livres a thousand. At such prices large quantities were put upon the market.[4] In 1763 the Jesuits sold at auction 97,000 brick. The price ranged from twenty-six livres, thirteen sols, four deniers to fifty-two livres, ten sols a thousand.[5]

[1] *A. N., C., Sér.* C^{13}, vol. xi, fols. 362-363.

[2] *Ibid.*, vol. xiv, fol. 142.

[3] *Ibid.*, vol. xvii, fols. 192-195.

[4] *Ibid.*, vol. xxx, fol. 276.

[5] *Ibid.*, vol. xliii, fols. 315-351.

Number in lot.	Cost of lot in livres.	Cost per 1000 liv.	sols.	den.
6000	250	41	13	4
6000	250	41	13	4
6000	255	42	15	0
6000	260	43	6	8
6000	260	43	6	8
6000	270	45	0	0
6000	275	45	16	8
6000	280	46	13	4
6000	280	46	13	4
6000	300	50	0	0
6000	300	50	0	0
6000	300	50	0	0
6000	305	50	16	4
6000	315	52	10	0
4000	200	50	0	0
3000	105	35	0	0
3000	90	30	0	0
3000	80	26	13	4
97000	4375			

Lime in this part of the province was scarce. In 1733 it retailed at the capital at ten sols and twelve sols, eight deniers a pound.[1] For use in building fortifications, the officials the next year bought 2,139 barrels, paying for it thirty sols a barrel, two deniers a pound.[2] Prices for building materials, such as nails, tacks, hinges and shutter hooks were, in 1733, ten sols a pound, one livre a pound, five livres, ten sols a pair, and four livres a pound, respectively.[3]

The sparseness of settlement and the great areas of idle land in all parts of the province made the traffic in real estate small. Nevertheless there were some such transfers. As early as 1717 a house at Natchez was valued at fifty livres, and in 1719 at 1,000 livres.[4] At this same settlement, in 1721, a large, well-equipped plantation sold at 50,000 livres.[5] Then, too, many Germans bought from former owners part or all of the land they owned above New Orleans. In the instances where prices are quoted, the land sold at 105 livres and sixty-two livres, ten sols an arpent.[6] There were still other such exchanges. The Jesuits, in 1726, for example, purchased from Bienville land adjoining their property and in 1751 the Ursuline order bought a plot of ground that lay next to its establishment. The amount given in these exchanges is not stated.[7]

[1] *A. N., C., Sér.* C^{13}, vol. xvii, fols. 192-195.

[2] *Ibid.*, vol. xviii, fols. 89-90.

[3] *Ibid.*, vol. xvii, fols. 192-195.

[4] *A., B. de l'Arsenal,* vol. 4497, fol. 55.

[5] *A., M. des C., Sér.* G^1, vol. 464.

[6] *Ibid.*

[7] *A. N., C., Sér.* C^{13}, vol. xxxv, fols. 5-6.

CHAPTER XVII

The Trade of the Illinois Country

THE French colony on the Gulf coast had scarcely been planted when "voyageurs" from the Illinois country arrived with their boats loaded with peltry.[1] At first the trade consisted only of skins. The traffic soon was extended to other things and in a short time all sorts of products were being carried down the Mississippi to the Gulf coast market. The Jesuits at an early date introduced the growing of wheat into the Illinois country. By 1721 that part of the province was producing a fine grade of it, which commodity had put the French in that region "pretty much at their ease".[2] As yet, however, there was not enough home-grown wheat to furnish Louisiana with all that was needed.[3]

Convoys of boats in 1721 went from the Illinois country to New Orleans loaded with all sorts of products. The wheat of the cargo, it was asserted, was of a very fine quality. Bienville, in fact, ordered the posts along the Mississippi to give all possible protection to the freight convoys from the Illinois and to furnish them with needful supplies.[4] Up to this time the Company of the Indies had sent to the Illinois French merchandise to the amount of 25,000 pounds annually. While there was some tendency on the part of the traders, there, to make the journey

[1] Margry, vol. iv, p. 364.

[2] Charlevoix, *A Voyage to North America,* vol. ii, p. 166.

[3] *A. N., C., Sér.* C^{13}, vol. vi, fol. 332.

[4] *Hist. Coll. of La.,* pt. 3, pp. 105-106.

to New Orleans themselves for the goods they desired, the officials believed it was not wise to encourage them in the practice since their time could be employed more profitably otherwise.[1] In August, 1725, however, two convoys, one from the Illinois and the other from Natchitoches arrived at New Orleans. Henceforward it became a regular occurrence for men at those posts to send to the capital their annual shipments of products.[2] In 1729 the Illinois country had a fine harvest. It began to be asserted that as soon as that part of Louisiana had become well established and free from Indian turmoil, it would be able to furnish flour and salt meat sufficient in quantity to supply the whole colony. This belief was strengthened by the large quantities of both of these products then being brought to New Orleans from the Illinois country.[3]

By 1732 there was a well-established trade between the Illinois country and Louisiana proper. The convoy that was expected at the capital about March did not arrive until May, thereby causing a shortage of provisions. This year it was composed of from twenty-five to thirty boats on which the farmers had shipped, at their own risk, products amounting in all to about 2,000 quintals of flour, 120 of lard, 200 quintals of beef and 160 of tallow, 600 or 700 hams, and 6,000 pots of bear's oil. In order to avoid a double shipment, when provisioning the posts between the Illinois country and New Orleans, the "ordonnateur" directed the several commandants to take from the convoy as it passed what flour and salt meat they needed for the year's subsistence.[4]

[1] *A. N., C., Sér.* C^{13}, vol. ix, fol. 240.

[2] *Hist. Coll. of La.*, pt. 3, p. 110.

[3] *A. N., C., Sér.* C^{13}, vol. xii, fols. 15-16, 19.

[4] *Ibid.*, vol. xv, fols. 133-136.

In compliance with the order just mentioned the commandant at Natchez secured 548 quintals of flour, fifty-five of lard, 200 of beef and 255 pots of bear's oil. The commandant at the posts at the Arkansas, the Tonicas and Pointe Coupée secured enough food for six or seven months, viz., at the Arkansas, sixteen quintals of flour; at the Tonicas and Point Coupée, each, thirty quintals, making a total for the four posts of 624 quintals. The remainder of the produce was sold at New Orleans, the officials buying 125 quintals of flour for the royal storehouse, making in all 749 quintals purchased by the government. Of this amount 340 quintals were of the better grade, " mieur blutee (*sic*)", and sold at twelve livres, ten sols a quintal; 409 of a poorer quality cost but eleven livres. These prices did not suit the shippers, who the year before had received twenty-five livres for such flour.

In explanation the officials stated that the difference was apparent rather than real and was due entirely to a change in the paper money of the province. The remainder of the shipment was sold to the merchants of New Orleans, where flour from the Illinois never sold as well as the French commodity, since even the best grades of the former flour would produce only an equal weight of bread, hence could not be mixed advantageously with rice in making it. The supply of provisions sent to New Orleans from the Illinois country in 1732 indeed was so considerable that the officials informed the crown that, if it were kept up every year flour shipments from France might well be discontinued. It was further asserted that it was not wise to make any reduction even, because that part of the province was still disturbed by Indian wars.[1]

Notwithstanding Indian hostilities, the output of the

[1] *A. N., C., Sér.* C^{13}, vol. xv, fols. 133-136.

products of the Illinois country increased annually. In 1733 the convoy reached New Orleans on May 10, six weeks later than usual. On the way down the river it left 6,000 quintals of flour at the Arkansas and 32,120 pounds at Natchez for the respective garrisons. The past season had been hard on the Illinois crops; half the grain that matured was swept away by storm before it could be harvested. Therefore after the posts had received an allowance there was not a large supply left for New Orleans.[1]

Lower Louisiana secured quantities of foodstuffs from the Illinois country in 1734. The " voyageurs ", too, were making yearly trips to New Orleans for a supply of merchandise.[2] By July of the following year two convoys had reached the capital. One of these consisted of twelve boats and carried 1,500 quintals of flour, some peltry and 200 hams.[3] Prices in the Illinois country at the time were as follows: flour, two sols a pound; hams, four livres, each; bear's oil, forty sols a pot; frogs, two livres each; tobacco, two livres a pound; brandy, five livres a pot; and salt, fourteen livres a minot (70 pounds).[4]

In 1736 the harvest in the upper part of the Mississippi valley was light.[5] That of 1737 brought forth an abundance of every thing, therefore the consignments the next winter were correspondingly large. The first shipment, containing 100,000 pounds of flour alone, reached New Orleans in April, 1738. It was carried thither by a convoy, part of the boats composing it belonging to the government, the remainder to private persons. The second, comprising

[1] *A. N., C., Sér.* C^{13}, fols. 166-168; vol. xvii, fol. 147.

[2] *Ibid.,* vol. xix, fols. 18-20, 25-29, 69-70.

[3] *Ibid.,* vol. xx, fols. 238-239; *Sér. B,* lxiii, fol. 608.

[4] *Ibid., Sér.* C^{13}, vol. xx, fols. 250-251.

[5] *Ibid.,* vol. xxi, fol. 260; vol. xxii, fol. 121.

between 50,000 and 60,000 pounds of flour and many other commodities arrived in May. The men in charge of the convoy brought the news that a third shipment was en route. Its consignment of flour brought the amount supplied to New Orleans that year up to 300,000 pounds.[1]

In 1738 the crops of the Illinois country were poor. Yet before the end of the year 1739, 300,000 pounds of flour, of which 12,000 pounds came from the Illinois and 17,000 from the Wabash, were used in provisioning the troops engaged in a war against the Chickasaw.[2] Some "voyageurs" who carried flour to New Orleans in 1739 received for it twenty-two livres a quintal.[3] In 1740 lower Louisiana received from the Illinois country 6,000 quintals of flour;[4] in the following year 125,000 pounds more flour and large quantities of peltry.[5] In 1742 the "ordonnateur" instructed the government convoy to bring to New Orleans oak lumber from the Illinois. In June it had not reached the capital and it is not stated whether the order ever was carried out. At any rate no such trade developed.[6]

The harvest in 1745 in the upper district of the province was not good. The convoys were dispatched as usual but no statement is made concerning the shipments.[7] In April, 1746, a convoy of "voyageurs" arrived at New Orleans with cargoes of flour amounting to 100,000 pounds which put the colony beyond immediate want.[8] In Septem-

[1] *A. N., C., Sér.* C^{13}, vol. xxiii, fols. 48-51, 77-81.

[2] *Ibid.*, vol. xxiv, fols. 3-7, 128; *Journal of the Chickasaw War, etc.*, p. 80.

[3] *A. N., C., Sér.* C^{13}, vol. xxiv, fol. 128.

[4] *Ibid.*, vol. xxv, fol. 22; vol. xxiv, fols. 3-7.

[5] *Ibid.*, vol. xxvi, fol. 97.

[6] *Ibid.*, vol. xxvii, fols. 37, 113.

[7] *Ibid.*, vol. xxix, fol. 89.

[8] *Ibid.*, vol. xxx, fol. 57; Pownall, App., p. 25.

ber the government convoy reached the capital with another consignment of flour, and the news that the growing crops were very promising when it left the Illinois.[1] Although the prospects for large consignments of produce from the upper part of the Mississippi valley in the ensuing year were flattering, the outlook for the whole province was not happy. The output of colonial flour as yet, was not equal to the amount consumed and the English war, practically, had shut off the annual supply from France.[2]

The convoys from the Illinois country carried to the Gulf settlements, in 1748, 800,000 pounds of flour alone.[3] Besides the flour the cargoes were made up of corn, bacon, hams from the bear as well as the hog, salt pork, buffalo meat, tallow, hides, tobacco, lead, copper, small quantities of buffalo wool, venison, bear's oil, tongues, poultry and peltry, chiefly, however, the loads were made up of pork and flour.[4] The government convoys carried up the Mississippi consignments of brandy, cloth, made clothing and other European goods. They left New Orleans usually some time in August. In 1748 the first convoy set out up stream early in July. Notwithstanding the gain in time in starting there was a great shortage in all kinds of foodstuffs before it returned with supplies from the Illinois country.[5]

During the continuance of the war, to bring down the Mississippi at flood time the entire output of bear's oil, tallow, salt beef, tongues, hams, peltry, lead and other produce of the region required only twenty-five or thirty

[1] *A. N., C., Sér.* C^{13}, vol. xxx, fols. 71, 110-112, 144.

[2] *Ibid.*, vol. xxxi, fol. 72.

[3] Le Page du Pratz, vol. i, p. 331.

[4] *A. N., C., Sér.* C^{13}, vol. xxxii, fols. 63, 113-121, 196-197.

[5] *Ibid.*, fols. 24-25; vol. xxxiii, fol. 168.

men. To return, including the escort carried along to give protection from Indian attacks, 150 to 200 men were needed.[1] In 1749 New Orleans received from the Illinois country a large consignment of flour and of peltry. The governor was of the opinion that the former commodity could be augmented considerably. To this end it was proposed to increase the number engaged in agriculture by men drawn from the Gulf coast settlements and from New France; to improve, also, the methods of production employed by the farmers and millers, and the manner in which the latter prepared the flour for shipment. Heretofore it had been sent to New Orleans in skin or cloth bags, much of it being damaged by water en route.[2] No plans were ever formulated by the colonial officials to carry out systematically any part of the above proposal. In 1750 the last of the annual convoys reached New Orleans in July. How many there were or what were their size and composition is not stated.[3] The crops this year were very short, therefore the consignments to New Orleans the next year were smaller than they had been for some time.[4] Flour at the time sold there at eighty and one hundred livres a quintal.[5]

By this time the abuses in the trade carried on between New Orleans and the Illinois country, it was declared by the "ordonnateur", had become intolerable. A man who had received his appointment as a gratuity from the governor, the usual practice, was in command of the government convoy. In making up the cargoes for the voyage his own merchandise took first place, that of private persons

[1] *A. N., C., Sér. C13*, vol. xxxii, fol. 116; vol. xxxiii, fol. 168; *Jes. Rel.*, vol. lxix, pp. 147, 213.

[2] *A. N., C., Sér. C13* vol. xxxiii, fols. 57, 152, 153.

[3] *Ibid.*, vol. xxxiv, fcl. 321.

[4] *Ibid.*, vol. xxxv, fols. 24, 195.

[5] *A., B. N.*, Joly Coll., vol. 1726, fol. 119.

second, and lastly that of the crown, if there still remained space for it. Frequently it happened that the "ordonnateur" was obliged to add a boat and more men in order to have the royal freight carried along, the commander being interested, naturally, in the merchandise from which he would derive extra profits. The arrival of the convoy was announced at each post in advance in order to give time to get ready for a trade with the captain when he reached the particular post. The government consignment was put on sale, and part of the profits found their way into the pockets of the commander. In 1748 the captain had been well supplied with provisions for the entire trip before he left New Orleans. At Pointe Coupée, on the way up the river, he purchased further supplies amounting to 1,150 livres; during the voyage he incurred a bill of 1,200 livres for his daily supply of game [1] and an additional bill of 2,000 livres for other foodstuffs.[2]

In 1749 the convoy under the same commander left New Orleans in August; in January, 1750, it had not reached the Illinois country and it was feared it would not do so before the river was blocked by ice. Because of the length of time taken to make the voyage the "ordonnateur" prophesied that the receipts would show a great leakage in the liquor he had placed on board. His belief was based on the fact that the previous year the government liquor consignment on delivery in the Illinois country was considerably less than the amount shown in the bill of lading. The "ordonnateur" learned, from what he considered good authority, that the commander and crew were drunk during the entire journey. At each of the posts en route the commander drank and caroused indiscriminately with soldiers

[1] *Supra*, p. 259.

[2] *A. N., C., Sér. C*[13], vol. xxxiv, fols. 291-296.

and civilians. It was further asserted that there was not a day that he did not lose his reason from the effects of the "guildive" he had consumed. From the beginning to the end of the voyage the government was "pillaged and robbed". Each year the expense for the convoy had increased. Michel, however, was unable to find any one better with whom to replace this commander, or to find a way to punish him for his business irregularities, due to the fact that almost every one in New Orleans was interested in him, some member of his crew, or in one of the private consignments, hence would not tolerate his prosecution.[1]

The next year the governor informed the crown that ever since the coming of Michel he had heard complaints about irregularities in the shipments of supplies to the Illinois country. He further asserted that he had heard them at no time except from the "ordonnateur" himself, a statement that was perhaps true. Notwithstanding his one source of information, the governor endeavored to find ways and means to decrease the expense of the convoys. For the coming year he proposed to offer the contract to the general public and to let it to the lowest bidder. He had small hope that anyone would be found to do the work for less than it had been done. In the first place there were very few men in the province in a position to undertake the risk. In the second place such service in Louisiana had always been expensive. The governor was of the opinion the price demanded was not excessive, since laborers were scarce and wages high. Moreover, it was difficult, at any price, to secure crews for the government boats which were large, requiring at least twenty-four men each. The efforts of the governor resulted as he had predicted; apparently, therefore, the matter seems to have been dropped.[2]

[1] *A. N., C., Sér. C^{13}*, vol. xxiv, fols. 291-296.

[2] *Ibid.*, vol. xxxv, fols. 8-12.

In 1752 the annual shipment from the Illinois country to New Orleans were unusually large. The posts en route, even including that of Natchitoches, were provisioned. Notwithstanding the amount given out the convoys on reaching the capital still had between eighteen and twenty cargoes of flour, pork and peltry.[1] Moreover, the commandant of the Illinois, in March, sent a consignment of lard, flour, corn, tallow and tobacco to Ft. Ouiatanon and Detroit. The entire order for the troops of New France had not been filled, due to the fact that there was a shortage of boats and men to transport it. The past harvest had been large but the growing crop indicated that there would be a greater output the coming year.[2]

Up to 1752 the English intrusions into the Mississippi valley had been troublesome enough to the French. Nevertheless they became more and more unbearable until the rupture came in 1754. Before the latter date the enemy seemed to be determined to take possession of the Ohio valley. Therefore, in order to prevent it, the French built Fort Du Quesne on the upper Ohio river. In 1753 it began to be provisioned with supplies drawn from the Illinois country. As the convoy was unable to pass the Falls of the Ohio, it was delayed through being forced to make a portage. After this experience it was despatched in time to pass the falls while the water was high enough to allow of it. The Ohio convoys were made up of from fifteen to sixteen boats, loaded with wheat, biscuit, corn, bear's oil, lard, tallow, salt meat, tobacco, bullets and some other commodities.[3]

[1] *A. N., C., Sér. C[13]*, vol. xxxv, fol. 126; vol. xxxvi, fol. 271; *Rec. Am. Cath. Hist. Soc. of Phila.*, vol. x, p. 206.

[2] *A. N., C., Sér. C[13]*, vol. xxxvi, fol. 309; vol. xxxvii, fol. 188.

[3] *Ibid.*, vol. xxxviii, fol. 99; Kerlérec, *Report, 1758*, p. 70; Bossu, vol. i, p. 179.

For three years the harvests in the Illinois country had been adequate to the demands put upon them. In July, 1754, the last of the annual convoys reached New Orleans, bringing with it the news of a fine growing crop in that district of the province.[1] Therefore the next year the settlements on the Gulf coast received from the Illinois country the usual shipments. From the same region other consignments were sent up the Ohio to the garrison stationed at Ft. Du Quesne.[2] During the progress of the war, due to the transportation of troops and munitions, the number of official convoys plying between New Orleans and the Illinois country had to be increased. Formerly one was sent out annually; now there were two regular ones and frequent special convoys, each being composed of double the number of boats.[3]

After 1755 it became increasingly difficult for the frontier posts to procure supplies from New France, therefore the bulk of the provisions for the troops in such places was drawn from the Illinois country. In response to a call for food, Captain Villiers with a company of men left Fort Chartres, in 1755, for Fort Du Quesne with 18,000 pounds of provisions.[4] The next year a similar consignment was carried to that post.[5] Governor Kerlérec, in his report of 1758, states that the Illinois country, from the beginning of hostilities, sent annually a convoy of about sixteen boats loaded with wheat, biscuit, corn, oil, lard, tallow, tobacco, salt, powder and bullets to the French posts that were surrounded by hostile Indians.[6] The next year Captain Audry, with 300 soldiers, some militia and 600 Indians,

[1] *A. N., C., Sér.* C^{13}, vol. xxxviii, fol. 26.

[2] *Ibid.*, fol. 170; Bossu, i, 159.

[3] *A. N., C., Sér.* C^{13}, vol. xxxvi, fol. 285.

[4] *Trans. Ill. St. Hist. Soc.*, 1907, No. 11, p. 222.

[5] Bossu, vol. i, p. 179.

[6] Kerlérec, *Report of 1758*, p. 70.

set out from the Illinois over the Maumee-Wabash route to reinforce the outlying posts of New France. For the support of themselves and the garrisons they carried along 200,000 pounds of flour and a considerable quantity of other provisions.[1]

The Illinois trade, to be sure, suffered from the war; perhaps even more from the irregularities in the traffic itself that it seems the officials were powerless to eliminate.[2] These obstacles were offset to some extent by men migrating from the Gulf region and from New France to the Illinois country where they established themselves either in trade or agriculture. In 1755, for example, a young merchant, Gabriel Carré, from Montreal, began business at Kaskaskia, continuing there until 1781 when he removed to St. Louis.[3] At the end of the French control a trading company, "Boyton, Wharton and Morgan", had one store at Kaskaskia and another at Fort Chartres, where it carried on trade in cattle and all kinds of produce.[4] Beauvain, who, in 1763, bought the property of the Jesuits at Kaskaskia, also, was an energetic and capable business man. He supplied the royal storehouse at Fort Chartres in one year alone with 86,000 pounds of flour. He also had more flour and other products ready for the market.[5] Valet, at St. Geneviève, on the west side of the Mississippi, annually put large quantities of produce upon the market, together with shipments of lard and salt. For some time after St. Louis was founded its entire supply of food was drawn from St. Geneviève.[6] On November 3, 1763, Captain Villiers reached Fort Chartres from the Gulf with a boat heavily laden

[1] *Coll. Ill. St. Hist. Lib.*, Va. Ser., vol. i, p. 165.

[2] *Supra*, pp. 259, 294.

[3] Billon, *Annals of St. Louis, etc.*, p. 452.

[4] *Chicago Hist. Soc. Coll.*, vol. iv, p. 421.

[5] Pittman, p. 85.

[6] *Ibid.*, p. 95.

with merchandise sent by the firm "Maxent, Laclède and Company", of New Orleans; Pierre Laclède, a member of the company, being in charge of the goods. The next year he began operating a branch trading-house in St. Louis.[1] Because of the scarcity of records on the subject no account can be given of the business methods employed by these companies.

The legal prices for European goods in the Illinois country were higher than on the lower Mississippi.[2] The law evidently had little effect; for example, brandy, in 1723, sold there at 5,000 livres a "quart", when paid for in bills of exchange;[3] in 1735, at five livres a pot.[4] Whatever the cost of brandy, much of it was consumed by the French themselves, and a far larger quantity used in the Indian traffic.[5] Information about the sort of European goods and their cost in the Illinois country is impossible to obtain. In 1738, however, a glimpse of the kinds of merchandise that changed hands in the upper district of the province and the prices they brought is available from the record of a sale that took place at Kaskaskia.[6]

[1] *Trans. Ill. St. Hist. Soc.*, No. 8, p. 111.

[2] *Supra*, p. 252.

[3] *A. N., C., Sér. C*[13], vol. vii, fol. 15; *supra*, p. 120.

[4] *Ibid.*, vol. xx, fols. 250-251.

[5] *Ibid.*, vol. xxxi, fols. 47-48; vol. xxxvi, fol. 228.

[6] Kaskaskia Papers, 1737-1784, MS. Chicago Hist. Soc. Lib.

The names and prices of the articles sold follow:

Wearing apparel.	*Liv.*	*Sol.*	*Wearing apparel.*	*Liv.*	*Sol.*
Breeches (sheepskin).....	15	..	Jacket (sheepskin).......	16	..
" "	7	10	" "	15	5
" "	7	..	" " (4) each	15	..
" (2 pairs) (sheep-			" " (3) each	13	00
skin) each	6	10	" " (2) each	11	15
Breeches (2 pairs) (sheep-			Coat (sheepskin)	21	..
skin) each......	6	..	Coat and jacket (sheepskin)	30	..
Breeches (3 pairs) (cloth)			" " " "	21	10
each	7	..	Soldier's uniform	18	..
			" "	11	..

Records of the trade in live stock in the Illinois country are also scant. The French drew their supply of horses, in part at least, from the Indians to the west of the Mississippi who in turn secured them from the Spaniards of New Mexico. In 1719 a trader exchanged three muskets, some powder, knives and a few trinkets with the Osage Indians on the upper Missouri for two horses and a mule, all bearing the mark of a Spanish branding iron. He also procured fourteen other horses, and on his failure to secure an Indian to guide him back to the Illinois country made his

Wearing apparel.	*Liv.*	*Sol.*
Hat	5	..
Dress	50	..
Skirt (blue)	29	..
" (gray (2) each	22	5

Dry-goods.	*Ells*	*Liv.*	*Sol.*
Limbourg	2	34	05
"	2½	19	10
"	1	16	10
"	1¼	16	..
"	1¼	15	..
Cloth (white)	2½	16	..
" "	4	21	..
" (red)	4	21	..
" (linen)	2½	34	..
" "	5	27	..
" (cotton)		21	..
" "	2	..	..
" (wool)	3	10	05
Cloth cover		29	..
" " (white)		20	5
" "		16	..
Cover (red limb.)		16	5
Napkins (half doz.)		29	10
" (doz.)		49	..
Yarn		8	10
" (1 lb.)		3	..

Hardware.	*Liv.*	*Sol.*
Sieves (two)	20	10
" "	7	10
Kettles (7 or 8 pots)	25	..
"	22	..
"	17	..
" (copper)	16	..
" " (6 pots)	12	..
" " (4 pots)	10	..
" (iron)	10	..
" (with cover) (4 pots)	10	..
Stove (iron)	30	10
Candlestick	10	..
Axes with handles (two)	10	..
Adzes (two)	12	..

Miscellaneous.	*Liv.*	*Sol.*
Table	25	..
" (two small round)	20	..
Chairs (8), (2 rockers)	25	..
Cart (iron tires)	40	..
Harness (2 sets)	60	..
Dishes (12 plates)	8	..
" (2 large, 10 medium), 2 small plates, a 2 qt. pot	50	00

way alone by the aid of a compass. En route, however, he lost six horses and a colt in attempting to cross a stream, a loss estimated at more than 900 livres.[1] By 1738 the Illinois country had horses to sell; forty-six, at 200 livres a head, being provided the government for use in the Chickasaw war.[2] At the sale mentioned above,[3] horses sold somewhat cheaper.[4] 135 yoke of oxen supplied the officials for the Indian war in 1738 cost 450 livres a pair.[5] Other exchanges of live stock at the sale just referred to brought quite good prices.[6]

Records of transfers of real estate, furthermore, are as rare as those of personal property. In 1738, however, a house and grounds, including a garden, near Fort Chartres, sold at 650 livres. At the same settlement a horse-mill and two arpents of land brought 900 livres.[7] In 1755 a house

[1] Margry, vol. vi, pp. 314-315.

[2] *A. N., C., Sér.* C^{13}, vol. xxiv, fol. 135.

[3] *Supra*, p. 300.

[4] See note 6 below.

[5] *A. N., C., Sér.* C^{13}, vol. xxiv, fol. 135.

[6] Kaskaskia Papers, 1737-1784, MS. Chicago Hist. Soc. Lib.

Price of live stock:

Kinds	Age	livres	sols
Bull	3 years	75	..
Bull	2 years	52	..
Bull	1 year	62	..
Bull (one large, one small)	.....	185	..
Cow (black)	8 years	99	..
Cow (black)	5 years	96	10
Cow (black)	5 years	86	..
Heifer (red)	2 years	50	..
Hogs (10)	5 or 6 months	77	..
Horses (3) mare and colt	......	400	..
Horse	......	300	..
Dogs (bull, mother and 4 pups)	......	15	..

[7] *Kaskaskia Papers*, 1737-1784, MS. Chicago Hist. Soc. Lib.

and its adjoining fields located near Kaskaskia sold at 6,500 livres, 3,000 livres being paid at the time of the transfer.[1]

Building materials were plentiful in the Illinois country, therefore few sales are recorded for lumber and stone. In 1737, for the construction of the fortifications at Fort Chartres, the crown paid from 130 to 135 livres a cubic "toise" for the masonry, 185 livres for the brick and ten sols a foot for the carpenter work, which prices the officials considered too high.[2]

Up to 1724, the lead mines of the Illinois country had supplied only local needs. That year 20,000 pounds, at fifty-five livres a quintal, payable in paper currency, were sold to the government for the use of the garrison at Fort Chartres.[3] In 1744, 30,000 pounds of lead from the Illinois mines was sent to New Orleans.[4] After 1750 enough lead was procured from these mines to supply both the French and Indians there, also to send annual shipments to the frontier posts of New France. The output was incapable of further expansion at this time, because there were in the colony no men with capital willing to invest in such an enterprise.[5]

[1] *A. N., C., Sér.* C^{13}, vol. xxii, fols. 51-54.

[2] MS. 1755, Courthouse, Belleville, Ill.

[3] *A. N., C., Sér.* C^{13}, vol. viii, fol. 103.

[4] *Ibid., Sér. F*, vol. lxxviii, fol. 16.

[5] *Jes. Rel.*, vol. lxix, pp. 221-223.

CHAPTER XVIII

New France in the Fur Trade of the Mississippi Valley

Ever since the establishment in New France of "The Company of the Hundred Associates", in 1626, the traders sent out under its direction pushed westward into new and unknown lands. On July 4, 1634, Jean Nicolet left Three Rivers to go among the Indians on the upper Great Lakes and before returning went on as far as the present state of Wisconsin.[1]

The coming in 1654 of a convoy of fur-laden canoes from a point 400 leagues to the westward stimulated interest in the trade, and in September of that year, Father Mercier wrote that, if thirty Frenchmen could be sent to the upper Lakes, "not only would many souls be won to God but also a profit would be derived in excess of the outlay required for the maintenance of the Frenchmen sent out, since the best furs come in greater abundance from those regions".[2] The French government did not respond to this call, but in the winter of 1658-1659, Radisson and Groseilliers, two traders who desired "to travel and see countreys" and "to be knowne with remotest people",[3] went westward as far as Lakes Michigan and Superior, on the latter of which they built a fort.[4]

[1] *Coll. St. Hist. Soc. Wis.*, vol. viii, pp. 188, 191-192; vol. xi, pp. 1-24.

[2] *Jes. Rel.*, vol. xli, pp. 77, 185.

[3] Thwaites, *The Colonies*, p. 247.

[4] *Pub. Prince Soc.*, vol. xvi, p. 31; *Coll. Minn. Hist. Soc.*, vol. x, pt. 2, pp. 457-553.

In time the traders became better acquainted with the region between Lakes Michigan and Superior. From twelve to fifteen Indian tribes made regular trips to the upper waters of the former for the purpose of securing food and of engaging in trade with one another. There the French established in 1670 a post named Michilimackinac that became the center of the western fur trade. From this post, in 1673, Joliet and Marquette set out on their journey in search of the Mississippi.[1] The traders, however, had reached the valley of that river ahead of them, for while on the Illinois Joliet met La Taupine whom he had known at Sault Ste. Marie in 1671.[2]

The work delegated to the Company, and its successors after 1663, and that assigned to the Church in New France sometimes was carried on by the traders in conjunction with the churchmen, while in other cases the former pushed on a little in advance. Nor did the task of establishing commerce with the Indians and the duty of converting them to the Christian faith always harmonize, as is shown in a letter in 1672 to Colbert by Governor Frontenac, stating that the Jesuits "think as much about the conversion of beaver as of souls; for the majority of their missions are pure mockery".[3] Other complaints evidently reached the royal government. In 1676, Governor Frontenac received the following instructions: "you must not suffer any person, invested with Ecclesiastical or Secular dignity or any Religious Community, to follow it (the fur trade) in any wise, under any pretext whatsoever, or even to trade in any peltries; and I consider it necessary to tell you that, for the sake of the example,

[1] *Jes. Rel.*, vol. lix, p. 91.

[2] Winsor, *Nar. and Crit. Hist. of America*, vol. iv, p. 179; *Mag. West. Hist.*, vol. ix, p. 432.

[3] *Doc. Rel. Col. Hist. N. Y.*, vol. ix, p. 93.

you ought not to allow any of your domestics, or any other person, in your name or by your authority, to do so; and I even forbid you to issue any license or permit for the (Indian) trade." [1] Had the crown been able to enforce this command it would have protected the fur trade of the Company organized for the purpose from inroads by the officials and independent traders as well as by the missionaries.

At the request of Governor La Barre the home government granted to La Salle, in 1678, a trading privilege that caused the existing Company much uneasiness. The patent from the standpoint of the officials of New France was given for a most worthy purpose, that of protecting the province and its fur trade from the hostile attacks of the Iroquois. The crown issuing the patent had attempted to preserve the rights of the Montreal fur traders by permitting La Salle to buy buffalo skins and peltry only from the territory not belonging to the Company.[2] La Salle gave the home government assurance that any bad effects that his grant might have upon the trade of those men would be more than balanced in the first place by the added security that it would give to his majesty's American possessions. In the second place it would increase the output of peltry, since his post on the upper Illinois river would intercept the skins that the Iroquois heretofore had carried to the English market.[3]

After receiving this grant La Salle ill-treated the Iroquois, avowing he would convey arms and ammunition to the Illinois and would, himself, if need be, die in assisting those tribes in carrying on war against them. The Iroquois, however, were not intimidated by his threats, and

[1] *Doc. Rel. Col. Hist. N. Y.*, vol. ix, p. 126.

[2] Margry, vol. i, pp. 337-338.

[3] *Hist. Coll. of La.*, pt. 1, p 42; *Coll. Ill. St. Hist. Lib.*, vol. i, p. 122.

in 1680 they returned from the Illinois carrying with them large quantities of skins.[1] These successes led them to plan larger campaigns. In 1683, they were engaged in a war against the Miami, Ottawa, Huron and Illinois, in the hope of taking possession of Michilimackinac, thereby cutting off French communication with the Indian tribes to the South and rendering themselves masters of the fur trade in the west.[2]

In order to combat this movement, La Salle established a sort of confederacy at Fort St. Louis on the upper Illinois river. Before the French and their Indian allies were able to check them, the Iroquois had pushed their incursions almost to the Mississippi.[3] The ferocity and extent of such attacks no doubt were due in part at least to the fact that the English fur fields were already practically exhausted.[4] La Salle at this time also pointed out to the home government the necessity of protecting its American fur trade from encroachments from the Hudson's Bay Company.[5] The crown, however, did not heed the warning; therefore very soon that Company had perceptibly decreased the amount of furs carried to Quebec. The French accordingly began to understand that in their struggle for control the Hudson's Bay Company would have to be reckoned with.[6]

The fight for full possession of the fur trade fell primarily upon the agents of the Company at Montreal and the traders with special permits from the crown. Tonty had been left in charge of the affairs at La Salle's post on the

[1] *Penn Arch.*, 2nd Ser., vol. vi, p. 9.

[2] Margry, vol. v, pp. 7, 48-49.

[3] *Ind. Hist. Soc. Pub.*, vol. ii, p. 327.

[4] *Coll. of Ill. Hist. Lib.*, vol. i, p. 122.

[5] *Ibid.*, p. 121.

[6] *Penn. Arch.*, 2nd Ser., vol. vi, p. 13.

upper Illinois and here aided the Illinois Indians in defending themselves against the attacks from the Iroquois. In 1687, after paying his trading dues to the government, amounting to 4,000 livres worth of beaver skins, he still had left in the storehouse between 1,000 and 1,200 livres worth of peltry.[1] Tonty and La Forest became the sole proprietors of the trade at Fort St. Louis; but the Iroquois and Fox hostilities greatly interrupted it.[2]

Apart from the trouble caused by the savages the condition of the fur trade in the Illinois country was not entirely satisfactory. Many of the skins sent to Montreal and Quebec were not properly cured; others were of poor quality. The officials thought it was wise to take all the peltry the Indians offered. They desired to improve the situation, and to this end requested Tonty and La Forest "to excite the savages to dress their skins well". At the same time it was proposed to make the conditions in the Illinois country such that there would be no need to buy skins in such abundance. It was decided to limit the number of permits to traders to twenty-five; to pay the soldiers of the garrison at Fort St. Louis in order to keep them out of the traffic, and to send presents to the Indians for the purpose of appeasing them for any shortage in a market for their peltry. Tonty, however, was permitted to go 500 leagues west of Michilimackinac in order to build up trade among the Indians of the region in question.[3] Still other Frenchmen from the Illinois country were exploring the territory on the upper Missouri, where they formed alliances with the Indians, the aim being to build up an advantageous fur trade.[4]

[1] Margry, vol. iii, p. 499.

[2] *Early Voyages up and down the Miss.*, p. 49.

[3] Margry, vol. v, pp. 65-66.

[4] *Jes. Rel.*, vol. lxiv, p. 161; *supra*, p. 30.

By this time the French were feeling the pinch of competition from the Hudson's Bay Company. In order to relieve the situation, Le Sueur began his voyages to the upper Mississippi valley among the Sioux. Before the end of the century he had made a number of such trips and had learned their language.[1] This accomplishment greatly increased the value of Le Sueur's services among the Sioux. In 1690 he was sent among them to restore peace. In five years the work was accomplished and a French post established there. In accomplishing the task Le Sueur received considerable aid from the presents that Perrot carried to Michilimackinac for distribution among the Indians of the northwest.[2]

Le Sueur, meanwhile, had become interested in the possibilities of the fur trade in this region. He told the officials that the bear, lynx, wild cat, martin and badger skins found there were incomparably more beautiful than those elsewhere, and requested that he be given the exclusive trade with the Sioux for a period of ten years, together with men and supplies for carrying on the traffic with Montreal. He further requested that he be allowed to supply those tribes with guns and ammunition. His proposition was rejected. Le Sueur, nevertheless, did not lose his interest in the commerce. In order to impress the officials with the abundance and wealth of the furs in the Sioux country, he stated that these savages dressed themselves entirely in beaver skins which were soon discarded and replaced by fresh ones, simply because of the lack of a market.[3]

[1] Margry, vol. vi, pp. 57-65.

[2] *Ibid.*, vol. vi, pp. 55-56; *Doc. Rel. Col. Hist. N. Y.*, vol. ix, p. 478; *Coll. Minn. Hist. Soc.*, vol. ii, pp. 94-95.

[3] Margry, vol. vi, pp. 60-64.

Le Sueur's appeal failed to move the officials of New France to undertake the establishment of such a trade. In some measure the rejection of the scheme was due to the opposition to it from the friendly Illinois, who looked with disfavor on a strong alliance with the Sioux, their enemies. Then too the opinion and action of the officials of New France at the time were influenced by men who hated Le Sueur because of his success and were doing what they could to thwart his plans and bring about his political and financial ruin. In part, as has been shown, they succeeded in the task assigned themselves. Misfortune completed the work. In 1698 Le Sueur was captured by the English, lost 10,000 livres, and finally made his way to France. On his return to New France he found his enemies bitterly hostile, he therefore soon decided to go back to France. He secured from the crown a mining and trading grant for the Sioux country, to be operated from Iberville's settlement on the Gulf of Mexico.[1] Although many of Le Sueur's personal schemes failed, the work that he and others did among the Indians of the Northwest succeeded in reviving the fur trade of New France. In August, 1690, five hundred Indians from Michilimackinac were at Montreal. The merchants of the village were very happy. It had been a long time since they had seen there so large a number of these savages. In order to induce them to repeat their visit, Governor Frontenac, August 25, gave them a great feast consisting of " two oxen, six large dogs, two barrels of wine, some prunes and tobacco to smoke ".[2]

The frequent conflict with the Iroquois finally led the officials of New France to conclude that the only way to put an end to the trouble was to remove the cause. To this

[1] Margry, vol. vi, pp. 90-92.

[2] *Doc. Rel. Col. Hist. N. Y.*, vol. ix, pp. 478-479.

end, in 1685, they informed the home government "the English both to the north and south of us as well as the Iroquois be to us as a constant threat, and it is our belief that something should be done to remove this enemy". They informed the royal government, also, that a great deal of uncertainty would be cleared up if only it could purchase the region dependent upon Albany.[1] This proposal, however, was not the first of its kind. In 1666, a colonial official had suggested to the crown the buying of the colony of New York, whereby his majesty "would have two entrances into Canada, and by which he would give to France all the peltry of the north, of which the English share the profits through communication they have with the Iroquois by Manhattan and Orange".[2] The argument was sound. Not only would it have given New France a second waterway to the sea and considerable influence over the Iroquois, but it would have closed one of the easiest English routes into the Mississippi valley. Moreover, during the reign of Charles II it is probable that such a purchase could have been made had the French government been persevering enough. Through lack of alertness their competitors, the English, again were left in a position to continue their formidable rivalry for the possession of the western trade.

At the beginning of 1687, New York, in order to aid the Iroquois in their wars with the French, and incidentally to increase its output of fur, made them a present of a barrel of powder.[3] The next year, through the artifice of the French, as the English claimed, a treaty of commerce between the subjects of the two crowns was signed, giving the French trader a decided advantage over his English

[1] Winsor, *Cartier to Frontenac*, p. 329.

[2] *Doc. Rel. to Col. Hist. N. Y.*, vol. ix, pp. 56-57.

[3] Colden, vol. i, p. 73.

rival. Moreover, Governor Andros saw to it that the treaty was obeyed, but the English asserted that the French did not.[1] Whatever the disadvantage from this source, the English were able to push forward to the great discomfort of the French. In 1692, the latter claimed the former were among the Miami and predicted the loss of the whole of New France if the English became masters of the Mississippi fur trade. In fact English influence among the western Indians already had caused the Fox, who wished to trade with them, to become hostile to the French. Moreover, it had caused outbreaks among the Miami. The French, therefore, were obliged, in 1692, to send out Nicholas Perrot for the purpose of pacifying the latter tribes.[2] Then too French legislation enacted for the purpose of regulating the fur trade had been decidedly useful to the English. The restrictions on the quantity of skins bought annually and on the number of permits issued, together with the actual extent of the fur territory, had caused the Company's agents to carry peltry to the English market.[3] In 1695, the fur output of New York, the only province at the time drawing furs from the Mississippi valley, amounted to about £10,000 sterling a year.[4]

The close of the seventeenth century, therefore, presented an interesting situation in the struggle for control of the western fur trade. The work of the French was beset with difficulties both internal and external. The English had as allies the Iroquois and Fox and were making headway among some of the other tribes of that area. They seemed, however, to have dreaded the Jesuits more

[1] *Pub. of Prince Soc.*, vol. vii, p. 229.

[2] *Parkman Club Papers*, 1896, p. 12.

[3] Margry, vol. v, p. 65.

[4] Halsey, *Old New York Frontier*, p. 8.

than they did the French traders. In 1700, Robert Livingston declared the "Jesuits at Canada are so cunning to have their share of whatever an Indian hunts, which is brought and laid before the image of the Virgin Mary in the Church, and this being done they have not only remission of their sins, but her prayers to the bargain for good luck when they go out a hunting next time".[1]

To these external problems of the fur trade of New France must be added the troubles that arose within. The officials complained of the men to whom special trading permits had been granted by the crown and they in turn complained that other persons with similar privileges were infringing upon their rights. For example, as early as 1682, La Salle asserted that Du Lhut and others working among the Sioux were ruining the trade belonging to him.[2] Legislation, added to extortion on the part of the officials themselves, brought bankruptcy to many of the Indian traders, who thereupon entered into direct commerce with the English. By the time Biloxi was founded they had become independent and at once opened up a traffic with the new French settlement.[3]

Before Louisiana was a year old New France asked the home government for protection against encroachments from the colony on the Gulf.[4] The governor of the former sent Tonty to Michilimackinac to induce the agents of Montreal merchants to return. Tonty succeeded with only 20 out of 104. The others to the number of eighty-four made their way to the Gulf, whither thirty more had gone some time before with ten canoes laden with beaver skins

[1] *Doc. Rel. to Col. Hist. N. Y.*, vol. iv, p. 649.

[2] Margry, vol. ii, pp. 253-254.

[3] *Supra*, p. 288.

[4] *A. N., C., Sér. C*[13], vol. i, fol. 29.

belonging to the Montreal dealers. The officials of New France at once informed the home government that it was very necessary to have this barefaced robbery stopped. To this end they desired the crown to limit the Louisiana trade to buffalo skins or other peltry found in that province itself.[1]

Instead of checking these traders, the home government sent out additional ones with special permits. Le Sueur was among the Sioux in 1700 where the officials of New France complained he was buying beaver skins contrary to the terms of his grant.[2] The crown was thereupon informed that it would be better to allow a few skins to go to the English than to ruin New France entirely by putting the whole trade in furs into the hands of persons who would carry it to Louisiana.[3] Le Sueur bought 3,600 beaver skins in eight days and sent them in three canoes down the Mississippi to Biloxi,[4] a fact that perhaps gives the above statement, in some measure at least, the appearance of being true.

The French government not only did nothing to restrain Le Sueur's traffic but actually increased the trouble of the Montreal merchants by issuing to Juchereau a permit to establish on the lower Wabash a tannery and there allowed him to buy buffalo hides and other peltry, except beaver skins. Thereupon the officials of New France began to make complaints against him similar to those previously directed against Le Sueur. They claimed that the three canoes of merchandise that Juchereau's grant allowed practically gave him control of the western trade. They as-

[1] *Rep. and Coll. St. Hist. Soc. Wis.*, vol. xvi, pp. 201-202.

[2] *Infra*, p. 336.

[3] Margry, vol. vi, pp. 68-69.

[4] *Ibid.*, vol. v, p. 417.

serted further that this traffic would make it impossible for the Company at Montreal to fulfill the terms of its contract with the crown, such as paying in its name the 6,000 livres it had agreed to distribute among the poor families of the province and its obligation to build a post at Detroit. In spite of a denial from Juchereau, they declared that it was utterly impossible for a trader to go among the Indians as he did without being obliged to buy all the peltry the savages offered.[1] The home government took no action in the matter, therefore it continued to receive complaints against Juchereau until his death in 1703.[2]

Although encroachments came chiefly from the English side yet the French did not abstain from retaliation. In 1700, Martin Chartière went into Pennsylvania without a permit and opened up trade with the Shawnee and Delaware. He built a post on the Susquehanna, married an Indian woman and reared a family. He and his sons became owners as well as fur traders. They always remained friendly to the French and regarded themselves as French subjects.[3]

Since the abolition of the "Company of the Hundred Associates", in 1664, a number of different companies had tried in vain to build up in New France a profitable fur trade. At the beginning of the eighteenth century it was in the hands of the "Company of Canada", having an exclusive traffic in beaver skins, and being permitted to send to France 150,000 a year.[4] The traffic at the Detroit post, in 1701, fell to the Company of Canada's privilege, for which it paid 70,000 francs annually. The permit included also

[1] Margry, vol. v, pp. 357-358, 360-365.

[2] *Ibid.*, vol. vi, p. 180.

[3] *Lancaster County Hist. Soc. Papers*, vol. ix, pp. 305-306.

[4] Kingsford, *The Hist. of Canada*, vol. ii, pp. 504-506; Margry, vol. v, pp. 360-361.

Fort Frontenac which was so close to the English that soon there was an illicit trade established with the merchants at Albany.[1] In order to protect the rights of the Company, the officials of New France, as has been seen, made violent protests to the home government against such men as Le Sueur and Juchereau,[2] hoping no doubt, to force them out of the business, thereby shutting off competition and forcing down the prices of skins demanded by the Indians. In order to prevent the traders of New France from carrying their peltry to the Louisiana market, also, the director of the "Company of Canada" proposed that all beaver skins shipped to France on vessels from Louisiana should be seized at Rochefort and sold at the same price as the Company was paying for them at Quebec.[3]

About the same time the officials of New France suggested to the crown that the boundary between the two French colonies on the continent of North America be made the Ohio river, it being claimed that definite limits would enable them better to control the fur trade. In order to make the dividing line effective, it was further recommended that the following posts should be built, namely, one among the Miami; another on the Wabash (Ohio) where it empties into the Mississippi; a third on the Wisconsin; and a fourth in the country of the Sioux. It was further suggested to the home government that Detroit be made the center for the trade of the west. With headquarters at the latter post it was believed to be possible to unify the whole fur traffic of New France, since the colonial officials would then be able to force the Indians in that area to carry their peltry directly to Detroit, enabling them,

[1] Margry, vol. iv, pp. 589-592; Winsor, *The Miss. Basin*, p. 73.

[2] *Supra*, p. 314.

[3] Margry, vol. iv, pp. 611-612.

therefore, to keep the savages under more effective control.[1]

The affairs of the Company passed from bad to worse. On October 5, 1701, it was asserted that the disorder among their Indian agents had reached such a state that those in the interior did not come back. In the previous September twelve men, with four canoes, made their escape and since almost their entire stock of merchandise consisted of brandy, they presumably were well received by the savages. The peltry they procured in exchange, it was believed, passed to the colony of Louisiana. The Company had not increased the number of its traders because the quantity of the beaver skins permitted to send annually to France was limited. It was claimed, nevertheless, that there were more of these persons than ever before engaged in the interior traffic, from whom, naturally, the Company derived no profit. The peltry they collected passed to the English market or was carried to the French at Biloxi.[2]

The next year, 1702, the royal government was informed that so many men had left their homes in New France, for the purpose of entering the Louisiana fur trade, that many of the merchants of Montreal and Quebec were financially ruined and asked that the practice be stopped.[3] The Louisiana officials, however, stated in reply that the difficulty rested entirely with these merchants themselves, because they provided the men with merchandise and sent them into the woods to buy peltry which would have gone over to the English if the French of Louisiana had not received it.[4]

In 1706, the "Company of Canada" became bankrupt.

[1] Margry, vol. iv, pp. 588-590; vol. v, pp. 359-362.

[2] *Ibid.*, vol. v, p. 358.

[3] *Ibid.*, vol. iv, pp. 610-611.

[4] *Ibid.*, pp. 628-629.

The fur trade of New France passed to "Aubert, Neyret and Gayot", who were often forced to pay more for peltry than they were able to secure for it in France. The firm spent lavishly, always having more traders in its employ than the traffic would warrant. Each year therefore the profits fell more or less below the expenses. Its credit collapsing brought on the ruin of its business, which in 1718 was given to a new company for a term of twenty-four years.[1] The prospects for the new organization, however, were not flattering, since the failure of the earlier company had occurred at a time when the traffic in peltry was said to be worth annually 2,000,000 livres. To increase that output was not an easy task.[2] The company also was given the exclusive beaver trade of the province. As a means of protection, the discovery of one beaver pelt on board a vessel not belonging to it was to be considered sufficient proof to warrant confiscation of both ship and cargo.[3]

Nothing the officials of New France did to regulate the fur trade of that province seems to have succeeded. The independent traders became yearly more numerous, their ranks being swelled by soldiers sent to the frontier posts who soon became traders there. When their commerce was interfered with officially, they deserted and began trafficking with Louisiana or the English. Other recruits came from among the settlers of New France who believed it less profitable to till the soil.[4]

Such difficulties were trifling in comparison with the in-

[1] Kingsford, vol. ii, pp. 505-507.

[2] *Doc. Rel. to Col. Hist. N. Y.*, vol. ix, p. 757; Charlevoix, *A Voyage to No. Am.*, vol. i, p. 52; Le Page du Pratz, vol. i, p. 48.

[3] Kingsford, vol. ii, p. 507.

[4] *Coll. Mich. Pioneer and Hist. Soc.*, vol. xxxiii, p. 243.

termittent wars that for years the Fox and Iroquois had waged against the French and their savage allies, at times with such fierceness as to threaten to destroy the entire traffic.[1] In 1716, the government of New France offered amnesty to the illicit traders on condition that they would agree to defend the province against these hostile savages.[2] Moreover these attacks of the natives brought the officials of New France to understand that in order to keep intact the fur trade of that province it was necessary to drop the quarrel with Louisiana concerning it and unite with that colony in combating English aggression. To that end the governor of New France proposed to give more attention to the garrisons at the frontier posts where the English of Pennsylvania, Virginia and Carolina were anxious to pass into French territory by means of rivers that furnished easy communication with the Mississippi, the very center of the French fur traffic.[3] In 1717, therefore, when New France lost control of the Illinois country the circumstance did not affect the fur trade to any extent.

In 1700, it was asserted that "the English do not discriminate in the quality of the beaver; they take all at the same rate, which is more than 50 per cent higher than the French, there being, besides, more than 100 per cent difference in the price of their trade and ours."[4] To a considerable extent the variance in rate paid was due to the fact that English goods were preferred by the savages and could be procured in Europe cheaper than could the similar French merchandise. As a result many of the French

[1] *Rep. and Coll. of Hist. Soc. Wis.*, vol. xvi, pp. 289-300; Neill, *Hist. of Minn.*, pp. 177-179.

[2] *Coll. Mich. Pioneer and Hist. Soc.*, vol. xxxiii, p. 573.

[3] *Rep. and Coll. Hist. Soc. Wis.*, vol. xvi, pp. 345-346.

[4] *Doc. Rel. to Col. Hist. N. Y.*, vol. ix, p. 409.

traders sold to the natives goods of English make.[1] The advantage in price increased English influence among the Indians year by year. By 1705, many of the Miami tribes had been won over, Juchereau's post on the Wabash was destroyed, and Governor Vaudreuil found it necessary to send Vincennes to arrange a treaty with the natives in question. Under existing conditions such a mission was not easy. In 1708, the Miami came to trade at Albany to the joy of the English who for five years had been working to that end.[2]

Encouraged by this accomplishment, the people of New York now began to make plans to drive the French from Canada as the only way to establish peace with the Indian tribes of the Mississippi valley. Moreover they were of the opinion that the expulsion would be neither a difficult nor an expensive undertaking, since whatever debt was incurred in the conflict could be paid for in a short time by the Indian trade thus acquired.[3]

By 1715, the English traders had penetrated as far as the Wabash.[4] The next year an "Ohio Company" was formed in Virginia for the purpose of promoting the western traffic. The Board of Trade, however, withheld its approval by laying the proposal aside. The English government at the time was indolent and much "afraid of giving umbrage to the French"; therefore until 1748 it made no attempt to help the American colonies extend their trade and settlement into the Mississippi valley. Interest in such a movement, however, seems to have kept alive, for in 1729 Joshua Gee published an ingenious discourse

[1] *Doc. Rel. to Col. Hist. N. Y.*, vol. ix, p. 409.

[2] *Journal of Captain Wm. Trent*, pp. 10-11.

[3] *Doc. Rel. to Col. Hist. N. Y.*, vol. iv, pp. 1054-1055.

[4] *Journal of Captain Wm. Trent*, p. 12.

on trade, in which he urged the planting of colonies as far west as the Mississippi river.[1] The English traders meanwhile had not waited for encouragement from the home government. In 1716, they sent to the mother country 72,000 deer skins;[2] and from 1717 to 1720 the total exports from New York alone were worth £8,443 sterling, most of it coming from the territory belonging to New France.[3]

Up to this time the struggle with the French had been carried on chiefly by fur traders from New York; after 1716, however, Virginians and Pennsylvanians became increasingly active in the Mississippi valley. In the year 1716, Governor Spotswood, of Virginia, sought to extend the boundary of that province westward far enough to break the communication along the Mississippi between New France and Louisiana.[4] He wrote to the Board of Trade that the British dominions were surrounded by French territory in such a way as to enable the French to secure the whole Indian trade on both sides of the Great Lakes. This position, moreover, made it possible to send out bodies of Indians for the purpose of attacking the English frontier settlements. Fortunately for the latter, he declared, the mountains in the rear had passes unknown to the French; hence he proposed that these passes be seized by the English before they should become known.[5] New York also urged upon the home government the necessity of strengthening the American colonies against the French, who were said to be fortifying themselves by making

[1] Dillon, *Hist. of Ind.*, p. 47.

[2] *A. N., C., Sér.* C^{13}, vol. iv, fol. 914.

[3] Roberts, *New York*, vol. i, p. 233.

[4] *Trans. Ill. St. Hist. Soc. Lib.*, No. 8, p. 40.

[5] *Board of Trade Papers*, 1718-1720, Pa. Hist. Soc. Trans.

stronger and better connections between New France and Louisiana.[1]

New York was becoming more and more convinced that the only way for the English to win control of the fur trade of the northwest was to secure the Indians as allies, through a recognition of the fact that it was useless to attempt "to persuade an Indian otherwise than that they are his best friends who can help him to the best bargains".[2] By such a policy New York for years had usually kept the friendship of the Iroquois, yet at times some of the tribes, through the influence of the Jesuits, had shifted over to the French for short periods of time. These exceptions, however, simply strengthened the English in their belief that the confidence of an Indian could be acquired and held only by affording him advantageous commercial opportunities.[3] The English traders, therefore, were encouraged to deal fairly with all the savage tribes, and each of the provinces was to bear its proportional share of the expense of building posts to the westward in order to advance the traffic.[4]

In spite of the active interests the merchants of New York had had in the western fur trade up to 1720, they were still unable to compete with the Indians and French. Since the beginning of the century, however, the New York merchants had derived handsome profits by selling to the French almost all the merchandise, except a small amount of brandy, that they used in their transactions with the natives. Such goods could be bought at Albany easier and cheaper[5] than they could be imported from Europe, a circumstance due in part to the impossibility of navigating the

[1] *Doc. Rel. to Col. Hist. N. Y.*, vol. v, p. 502.

[2] *B. of T. Papers*, pt. 2, vol. x, 1718-1720, Pa. Hist. Soc. Trans.

[3] *Ibid.*

[4] *Ibid.*

[5] *Supra*, p. 319.

St. Lawrence during a number of months in the winter season.[1]

At this time some of the inhabitants of New York felt that direct trade with the Indians would be much more advantageous to the province as a whole. To this end laws were passed in 1720, 1722 and 1724 prohibiting the sale of Indian goods to persons from New France. This action, it was claimed, would ruin Montreal to the corresponding benefit of New York. Strouds that cost £10 sterling at the latter sold at the former at £25. The difference, it was claimed at the time the bills were pending, would enable the English to sell the goods directly to the natives 50 per cent cheaper, and give their traders the same profits that the French were getting.[2] As late as 1739 the New York officials asserted the prohibition laid on the trade with New France was working well, and informed the home government that presents should be sent to the Iroquois for the service they rendered in making it effective.[3]

There was, however, a considerable number of persons who did not view the arrangement with favor. They were satisfied with the trade as it had been and had no desire to incur the risk that would be necessary in order to carry it on directly in the Indian country. An illicit traffic sprang up with New France which was most exasperating to those who had promoted the enactment of the laws in question. On the other hand, October 28, 1748, they were encouraged in this regard by the news that the Indians had killed two Frenchmen who had tried to prevent them from carrying peltry to the English. Governor Clinton at once began to

[1] *Doc. Rel. to Col. Hist. N. Y.*, vol. v, p. 577; Colden, vol. i, pp. 103-105.

[2] *Doc. Rel. to Col. Hist. N. Y.*, vol. v, p. 757; Colden, vol. i, pp. 103-105.

[3] *Doc. Rel. to Col. Hist. N. Y.*, vol. vi, p. 157.

use all his influence to shut off the clandestine trade. The assembly, however, was controlled at the time by men who favored it, hence nothing effective could be done in restraint.[1] At the opening of the second war with England, therefore, this traffic between Albany and New France was still being carried on. In 1756, Governor Shirley renewed Governor Clinton's proposal to establish direct trade with the Indians at Oswego, but the war made it impossible to adopt and carry out vigorously any trading policy whatever.[2]

New France, on the other hand, succeeded in persuading the Indians to allow a fort to be built on the Great Lakes that, it was hoped, might cut off to some extent the English trade at Oswego.[3] On May 14, 1726, the French entered into a treaty of commerce and friendship with the Sioux. To that end an exclusive right of trade with these tribes for three years, also, was given to a company protected by an order to commanding officers at the French posts in that territory to confiscate the merchandise of all persons guilty of interference with it, one-half of the goods thus forfeited to go to the company, the other to the crown. It was permitted to build storehouses at places where there was such an officer, but nowhere else. It was to be allowed 1,350 livres worth of merchandise annually and as many boats to carry on the traffic with Montreal as the trade would warrant. Its agents, however, were not to engage in commerce with the natives on the way to or from Montreal. At the end of the three years the government of New France reserved the right to assign the privilege to the highest bidder or to whomsoever it saw fit; meanwhile no

[1] *Doc. Rel. to Col. Hist. N. Y.*, vol. vi, pp. 371-374, 455.

[2] *Bancroft Papers*, 1755-1757, Jan. 5, 1756, N. Y. Pub. Lib.

[3] Parkman, *A Half-Century of Conflict*, vol. ii, p. 52.

member of the company should sell or transfer his stock to an ecclesiastic or any one whose activities might lead to competition with that organization.[1] A right so restricted seems not to have appealed strongly to other merchants in Montreal, for when the grant expired it was renewed in favor of practically the same persons as before.[2]

From 1730 to the outbreak of the war with England in 1744 there was no change by either the French or English in the methods employed in the western fur trade. Each side worked to strengthen its alliance with its own Indians and to increase the number won over from the allies of its opponents.[3] The English at the time, however, were not well organized to meet aggression, and on September 20, 1731, the governor of Pennsylvania recommended to the Board of Trade that it instruct the governor in the several provinces to take especial care of the commerce with the western Indians, but in the endeavor to promote the welfare of a particular province the governor there should see to it that nothing was done that would weaken the trade of an English neighbor.[4]

The activities of the French traders up to 1720 had had little effect upon the provinces of Pennsylvania and Virginia, except perhaps to draw away a few of their allies.[5] By this time they had carried the work of alienating the savages so far that they had been able to prevail upon the Iroquois to make groundless complaints against the people of Pennsylvania, who, the Indians were led to believe, were a mild and defenseless folk. It was asserted, further,

[1] Margry, vol. vi, pp. 547-552.

[2] *Ibid.*, pp. 563-567.

[3] *A. N., C., Sér.* C^{13}, vol. xvi, fols. 184-185.

[4] *B. of T. Papers,* vol. xiii, Sept. 28, 1731, Pa. Hist. Soc. Trans.

[5] *Ibid.*, 1720-1727, vol. xi, Nov. 30, 1720.

that the French had instigated inter-tribal wars for the purpose of drawing all of the English colonies into a war with the western tribes.[1] In 1721, accordingly, Governor Keith asked the home government "to fortify the passes back to Virginia", "to build forts on the Mississippi".[2] During the year Spotswood wrote to Keith asking him to make an agreement with Virginia to unite in an effort to hold the loyalty of the Indians east of the mountains.[3] At this time the English, in order to offset French influence among the tribes of the Ohio valley, decided to push more vigorously the old principle of furnishing them with goods at fair prices. In spite of this decision and active endeavors to carry it out, the avarice of the traders led them to impose upon the Indians, thus arousing their hostility rather than winning their friendship.[4]

About 1740, the Pennsylvania and Virginia traders began to be much more keenly interested in the western traffic.[5] In order to safeguard Pennsylvania at least, a treaty with the Indians at Lancaster was made in 1744.[6] After that agreement the Pennsylvanians became bolder. From 1745 to 1753 sixty of them were busy in the west where they bought thousands of skins from the Indians. Some of the traders sent out regular trains of fifteen and twenty pack-horses that made several trips each year.[7] Some of them also passed up the Alleghany river and westward to Lake Erie, whence they drove their pack-horses across country

[1] *Penn. Col. Rec.*, vol. iii, p. 98.

[2] Thwaites, *Wisconsin*, pp. 88-89.

[3] *The American Weekly Mercury*, No. 75, p. 51, May 25, 1721.

[4] *Coll. and Res. Mich. Pioneer and Hist. Soc.*, vol. xix, pp. 12-13.

[5] Gordon, *Hist. Penn.*, pp. 249, 259-260.

[6] *Penn. Col. Rec.*, vol. iv, pp. 698-699; vol. v, p. 24.

[7] *Journal of Captain Wm. Trent*, pp. 42-43.

to the Scioto river. Others, even more venturesome, went on to the Wabash where they traded with the Miami, thereby tapping the rich fur-producing region between Lake Michigan and Lake Erie; a territory up to this time entirely controlled by New France.[1]

The French found it most difficult to make headway against these English traders who paid the Indians twice as much and gave them more presents.[2] Thereupon the French called to their assistance Peter Chartière, son of Martin,[3] and a band of Shawnee Indians who at once began to rob the Pennsylvanians. By 1747, almost the entire Miami trade again came under the control of the French who, however, did not use their influence wisely. They lowered the price of skins and vainly tried to induce the Indians to believe that the decline was caused by the war. Finally, when the offer for peltry in one case fell so low that a single charge of powder and a bullet was all the Frenchman would give for a beaver skin, the Indian promptly buried his hatchet in the head of that individual and scalped him. Five others of that nationality also lost their lives while engaged in trade with the natives to the south of Lake Erie, and it is more than likely that the savages had been encouraged in such hostilities through the influence of the Pennsylvanians.[4] The latter continued warring on the French competitors.

In May, 1747, a letter was sent to the governor of Pennsylvania from the Indians around Detroit, the spelling and construction of which seemed to show the earmarks of a jealous Pennsylvania trader. George Croghan, "prince of

[1] *Journal of Captain Wm. Trent,* p. 12; *Penn. Col. Rec.,* vol. v, pp. 24, 87.

[2] *Doc. Rel. to Col. Hist. N. Y.,* vol. x, pp. 115, 119, 144.

[3] *Supra,* p. 315.

[4] *Penn. Arch.,* vol. i, pp. 741-742.

the Pennsylvania traders ", told the governor that the Indian allies of the French had been won over and that it was now feasible to reinforce the English influence over them by sending them presents. The policy of Pennsylvania, however, was opposed to using the western tribes for warlike purposes, but not averse to widening the area of the fur trade.[1] Croghan and his fellow traders nevertheless began to urge that arms be furnished to the natives around Lake Erie. The colonial council and assembly hesitated to take the step, whereupon, in September, 1747, Croghan wrote to the Governor: " The Inguns att this side of Lake Eary is Making warr very Briskly Against the French, Butt it is very impatiant To hear from there Brothers, ye English, Expecting a Present of powder and Lead, which if they Don't gett, I am of Opinion, By the Best Accounts I can gett, That they will Turn to the French, which will be very willing to make up with them again. Sr, if there be no provision Made for to Send them a present by some of the Traders Directly, Send Me an account by first opportunity, for if there be Nothing Sent I will not Send any Goods or Men this year for fear of Danger." [2] Croghan, it seems, struck the one vulnerable spot. Presents for the western Indians were immediately provided, the tribes around Lake Erie receiving powder and lead worth £30 or £40 sterling.[3]

Croghan thus had won his point with the Pennsylvania officials, and on August 10, 1748, nine licensed and forty-nine unlicensed traders left for the interior.[4] The augmentation of the number of men in the western traffic of the Quaker province was due to the fact that the Twight-

[1] *Penn. Arch.*, vol. i, pp. 741-742.

[2] *Ibid.*, p. 770.

[3] *Ibid.*, pp. 771-772.

[4] *Ibid.*, vol. ii, p. 14.

wee were aware that the French paid poor prices for peltry in places where there were no English competitors, hence were encouraging the latter to come among them. The growth of friendship between the Pennsylvanians and the savages resulted in a treaty at Logstown, in 1748, which virtually gave the former control of the Indian traffic as far west as the Mississippi. Moreover is was now possible for the English to interrupt French communication between Louisiana and New France.[1] On July 23, 1748, Pennsylvania strengthened its position still further by making a treaty of commerce and friendship at Lancaster with representatives of the Miami tribes. The agreement was particularly advantageous to Pennsylvania and Virginia and of some value to the other English colonies.[2]

The safety that these arrangements with the Indians afforded to the traders stimulated them to advance farther and farther into French territory. The next year, Céleron, August 6, 1749, on meeting some of these Pennsylvanians in the Ohio valley, sent word by them to the officials of their province that their traders were to be kept out of the Mississippi valley.[3] Little heed was paid to this demand. On the contrary, the governors of Pennsylvania, Maryland and Virginia caused the trail that ran from the Miami country to the forks of the Ohio and from there to Will's Creek on the Potomac to be cleared in order to make the journey thither for the traders and Indians easier.[4] The improvement of this highway into the Indian country was a hard blow to the French in the Ohio valley, and was perhaps the most important move made by the English up to

[1] *Penn. Col. Rec.*, vol. v, pp. 315, 322.

[2] *Ibid.*, vol. v, pp. 316-319.

[3] Walton, *Conrad Weiser*, pp. 229- 231.

[4] *Journal of Captain Wm. Trent*, p. 24.

this time in their endeavor to get control of the western fur trade.

With the development of the Pennsylvania and Virginia traffic with the Indians, the settlements gradually advanced westward and by the end of the war in 1748 had reached the foothills of the last range of mountains separating those colonies from the Mississippi valley. In 1748, Thomas Lee, of Virginia, in conjunction with twelve other men from that province and Maryland, and Handbury, a London merchant, formed "The Ohio Company" for the purpose of stimulating progress in that direction and promoting trade.[1] Dr. Thomas Walker, Christopher Gist and others were sent out in the following year to explore the western country which they traversed as far as the Falls of the Ohio.[2] The Company also despatched Barney Curran, a trader, with goods to exchange for peltry with the natives there.[3]

Between the Pennsylvania traders and those of Virginia and Maryland so much jealousy and rivalry in the fur trade developed as to threaten to destroy the effectiveness of the Logstown treaty.[4] Because of the greater distance to be covered those from the two latter provinces were put to much more expense and hence were readily undersold by the Pennsylvanians. The Virginians and Marylanders complained bitterly of this disadvantage, and differences often arose between them and the traders from Pennsylvania while actually at work among the Indians. This lack of unity greatly weakened the English encroachment upon the French territory.[5] During the recent war the French

[1] *Penn. Col. Rec.*, vol. v, pp. 422-424; Dillon, p. 50.

[2] *Filson Club Papers*, No. 13, pp. 1-83; Dillon, pp. 50-51.

[3] *Mag. West. Hist.*, vol. vi, p. 105.

[4] *Penn. Arch.*, vol. ii, pp. 31, 46-49.

[5] *Journal of Captain Wm. Trent*, p. 25.

had lost many of their Indian allies. Until its close there was little opposition to English aggression further than protests sent to the governor of Pennsylvania, who was asked to recall the traders.[1]

In 1749, Governor Vaudreuil was instructed to do what he could to stop the English advance into the Ohio valley. To this end a union of the Indian tribes was proposed, and also the building of one or two posts on the upper Ohio for the purpose of preventing the English from doing so, in which case they could easily carry on the trade in all parts of the French fur fields.[2] The next year New France warned the English of Pennsylvania that their people were trespassing on French soil where, if they persisted, their goods would be seized and confiscated.[3] Moreover, the French had bettered their organization and were energetically at work winning back the friendship of the Indians whom they had lost for a while.

By December 17, 1750, the Pennsylvania traders began to feel the results of the renewal of French activity in the Ohio valley. Croghan's men, for example, reported that two of their number and seven horses loaded with skins had been seized and carried to a new post being built on an arm of Lake Erie (probably Sandusky).[4] The English on their part were striving to counteract the growing French influence with all the force they could muster. In May, 1751, they were still holding the trade of many of the savages.[5] The next year Pennsylvania and Virginia traders met the Ohio Indians at Logstown where the tribes con-

[1] *Penn. Col. Rec.*, vol. v, p. 425; *Mag. West. Hist.*, vol. ii, pp. 369-373.

[2] Margry, vol. vi, p. 727.

[3] *Doc. Rel. to Col. Hist. N. Y.*, vol. vi, p. 565.

[4] *Journal of George Croghan*, Dec. 17, 1750; in Taylor's *Ohio*, p. 61.

[5] *Early Western Travels*, vol. i, p. 59.

firmed the Lancaster treaty and agreed to further the operations of the "Ohio Company".[1]

The treaty, however, did not assure full protection. On December 10, 1753, some of the English found on French territory were robbed of their merchandise, others were killed and still others carried away as prisoners. At the time the English claimed that the officials of New France and Louisiana were paying 100 crowns for each English scalp brought in. This information no doubt was derived from their spies whom they kept among the western Indians, for the purpose of inciting the tribes to war against the French.[2]

The English traders among the natives there nevertheless did not work as effectively as they might have done. As early as 1753 the savages complained these traders brought them "scarcely anything but Rum and Flour; They bring little Powder and Lead or other valuable goods. The rum ruins Us. . . . When these whiskey traders come they bring thirty or forty Caggs and put it down before Us and make Us drink and get all the Skins that should go to pay the Debts We have contracted for Goods bought of the Fair Traders. . . . The wicked Whiskey Sellers when they have once got the Indians in Liquor make them sell their very Clothes from their Backs. . . ."[3] Such behavior was not conducive to the building-up of a strong influence over the western tribes, hence by 1755 the English had lost much of their power over the Ohio Indians, and the Delaware were already at war with them.[4] The next year they lost both the Twightwee and the Jachquai (sic).[5]

[1] *Mag. West. Hist.*, vol. vi, p. 335.

[2] *Journal of Captain Wm. Trent*, pp. 73-74.

[3] *Penn. Col. Rec.*, vol. v, p. 676.

[4] Walton, p. 227.

[5] *Board of Trade Papers*, 1754-1757, Pa. Hist. Soc. Trans.

At the renewal of war with Great Britain, therefore, the French had much support from the natives. In 1758, the savages of the upper Ohio were carrying most of their peltry to Detroit where they always found plenty of French traders ready to buy it. French brandy, however, was not so plentiful as English rum. At times the Indians found it necessary to call a council in order to decide who should be the ones to get drunk.[1]

Regarding the amount of peltry that passed from the Mississippi valley to New France and to the English colonies during the period in question, few statistics are available. On August 20, 1749, there were at Oswego 193 canoes manned by 1,557 men who had carried thither 1,185 packs of skins of which 1,049 came from the western country. Out of this number of canoes three were manned by thirty-six Frenchmen who brought thirty-five packs. The value of the peltry thus carried to this post was £21,406 sterling.[2] The Miami alone brought seventy-seven packs in eleven canoes manned by eighty-eight men.[3] By 1761, the value of the goods necessary to carry on the Indian trade in the upper Mississippi valley amounted to 1,500,000 livres, when sold at an advance of 30 per cent to cover freight charges. It was asserted at this time by the English that the French "computed the value of all kinds of skins imported from Canada to amount to £135,000 sterling per annum".[4] At the same time all the northern English colonies did not export to the mother country more than £90,000 sterling. The next year the peltry that

[1] *Ohio Valley Hist. Series*, No. 5, pp. 75-76.

[2] *Doc. Rel. to Col. Hist. N. Y.*, vol. vi, p. 538.

[3] *Journal of Captain Wm. Trent*, p. 25.

[4] *Coll. and Res. Mich. Pioneer and Hist. Soc.*, vol. xix, p. 14; *The Present State of the British and French Trade, etc.*, 1745, p. 9.

reached Montreal from the upper Mississippi valley was worth 146,000 livres.[1]

Notwithstanding the fact that the output of furs from New France was greater than that from its English rival, and the further fact that in 1763 Fort Ouiatanon alone sent to Detroit 80,000 pounds of peltry, the French had lost to the English in the struggle for the control of this traffic. The latter were at this time trading in Wisconsin. For example, Denis Croghan, in the spring of 1763, arrived at Green Bay with seventy packs each weighing thirty pounds.[2]

In short, then, the account of the peltry that passed from the Mississippi valley to New France and to the English colonies during the period under consideration shows that up to 1720 the greater part of the skins from that region were despatched to Europe by way of Montreal and Quebec. From the beginning of the century at least many pelts passed from these two markets to Albany and from there were shipped to Europe. From this time to the opening of the first war with England the French continued in the ascendancy, but all the while were gradually letting that power pass into the hands of their rival. Between 1744 and 1750 the English merchants received a larger quantity of the peltry from the region in question than did the French. Before the opening of the Seven Year War, however, the latter had regained much they had lost. For the remainder of the time the trade was in such great confusion that not much definite knowledge can be ascertained concerning it. The few facts available, at all events, show that the French obtained peltry in considerable quantities up to the time the province was ceded to the English.

[1] *The Present State of the British and French Trade, etc.*, 1745, p. 9.

[2] *Coll. and Rep. St. Hist. Soc. Wis.*, vol. viii, p. 235.

CHAPTER XIX

The Fur Trade of Louisiana, 1699-1763

Among Iberville's schemes for the development of the province was one for the promotion of a trade in skins with the natives. As early as 1700, he had received some buffalo hides from the Illinois country and had engaged the " voyageurs " returning thither to procure more of them in order to ascertain their possible value in the markets of France. For each skin the hunters were to receive seven livres; in order to secure the skins more rapidly they were instructed to do what they could to induce the Illinois Indians to abandon the beaver for the buffalo hunt. In Iberville's opinion the savages would prefer the latter if the hides would bring as large returns as the skins of the former did. In order to carry on this traffic on a large scale it was further proposed to have a number of large flatboats constructed, on which considerable quantities could be sent down the Mississippi,[1] there to be placed on ocean vessels and shipped to France.[2]

Iberville's previous knowledge of the fur trade about the Hudson Bay[3] led him to believe in the possibility of persuading the natives of that region to sell the peltry to traders from Louisiana whom he proposed to station on the upper waters of the Mississippi river. With prices the same and French merchandise as attractive as that offered

[1] *Supra*, p. 59.

[2] Margry, vol. iv, p. 376.

[3] *Ibid.*, vol. vi, pp. 497-500.

by the English, the Indians undoubtedly would prefer to dispose of the pelts in this fashion rather than to carry them miles over a difficult and dangerous country in order to exchange them for the latter's goods. If workable the scheme would completely destroy the traffic of the English in that region since none of their traders could be induced to follow the savages into the interior. Iberville asserted that if such a traffic were established, within four or five years it would draw away from Fort Nelson annually between 60,000 and 80,000 buffalo skins, worth four or five livres each; 150,000 deer skins, worth 2,500,000 livres; and other peltry, such as that of the bear, wolf, otter, lynx, wild cat, fox and martin, worth at least 200,000 livres.[1] The proposal seems to have had no effect on his own government, whereas the agents of the Hudson's Bay Company, in order to strengthen their influence over the Indians with whom they traded, speedily began to supply them with guns.[2] For some time the energetic way in which the English carried on their work made it impossible for the French to make any advance in the field.

In 1700, Le Sueur [3] left Biloxi with two boats, manned by nineteen men; [4] on reaching the territory in the Sioux country assigned him by his patent, he began operations by establishing a post on the Blue river which he named Fort l'Huillier.[5] During his stay he bought 3,600 beaver skins [6] and many other pelts, for which he gave in exchange merchandise, including some Brazilian tobacco that was much appreciated by the savages.[7] Trade in beaver was

[1] Margry, vol. iv, pp. 600-601.

[2] *Ibid.*, vol. vi, p. 82.

[3] *Supra*, p. 314.

[4] Margry, vol. vi, p. 70.

[5] *Ibid.*, p. 80.

[6] *Supra*, p. 314.

[7] Margry, vol. v, pp. 417-419.

contrary to Le Sueur's grant; but he justified the purchase on the ground that the Indians had pillaged his canoes and that he had taken the pelts in compensation for his losses. The officials of New France, however, asserted that the robbery was preconceived by Le Sueur in order to have an excuse to seize the skins.[1] On returning to Biloxi he soon sailed for France. Nothing more was done with his grant in the Sioux country, due perhaps to the fact that the Illinois opposed the French going there to trade, fearing they might supply the Sioux with firearms; the very thing Le Sueur, himself, would have done had the officials permitted it.[2] The Illinois, in fact, robbed eleven Frenchmen who were returning from that region of beaver skins to the value of 33,000 livres.[3]

During the very first year of the existence of the little French settlement on the Gulf of Mexico quite a traffic in skins was established with the traders coming from the upper part of the Mississippi valley.[4] On February 16, 1700, Tonty and others from the Illinois country sold at Biloxi six canoe loads of beaver pelts.[5] As has been shown,[6] this commerce, of an illicit sort, was stimulated by the attitude in New France toward it. But neither length nor the hardships of a voyage to the Gulf were great enough to stop the traffic in question. Therefore both buffalo hides and peltry found their way to that market in prodigious quantity.[7] For some of the beaver skins Iberville gave in return 1,200 to 1,500 pounds of powder,

[1] Margry, vol. v, p. 357.

[2] *Ibid.*, vol. vi, p. 89.

[3] *Ibid.*, vol. iv, p. 366.

[4] *Supra*, pp. 313, 314.

[5] Margry, vol. iv, p. 364.

[6] *Supra*, pp. 313, 314.

[7] Margry, vol. iv, pp. 521, 606-607.

and "some of his people have also given them other goods in trade".[1]

On February 22, 1702, Iberville conferred with certain traders from the Illinois country who wished to sell him the beaver skins they had in storage there. They had received flattering offers from the English, but the risk to be incurred in the transaction made them prefer to sell to the French at Biloxi.[2] Encouraged by this opportunity, Iberville began to consider the feasibility of increasing the fur trade at Biloxi to at least 45,000 pounds of skins annually.[3] This he proposed to bring about by a readjustment of the position of the Indian tribes in the upper valley. The scheme aroused no interest on the part of the home government, yet a royal grant at this time was made to Juchereau[4] who soon collected 15,000 skins which contributed in some measure to an enlargement of the quantity of skins sent down the Mississippi from the Illinois country.[5]

In 1704, Bienville tried to increase the trade still more by attempting to induce about 110 Frenchmen who were at work in bands of seven or eight in the Missouri region to come down with their peltry.[6] About this time a quarrel broke out among the savages of the Illinois that destroyed Juchereau's post on the Wabash, involving a loss of 13,000 buffalo hides that would have gone to the same market.[7] The peltry trade of the French was further disturbed by hostilities between the Alibamon and Mobile Indians.[8]

[1] *Rep. and Coll. St. Hist. Soc. Wis.*, vol. xvi, pp. 201-202.

[2] Margry, vol. iv, pp. 509-510.

[3] *Ibid.*, p. 598.

[4] *Supra*, p. 314.

[5] *A. N., C., Sér. C13*, fol. 458; La Harpe, p. 367.

[6] Margry, vol. v, p. 368.

[7] *A. N., C., Sér. C13*, vol. i, fol. 225; *Trans. Ill. St. Hist. Soc.*, pt. 1, p. 43; *Journal of Captain Wm. Trent*, pp. 10-11.

[8] *A. N., C., Sér. C13*, vol. ii, fol. 398; Margry, vol. v, pp. 435-436.

Louisiana, like New France, had English rivals to reckon with. In 1699, traders of that nationality had given the Indians near the mouth of the Arkansas guns and other presents in order to alienate them from the French and especially from the Jesuits.[1] A year later Penicaut, on passing up the Mississippi found an English trader also among the Arkansas Indians. He was kindly disposed toward the French and rendered them much assistance in securing food of which the latter were much in need.[2]

These Englishmen, however, were evidently not the first visitors of their kind to the valley. Delisle's map of 1701 shows Carolina trade routes as far west as the Chickasaw, and on a map of 1703 the Tennessee river is marked as the chief thoroughfare.[3] Carolinians in fact were much ahead of their northern neighbors in crossing the mountains. It is claimed that they were trading with the Indians on the Cumberland and Tennessee when La Salle made the discovery of the mouth of the Mississippi, and that by 1700 were passing down these rivers to the Ohio, Wabash and Mississippi.[4]

In 1701, the French government was informed that English traders were among the Chickasaw, and was advised to establish a post at the mouth of the Wabash in order to prevent trade from being developed over that route between the English and the French.[5] The post was not built. Before the end of the year one Frenchman was killed on this route, though five others made successful trips to Carolina and brought back quantities of English merchandise.

[1] *Jes. Rel.*, vol. lxv, p. 117.

[2] *Hist. Coll. of La. and Fla.*, vol. i, p. 63.

[3] Winsor, *The Miss. Basin*, p. 20.

[4] Coxe, *Description, etc.*, pp. 109-122; King, *Ohio*, pp. 48-49.

[5] Margry, vol. v, pp. 354-355.

This traffic explains why Iberville wished to shift the relative position of the native tribes in the Illinois country to block it and at the same time to protect the French against attacks from Indian allies of the English.[1]

On May 7, 1707, it was stated that the Carolinians were receiving from the western Indians, including the Chickasaw, about 50,000 skins annually, in exchange for broad cloth, red and white beads, knives, guns, powder and bullets worth between £2,500 and £3,000 sterling.[2] About this time the Board of Trade was informed that English merchandise was attractive to the Indians and held the savages to alliance and obedience provided its price were low enough; on the principle that "they affect them most who sell the best cheap". It was indispensable to the success of the traffic, also, that Indian traders should be enabled to buy their merchandise at as low a rate as possible, because they were often forced to take small skins at double their real value in order to maintain friendly relations with the savages.[3]

The influence exercised by the Carolinians over a number of tribes in the lower Mississippi valley led them to believe it possible to control all, hence, July 10, 1708, the Board of Trade was informed that all the Indians of the "back country" could be made English subjects by placing the Yassas and other friendly tribes on the Cussate river, and by building a few small forts on the frontier where English merchandise could be stored. The home government was further informed that the Cherokee were an adequate protection for Carolina against the Illinois and

[1] Margry, vol. iv, pp. 599-600.

[2] *Bancroft Papers,* MSS., 1662-1679, N. Y. Pub. Lib.

[3] *Public Records of South Carolina,* MSS., vol. v, p. 196; Trans. B of T., Columbia, S. C.

other Indians well disposed toward the French from the north, but that the Cherokee were greatly harrassed by the Iroquois. To that end it was requested that New York be instructed to intercede with the latter to cease their raids.[1]

The Carolinians themselves at the time were endeavoring to bring about peace with the Choctaw and wean them away from the French. A trader in fact proposed to pass down the "Talapotires" (Talapoosa) with a fleet of eight canoes and an army of 500 Indians for the purpose of destroying all tribes that refused to enter into a treaty with the English. However, just as the scheme was ready to be carried out news reached him that the French and Spaniards were about to invade Carolina; whereupon he abandoned the warlike phase of the project, and proceeded in a peaceable fashion to do what he could to secure an alliance with the Choctaw.[2] Meanwhile the Cherokee, instigated no doubt by the English, becoming hostile killed two French traders.[3] In order to defend themselves and their Indian allies, accordingly, the French, in 1710 or 1711, built Fort Massac on the Ohio river.[4]

The patent of Crozat gave him an exclusive right of trade in all peltry, except beaver, which was reserved to New France.[5] When his agents took control of Louisiana they found the English of Carolina among the Natchez and in possession of storehouses among the Choctaw.[6] These traders, it seems, had been instructed immediately to make

[1] *Public Records of South Carolina*, MSS., vol. v, p. 198.

[2] *Ibid.*, p. 195.

[3] *A. N., C., Sér.* C^{13}, vol. ii, fols. 5-32; *Sér. B*, vol. xxix, IC, Louisiane, fols. 9-19.

[4] *Chicago Hist. Soc. Coll.*, vol. iii, p. 55; *Trans. Ill. St. Hist. Soc.*, pt. 8, p. 43.

[5] *A. N., C., Sér. A*, vol. xxii, fols. 1-8; *Hist. Coll. of La.*, pt. 3, p. 40.

[6] Margry, vol. v, p. 507.

a study of the French and Spanish settlements, and send home detailed reports of their observations.[1]

To offset these intrusions on the part of the English, Crozat's officials sent out twelve men with two canoes to the Natchez country, where they were ordered to establish a post where trade might be carried on with these savages.[2] Others were despatched to the Illinois country, who on their return brought to Mobile bear, wild cat, and similar skins.[3] The trade carried on by the new régime was not destined to prosper because the officials offered such low prices,—fifty sols for bear skins and fifteen for deer skins,—that most of the peltry either passed into the hands of the English or up to New France. Traders who formerly brought many skins to Mobile did so no longer, and declared that while Crozat remained in control of affairs they would continue to stay away. Moreover the official price demanded for Indian goods robbed them of all their profits.[4] The settlers in lower Louisiana, however, continued to receive a few pelts with which they carried on an illicit trade with vessels that chance brought to their shores. For beaver skins they received three livres each and for deer skins fifty sols, but in waiting for the arrival of such vessels they were apt to lose much peltry on account of damage by worms.

The work of Crozat's traders in the Illinois country was interrupted by the hostilities of the Natchez who, in 1714, began to kill them in order to secure their merchandise.[5] Notwithstanding the danger they encountered in going up

[1] *Indian Book*, 1710-1718, vol. i, p. 56. Columbia, S. C.

[2] Margry, vol. v, p. 506.

[3] *A. N., C., Sér. F*[3], vol. ccxli; *Sér. C*[13], vol. iii, fols. 269-270.

[4] *Ibid., Sér. C*[13], vol. iii, fols. 209-223.

[5] Margry, vol. v, pp. 512-513.

and down the Mississippi, they made some headway in the traffic form their post of Charville on the Tennessee river.[1] The same year Bienville built Fort Toulouse, so as to strengthen the French trade on the east and also to drive back the English traders.[2] Since the friendship of the Choctaw had already been gained, attention was then given to winning over as many as possible of the Chickasaw.[3]

On May 4, 1716, six traders with three canoes laden with peltry reached the Gulf coast, and in September of the same year Bienville sold 800 deer skins to a French vessel for four reaux each.[4] The traffic was still hampered by the hostilities of the Chickasaw and Natchez, resulting in the death of a numuber of Frenchmen.[5] Some peltry was obtained from the Red river district and some from the Creeks, despite the presence among them of English traders who were doing business on a much larger scale.[6]

The English traders held large debts against many of the Indians. For payment they seized the chickens and hogs, reaped the fields and took away the crops of grain and peas. Moreover they forced the natives to carry heavy burdens for them over long distances. When the savages protested they were cruelly beaten and otherwise treated in a most brutal manner, a course of behavior that caused the Indians to retaliate in kind.[7]

The French were not slow to take advantage of this

[1] *Supra*, p. 29.

[2] *Pub. Rec. of S. C.*, vol. vii, p. 237; Coxe, *Desc. of the Eng. Prov. of Carolana*, pp. 26-27.

[3] *Hist Coll. of La.*, vol. ii, p. 236; vol. iii, pp. 43-46.

[4] Guénin, *La Louisiane*, p. 125.

[5] *A. N., C., Sér.* C^{13}, vol. iv, fols. 355-365.

[6] *Ibid.*, fol. 914.

[7] *Letters of Governor Spotswood*, vol. ii, p. 94; *B. of T. Papers, Prop.*, vol. x, p. 51, Columbia, S. C.

break between the English and their savage allies. Soon they had won over the Chickasaw, Alibamon, Jalipoosa, Abicaw, and some other tribes that had been trading with the English for thirty years. The Carolinians naturally were alarmed at such a possibility of losing their entire hold on the western traffic which was variously estimated at from £1,000 to £6,000 sterling a year reckoned in terms of cloth, guns, powder, bullets and ironware that were exchanged for buck skins, deer skins, and other peltry. Further distress was caused by the fact that about 200 persons who were occupied wholly in the Indian trade were thrown out of employment. The Cherokee continued faithful, but the colonial officials wrote to the home government that "God only knew how long they would remain so". By 1719, indeed the English had lost more than half of their Indian traffic, and the next year it was still further embarrassed when some of their pack-horse drivers deserted to the French.[1]

Although the Crozat régime had been very discouraging to trade as such, it had considerably increased French influence among the Indian tribes of the lower Mississippi valley. Traffic improved when the Company of the West took over Louisiana. During the first year of the control at least 1,000 deer skins were shipped to France.[2]

The Company soon began to make plans to better the conditions of the fur trade. To this end it sent men to the upper Missouri for the purpose of entering into treaties of commerce and friendship with the Indians there. The erection of Fort Chartres[3] also gave considerable strength to

[1] *B. of T. Papers*, vol. x, pp. 1718-1720, *Trans. Penn. Hist. Soc.*; *Pub. Rec. of S. C.*, vol. vii, p. 237; vol. viii, pp. 72, 240.

[2] *A. N., C., Sér. C13*, vol. v, fol. 16.

[3] *Supra*, p. 29.

the trade in the Illinois country, and from this time onward a great deal of peltry was collected there for the Gulf coast market.[1] In like fashion Fort Assomption[2] served to make transportation to lower Louisiana safer, and to hold the hostile Chickasaw in check.[3] By 1721, the French were able to adjust certain differences that had arisen with the Choctaw[4] over presents and prices; accordingly, in December, La Harpe started on a journey westward with the object of making treaties of friendship with the Indians on the Arkansas.[5]

The acquisition of the Illinois country[6] did not increase the Gulf trade in beaver skins, because the animals found there were almost of a straw color. The value of pelts of the sort depended upon their darkness of hue, whereas in the case of light shades the fur was thin and of little value.[7] Other kinds of peltry, however, were sent down in great quantities. Before the skins could be shipped to France they were often badly damaged in the warm climate because of the crude system of tanning.[8] On September 15, 1720, the Louisiana officials informed the home government that they were able to provide large numbers of buffalo skins from the Wabash country, but that it was needful to tan the skins carefully in order to prevent their destruction on the way to France. To this end it was proposed to erect tanneries on the Wabash and to send thither

[1] *Chicago Hist. Soc. Coll.*, vol. iii, p. 55; *Am. St. Papers, Pub. Lands*, vol. i, p. 80.

[2] *Supra*, p. 28.

[3] *A. N., C., Sér.* C^{13}, vol. vi, fol. 146.

[4] *Ibid.*, vol. vi, fols. 146-147.

[5] La Harpe, pp. 282-284.

[6] *Supra*, p. 26.

[7] Charlevoix, *A Voyage to North America*, vol. i, p. 54.

[8] *A. N., C., Sér.* C^{13}, vol. vi, fol. 20; Margry vol. v, p. 626.

soldiers who understood the processes involved.[1] Moreover in the effort to develop the fur trade of the upper part of the valley, traffic with the Indians about Mobile, consisting in an exchange of knives, hatchets, guns, powder, mirrors and brandy for deer skins and corn, was not overlooked.[2] In 1721, the Company endeavored to systemize the commerce in peltry by fixing the prices of it at the various storehouses.[3]

In spite of the recent setback the English of Carolina soon became active again in the Louisiana trade. The colony had returned to the old English principle of buying up skins at fair prices. This, it was believed, would eventually bring back their former allies, since the French could not undersell their English competitors because the French market for deer skins was inferior.[4] At this time there were probably 2,000 Indians located between the English and French settlements in lower Louisiana who were trading indiscriminately with both. The Carolinians, however, were fearful lest these natives should go over entirely to the French; for the only savages upon whom the English

[1] Margry, vol. v, p. 626.

[2] Chaville, p. 131.

[3] La Harpe, pp. 176-178.

The following are prices fixed for Biloxi, Mobile and Fort Louis; delivered elsewhere they were diminished by the cost necessary to ship them to the coast. They were to be paid for in bills on France, having two months' time, with discount at ten per cent.

Kinds	Best grade			Good grade		
Beaver	3 livres a pound			34 sols a pound		
Buffalo	4 livres each					
Cow	2 livres, 10 sols, each					
Deer skins	With head and tail			Without head and tail		
	Large	medium	small	Large	medium	small
	25	20	15	20	15	10 sols, each

[4] *Supra*, p. 319; *Pub. Rec. of S. C.*, vol. viii, p. 227.

at this time could rely were the Cherokee who were at war with the French.[1] Notwithstanding the confidence of the English in their ability to undersell their rivals, the prospects of regaining their former prestige in the western trade were not especially flattering.

Just at the time when the outlook was darkest for the English, the French officials began playing into the hands of their rivals by trying to persuade the traders to take up agriculture, which they believed was more essential to the welfare of Louisiana. The traders, too, on their part were furthering the English advantage by demanding of the Indians high prices for French goods.[2] In 1723, trouble with the Natchez led to the issuance of an order suspending all commerce with them. This command widened the breach between the officials and the traders, who continued their operations much as before in utter disregard of instructions from New Orleans.[3] The Indians on the Missouri also went on the war path, robbing the Frenchmen in their territory.[4]

Fort Chartres was the starting-point of the traders going to the Missouri, as well as the place from which voyages to the lower Mississippi began, and hence was a post of considerable importance.[5] On October 7, 1724, the Osage Indians sent word to the Louisiana officials that they had quantities of peltry, especially beaver skins, which they desired to exchange for French merchandise.[6] The year had opened with some of these savages still unfriendly, due

[1] *Pub. Rec. of N. C.*, vol. ii, p. 422.

[2] Margry, vol. v, p. 654.

[3] Pickett, *Hist. of Ala.*, vol. i, pp. 232-233.

[4] *A. N., C., Sér.* C^{13}, vol. vi, fol. 299.

[5] *Ibid.*, fols. 362-363, 365.

[6] Margry, vol. vi, p. 427.

in part to the fact that the French were short of goods with which to trade. Before the close of the year, however, Fort Orleans [1] had been established and Bourgmont, who was placed in command, was able to arrange treaties with some tribes and to open trade with the Kansas Indians in particular.[2] Even earlier than this the French had attempted to increase their influence among the Sioux. In 1722, they were dealing with five of the twenty-five or twenty-six tribes.[3] Much of the trade of the others passed to the English posts on Hudson's Bay; accordingly, in order to break it up a post was established, in 1724, at "Tekamamiowen" in the Sioux country.[4]

By 1725, the Company was thoroughly convinced that it could not carry on the Indian trade by sending out agents of its own, hence decided to put the traffic in the hands of men already skilled in the service. Otherwise the risk and expense were too great. The number of skins obtained in the province at the time was estimated to be about 50,000 annually, exclusive of the peltry drawn from the Sioux, Missouri and Illinois Indians.[5] Of this amount the natives on the Red river, the Tonica and the tribes on the Arkansas furnished 1,000 deer skins each; the Yazou and Ossagoulas similarly 2,000, of a very good quality; the Alibamon, 3,000; the Chickasaw and Choctaw, 4,000 each; the Talapouches, 5,000; the Abikas, 8,000, and the other tribes in lower Louisiana smaller amounts.[6]

In 1727, the fur trade in the upper part of the province

[1] *Supra*, p. 30.

[2] Margry, vol. vi, pp. 396-447.

[3] *Ibid.*, p. 518.

[4] *Ibid.*, pp. 505, 509, 513-514.

[5] *A., A. E., Am.*, vol. i, fols. 6-50.

[6] *Ibid.*

was much disturbed by wars with the Fox. Since the beginning of the century these tribes had been frequently hostile to the French, and it was the opinion of the commandant at the Illinois post that there would be no end to the outbreaks until these savages had been annihilated. A proposition was made to New France that the destruction be undertaken jointly, but the plan was rejected as being too hazardous, since the Fox were a very fierce and warlike people.[1] While these proposals were under consideration, the unjust action of the commandant at Fort Rosalie, by taking their lands for the purpose of making himself a handsome estate, aroused the Natchez[2] in turn to a violent state of resentment. They attacked and came near destroying the French settlement which was one of the best trading posts in lower Louisiana.[3]

The English were as quick to take advantage of these Indian outbreaks as the French had been in 1715. From 1721 onward their traders among the Chickasaw and Choctaw had been increasing year by year. While among these tribes they had been encouraging them to take up arms against the French, and by way of influence were affording them exceptional trading opportunities, much better than the French could offer.[4] In 1726, Carolina exported 73,790 deerskins and 1,965 pounds of leather.[5]

Five years later the French share in the western fur trade had fallen into a most critical condition. In 1732, a Choctaw brought the news that English traders were among his people with fifty horses loaded with goods, and operating

[1] *Rep. and Coll. St. Hist. Soc. Wis.*, vol. iii, pp. 161-165; vol. xvii, p. 69.

[2] *Supra*, pp. 45, 88.

[3] Le Page du Pratz, vol. iii, pp. 230-231.

[4] *A. N., C., Sér.* C^{13}, vol. vi, fols. 146-147.

[5] *Bancroft Papers*, vol. i, pp. 1662-1679, 1726, N. Y. Pub. Lib.

in an area thirty leagues in extent.[1] On May 12, the provincial officials informed the home government that they were buying up all the deer skins the Choctaw offered, so as to keep these Indians from becoming allies of the English. From January 1 to March, they had obtained 2,200 skins weighing about 25,000 pounds and placed them in the royal storehouse ready for shipment to France. On July 18, the "ordonnateur" sold at twenty-five sols a pound deerskins to the amount of 5,082 pounds. This was considered a good bargain since many of the skins were already damaged by worms, and were sure to depreciate still more were they allowed to remain packed away in the storehouse.[2]

These purchases were a great drain on the colonial treasury since the officials were obliged to pay at English rates. On July 24, 1733, accordingly, they requested the home government to instruct them as to the price, in munitions of war and other sorts of merchandise, they should pay for deer skins, in view of the fact that the French market for them was very poor. Nevertheless it was declared to be necessary to pay good prices since the Choctaw had deerskins ready for the market and the Alibamon had declared that they could secure better rates from the English than the French. The crown was therefore urged to secure the trade of these Indians even at a considerable sacrifice.[3]

The next year the officials at Mobile secured some English merchandise from a vessel trading there which was used to great advantage in dealing with the Choctaw. The English, on their part, tried to make capital out of the incident by telling the savages that the French would be unable

[1] *Bancroft Papers*, vol. i, MSS., N. Y. Pub. Lib.

[2] *A. N., C., Sér.* C^{13}, vol. xv, fols. 107, 174.

[3] *Ibid.*, vol. xvii, fols. 163-164.

to supply them with limbourg unless other English vessels brought it to Mobile. This source of supply was very unlikely since the provincial government of Carolina was going to make such a trade impossible.[1] As Carolina did not do so, the English in the Choctaw country were unable to make this prophecy effective. Besides supplying the French with limbourg for the Indian traffic English vessels also gave them a better market for deerskins than France itself offered.[2]

During the last year of the control of Louisiana by the Company of the Indies the traders at Mobile had been fairly prosperous. They were able to dispose of their peltry at twenty-five sols a pound and on the merchandise they took in exchange they made a profit in trading it to the natives of from 20 to 50 per cent.[3] On February 28, 1734, from ten to 12,000 deerskins were shipped from Mobile to foreign markets.[4] In order to increase this trade, it was proposed to establish a French post among the Chickasaw. Such an establishment would serve to maintain good order on the part of the French trader and help to bring those Indians into alliance. It was claimed that dealers from Mobile were carrying to the Chickasaw and Choctaw large quantities of English goods. This traffic the officials denounced on the ground that the English were gaining a profit on their merchandise and at the same time were securing at first hand the best peltry the Chickasaw had, at thirty sols a pound, thereby forcing the French to pay the same price for inferior skins. Moreover it was claimed that the sale of English goods weakened French influence

[1] *A. N., C., Sér. B,* vol. lxi, fol. 631.

[2] Force, *Tracts,* App., No. 5, vol. i, pp. 45, 46, 49.

[3] *A. N., C., Sér.* C^{13}, vol. xviii, fols. 62-68.

[4] *Ibid.,* fols. 8-12.

correspondingly.[1] The commandant at Mobile was interested personally in the fur traffic to such an extent as to require a legal investigation of his activities. The case was carried to the superior council where it was decided against that officer, who thereupon was ordered to reimburse the Company for the damages caused by his dealings.[2]

The difficulty in holding the Choctaw as allies was perhaps somewhat less than in the case of the Chickasaw, yet the trade and friendship of those tribes cost heavily in presents.[3] The French tried to make the Choctaw believe there was an advantage in dealing with them which could not be gained in trade with the English. The facts of the matter scarcely bore out the French assertion, a circumstance that the Indians were quite clever enough to discern.[4] The French were giving five quarters of limbourg for five large or ten medium-sized deer skins, and a gun for ten large or twenty medium-sized pelts, which price, the French asserted, could not be gotten from the English. Whether this statement was true or false matters little; the Indians knew that such rates could be maintained only by having the English as competitors and accordingly were not anxious for either rival to be driven from the trade.[5]

On July 4, 1734, the English were at Mobile buying up deer skins.[6] The inhabitants encouraged this traffic since by it they were able to pay English prices for peltry with much more ease. By it also they had been able to secure the greater part of the Choctaw trade and of many of the

[1] *A. N., C., Sér.* C^{13}, vol. xviii, fols. 138-141.

[2] *Ibid.*, vol. xv, fol. 33.

[3] *Ibid.*, vol. xviii, fols. 177-178.

[4] *Ibid.*, vol. xix, fols. 95-96.

[5] *Ibid.*

[6] *Ibid.*, vol. xviii, fol. 205.

Creek as well, who informed the Carolinians among them that they could procure all the English goods they wanted from the French.[1] In order to drive the English dealers from the Choctaw trade entirely the French, in 1736, built Fort Tombecbée.[2]

Returning to the Illinois country, in 1730, it was said that 100 men could be found there able to bear arms. This number was increased at certain times of the year by as many as 200 on their way back from their annual hunting trips among the surrounding tribes.[3] This number, however, the English authorities placed at 500,[4] some of whom dealt with the natives on the Missouri where they had caused much trouble by the licentious habits they practiced.[5]

About this time also it was asserted of the Illinois trade that it would be benefited by the establishment of a French post at the mouth of the Wabash.[6] The Illinois themselves were the firm friends of the French with whom they had been on good terms since the latter took possession of the Mississippi valley. Moreover they had not only assisted in driving back the Iroquois and Fox, but had aided in the war against the Chickasaw, Cherokee and Natchez.[7]

In 1735, again, the French and Illinois Indians were at war with the Fox.[8] This hostility considerably disturbed the trade with the Sioux, yet in 1735 the French were able

[1] *Coll. Ga. Hist. Soc.*, vol. ii, p. 319; Force, *Tracts*, App., No. 5, vol. i, pp. 45, 46, 49.

[2] Le Page du Pratz, vol. ii, p. 255; *supra*, p. 25.

[3] *A. N., C., Sér. F³*, vol. xxiv, fols. 235-241.

[4] *Pub. Rec. of S. C.*, vol. xvi, p. 390.

[5] *A. N., C., Sér. F³*, vol. xxiv, fols. 235-241.

[6] *Ibid.*

[7] *Ibid., Sér. C¹³*, vol. xvi, fols. 178-188, 193, 227; *Rep. and Coll. St. Hist. Soc. Wis.*, vol. xvii, pp. 179-181, 213.

[8] Margry, vol. vi, pp. 570-571; *Rep. and Coll. St. Hist. Soc. Wis.*, vol. xvii, pp. 183-185.

to buy from them 100,000 beautiful beaver skins.[1] The next year the quantity of pelts secured from that source was considerably reduced by unfriendliness on the part of the Sioux themselves. The danger involved in a trade with these tribes was at the time too great even for the venturesome Frenchmen to attempt.[2] Traffic with the other tribes about the Illinois country was fairly normal, consequently the annual shipments were made as usual to New Orleans.[3] The carrying of the peltry to the capital was relieved of attacks from the Natchez Indians who had now been practically destroyed; but the danger from the Chickasaw was still very formidable.[4]

The natives of the lower part of the Mississippi valley, in 1735, were securing such good prices for their peltry that the French traders were unable to make any profit unless they gave limbourg in exchange. For an ell and a half of this cloth costing fifteen livres, English price, they received five large or ten medium-sized deerskins.[5]

The French also entered into an agreement with the Alibamon whereby they were to be allowed to settle among them provided the traders would pay the same prices for peltry as the English did and in accordance with the latter's method of classifying deerskins. Hides of the first class were to weigh not less than two pounds; those of the second, twenty ounces, or less than two pounds, and those of the third class under twenty ounces; the first class equaling two of the second and three of the third. Few of the last-named were accepted because of their inferior qual-

[1] Margry, vol. vi, p. 574.

[2] *Ibid.*, pp. 574-575.

[3] *A. N., C., Sér. C*[13], vol. xx, fols. 85-91; *Sér. B*, vol. lxiii, fol. 608.

[4] *Pub. Rec. of S. C.*, vol. xix, p. 153.

[5] *A. N., C., Sér. C*[13], vol. xx, fols. 25-27.

ity. An ell and a half of limbourg costing twelve livres was to be exchanged for five large skins or an equivalent number of the smaller sizes. In the English market these would bring fifteen livres,[1] thereby netting the trader three. A gun worth eleven livres would sell for ten deerskins, and a shirt worth three livres for two. Were such prices to be paid by the French their profits would be very small indeed. Moreover it was claimed that since the English received most of the large skins the French had to buy second grade pelts at almost the same rate as that the English paid for those of the best grade.[2] However many of the skins collected by the French indirectly passed to the English markets. On August 25, 1735, 5,000 deer skins were sold at Mobile to one English trader alone.[3]

As already observed,[4] the English had not always treated the Indians fairly, hence in 1734 a deputation of natives went with Governor Oglethorpe of Georgia to England to arrange a treaty that would fix the weight and prices of English goods, and for an understanding that no more than one storehouse should be permitted in a village.[5] The English trade with the western savages, nevertheless, prospered. In 1735, about 100,000 pounds of pelts were collected at Augusta alone.[6] Forty miles from the French post of Toulouse the English now had a garrison beyond which the traders of the former could not pass without arousing English hostility.[7] The fact did not prevent those of the latter from passing beyond the Fort Toulouse limit.

[1] *Supra*, p. 352.

[2] *A. N., C., Sér. C*[13], vol. xx, fols. 145-149.

[3] *Ibid., Sér. C*[13] *vol. xx*, fols. 160-167.

[4] *Supra*, p. 343.

[5] Force, *Tracts: An Account Showing the Progress of the Colony of Georgia, etc.*, vol. i, p. 15.

[6] *Ibid.*, p. 6; *Coll. Ga. Hist. Soc.*, vol. i, p. 179.

[7] *Coll. Ga. Hist. Soc.*, vol. i, p. 182.

Therefore the trade of Augusta, in 1736 alone, required the use of five large boats to take the peltry to Savannah. These boats were able to carry about 9,000 pounds of deer skins and each boat made annually four or five voyages to the coast with a cargo worth between £1,200 and £1,500 sterling.[1] In 1739, it was stated that the traders, pack-horse men, servants, townsmen and other persons living on the fur trade from Georgia and the Carolinas and centering their activities at Augusta, numbered about 600. Each hunter, it was asserted, furnished the market annually with about 300 pounds of skins that had been given in exchange for woolen goods and ironware.[2]

There were other traders who only passed through Augusta on their way to the Creek. In 1741, there were forty-six of them, along with 305 pack-horses, employed in traffic with the Creek and Chickasaw.[3] Up to this time Augusta was considered the key to the Creek, Cherokee and Chickasaw trade, although not more than 500 horses were employed in it. At this time as many of the traders set out from New Winsor, South Carolina, as from Augusta. At the latter place there were but three trading houses and everything was in a languishing condition due to the poor system of regulation.[4]

During these years the French on their part had not been inactive. In September, 1736, 7,000 ells of limbourg were required for the trade. The home government was requested to send only the blue and red varieties; 3,000 ells of the former and 4,000 of the latter, but none of the black and white since it could be used for the negroes only. This

[1] *Coll. Ga. Hist. Soc.*, vol. i, p. 179; Force, *Tracts: An Account, etc.*, vol. i, p. 6.

[2] *Coll. Ga. Hist. Soc.*, vol. i, p. 179; Force, *op. cit.*, vol. i, p. 6.

[3] *Coll. Ga. Hist. Soc.*, vol. ii, p. 124.

[4] *Ibid.*, vol. i, p. 179; vol. ii, p. 126.

amount of cloth, is was claimed, would enable the traders to net an annual profit of between 150 and 200 livres.[1] 9,000 deerskins left Louisiana in 1738 by one vessel alone,[2] and the next year about 50,000 such pelts were procured in exchange for bullets, powder, guns, flints, blankets, vermillion, mirrors and hardware.[3]

In June, 1740, it was asserted by the English that the French traders among the natives were urging the savages to kill their English rivals and to carry away their merchandise. A proposition like this was no doubt tempting to the Indians, since the English were sending into the interior large pack-horse trains heavily loaded with all kinds of goods.[4] The French were unable to make an impression upon the Cherokee; hence they determined that if the tribes could not be brought over wholly or mainly to the French side, they would endeavor to destroy them. They met with small success in this undertaking, however, because the Cherokee could easily secure from the English what ammunition they needed for defense.[5] With most of the tribes French influence was on the increase. It was strong among the Creek. The Alibamon were entirely under French control, whereas the Choctaw were trading with both the French and English, though with their affections thrown into the balance against the latter.[6]

At the beginning of the war, in 1744, Louisiana obtained about 100,000 deer skins [7] as well as many buffalo, kid,

[1] *A. N., C., Sér.* C^{13}, vol. xxi, fols. 111-113.

[2] *Ibid.*, vol. xxiii, fols. 195-196.

[3] *A., B. de l'A.*, vol. 4817, fols. 193-199.

[4] *A. N., C., Sér.* C^{13}, vol. xxi, fols. 111-113.

[5] *Coll. Ga. Hist. Soc.*, vol. i, p. 180.

[6] *Pub. Rec. of S. C.*, vol. xx, p. 288.

[7] *A. N., C., Sér.* C^{13}, vol. xxviii, fols. 35-36.

otter and beaver skins for which the French traders gave in exchange guns, powder, bullets, knives, needles, razors, vermillion, woolen goods, ribbons, blankets, shirts, blue and red limbourg and brandy well mixed with water.[1] At the same time the English were exporting about 100,000 hogsheads (800 or 900 lbs. each) of skins a year, for which they were receiving sixteen shilling, nine pence a pound.[2]

After hostilities had started the French were unable to provide the traders with European goods in sufficient quantity to carry on their business successfully. Moreover the French prices for peltry decreased by three-fifths of their former value while English prices advanced. A deer skin would sell in England for five livres while in France one of the same quality would bring but two. Then, too, English goods were of much better quality than those imported from France. The English traders, however, were not satisfied with this difference in price alone. As a means of promoting their operations, they began to imitate the French traders in their liking for Indian girls and to eat and drink with the natives in a most friendly and familiar fashion. This kind of sociability coupled with tempting prices won many new allies, some of whom maltreated and in some cases killed the French traders. The French on their part claimed that the "insinuating" English were unable to gain the real affection of the Indians who instead secretly hated them. This deep-seated dislike for the English the French claimed made it impossible for many of the natives to abandon the latter completely.[3]

The French had still another sort of hold on the faithfulness of the savages of the lower Mississippi valley. French powder was more easily obtainable and of a quality quite

[1] *The Present State of the Country, etc.*, 1744, p. 11.

[2] *The S. C. Gazette*, Jan. 6-Nov. 26, 1744.

[3] *A. N., C., Sér. C*[13], vol. xxviii, fols. 24-27.

superior to that provided by the English. The latter attempted to offset French powder and lead with English rum, making the Indians crazed and turning their fury against their opponents. While the Indians were drunk they fought among themselves and with the French soldiers and missionaries whose houses they attempted to enter and pillage. In forcing the savages back the French were often wounded and some of them were killed. During these drunken bouts the English traders secured all the peltry the Indians had collected and at times actually bought up the next year's assortment on the basis of credit for rum. Credit of this sort, however, was not forthcoming where the trade of a particular tribe was negligible. For example, the Alibamon complained that the English furnished rum to the Choctaw but refused to advance it to them. The French tried to show them the evil wrought by English rum, at the same time endeavoring to establish among them trade in merchandise of a more useful sort.[1]

The external difficulties that stood in the way of the advancement of the French fur traffic were very little less formidable than the internal obstacles. The trade was hampered by the excessive number and by the low character and ability of many of the men engaged in it. All sorts of persons had gone into the business. These circumstances created dissensions among the savages most prejudicial to the building-up of a flourishing trade. Crimes were committed that often involved the Indians in actual war with the provincial government. Such disorders were especially pronounced among the Indians on the Missouri. The excessive number of the traders, also, led each of them to promote his individual advantage at the expense of his fellows. As a result each tried to undersell his rival, and

[1] *A. N., C., Sér.* C^{13}, vol. xxviii, fols. 24-27.

some even resorted to buying peltry in advance, hoping thereby to force others out of the field. The whole trade on the upper Missouri and Mississippi was in a fair way to ruin.[1]

In order to improve matters it was proposed to assign boundaries to Louisiana, or to form a company composed of twenty of the best men of the province who should take over for a stated number of years the entire control of the fur trade. Some such an arrangement, it was believed, would be for the general good of the province and would at the same time increase the output of peltry by at least 600 packs a year.[2] Neither of these schemes was adopted; instead, action was taken to have the traders kept in check by placing the officials of outlying posts under the supervision of the Illinois commandant in all matters relating to the fur trade.[3]

During the years of the war, 1744-1748, notwithstanding the shortage in French goods the fur trade of Louisiana was by no means destroyed. At this time it was estimated that there were 1,600 Frenchmen engaged in it.[4] However generous this estimate, each year large quantities of skins were sent down to New Orleans. In 1745, the value of furs at the capital was given as 9,621 livres.[5] As it was difficult for the governor to supply the Indians with their usual presents, in 1746 the Choctaw and Creek were impatient concerning the delay and the Choctaw that year made a special visit to Mobile for them. In 1749, the gifts to these savages cost 62,000 livres.[6] Although the French

[1] *A. N., C., Sér. C*[13], vol. xxviii, fols. 82-85, 224-232; vol. xix, fols. 82-83.

[2] *Ibid.*, vol. xxviii, fols. 224-232; vol. xxix, fols. 82-83.

[3] *Ibid.*, vol. xxix, fols. 85-86.

[4] *Ibid.*, vol. xxx, fol. 268.

[5] *Ibid.*, vol. xxix, fols. 109-111; vol. xxxii, fols. 222-227.

[6] *Ibid.*, vol. xxx, fols. 49-52.

had been at great pains to win the trade of the Choctaw and Creeks the shortage of presents during the war had caused them to share the traffic with the English.[1]

The disorder caused by the dissolute habits of some of the French traders continued throughout the war. Governor Vaudreuil, in 1747, undertook to suppress the disturbances in the Illinois country and at Natchitoches, but his efforts met with small success.[2] Between New Orleans and the Illinois country, furthermore, the fur trade was greatly impeded on account of attacks made on the convoys by hostile Chickasaw.[3] In fact it became necessary to keep men on guard day and night to repulse them.[4]

With the restoration of peace came renewed effort from both the French and English to secure possession of the whole of the Indian trade of the lower Mississippi valley, each stimulated by the aggression of the other.[5] In 1751, the Carolinians were among the Alibamon ready to stir up trouble.[6] The French on their part were inclined to allow the natives to deal with both English and French traders, because of the difference in the kinds of peltry sought, but the English were not satisfied with any such arrangement. The latter claimed as allies all the tribes of the southwest and hoped to unite them with the Iroquois in a supreme effort to seize the fur trade entire. They claimed that the French were busy among the Indians under English influence trying to establish storehouses, or in reality forts, and offering to pay well for English scalps.[7] Yet despite this

[1] *Coll. S. C. Hist. Soc.*, vol. ii, p. 294.

[2] *A. N., C., Sér.* C^{13}, vol. xxxi, fols. 47-48.

[3] *Ibid.*, vol. xxxii, fol. 116.

[4] *Ibid., Sér.* F^{3}, vol. xxiv, fols. 361-371.

[5] *Ibid., Sér.* C^{13}, vol. xxxvii, fol. 68.

[6] *Jes. Rel.*, vol. lxix, p. 205.

[7] *Doc. Rel. Col. Hist. N. Y.*, vol. vi, pp. 709-710.

rivalry the trade had advanced considerably since the close of the war, and by 1752 the supply of peltry increased accordingly.[1]

The fur traffic in the portion of Louisiana drained by the Missouri and its branches was placed under the monopolistic control of Déruisseau.[2] The new official was not able to end the trouble created by the traders among the Indians there, corrupting the savages by their evil ways, stealing and carrying away the Indian girls. The excesses of these men even had gone so far as to provoke the natives into destroying the French post, Fort Orleans, upon the upper Missouri. Besides their own misdeeds the Frenchmen defrauded the natives most shamefully. For example, for 1,000 crowns worth of fine beaver skins they paid a small amount of powder which they told the Indians was a new variety that, if planted, would produce all the powder they would want. As soon as the natives discovered that they had been defrauded they were infuriated against the French in general, believing them in sympathy with the behavior of the traders.[3]

When hostilities with England began again in 1754, Governor Kerlérec was greatly in need of merchandise for the traffic, hence could not give the Indians their usual presents. Failing to receive them, the savages threatened to call in the English.[4] Later in the year, when the governor was able to distribute gifts to the value of 62,000 livres he succeeded for a while in allaying the discontent.[5] In return for this expenditure the French received a quantity of peltry worth 30,000 livres and were able to keep the Choctaw faithful.[6]

[1] *A. N., C., Sér. C*[13], vol. xxxiii, fols. 166-168; vol. xxxvi, pp. 269-275.

[2] Gayarré, *Hist. of La.*, vol. ii, p. 23. [3] Bossu, vol. i, pp. 145-149.

[4] Gayarré, Hist of La., vol. ii, pp. 73-74.

[5] *A. N., C., Sér. C*[13], vol. xxxvii, fols. 164-174.

[6] *A., B. N., Fr.*, vol. 12424, fol. 341.

From Fort Tombecbée the French made strenuous endeavors to hold as allies not only the Choctaw but as many as possible of the Chickasaw.[1] Five of the Creek towns also, it was claimed, were entirely under French control.[2] At all events when, in 1756, the Cherokee asked the Creek to join them in a war with the English against the French, they met with a refusal. This shows that two years after the opening of the war the French at least could still count on Creek neutrality. This stand on the part of the Creeks, the English interpreted to mean that the Indians intended to play off the two Europeans against each other and to receive presents from both. It was the opinion of the governor of South Carolina that if the Creek were forced out of their neutrality, they would take sides with the one they deemed the stronger.[3] South Carolina had already secured itself on the northeast against attacks from the French by treaties with the Cherokee and Catawba.[4] By October, 1758, however, it seems they had lost some of the Cherokee, for according to the governor "the Cherokee, Creek and other of the southern Indians who came to Charleston last winter and early in the spring under the pretense of joining us in the war against the French; as soon as they had secured from us everything they could expect, by all the art they were masters of, left us without the least remorse when they found they were not likely to get any more presents. I am now left with about fifty Indians." [5]

Governor Kerlérec certainly did well in the management

[1] Bossu, vol. i, pp. 278-279; Pownall, App., p. 22.

[2] *Bancroft Papers*, 1755-1757, N. Y. Pub. Lib.

[3] *Ibid.*, Dec. 25, 1756; *A. N., C., Sér.* C^{13}, vol. xxxix, fols. 84-98.

[4] *The Va. Mag. of Hist. and Biog.*, vol. xiii, pp. 225-226.

[5] *Bancroft Papers*, Jan., 1758-Dec., 1760.

of the Indian trade during such trying times. The year 1757 opened with all of the royal storehouses empty, nothing in the hands of private merchants suitable for the traffic and presents to the Choctaw and Alibamon lacking.[1] As the war progressed it became constantly more difficult for the governor to placate the natives with the customary gifts. As a result the Alibamon, in 1759, were trading indifferently with the French, Spanish and English, though they liked the Spanish least and called them cruel.[2] In 1760, the French were still on the Tennessee river dealing with the Cherokee under an assurance that the post on that river had been established for the purpose of bringing supplies to them. The English on their part declared that the French succeeded quite well in amusing and deceiving the natives, while other compatriots of theirs were carrying on hostilities against the Carolinians.[3] By 1761, the governor was indeed in a difficult position. He asserted the "Choctaw and Alibamon harass us daily to have supplies and merchandise. They threaten to go over to the English, if we cannot relieve them, and, in the meantime, by their frequent visits they devour the little that remains of our provisions and exhaust our meager stock of merchandise. We have just ground to fear and expect hostility from them. Therefore our situation is not tenable, and the whole population is in a state of keen anxiety."[4]

A year later, June 24, 1762, Kerlérec informed the home government that the ships from France "brought none of the articles we wanted most and hardly any of the things in the invoice. What they have brought is either not to the

[1] *A. N., C., Sér. C[13]*, vol. xxxix, fols. 258-259.

[2] Bossu, vol. i, p. 256.

[3] *Pub. Rec. of S. C.*, 1716-1763, vol. xxix, p. 2.

[4] Gayarré, *La.: Its Hist., etc.*, p. 89.

taste of the Indians, or is so inferior or bad quality, that it is without value. I am therefore under the shameful and humiliating necessity of not keeping my plighted faith to the savages. What shall I do with these Indian tribes I had convened, under the expectation of the supplies which I was led to believe would be at hand? What will be their feelings? How shall I keep them quiet? I am in a frightful position. Is the province of Louisiana destined to be the sport of cupidity and avarice"?[1]

During the closing years of the war the conditions in the Illinois country were less critical. Since the beginning of hostilities the demand on Fort Chartres for men and material aid had been frequent and pressing. As has been shown the commandant of that post labored to meet them, sending quantities of supplies both to New France and to lower Louisiana. At the end of the struggle the fur trade of this part of the province was still intact and even growing. In 1762, "Maxent, Laclède and Company" of New Orleans received a permit from Governor Kerlérec to establish trading operations on the Missouri river. The next year the Company sent one of the members of the firm to the Illinois country to select a site and establish a base of operation for the trade. Around this trading post later grew the city of St. Louis.[2]

In their struggle for the control of the fur trade of Louisiana the French and English employed practically the same methods, some devised by the former, others by the latter. Neither was slow to adopt the good points in the activities of the other. The English, however, had better support from the mother country and were always well pro-

[1] Gayarré, *op. cit.*, p. 91.

[2] *Trans. Ill. St. Hist. Soc.*, pt. 8, p. 111; *Mag. West. Hist.*, vol. ii, pp. 303-305; *supra*, p. 300.

vided with Indian goods and presents when needed. This advantage was unsurmountable, for an Indian's friendship could be held in such a fashion. Had each of the contestants been furnished with the same quantity and quality of merchandise, the results might have been different. At any rate the English would have found in the French a much more powerful rival than was actually the case.

CHAPTER XX

TRADE WITH THE FRENCH WEST INDIES

THE advantages of commerce between Louisiana and the French West Indies were early taken into consideration. Father Hennepin, in 1683, prophesied that in a short time the province could supply the islands "with bread, wine and meat". The French filibusters and buccaneers, he added, would be able to kill more wild cattle in Louisiana than in their existing haunts.[1] This intercolonial trade began in 1700 when Iberville bought at St. Domingue goats, hogs and many kinds of useful plants for the establishment of the settlement on Biloxi Bay.[2] The next item recorded seems to be that of 1703, when Iberville intimated to the home government that sugar for Louisiana should be carried to the colony from St. Domingue instead of directly from France, thereby saving one-fifth of the freight charges.[3] On this suggestion no comment was made. However, Iberville was informed the royal vessels were not expected to carry European goods from Louisiana to the islands but instead the cargoes were to be made up of lumber and other products of the colony.[4]

For a time such articles were very scarce. Lack of funds, also, made it necessary to send to the islands for supplies. In September, 1705, a filibuster's ship from

[1] Hennepin, *A Description of La.*, p. 151.

[2] Margry, vol. iv, p. 376.

[3] *Ibid.*, p. 625.

[4] *Ibid.*, p. 623.

Martinique, evidently directed toward Louisiana, was wrecked, causing a loss of ninety persons and 72,000 piastres.[1] Two years later a boat laden with supplies from the West Indies reached the province and brought the news of the death of Iberville.[2] Louisiana at this time was in most straitened circumstances; hence in order to tide it over Bienville borrowed 2,000 piastres from a merchant of Martinique.[3] So far the province had made its appeal for succor only to St. Domingue.[4] Such were the faint beginnings of commerce with the French islands.

In 1708, the Louisiana officials proposed to attempt building up trade by means of ship timber; but when the captain of a vessel from Cape Français brought to the province a cargo of island merchandise he found no such material on hand and a poor market for his goods besides. In time, however, he disposed of the cargo and was entrusted with a commission to procure and bring thither a dozen or more mares.[5] His experience seems not to have discouraged others, for in 1710 a boat from Martinique was at Dauphin Island with foodstuffs.[6] As a rule the officials of both Martinique and St. Domingue had not been favorable to provisioning the continental province. They already had become fearful lest the better soil and climate of Louisiana should draw thither the more ambitious and prosperous inhabitants of the islands, and accordingly were unwilling to furnish such things as would aid in the growth of that colony. Even in 1712 the officials of Louisiana were unable to procure wheat for sowing.[7]

[1] La Harpe, pp. 93, 97.

[2] *A. N., C., Sér. C*[13], vol. ii, fols. 5-32. [3] *Ibid.*

[4] Villiers du Terrage, p. 7.

[5] *A. N., C., Sér. C*[13], vol. ii, fols. 356-362, 427-438.

[6] *Ibid.*, fols. 567, 641.

[7] *Ibid.*, fols. 803-809.

The Crozat régime scarcely had been established when the few vessels from the islands ceased to appear. With their captains the settlers of Louisiana had been accustomed to exchange peltry and a little lumber for sugar, tobacco, cocoa, molasses and other island products as well as for European goods, which were often long delayed if brought directly from France. The checking of this trade greatly disturbed the people of the province who almost from the beginning were more or less hostile to Crozat's agents.[1] They believed that one of the chief reasons for the founding of the colony was trade with the islands, and hence strongly opposed interference from the new officials who wished to manage it solely in the interests of the proprietary himself.[2]

Du Clos, on his arrival as "ordonnateur", took sides with the Bienville faction upholding the cause of the colonists, and accordingly was soon at loggerheads with Governor Cadillac. Early in his term of office, also, he proposed the establishment of an exchange of lumber for tobacco, brandy, molasses and other island products, especially with St. Domingue and Martinique, where European merchandise could be obtained quite as satisfactorily as from France itself.[3] This trade, he claimed, would promote the growth of Louisiana and put a formidable obstacle in the way of English colonial expansion. To this end it was suggested that boats be sent to the islands three times a year with local products with which to buy domestic animals. The latter were to be sold at a fixed and moderate price to the inhabitants directly, and not through the Crozat agents who were apt to dispose of them at very high rates,

[1] *A. N., C., Sér.* C^{13}, vol. iii, fols. 212-213; Charlevoix, *Hist. and Gen. Des. N. Fr.*, vol. vi, pp. 32-34.

[2] La Harpe, p. 122; *Coll. La. Hist. Soc.*, pt. 3, pp. 39-44.

[3] *A. N., C., Sér.* C^{13}, vol. iii, fols. 97-107, 209-310.

while receiving substantial profits from the peltry and other goods taken locally in exchange.[1]

Commerce of this sort would be a violation of the proprietary rights, and, unless approved officially, would have to be carried on clandestinely. In September, 1714, it seems, a vessel bearing a permit from the governor of St. Domingue came to Mobile for "repairs" after encountering a storm. There is no record of any trading transactions, but "disabled by storm" was so common a pretext for illicit traffic that the statement at once makes one suspicious.[2] Commercial disputes yearly widened the breach between the Louisiana settlers and the Crozat agents, and in 1715 the crown sent out instructions to the governor and "ordonnateur" in connection with the purchase of domestic animals which were to be sold to the colonists at moderate prices.[3]

The next year a brigantine came to the province from Martinique. The governor would not allow it to do any trading.[4] This act increased the popular ill-will because of the great need at the time of foodstuffs. Early in 1716 a request for them was sent to St. Domingue.[5] Part of the return cargo consisted of two barrels of rice for planting, bought at a cost of twenty-five livres; ten "quarts" of brandy, and two casks of wine, at 1,000 livres.[6] The immediate needs of the colony, however, were satisfied. In order to prevent a repetition of such requests, it was proposed that, since St. Domingue was a port of call for all ships coming

[1] *A. N., C., Sér.* C^{13}, vol. iii, fols. 209-213, 216-217.

[2] *Ibid.*, fols. 511, 791.

[3] *Ibid., Sér.* F^3, vol. ccxli, M. S. S. M., Dec. 27, 1715.

[4] La Harpe, p. 122.

[5] *A. N., C., Sér.* C^{13}, vol. iv, fols. 355-356.

[6] *Ibid.*, fols. 445-446.

to Louisiana, and lay only eight or ten days' journey away, it be made a general depot of food supplies for the province.[1] Nothing was done with the suggestion and smuggling seems to have become more common than ever. At any rate in September, 1716, Bienville on his own account sold 800 deerskins at four reaux each and a considerable amount of lumber. Governor Cadillac determined to invoke the protection of the crown against such traffic.[2] Accordingly he proposed that this particular boat on its return be confiscated as a means of deterring others that might be similarly engaged.[3] The Crozat agents, however, refused to alter the conditions that had caused the development of an illicit traffic, therefore they were unable to suppress it.

Fortunately for Louisiana the Company of the West held more liberal views than Crozat had done on the subject of trade, hence from the outset better feeling prevailed between the officials and the people.[4] Enterprises beneficial to the province as a whole and undertaken by the inhabitants themselves, were often encouraged. When, in 1720, for example, certain settlers asked for permission to construct a boat of sixty tons to be used in carrying domestic animals from St. Domingue, the request was granted.[5] Little by little the island trade developed until, in 1722, there were three elements at work: Louisiana ships that made voyages to both Martinique and St. Domingue, where they exchanged corn, lumber and peltry for brandy and flour; island boats carrying on a similar trade; and vessels from France that took on the return trip cargoes of products from the province to the islands.[6]

[1] *A. N., C., Sér.* C^{13}, vol. iv, fols. 393-394, 847.

[2] *Ibid.*, fols. 355-356.

[3] *Ibid.*, vol. v, fol. 5.

[4] *Ibid.*, fols. 46-47.

[5] *Cotte G*, Feb. 6, 1720, La. Hist. Soc. Trans., N. O.

[6] Béranger, *Mémoire de la Louisiane*, p. 89. Newberry Lib., Chicago.

Of the persons interested in the three forms of venture, Louisiana settlers were the first to take advantage of the commercial opportunities thus presented. In 1722, on being given permission by the Company so to do, they despatched a cargo of lumber to Cape Français and there exchanged it in part for indigo seed.[1] The same year, however, the manager of one of the large landed concessions of Louisiana was refused permission to imitate this example on the ground that it would serve merely as a pretext to trade with the Spaniards to the serious injury of the Company.[2] About this time, also, the provincial officials received a communication from Cape Français urging them to establish better commercial relations with it. The superior council, convinced of the soundness of the argument presented, decided to allow the colonists to send thither lumber, tar, pitch, brick and other products, and those persons who had the means at once availed themselves of the permission.[3]

In 1726, the officials of the areas concerned held a conference on the matter of trade, and formulated a plan to exchange Spanish silver for rice, corn, lumber and other local wares. The scheme met with general approval, since it would help to put silver money into circulation, and could easily be carried into effect by the vessels coming to Louisiana from France.[4] In 1728, furthermore, the attention of the home government was called to the great advantage, both to the Company and the colony, which might be derived from such traffic. Assenting to the plan the French authorities despatched an order to Louisiana that three vessels be employed forthwith in the island trade; two to

[1] La Harpe, p. 342.

[2] *A. N., C., Sér.* C^{13}, vol. viii, fols. 88-91.

[3] Le Page du Pratz, vol. iii, pp. 387-388.

[4] *A. N., C., Sér.* C^{13}, vol. x, fol. 310.

Cape Français and the other to Martinique, carrying cargoes of laths, shingles and other forms of lumber as well as pitch and tar.[1] The next year the crown was informed that the province had already received much benefit from the process, through an increase in the supply of domestic animals, whereas the islands in turn obtained considerable quantities of rice, corn and beans.[2]

On resuming possession of Louisiana, in 1731, the crown began at once to remove some of the restrictions on the island trade. From July onward all duties on such commerce were to be removed. Moreover the insular officials were instructed to do what they could to interest local merchants in the traffic and the provincial authorities, similarly, were directed to urge the colonists to produce commodities suited to the purpose and to see to it also that every available boat was actively employed in the trade. A traffic in lumber with Martinique, where it was said to be rare, was especially insisted upon. The governor of Martinique likewise was shown the advisability of promoting the commerce in question, because the products of that province and Louisiana were readily exchangeable.[3]

One of the passengers of the royal vessel that left France bearing the above instructions was Salmon, the new "ordonnateur", whom the crown directed to confer with the governor of the "Isles du Vent" (Windward Islands) about ways and means to foster trade between that French province and the one on the mainland. The governor was informed that through it the island could be supplied with all kinds of lumber and at the same time would secure a market for its syrup, "tafia", flour, sugar, horses, mules,

[1] *A. N., C., Sér.* C^{13}, vol. xi, fols. 111-112.

[2] *Ibid.*, fols. 117-118.

[3] *Ibid., Sér. B*, vol. lv, fols. 585, 596.

cattles and piastres. Salmon was instructed similarly to do what he could to develop the trade of Louisiana with other French island settlements, especially Cape Français. If possible he was to induce merchants from the latter to send a boat to the former on a trial trip, and before leaving Cape Français he should notify the crown of the results of his efforts.[1]

On his arrival in Louisiana the "ordonnateur", in conjunction with Governor Périer, publicly announced that trade with the islands, especially in cattle and horses, was to be open to all settlers alike. On January 20, 1732, it was asserted that the province would soon be in a position to supply the insular colonies with cordage, flour, lard, beef, pitch, tar, pine, cypress, oak and walnut planks, weather-boarding, all kinds of timber for building purposes and some oak lumber as well, suited for the making of furniture, in fact, to enter upon commercial relations similar to those carried on by New York and Carolina with the English islands.[2] This was a rather sanguine opinion, however, in view of the fact that on March 30, 1732, all the "ordonnateur" could report was some advance in the trade with St. Domingue and "Isle Royalle"[3]

During the same month further interest was manifested in the development of commerce with the islands, when a proposal was made that new boats, and even many new ones if the trade with the islands warranted it, should be constructed in the ship yards of Louisiana.[4] Until the colonial boats could be built it was proposed that the traffic be carried on in any that could be provided. Before the

[1] *A. N., C., Sér. B*, vol. lv, fols. 384, 615.

[2] *Ibid., Sér. C*[13], vol. xiv, fol. 244.

[3] *Ibid.*, vol. xv, fols. 77-78.

[4] *Ibid.*, fols. 54-56.

end of the year a French merchant craft took over a special cargo of brick and lumber to the islands where it was exchanged for sugar and syrup. In other cases ships of the sort usually took on cargoes of Louisiana products for the West Indies only to return to France.[1] On September 2, 1732, a royal vessel left the province for St. Domingue with a cargo of brick and lumber belonging partly to the crown and partly to the settlers.[2]

On October 8, 1733, the home government expressed to the " ordonnateur " and the governor a hope that the trade between Louisiana and the island provinces would soon be firmly established. It was the royal wish, also, that the inhabitants be induced to make a thorough test of the possibilities of the traffic in order to ascertain what benefit might be expected from it. To this end, as soon as completed, the boat then under construction was to be freighted with local products and despatched to the islands.[3] At this time it seems an English company offered the Louisiana officials to provide a supply of boats for the French West Indies trade; but on reference to the crown the proposal was rejected on the ground that it might lead to evil results. From the royal standpoint it was declared better policy to attempt to use insular boats for the purpose. However, if the Louisiana officials felt reasonably sure that the English offer was entirely safe, the home government might withdraw its refusal.[4]

In 1734, the crown had three vessels in Louisiana fit for the island trade,[5] but before they had been long in the service one was wrecked by a storm, and only one of the

[1] *A. N., C., Sér.* C^{13}, vol. xv, fol. 71.

[2] *Ibid.*, fols. 77-78, 127; vol. xvi, fols. 83-84; *Sér. B*, vol. lvii, fol. 801.

[3] *Ibid., Sér. B*, vol. lix, fols. 573-574.

[4] *Ibid.*

[5] *Ibid., Sér.* C^{13}, vol. xvi, fols. 122-124.

others was engaged in the traffic.[1] At yet the major part of the commerce was carried on by the merchant vessels from France on their return trips.[2] The islanders on their part had one ship concerned in it.[3] Interested as they were in any possibility of promoting trade with the West Indies, few of the Louisiana settlers were able to furnish the needful financial backing. In 1735, two of them fitted out a boat with a cargo for Martinique consisting of tar, pitch, hulled rice, peas, beans, lumber, brick, and floor tiles. On account of a fire that broke out on board the captain was forced to carry the goods to Cape Français instead.[4] An English vessel, similarly, which had been confiscated at Mobile, was despatched with a cargo for the islands, but on arriving at Cape Français was condemned as unseaworthy and retired from the service. Thus in a single year two vessels were lost to the trade.[5]

Disasters like these were discouraging not only to the Louisiana settlers, but they added to the disinclination felt by the insular merchants for voyages to the continental province. The feeling was due partly to dread of the sea and partly to the danger of capture by pirates. Then, too, boats in the islands as well as Louisiana were not plentiful, and there was a shortage of money and sailors with which to equip them.[6]

About the end of August, 1735, a small ship of twenty-five tons laden with crude sugar reached Louisiana, supposedly from St. Domingue. During its stay at New Orleans a report got abroad that the owner was a Canadian

[1] *A. N., C., Sér. C*[13], vol. xix, fols. 8-10; vol. xvi, fols. 122-124.

[2] *Ibid.*, vol. xix, fols. 3-5, 104-105, 106-107.

[3] *Ibid.*, fols. 90-91.

[4] *Ibid.*, vol. xx, fols. 52-56.

[5] *Ibid.*

[6] *Ibid., Sér. B,* vol. lxiii, fol. 596.

freebooter who had secured his cargo in an exchange for negroes obtained through a piratical venture. Though the truth of the story could not be ascertained, the character of the captain seemed to vouch for it. At all events, regardless of the way in which the merchandise had been acquired, he was allowed to sell it.[1]

In compliance with royal instructions to that effect, the Louisiana officials tried to do what they could to replace the local boats that had been lost by accident during the year but without immediate success. Meanwhile the trade was carried on as usual by the French merchant vessels. Toward the end of the year 1735 an insular merchant came to New Orleans on one of these ships with some wine and flour which he exchanged for bricks, joists, laths and other lumber. The venture was profitable and the Louisiana settlers hoped the merchant in question would soon put a boat of his own in the trade.[2] In the same year, also, the crown approved a plan to create commerce with Guadeloupe, and directed the officials to offer every encouragement to it. Even in the face of the fact that the trade must necessarily be small and that there would be no cargoes for the return trip, the home government urged the establishment on the ground that in any case it was too important to be neglected. The crown communicated with the governor of Guadeloupe also on the matter. From him a reply was received, stating that a ship had been there from Louisiana, and its owner had sold the cargo advantageously. Moreover, it was further asserted that the captain had made arrangements to continue trading with that island. The French authorities, therefore, were convinced that such a venture was sufficient proof to warrant an energetic effort to promote the commerce in question.[3]

[1] *A. N., C., Sér.* C^{13}, vol. xx, fols. 101-104.

[2] *Ibid.*, fols. 85-91; *Sér. B*, vol. lxiii, fols. 587, 596.

[3] *Ibid., Sér. B*, vol. lxii, fols. 313, 315-316; vol. lxiii, fols. 624, 629.

In 1736, a French merchant craft made the homeward voyage by way of Martinique carrying to the island a cargo of lumber, tobacco and tar.[1] Merchants of Martinique and Guadeloupe had at Mobile a vessel of forty tons that sold its cargo at a good profit and took back a load of pitch, tar and peltry, and a vessel from Cape Français was similarly engaged.[2] The officials of Louisiana hoped the success of these ventures would encourage other islanders to take up the work. In the latter part of the previous year a settler of the province bought a boat from a merchant of Bordeaux and at once put it into the island trade. Before the end of the year 1736 it was making its second trip to Martinique with a cargo of tar, pitch, hulled rice, peas and beans, notwithstanding the first consignment brought him small profit.[3]

The year 1737 opened with an apparent setback to the island trade. On January 19, a vessel of sixty tons from Cape Français when almost at the end of its voyage ran into a storm and was wrecked on one of the coastal islands near the mouth of the Mobile. The captain, crew and much of the cargo, which was made up of 300 "quarts" of flour and other merchandise, were saved, but the ship was damaged beyond repair. The accident was greatly deplored in Louisiana, because it was feared that, since the boat was only on its second trip, the disaster would discourage the islanders from further efforts to trade with the province.[4] To counteract this misfortune a Bordeaux boat of fifty tons was condemned by the colonial officials in 1736. A captain of the provincial army bought it, over-

[1] *A. N., C., Sér.* C^{13}, vol. xxi, fols. 25-30, 94-100.

[2] *Ibid.*, fols. 20-30, 250-253, 328.

[3] *Ibid.*, fols. 25-30, 94-100.

[4] *Ibid.*, vol. xxii, fols. 173-175.

hauled it and had it made seaworthy. Early in June, 1737, it was freighted with Louisiana products and despatched to Martinique.[1]

At this time the home government was actually endeavoring to build up trade between the Gulf coast province and the French islands. To this end it instructed its agents in the former colony to do what they could to interest the merchants there in such an undertaking. On its own part, by way of encouragement, it agreed to exempt for a period of ten years, beginning July 1, 1737, from all duties cargoes carried from Louisiana to the "Isles du Vent". The crown also commanded the intendant of the latter to have the ordinance registered with the superior council and publicly posted.[2]

Little is known about the trade for the years 1738, 1739 and 1740, beyond the fact that vessels from France carried colonial products from Louisiana to the islands and that the cargoes were composed of lumber, brick, peas, corn, "Appalaches" beans, and rice.[3] Much of the cypress lumber was cut and marked ready to put together into a house as soon as it reached the islands. Brick sold there at from fourteen to fifteen livres a thousand; beans at ten livres, and peas at from twelve to thirteen livres a barrel, weighing 200 pounds. A few islanders and Louisiana merchants were still occupied with a similar traffic. They took over like cargoes and brought back sugar, coffee, brandy and "guildive", gaining on such merchandise 100 per cent or more.[4]

In order to provide adequate protection against possible

[1] *A. N., C., Sér.* C^{13}, vol. xxiv, fol. 33.

[2] *Ibid., Sér.* F^{3}, vol. ccxlii, July 1, 1737; *Sér. B*, vol. lxv, fol. 506.

[3] *Ibid., Sér.* C^{13}, vol. xxiii, fols. 123-124, 134-137.

[4] Le Page du Pratz, vol. iii, pp. 387-388.

seizure by the English on suspicion of carrying contraband to the Spanish possessions, it was found advisable, in 1741, to have the ships go and come in convoys. As a result, Cape Français became a port of call for all vessels bound for and returning from Louisiana, because from that point onward they were accompanied by a man-of-war.[1] As hostilities between France and England had not yet been declared, the insular trade was not otherwise affected by the existing war.

In July, two settlers arrived in a small boat from Martinique, primarily for the purpose of trade. During their stay they bought a plantation three leagues below New Orleans and returned home with the intention of coming back with their slaves and other property.[2] In this connection the crown was petitioned to allow 1,500 small farmers to migrate from Martinique and St. Domingue to Louisiana; but since departures of the sort had been put forth by the islanders as a risk likely to arise from trading with that province and might lessen such commerce as actually existed, the petition was denied.[3] Regardless of this phase of the situation, the traffic prospered. During the year in question five vessels came from Martinique and St. Domingue alone and their owners admitted their satisfaction with the profits obtained and expressed a willingness to continue sending vessels to Louisiana.[4] In 1742 more than a dozen ships brought cargoes of wine, flour and "guildive", for which they took in exchange lumber, planks, rice, peas, beans, tar, pitch and other products. French merchantmen also carried to the islands similar cargoes.[5] The island

[1] *A. N., C., Sér.* C^{13}, vol. xxvi, fols. 128, 178.

[2] *Supra*, p. 240.

[3] *A. N., C., Sér.* C^{13}, vol. xxvi, fols. 29-30, 108.

[4] *Ibid.*, fol. 108.

[5] *Ibid.*, vol. xxvii, fols. 38, 109; vol. xxviii, fols. 35-36.

trade for 1743 apparently was brisk. In July, a boat left the province for Martinique and another for St. Domingue, while one arrived from the former in the following month.[1] In September alone eight ships appeared, two of which were from Martinique and two from Cape Français.[2]

By 1744, the traffic with the " Americans ", as the people of Louisiana called the French islanders, had become quite considerable. Governor Vaudreuil states that at the time twenty vessels came from St. Domingue and Martinique with merchandise and rum, and received in exchange piastres, peas, beans and lumber.[3] The next year the ships from the islands and those from France left Louisiana in convoys in order to protect themselves against the English; otherwise the war seems to have had no effect upon the island trade.[4] During the year many merchant ships from " America " came to Louisiana with cargoes of liquor which, it was claimed, did more harm than good, in spite of the market it furnished for local products. The coming of these vessels, furthermore, gave the Louisiana officials greater opportunity to communicate with the home government. As this was especially desirable in war times, the opposition to the sale of " guildive " and other intoxicants was not particularly violent.[5]

By 1747, however, the war between England and France was having some effect on the " American " trade, which the English had been unable seriously to interrupt.[6] As

[1] *A. N., C., Sér.* C^{13}, vol. xxviii, fols. 84-85, 101-102, 117.

[2] *Ibid., Sér. B*, vol. lxxviii, fol. 25.

[3] *Ibid., Sér.* C^{13}, vol. xxviii, fol. 219; *The Present State of the Country, etc.*, 1744, pp. 8-9, 10, 33-34.

[4] *A. N., C., Sér.* C^{13}, vol. xxx, fols. 34-35.

[5] *Ibid.*, fols. 110-112; vol. xxxi, fol. 98.

[6] *Ibid.*, vol. xxxi, fols. 85-86.

before the commodities sent to the islands consisted of lumber, pitch, tar, brick, floor-tiles, tallow, peas, beans, corn and other foodstuffs, and the return cargoes of molasses, sugar, coffee and silver.[1]

In 1748, the lumber, tar, pitch and tallow despatched chiefly on account of the settlers themselves, is quoted as worth about 38,750 livres. To this amount must be added 18,750 livres in lumber and 200,000 in pitch, tar and tallow sent by the French merchants.[2] Instead of destroying trade with the islands, therefore, the war had rather promoted it. The danger from seizure had been too great to make it advisable for the French merchants to take cargoes from Louisiana to France, accordingly the vessels carried cargoes to the West Indies where the risk was smaller.[3]

As had always been the case, any considerable impetus given to the traffic would have called for a corresponding expenditure, and there were few persons either in Louisiana or the islands in a position to make such an investment of capital. Then, too, the few who were able to do so had but one aim, that of securing for themselves a monopolistic control which would insure their own fortunes quickly, regardless of the possible loss to a development of the trade as a whole. Hence at the close of the war the prospects for rapid and healthy growth in the island trade on a large scale were not very favorable.[4]

By 1750, nevertheless, the traffic had become quite active. Over forty vessels came to Louisiana, most of which were

[1] *A. N., C., Sér.* C^{13}, vol. xxxii, fols. 222-227; *A., A. É., Am.*, vol. ii, fol. 108; *A., B. N., Fr.*, vol. 12224, fol. 112.

[2] *A. N., C., Sér.* C^{13}, vol. xxxii, fol. 41; *A., B. N., Fr., Joly Coll.*, vol. 1726, fols. 242-243.

[3] *A. N., C., Sér.* C^{13}, vol. xxxii, fol. 52.

[4] *A., A. É., Am.*, vol. ii, fols. 108, 120; *A., B. N., Fr.*, vol. 12224, fol 113.

from St. Domingue and Martinique. All of them carried back cargoes of lumber and brick for the rebuilding of villages that had been destroyed "by a fire from Heaven".[1] The traffic was especially encouraging to the people of Louisiana who had feared the English, who were reported to have brought lumber to the islands the year before, might supplant them. Their fear was allayed further by an assurance from the home government that a general permission had not been granted to the English to provide St. Domingue with lumber. The report that such a privilege had been conferred arose from the fact that an English ship had been permitted to sell material for the construction of a small church at Cape Français. The protection of their lumber trade so pleased the people of Louisiana that, on May 16, 1751, they sent to the crown, through their " ordonnateur ", an address of appreciation.[2]

In the following year the island traffic met with a slight misfortune. On April 28, 1751, it seems, a brigantin left Louisiana for Cape Français with a shipload of mules, and returned in January, 1752, with a cargo of insular products. After selling the latter the captain bought six mules and five Indian slaves and again set out for Cape Français. When about twenty leagues from its destination the vessel was seized by the Spaniards who carried it to a post in San Domingo where both ships and cargo were confiscated, on the ground that the mules had been procured in clandestine trade with a Spanish colony. The officials of Louisiana protested against the seizure without avail; hence in order to convince the Spaniards that Louisiana was able to export mules and to obtain reimbursement it became necessary to appeal the case to France. There is no evi-

[1] *Jes. Rel.*, vol. lxix, pp. 213-215.

[2] *A. N., C., Sér.* C^{13}, vol. xxxiv, fols. 298-299; vol. xxxv, fol. 204; *Sér. B*, vol. xci, fol. 8.

dence that the home government ever took up the matter with the Spanish authorities.[1]

For the year 1752, in general, the trade was encouraging. Large quantities of lumber found good prices at St. Domingue.[2] Here also was a market for myrtle-wax.[3] About this time, however, the trade with the islands began to assume a somewhat different form. Numerous vessels came thence to Louisiana with cargoes of European merchandise which was offered for sale at an advance of not less than 150 per cent on the purchase price. When the prospective buyers complained of so excessive a rate of commission the island merchant replied that the arrangement opened to them a market for their lumber and other products which the French merchants would not take if they brought these goods directly from France. The assertion was true to a certain extent, but the small boats from the West Indies were able to carry only from 3,000 to 4,000 livres worth of lumber, whereas the merchandise they brought over amounted in value to 40,000 or 50,000 livres. Were the latter fully disposed of, the difference was taken to the islands in bills of exchange on France, which in most cases was sufficient to enable the merchants concerned to buy there additional European articles for a new cargo to Louisiana. The province thus had to pay high prices for such wares in order to secure a small market for certain of its own products at the risk of being deprived correspondingly of its market in the mother country for tobacco, indigo and similar commodities in demand there.[4]

Though statistics for the period are scant, it seems prob-

[1] *A. N., C., Sér. C*[13], vol. xxxvi, fols. 62-63.

[2] *Ibid.*, fols. 228, 270.

[3] *Ibid.*, fols. 271-272, 275.

[4] *Ibid.*, fols. 327-328.

able that the trade with the islands in 1753 and 1754 differed little from what it had been for a year or two previous, for in September, 1754, the colonial officials informed the home government that the number of vessels coming to the province convinced them that the commerce between Louisiana and the Windward Islands was at last firmly established.[1] In some measure to relieve the settlers on the mainland from the excessive prices charged by the islanders, an order came from France at this time to send a royal ship, the "Rochefort", to St. Domingue with a cargo of lumber to be exchanged there for European merchandise.[2] Furthermore, the crown granted to a merchant from Bordeaux a permit to establish in Louisiana a lumber camp for the trade with the West Indies. On reaching the province, however, the grantee found that the settlers were in the habit of employing their negroes during the winter months in cutting wood and sawing it into lumber for the islands and accordingly were able to furnish all that they could get transported thither. Instead of establishing the camp, therefore, he proceeded to buy the lumber and ship it on his own account.[3]

At the close of the year 1754, therefore, the trade between Louisiana and the French islands was advancing. The journey required from twelve to fifteen days each way, with cargoes thither made up as heretofore, of lumber of all sorts, to the amount of 180,000 livres annually; pitch, tar and vegetables worth 30,000 livres; myrtle-wax, valued at about 25,000 livres; tallow and bear's oil estimated at 25,000 livres; and brick, salt meat, and grains, the value of which is not stated. On the return trip, as was usually the case, island products, such as sugar and liquors, were carried.[4]

[1] *A. N., C., Sér.* C^{13}, vol. xxxvii, fol. 83; vol. xxxviii, fol. 51.

[2] *Ibid.*, vol. xxxviii, fols. 84-85, 90.

[3] *Ibid.*, fols. 37-38.

[4] *Ibid.*, fols. 208, 265.

In January, 1755, the "Rochefort" was despatched to Port-au-Prince with a cargo of lumber, and returned the next year laden with merchandise for the royal storehouse.[1] Other vessels having pitch, tar, lumber, hams, salt beef, peas, beans, myrtle-wax, and corn on board sailed to the islands and brought back sugar, syrup, coffee, brandy and French merchandise in general.[2] Despite the vigilance of the Louisiana officials, abuses crept into the trade which required adjustment. Among other things the island merchants had fraudulently introduced flour into the province. So as to put an end to the practice so prejudicial to the commerce with the mother country, it became necessary to enact a law prohibiting it under penalty of confiscation of the entire cargo of the vessel concerned.[3]

From 1757 to the end of the French control of the Mississippi valley, the war between France and England greatly disturbed the trade with the West Indies but did not destroy it entirely.[4] In 1759, for example, Rochemore, the "ordonnateur", bought a cargo of "guildive"[5] from St. Domingue.[6] The captain of the boat that brought it, as well as the masters of all other vessels that came to Louisiana during the incumbency of that official, had little respect for him. Though compelled to secure their bills of exchange from the "ordonnateur", they usually, more or less openly, took sides with the governor's faction in the local broils of the time. This was natural enough in view of the fact that Rochemore cut deeply into the trade which up to this time they had all to themselves. The "ordon-

[1] *A. N., C., Sér.* C^{13}, vol. xxxix, fols. 76-77, 140, 223.

[2] *Ibid.*, fol. 170; Pownall, App., p. 20.

[3] *A. N., C., Sér.* F^3, vol. ccxliii, M. S. S. M., April 9, 1755.

[4] *Ibid., Sér.* C^{13}, vol. xxxix, fols. 258-259, 288; vol. xl, fols. 7-8.

[5] *Supra*, p. 220.

[6] *A. N., C., Sér.* F^3, vol. xxv, fols. 101-105.

nateur" forced them to sell to him instead of to whomsoever they saw fit, and in one instance a captain found it necessary to pay Rochemore's secretary 100 livres to get him to read his trade permit.[1] This situation in the province itself, added to that caused by the war at large, had a depressing effect upon the island trade, yet in 1760, 1761 and 1762, there were vessels still engaged in it.[2]

[1] *Ibid., Sér.* C^{13}, vol. xli, fols. 120-125.

[2] *Ibid.*, vol. xlii, fol. 68; vol. xliii, fols. 26, 103.

CHAPTER XXI

Trade with Mexico

When La Salle made his attempt to plant a settlement on the Gulf coast, trade relations between France and Spain were broken off, but it was the belief of the French that the weakness and corruption among Spanish colonial officials would make it easy to enter into trade with Mexico in spite of the legal restrictions. To this end it was proposed to keep at St. Esprit Bay (Muddy Lake), seventy leagues from Mexico, an abundance of merchandise better in quality than could be procured at Vera Cruz.[1] The death of La Salle, however, delayed the settlement of Louisiana until some of the restrictions on the trade had been removed, but as they were continued against the English the result was a double gain for the French.[2]

Iberville was also interested in the proposed trade. During his first visit to the Gulf of Mexico he found at Pensacola two Spanish vessels, from Vera Cruz and Havana, respectively.[3] This chance encounter was destined to produce important results. As early as 1703, one of the royal "traversiers" had made three trips from Louisiana to Vera Cruz in search of food supplies for the new colony, after which time boats from the former made frequent voyages to the latter on similar errands. On these

[1] Margry, vol. iii, pp. 568-569.

[2] Charlevoix, *New France*, vol. v, p. 128; *Hist. Coll. of La.*, pt. 3, pp. 40-41.

[3] Margry, vol. iv, p. 502; *Hist. Coll. of La. and Fla.*, vol. i, p. 20.

ships, however, the governor at Vera Cruz would allow only limited quantities of supplies to be taken, poor in quality and high in price.[1] That these voyages to and from Vera Cruz were not wholly for the purpose of securing supplies of food is evident from the fact that, in 1710, a complaint was made to the home government that the royal vessels in the province were used almost exclusively by the brothers of Iberville in carrying their peltry and other merchandise to the Spanish market, and that the cost to the crown for such transportation for the years 1702 to 1706 amounted to 71,750 livres.[2]

These activities on the part of the French aroused jealousy at Vera Cruz. It began to be harder for the former to secure there anything that could be used to develop the Louisiana industries. Wheat for sowing and animals for breeding purposes could not be purchased at Vera Cruz, and French merchandise could be exchanged only for foodstuffs in small quantities.[3] In 1710 a supply of flour for the sustenance of the province was brought from the town to a French vessel anchored just outside the harbor, even if foreigners were not allowed to enter or carry on trade in the harbor or outside of it. As soon as the flour was on board the governor demanded that the captain set sail for home at once.[4]

Even before the appearance of the Crozat agents in Louisiana, the governor of Vera Cruz no doubt had his suspicions that many of the requests for foodstuffs were merely pretexts for opening a traffic in all sorts of commo-

[1] Margry, vol. v, pp. 485-487; *A. N., C., Sér.* C^{13}, vol. i, fols. 387-396; vol. ii, fols. 586-602, 641-645.

[2] *A. N., C., Sér.* C^{13}, vol. ii, fols. 5-32; *Sér.* F^3, vol. ccxli, May 13, 1710.

[3] *Ibid., Sér.* C^{13}, vol. ii, fols. 803-809.

[4] Margry, vol. v pp. 485, 487.

dities, and hence adopted measures that would tend to thwart such schemes. From the beginning of the new régime in Louisiana, however, there was no attempt to disguise the intentions of the French traders.[1] No sooner had Governor Cadillac landed than he despatched the vessel on which he had come to the province on a voyage to Vera Cruz. Commercial relations at this time were openly proposed, but were rejected by the viceroy who presented the commander of the ship with a few cattle and some provisions and ordered him to leave the port.[2] The failure did not discourage the governor from making other attempts in the same direction. He began to construct on Dauphin Island a storehouse for European goods to be used in promoting the trade in question.[3] In all probability the Spanish opposition would have been overcome, if at the close of the last war Spain had not made a treaty with England to keep its ports closed to the French. Again and again the Crozat officials tried to break through the barrier at Vera Cruz only to meet with failure, so alert were the English in forestalling them.[4]

The scant success of the French at that Spanish port, nevertheless, was enough to keep their interest alive. In 1713 they were allowed to buy there a vessel of about seventy tons which they hoped to use in developing trade,[5] while at the same time they were endeavoring to make ready for the same service a royal boat of about sixty tons.[6] They were still further encouraged by the issuing of a trade permit to a merchant of Mexico to go to Louisiana to

[1] *A. N., C., Sér.* C^{13}, vol. ii, fols. 589-602, 641; vol. iii, fols. 126-127.

[2] Charlevoix, *op. cit.*, vol. vi, p. 18.

[3] *Hist. Coll. of La.*, pt. 3, pp. 40-41.

[4] *A. N., C., Sér.* C^{13}, vol. iii, fols. 159, 186, 223-224, 248-251.

[5] *Ibid.*, fols. 245-248.

[6] *Ibid.*, fol. 186.

manufacture hats from buffalo wool and catskin, under an agreement that one French vessel a year be allowed to enter the harbor at Vera Cruz with the ostensible object of procuring foodstuffs, but in reality for the purpose of selling merchandise and about 3,000 deerskins.[1]

The French now decided to try another method of action, that of offering the merchants in Mexico flattering inducements to bring their products to Louisiana. French merchandise could thus be sold more cheaply, since the risk involved in carrying it was avoided and the expense required to provide the needful boats was saved.[2] Scarcely had the new order of things been worked out when a Spanish merchant arrived at Mobile, where he bought 4,000 piastres worth of merchandise and would have made a purchase of 40,000 but for an irregularity in his letter of credit.[3] This sale raised the hopes of the Louisiana officials, who at once began to evolve other schemes to advance the trade more rapidly. To this end they looked about for some Canadians to establish a depot of supplies on the Madeleine river and from that point as a base of operation to break up the English control of the traffic there and in Vera Cruz. If this could be done it was believed that the resulting commerce would net the French 5,000 or 6,000 livres a year; the estimate being made on the supposition that Vera Cruz was the entrance to the riches of Mexico.[4] Like other French schemes of trade it was not workable; hence Governor Cadillac was forced to fall back on an occasional trading trip from Mexico to Louisiana and a certain amount of smuggling carried on under the cover of procuring food supplies.[5]

In 1717, the Company of the West returned to the old

[1] *A. N., C., Sér.* C^{13}, vol. iii, fols. 356-357.

[2] *Ibid.*, fol. 605.

[3] *Ibid.*, fols. 469-476, 512.

[4] *Ibid.*, vol. iv, fol. 54.

[5] *Ibid.*, vol. iii, fols. 69, 759.

method of carrying European merchandise to Vera Cruz and of openly offering it for sale there. Without unloading, one of its vessels from France sailed directly for the coast of Mexico. Reaching Villa Rica, not far from Vera Cruz proper, two of the crew able to speak Spanish were set ashore with a price-list of the articles in the cargo, which was to be shown to local merchants. The latter, after inspecting the merchandise, agreed to purchase it and gave Spanish silver in exchange. The vessel then departed for Dauphin Island and eight days later returned to France.[1]

The new régime was distinctly more successful in dealing with the Spanish in Mexico than its predecessor had been. On November 25, 1718, three vessels left Louisiana for France laden with upwards of 100,000 pounds of tobacco, logwood and peltry, the first two articles having been secured from Spanish ships that had found their way to the French settlement.[2] The Company, it seems, continued to attract the Spaniards to its province. In 1722, the statement was made that during the four years preceding many from Mexico had come to Mobile and that in consequence numerous commodities from that area were in use. The latter included tanned skins of which the best grades brought four livres ten sols a pound; cocoa that sold at eighteen and twenty livres a quintal; logwood worth ten to fifteen livres a hundredweight; Brazil wood, "a quality of logwood superior to that from Campeachy"; sarsaparilla in large quantities at thirteen to fifteen sols a pound; vanilla at different prices; and cochineal valued at fifteen livres a pound.[3] Moreover, on June 10 of the same year

[1] Margry, vol. v, p. 546.

[2] Le Gac, *Mémoire d'aprés les Voyages sur la Louisiane, etc.*, B. P. Lib.

[3] Le Page du Pratz, vol. iii, pp. 389-391; *A. N., C., Sér.* C^{13}, vol. vii, fols. 75-76.

a ship left Louisiana for Vera Cruz with a cargo of French merchandise worth 13,800 piastres, 12,000 piastres of which had been purchased directly from the settlers and the remainder from the royal storehouse.[1] That the commercial relations were improving is evident also from the fact that in September three vessels arrived from France with 315,000 livres worth of merchandise intended especially for the trade with Mexico.[2]

In May and again in August, 1723, several Spanish merchants reached Mobile with cargoes of tobacco, sugar and 2,000 piastres, amounting in all to 4,085 piastres. Since their trading permits were of but a month's duration, not enough time was available to enable them to remain until all the commodities were disposed of; therefore it was the custom to leave one of the merchants ashore while the other left for another consignment of goods. As they did not have sufficient time also to go to New Orleans, it was proposed to establish a supply depot at the Balise. This arrangement, it was believed, would be advantageous to both the Spaniards and the Company, for it would tend to give more of the commerce to the latter by shutting out private traders who were willing to pay higher prices for the Spanish goods than the Company was disposed to do. In one case, it seems, a woman at New Orleans had paid ten reaux for a pound of chocolate and a Spanish merchant had enriched private individuals at the capital to the extent of 2,000 piastres. In order to share in such benefits until the proposed storehouse could be built the Company sent a shallop laden with merchandise to Dauphin Island where, however, it arrived too late to be of any service.[3] In Oc-

[1] La Harpe, p. 327.

[2] *Ibid.*, p. 337.

[3] *A. N., C., Sér. C[13]*, vol. vii, fols. 31-35.

tober, three Spanish traders came thither with a cargo of tobacco and other merchandise, the former article alone being worth more than 4,279 livres. After completing their transactions at Mobile they left for New Orleans.[1]

Early in 1725 two more Spanish merchants arrived. They pretended to have come to Louisiana because of heavy seas that had prevented them from carrying their cargoes to the original destination. Anchoring off the "Island of Vessels", near the mouth of the Mobile, they asked to be given a supply of food, and seemed disinclined to do any other business, though merchandise was offered them at a reasonable price. They bought only 113 piastres worth, what they apparently needed, and left the village. They soon returned and continued buying with an indifference that had the desired result upon the French who sold them peltry very cheaply indeed. Still the bargain was not altogether one-sided; the skins were already damaged by rats and worms and were sure to depreciate further if not disposed of immediately. The French took chiefly logwood in exchange delivered at the Balise.[2] As the supply depot had not yet been established there, the home government was urged to hasten action in the matter. The colonial officials asserted that one could not expect a Spanish merchant to consume two months of his time going up the river in order to spend four days in trade, the probable result being that the Spaniards would retire from the business altogether.[3]

Commerce with Mexico was not lucrative, due to the fact that it could be maintained only at a great risk of having both vessel and cargo confiscated. So as to decrease

[1] *A. N., C., Sér.* C^{13}, vol. vii, fols. 75-76.

[2] *Ibid.*, vol. ix, fols. 26, 51-53.

[3] *A., A. E., Am.*, vol. i, fol. 19.

the danger from this source, it was proposed, in 1726, that the English method be adopted of meeting Spanish ships on the open sea and carrying on the trade there.[1] The rumor of war that at this time reached the colony, however, made this scheme look unattractive, and no further action was taken in the matter.[2] The French, also, began to let the supply of European goods suited to the Spanish traffic diminish, and by the middle of the next year the only thing available was some lace that was far too expensive to offer much chance of sale.[3] The colonial officials asked that the storehouses be replenished at once, in view of the fact that the arrival of Spanish merchants might be expected at any time. In November, a trader reached Louisiana, but, on finding there no merchandise to buy, left after receiving an assurance that there would be goods awaiting him on his return. He came again in July of the next year only to discover the storehouse still empty. Therefore he demanded that the French pay him 550 piastres for breach of agreement. He departed with a promise to return in November or sooner if the Louisiana officials would write him at Campeachy when the European merchandise arrived. On his part he agreed to bring with him some cochineal, the production of which was contemplated as a new branch of industry in Louisiana.[4]

In June, 1728, another Spanish merchant appeared, a fact that greatly embarrassed the provincial officials because they had nothing to sell him, excepting some scrap iron of a rather inferior quality for which the Spaniard offered four piastres a quintal. For the sake of keeping the trade alive

[1] *A. N., C., Sér.* C^{13}, vol. x, fol. 150.

[2] *Ibid.*, fol. 245.

[3] *Ibid.*, vol. x, fol. 188.

[4] *Ibid.*, vol. xi, fols. 54-56.

the officials felt obliged to accept the offer. They accordingly sold him about 16,000 pounds for 640 piastres. Of this sum 405 were represented by sugar which, as the price charged was ten sols a pound, increased somewhat the cost of the iron.[1]

By the beginning of October, 1728, the supply of French merchandise that had been looked for had been placed in the Louisiana storehouses where it was held to await the coming of the Spanish traders. The officials would sell none of it in the province in spite of the prevailing need. One of the Company's boats brought 70,000 pounds of merchandise and a message that, if more was required, to keep the foreigners in the colony until the arrival of three other ships that would soon be on the way.[2] According to the previous agreement, the Spaniards at Campeachy were notified that French goods valued at 100,000 écus were on hand. They were requested, furthermore, to bring with them some cattle and a considerable quantity of so-called "Ranier" tobacco of the best quality which would bring in Louisiana not less than two reaux a pound.[3]

The war that was rumored in 1726 had become by 1728 a reality, and imposed something of a check on the trade with Mexico. On December 9, in order to remove some of the obstacles, it was proposed to continue the traffic by means of Spanish vessels plying between Spanish ports on the Gulf of Mexico. The local governors, to be sure, did not allow French boats to enter the harbors, and watched trading permits closely. If a Spanish merchantman did not return to port within the time limit, both vessel and cargo were liable to confiscation and the commander to

[1] *A. N., C., Sér. C*[13], vol. xi, fols. 54-56.

[2] *Ibid.*, fols. 117-118.

[3] *Ibid.*, fols. 147-149.

penal service in the galleys. It was therefore proposed to establish a depot for French goods somewhere along the direct route from St. Augustine, Pensacola, Havana, Campeachy, Tuxpam and Tampico, where business could be done without loss of time or deviation from the legitimate course.[1] Nothing however, came of the proposal.

Meanwhile the "ordonnateur" had sent letters in triplicate to four merchants of Vera Cruz and Campeachy enclosing a statement of the merchandise then in the Louisiana storehouses and urging them to take immediate advantage of the opportunity.[2] By June, 1729, the officials had grown so impatient at waiting in vain for the coming of the Spanish traders that they resolved to carry some of their goods to Vera Cruz direct, under the pretext of informing the viceroy of New Spain of the danger that threatened the Florida coast, but in reality to do business there. Nothing very lucrative was the outcome of the venture, and during the remainder of the period in which the Company of the Indies controlled Louisiana, the trade with Mexico seems to have been too uninteresting to form any part of the correspondence between the provincial officials and the home government.[3]

Although in the instructions to the governor and "ordonnateur" at the time of the resumption of royal rule in Louisiana, the crown laid considerable emphasis on the importance of the trade with Mexico, nothing in this direction was accomplished during the first year, chiefly because of the scarcity of goods in the storehouses.[4] The home government, accordingly, was requested to remedy this defect

[1] *A. N., C., Sér.* C^{13}, vol. xi, fols. 175-176.

[2] *Ibid.*, fol. 309.

[3] *Ibid.*, vol. xii, fols. 61-63.

[4] *Ibid.*, vol. xiii, fols. 16-17.

as speedily as possible. Much of the lack of success of the Company in the trade, asserted the Louisiana officials, was due to the disappointment of the Spanish merchants at not finding on their arrival at New Orleans or Mobile the merchandise that had been promised them. Commerce, indeed, was especially difficult to revive at this time because commodities could be secured at St. Domingue at thirty per cent less than the people of Louisiana could afford to sell them.[1]

In August, 1732, a storm swept over the Gulf region causing much damage, among other things wrecking a Spanish vessel off the coast at ten leagues from the Balise. The ship and the entire cargo were lost but the crew of 120 men were saved. They were sent to New Orleans and distributed among the families of the village at the expense of 150 livres a day to the colony. Before their departure the cost of their maintenance reached 15,842 livres. Of this amount 6,000 livres was paid by the government of Pensacola before the sailors left for Vera Cruz.

The vessel that carried the Spaniards home accordingly took with it a bill for 9,842 livres to be collected from the viceroy of New Spain. For food and passage an additional expense of 2,364 livres, two sols, six deniers was incurred. The items were duly presented to the viceroy who at the same time was particularly informed of the good treatment his countrymen had received at the hands of the people of Louisiana. The French hoped in return the viceroy would not only pay the sum expended but would make them a loan of 50,000 livres, sell them 10,000 pounds of lead and allow them to purchase either at Vera Cruz or Campeachy a boat of about seventy tons for the provincial service. Some encouragement in entering upon this procedure arose

[1] *A. N., C., Sér.* C^{13}, vol. xiv, fol. 234.

from the fact that the viceroy already had written to the governor of Louisiana offering his help in time of need.

The French returned to New Orleans in May, 1733, with foodstuffs and ammunition for Pensacola. Following his instructions the captain had succeeded in purchasing the boat of seventy tons but had not secured the loan nor the lead. As to the loan the viceroy declared that he had no assurance that the obligation would be recognized by the successor of the present governor of Louisiana, should the latter leave office before the payment had been effected. He, however, presented the captain of the French expedition with thirty-five quintals of lead and 5,000 livres. Of this sum the governor of Louisiana took 3,696 livres, eighteen sols, nine deniers for the cost of transportation and freight for the return cargo; 600 livres and 350, respectively, were given to the first and second officers in charge of the affair; and 353 livres, one sol, three deniers were distributed among the crew. The amount held against the viceroy for the sustenance of the Spanish sailors while in Louisiana was given in payment of the boat that was purchased by the captain. At the conference with the viceroy the French had endeavored to open up trade between Louisiana and the Spanish ports under his jurisdiction, but very little in that direction was accomplished.[1]

During 1733, 1734 and 1735, despite their favorable geographical position, the French were not at all successful in promoting commerce with Mexico. They had been compelled, also, to revise the opinion about Spanish officials held in 1699, for none of their bribes had been able to open a single port. In 1736, indeed, treatment meted out to French crews entering Spanish harbors became so severe that it was useless to send any more vessels thither. The

[1] *A. N., C., Sér.* C^{13}, vol. xvi, fols. 7-10, 118-120, 122-124; vol. xvii, fols. 12-13.

sole hope left, therefore, lay in the possibility of attracting Spanish traders to Louisiana. To this end French merchandise was to be placed in the storehouses at the Balise and Dauphin Island, which were almost on the direct route of the Spanish vessels making their circuit of the Spanish ports in the Gulf of Mexico. For this purpose between 40,000 and 50,000 pounds of merchandise were sent from France. When the colonial officials saw the commodities untouched, they became impatient and despatched a boat from Mobile and another from New Orleans to Vera Cruz in the hope that this procedure might hasten the coming of the Spanish traders. The latter vessel carried a permit from Bienville and news of the hostilities of certain Indian tribes who were bringing Spanish scalps to the French settlements. These documents, it was thought, might break down the opposition of the Spaniards long enough to enable the captains to dispose of their cargoes. The governor of Vera Cruz declined absolutely to allow either ship to enter the port.[1] The captain from Mobile told that officer that he had come to Vera Cruz for the benefit of the Spanish post at Pensacola which was much in need of supplies. This plea the governor remarked was only a pretext for illicit trade and declared that his boat would be confiscated if he did not leave the harbor at once.[2]

In 1737, the situation became worse. French deserters were allowed to make their escape in Spanish boats from Pensacola.[3] Moreover the only trade that seems to have come to Louisiana during the year did not brighten the hopes of improved trade relations when the Spaniards de-

[1] *A. N., C., Sér.* C^{13}, vol. xvi, fols. 84-85; vol. xix, fols. 208-209; vol. xx, fols. 52-56, 102-104; vol. xxi, fols. 25-30.

[2] *Ibid.*, vol. xxi, fols. 94-100.

[3] *Ibid.*, vol. xxii, fols. 28-29.

manded reductions in the price of all French merchandise, making any profit for the seller impossible.[1] The conditions seem to have remained unchanged until May, 1739, when a Spanish vessel from Campeachy anchored off Dauphin Island, did a small amount of trading, and proceeded to New Orleans with the cargo of salt and logwood and 3,000 piastres.[2] Spanish interest in commerce with Louisiana was apparently increasing, for in January, 1740, a ship of that nationality touched at the Balise, whether for trading purposes or because of bad weather is not known.[3]

Improvement in the traffic, in 1741, became fairly marked. For the most part this was due to the war then prevailing between Spain and England. As early as March three or four vessels had come to Louisiana from Mexican ports. Ill luck or improvidence still pursued the French. They had to send the Spaniards away empty-handed, for there was nothing in the storehouses to sell them. Hardly had they left the province when a small Spanish bark arrived with four merchants on board possessing among them 50,000 piastres with which to buy French merchandise. These men had to be treated in like fashion.[4] The home government, thereupon, was urged to send the needful supplies at once.[5] It was further informed, also, that the Spanish ships brought large quantities of piastres, as well as cochineal, logwood and other commodities ready for sale. One of the boats, it was stated, stayed three weeks and another three months waiting for the arrival of French goods, but were obliged to leave the province, tak-

[1] *A. N., C., Sér.* C^{13}, vol. xxii, fols. 37-41.

[2] *Ibid.*, vol. xxiv, fol. 247.

[3] *Ibid.*, vol. xxv, fol. 143.

[4] *Ibid.*, vol. xxvi, fols. 127-130, 150-151.

[5] *Ibid.*, fols. 150-151.

ing their piastres along with them.[1] Accordingly, though the beginning of the year 1741 offered some prospects of betterment in the commercial relations with Mexico, its close saw almost nothing accomplished.

Much as both the home government and the provincial authorities realized that a favorable opportunity had arrived, they were unable to overcome the obstacles in the way of sending merchandise suited to the trade in question. The French merchants whom the crown had induced to carry the commodities to Louisiana demanded such exorbitant prices that the Spaniards declined to pay them.[2] Just at this time also some influential men of Vera Cruz asked permission to send their sons to New Orleans to learn the French language. Two boys actually came. They received a cordial welcome, for the officials professed to see in the scheme the possibility of strengthening the commercial ties between the two places.[3] Nothing further came of it. Instead the trade received a setback from the French merchants themselves who began anew to carry their merchandise directly to the Spanish ports.[4]

Despite all these misfortunes the traffic began to recover. In 1743 many French vessels brought to Louisiana goods that were readily sold to the Spaniards for cash. One of the royal ships alone carried to France 6,000 piastres thus derived. Too many boats, however, were engaged in the trade, hence the market soon was glutted with French merchandise.[5] The vessel that went from the province to Vera Cruz, on the other hand, met with little success because the

[1] *A. N., C., Sér.* C^{13}, vol. xxvi, fols. 178-179.

[2] *Ibid.*, vol. xxvii, fols. 127-128; *Sér. B*, vol. lxxiv, fols. 12-20.

[3] *Ibid., Sér.* C^{13}, vol. xxvii, fols. 27-29.

[4] *Ibid., Sér. B*, vol. lxxvi, fol. 2.

[5] *Ibid., Sér.* C^{13}, vol. xxviii, fol. 61.

trade permits were apt to be so costly as to rob the business of its legitimate profits. Regardless of this circumstance, the French continued to send boats thither. One of them carried a cargo of 55,000 pounds, from the sale of which a profit of only 300 piastres was made. With returns so small as this the French could not afford to send any more cargoes to Mexico, consequently they went back to the old plan of attracting the Spaniards to Louisiana.[1] Vaudreuil, in fact, prohibited such shipments altogether.

The war that began in 1744 stimulated the trade to the extent of 1,000,000 piastres a year.[2] In 1746, it was reported to the home government that, next to the islanders, Spanish merchants were most actively represented in Louisiana commerce. Furnishing a market for the abundant colonial products, they bought large amounts of flour, corn, rice and other commodities for which they paid in cash.[3]

During 1747 and 1748, the Spanish vessels continued to leave behind them considerable sums in Spanish money and quantities of logwood and sugar.[4] Governor Vaudreuil, however, believed the trade capable of further expansion. He carried on an extensive correspondence with the Spanish governors of the posts on the Gulf of Mexico and succeeded in establishing friendly relations even with the viceroy of New Spain, which the governor had not hesitated to turn to advantage.[5] So as to aid in the development of trade with Tampico, Campeachy, Vera Cruz and other Spanish ports, he advised the home government to be less strict in dealing with deserting sailors, because leniency in

[1] *A. N., C., Sér.* C^{13}, vol. xxviii, fols. 62-63.

[2] *The Present State of the Country, etc.*, 1744, pp. 9-10, 34.

[3] *A. N., C., Sér.* C^{13}, vol. xxx, fols. 110-112, 273.

[4] *Ibid.*, vol. xxxi, fols. 74-75; vol. xxxii, fol. 22.

[5] *Ibid.*, vol. xxxii, fols. 69-71.

this respect was the only available way to obtain crews for the vessels sent thither from Louisiana.[1]

Throughout the two years following, Vaudreuil continued his correspondence with the Spanish governors as before. Since the establishment of peace these officials had become somewhat reserved in manner but their attitude did not deter the Louisiana governor from proffering all sorts of service or aid.[2] As a result of Vaudreuil's tact and perseverance New Orleans became somewhat of a centre for Spanish trade. To it came merchants from Cuba, St. Augustine, Pensacola, St. Bernard Bay, St. Joseph Bay, Porto Bello, Santa Maria del Darien and Cartagena to buy cloth, lace, wine, brandy, and other merchandise from France, together with tobacco, indigo, hemp, rice, lumber, masts, pitch, tar, peltry, and other products of Louisiana itself. In order to enable the settlers more or less remote from the capital to derive greater advantage from the traffic, it was proposed to send special boats up the river to carry their wares to New Orleans. This would enhance the value of their share in the piastres, smoking tobacco, cocoa and logwood brought by the Spaniards.[3]

As early as 1750[4] the number of Spanish vessels coming to the province fell off because the French ships had glutted the Spanish colonial market with European merchandise that consequently had to be sold at a low price. The Spanish governors also had begun again to refuse the French boats admittance to ports under their jurisdiction. These circumstances afforded some hope that the tide would turn once more toward Louisiana. Four or five vessels, at all events, came from Campeachy and took on large quantities

[1] *A., B. N., Fr.*, vol. 12224, fol. 128.

[2] *A. N., C., Sér.* C^{13}, vol. xxxiii, fols. 64-66.

[3] *Ibid.*, fols. 166-167.

[4] *Supra*, p. 402.

of dry-goods and lumber which they carried to the Spanish West Indies. In 1752 there were four Spanish vessels in the province with cargoes of tobacco and logwood which they exchanged for European goods.[1]

As France was now drifting toward another war with England, for the next two years not much information is available about trade with Mexico. Mobile, it seems, enjoyed a fairly lucrative commerce with Spaniards who, under the pretext of going to Pensacola, came from various ports of Mexico, anchored off Dauphin Island, and bought up cargoes of French merchandise, thereby greatly increasing the amount of gold and silver in local circulation.[2] This illicit traffic was not interfered with. It seemed better to tolerate it, than by attempting to prevent it, to throw it into the hands of the English. The trade also had the further advantage of increasing considerably the chances of communication with the home government when war actually came on.[3]

The commercial activities of Mobile in this respect had developed rather rapidly since 1748. At the beginning those who entered upon them did so with a small capital in the shape of French merchandise. This stock they sold to Spaniards who occasionally anchored near the village. The sale usually netted good returns, a fact that enabled the participants to increase their stock for the next opportunity to do business. Before the beginning of hostilities with England, however, the authorities at New Orleans tried to draw some of the traffic to the capital. It seems natural enough that they should attempt it when Mobile was enjoying a trade valued at 50,000 piastres a year.[4]

[1] *A. N., C., Sér.* C^{13}, vol. xxxiv, fols. 250, 277.

[2] *Ibid.*, vol. xxxvi, fol. 270.

[3] *Ibid.*, vol. xxxvii, fol. 58; vol. xxxviii, fol. 209.

[4] *Ibid.*, vol. xxxix, fol. 50; vol. xl, fols. 246-247.

During the war Spanish vessels came to Louisiana from time to time, but the number naturally tended steadily to decrease as hostilities progressed. On August 28, 1758, it is stated that four months had elapsed since a boat had been sent to Vera Cruz for a supply of ammunition and that nothing as yet had been heard from it.[1] In May, 1759, a cargo of 250 hogsheads of salt from Campeachy was sold at New Orleans [2] for twenty deniers a pound.[3] As the war advanced to the disadvantage of France, the trade necessarily became more and more disturbed. In 1760, the merchants from Mexico found it correspondingly difficult to cash the bills of exchange they received in Louisiana, hence accepted them only with the greatest reluctance. This circumstance in turn hindered efforts to obtain ammunition for the province from the Spaniards.[4] The traffic seems not to have been entirely destroyed, however, for in 1764 an English estimate put the annual value of the trade with Vera Cruz, Campeachy, Havana and New Orleans at 60,000 pounds.[5]

[1] *A. N., C., Sér. F*[3], vol. xxv, fols. 34-35.

[2] *Supra*, p. 220.

[3] *A. N., C., Sér. F*[3], vol. xxv, fols. 101-105.

[4] *Ibid., Sér. B*, vol. cxiii, pt. 1, fols. 276-277; *A., B. N., Fr.*, vol. 10764, fols. 243-245.

[5] *B. of T. Papers*, Oct. 31, 1764, Ala. Hist. Soc. Trans. Montgomery, Ala.

CHAPTER XXII

TRADE WITH NEW MEXICO AND TEXAS

WHEN the French took possession of the Mississippi valley they believed that overland commerce with Mexico would enable them to share in the wealth of the gold and silver mines located somewhere in that vast province of Spain.[1] Excepting for an exploring expedition in 1701, made up of twelve Canadians under the command of Juchereau de St. Denis, and despatched by Bienville to the Red river, where they spent six months without acquiring any information concerning the Spaniards,[2] nothing in that direction was done until Louisiana passed under the control of Crozat, one of whose projects was the building-up of a trade with the Spanish settlements of the interior.[3]

In 1712, Governor Cadillac furnished a party of twenty-two men under the leadership of St. Denis with passports, gave them five canoes laden with 10,000 pounds of merchandise and sent them on a trading expedition to New Mexico.[4] The party passed up the Red river as far as practicable, and then proceeded across country to the Spanish settlements in New Mexico. Informed of the object of the visit the local officials declined to give any definite reply until the matter had been laid before their provincial superiors, an attitude necessitating a long delay. The next

[1] Margry, vol. ii, pp. 360-364.

[2] La Harpe, p. 34.

[3] *A. N., C., Sér.* C^{13}, vol. iii, fols. 223-224, 230; La Harpe, p. 113.

[4] La Harpe, p. 116; Margry, vol. v, p. 495.

year found St. Denis still awaiting an answer to his proposal. When vouchsafed it was in effect a refusal unless he could obtain permission from the viceroy at the city of Mexico. Here the French leader stayed a long time, but all his efforts were fruitless. Finally he was allowed to return to Louisiana after an absence of nearly three years.[1] On hearing the results of his efforts, Governor Cadillac was convinced that trade could not be opened in this fashion. He therefore contented himself with ordering a fort to be erected, 1717, on the Red river among the Natchitoches Indians so as to prevent the Spaniards from encroaching upon French territory.[2]

St. Denis had a different opinion. In conjunction with several Canadians he formed a commercial company, purchased of Crozat's agents 60,000 pounds of merchandise, which it was proposed to sell to the Spaniards in the province of New León, and on October 10, 1716, set out for the viceroyalty where he arrived in October of the next year, sold the goods at a good price to some merchants of Boca de León and started on the return to Mobile, arriving there October 25, 1717. En route he was seized, held as a spy and later sent in chains to the city of Mexico. Here he was forced to remain until 1719 when he was able to make his way back to Louisiana. The misfortune befell him because at the time of his visit in 1716 an agreement he had made with the viceroy had become ineffective through the death of that functionary and the unfriendly attitude of his successor toward the French.[3] The activity of this pioneer, together with the building of the post on the Red river, nevertheless alarmed the Span-

[1] Margry, vol. v, pp. 496-505, 526-537; La Harpe, pp. 129-131.

[2] La Harpe, p. 131.

[3] *Ibid.*, pp. 130, 134, 135-139, 145.

iards who, as a means of defense against further encroachments, on January 29, 1717, established the post of Adayes on the frontier not far from Natchitoches.[1]

In 1719, the leadership in the development of trade with the Rio Grande settlements was given to Bénard de La Harpe.[2] To this end he sent to the governor of Texas his passport and a letter in which he expressed his desires in the matter. These he set forth with deference yet at the same time with considerable confidence, as had been suggested to him by the Spanish missionary at Adayes. On May 28, 1719, La Harpe received a reply stating that he was intruding upon Spanish territory which he was commanded to leave at once. Trade with the Spanish in Texas, La Harpe now saw, was not feasible as yet; accordingly a second letter he despatched to the governor on June 9 was much less complimentary in tone. In it he asserted that Texas did not form a part of the viceroyalty of New Spain. As his honor well knew, that province was drained by rivers flowing into the Mississippi, a fact which by La Salle's work in 1684 made it a part of the possessions of the king of France.[3]

Failing in his attempt to persuade the governor, La Harpe next turned his attention to Father Marcello, the missionary at Assinais, and on April 26, 1719, wrote him as follows: Reverend Father, . . . "Your zeal as I well know is very great, but at times you must need help. Touched by these things and having in my possession the means to aid you in your work of the spreading of the Gospel, I make you the following offer. You write to your

[1] La Harpe, p. 139.

[2] *Ibid.*, pp. 144-146; Margry, vol. vi, pp. 241-242.

[3] La Harpe, pp. 189-192, 193-194, 196-197; Margry, vol. vi, pp. 253, 262-267, 274-276.

friends in New Mexico and the kingdom of León that they can find at Nassonites or Natchitoches all the European merchandise of which they have need, and, too, at reasonable prices, which will undoubtedly enable them to sell the merchandise at a good profit. With these merchants I will make an arrangement that you are to have five per cent on all sales." "This," La Harpe continued, "will be a sure means of establishing a trade between the two settlements, thereby rendering great service to many persons who otherwise for a long time would be deprived of all European merchandise. Moreover, this trade will make it possible for you to establish your mission solidly." La Harpe then asked the missionary to sell him ten cows and two bulls which he proposed to pay for with corn and beans. Along with this letter La Harpe sent the missionary a present of ten pieces of Bretagne and one of damask in order to insure a favorable reply.[1]

On May 24, 1719, Father Marcello replied to La Harpe thus: . . . "It is not proper for a priest to engage in trade. I propose, therefore, that our correspondence be kept secret, especially since I am on very friendly terms with the Spanish officials. The correspondence which you propose to open, however, meets with my approval and I shall write my friends of your wishes." The missionary then closed his letter with an assurance that he would keep La Harpe informed of "what passes" and a promise to send him four cows and a bull, all the animals that he at the time could provide.[2]

So far as the records show the correspondence ended here. What trade grew out of it there seems to be no way of determining. Evidence, however, is available that, if the

[1] Margry, pp. 268-269; La Harpe, pp. 190-191.

[2] Margry, vol. vi, pp. 274-275; La Harpe, pp. 194-195.

French on the lower Mississippi were much interested in the settlements on the Red river, it came more from hopes than from realities, so far as trade was concerned. At all events many of the settlers were anxious to accompany La Harpe in the belief they would be able quickly to make their fortunes. Most of them were not inclined to take up agriculture as a means of developing trade, and when pressed to do so deserted. The Indians, however, supported La Harpe, and captured and brought back a majority of the fugitives.[1]

Taking up the project launched by St. Denis and La Harpe, in 1720, the Company of the Indies proposed to establish a post on St. Bernard Bay, where they could put in a supply of merchandise to be used in promoting commerce with the Spaniards located near the upper waters of the rivers that flow into that bay. Up stream at a spot most conveniently situated a second post was to be built. From this point the French proposed to enter into alliances with the Indians of the region and use them as guides to lead the way directly to the gold and silver mines of Mexico. Moreover, it was asserted, French merchandise carried to the Spaniards would help operations very greatly, since all kinds of European goods were scarce in the interior settlements.[2]

The post on St. Bernard Bay was never erected, but by 1720 that at Natchitoches had thirty-three Frenchmen, thirty-four negroes and six Indian slaves. The colonists raised wheat, corn, rice, beans, tobacco, melons, potatoes and vegetables, and secured from the Indians peltry and bear's oil for export. With these commodities they managed to do a considerable amount of business. Corn and

[1] Margry, vol. vi, p. 270; Le Page du Pratz, vol. iii, pp. 272-273.

[2] *A. N., C., Sér.* C^{13}, vol. vi, fol. 22; Margry, vol. vi, pp. 233, 336.

beans sold at the French post at sixteen livres a barrel and tobacco at thirty sols a pound. At Adayes they sold annually about 200 barrels of corn, sixty of beans and 300 pounds of tobacco. For them they were paid in silver at the following prices: corn and beans at three piastres a barrel and tobacco at fifteen sols a pound. The French, however, had only a slight chance apparently of increasing the traffic in the face of the potentialities represented at Adayes by two plows and some ground already under cultivation. Besides the trade in colonial products, there was a small business, amounting to about 200 piastres a year, done in European goods. The reason for it was the inferior quality and the high price of French merchandise compared with what was offered in competition by the English traders.[1]

About this itme the English received an order to furnish 450 piastres worth of goods to each of the 100 soldiers stationed at Adayes who were no longer to be paid in silver. On the wares thus provided it was claimed that the Spanish commandant made a profit of at least 600 per cent. Since the viceroy was willing to tolerate the abuse, from this time onward the men of the garrison had no money with which to buy from the French, even had their goods been more desirable than the English articles. Accordingly, while this agreement with the English lasted, the trade with Natchitoches in this respect was reduced almost to nothing. Even after the expenditure of very considerable sums for the purpose of "closing the eyes of justice" the English, it seems, were able to undersell the French, and no improvement in the situation could be expected until the French could lower the price and better the quality of their merchandise. This reduction was impossible, due to the long distance the goods had to be carried on pack-mules.[2]

[1] *A. N., C., Sér.* C^{13}, vol. vi, fols. 50-51.

[2] *Ibid.*, fols. 51-52; Margry, vol. vi, pp. 231-232.

St. Denis, the one man in Louisiana who was at all well fitted to deal with the situation, the Company now, 1721, placed in charge of the post at Natchitoches with power over the surrounding territory. He had as his partner in this enterprise Weillart d'Anvilliers, chief clerk of the post, who was to share with him, equally, five per cent on all sales of merchandise made to the Spaniards. Just what they accomplished during their term of office, the former remaining until 1744, it seems impossible definitely to ascertain.[1] In 1722, however, a "visitador general", in the person of Captain Antonio Cobian Busto, made a tour of the viceroyalty in order to investigate the affairs of the interior provinces, and found a number of Spaniards engaged in illicit traffic with the French of Louisiana. He reported the fact to the viceroy who the next year received an order from the king of Spain to put a stop to it. The same year the governor of the province issued an order meant to regulate trade with "gentile tribes". Governor Bustamante affirmed that New Mexico traders went to Louisiana where they bought annually goods worth $12,000. The governor's prohibitory command, April 3, 1723, was to the effect that "The people were allowed to trade with gentiles who came to Taos and Pecos, but some were accustomed to go out in the plains to meet them",[2] the latter act evidently being the unpardonable sin. The remoteness of these provinces made it exceedingly difficult to fulfill the royal wishes and irregularities of the sort probably continued. At any rate in 1725 a small trade was still carried on between Natchitoches and the Spaniards of New Mexico.[3]

[1] *A. N., C., Sér. C*[13], vol. xiii, fol. 66; Margry, vol. vi, p. 222.

[2] Bancroft, *Hist. of Arizona and New Mexico*, pp. 238-239.

[3] *A., A. É., Am.*, vol. i, fol. 26.

In 1731, the officials of Louisiana recommended that the home government send merchandise for the Mexican trade but Natchitoches was not mentioned especially as one of the posts to receive it.[1] By 1733, however, they were convinced that traffic on a scale of any size was practically impossible on account of the strong opposition and great activity against it shown by the viceroy of New Spain.[2] Two years later the trade with Adayes through Natchitoches was said to be worth between 2,000 and 3,000 piastres annually. However the priest at the former post now asked Father Beauboise at the latter to send him a quantity of cloth, church ornaments, flour, wine and brandy. To use this request as a means of expanding trade in general involved great risk from seizure by Indians and Spaniards alike who were apt to treat intruders with great severity. Therefore the French were of the opinion that, to be profitable, the necessary dealings would have to be carried on entirely by the Spaniards themselves at Natchitoches.[3] As the latter could not be induced to go there in any considerable numbers, development in this direction would be very slow. In 1737, in fact, the father at Adayes had not received any of the supplies asked for.[4] Up to this time all restrictions on the traffic had come from the Spaniards. This year, learning of the existence of a small trade in meat between Natchitoches and Adayes, the French officials forbade it. Like many ordinances of the time the prohibition was so poorly enforced that substantially no change in the situation took place.[5]

The death of St. Denis, 1744, was a blow to the commer-

[1] *A. N., C., Sér. C13*, vol. xiii, fol. 13.

[2] *Ibid.*, vol. xvi, fols. 84-85.

[3] *Ibid.*, vol. xx. fols. 52-53.

[4] *Ibid.*, vol. xxii, fols. 37-38.

[5] *Ibid.*, vol. xxi, fols. 256-260; *Sér. A*, vol. xxiii, Oct. 30, 1737.

cial relations between Louisiana and the interior settlements of Mexico. Related by marriage to the local officials, he had always been able to carry on some trade there.[1] The commandant's influence with those at Adayes, however, was much less. Some business was still done but after 1747, when Spanish troops were paid with merchandise from Mexico, opportunities for enlarging it were scanty indeed.[2]

Under these circumstances Vaudreuil, in 1748, arranged with the viceroy for an exchange of deserters at Natchitoches and Adayes, respectively, a scheme that the governor believed would eventually lead to an increase in the trade.[3] Commerce with the whole of the viceroyalty passing through Natchitoches at this time was worth a little less than 14,500 livres a year.[4] Vaudreuil left Louisiana in 1752 without witnessing any material improvement in the situation. Nor were matters any better under his successor.

So far as New Mexico proper was concerned, as early as 1703, twenty Canadians started thither from the Illinois country with the idea of trading with the Spaniards for piastres and to find out what they could concerning the mines of New Mexico.[5] The attempt ended in failure. Two years later some "voyageurs" from the upper Missouri reached the Illinois country where they gave an account of the frontier settlements of New Mexico, which, however, was too vague to arouse French activity in that direction.[6]

[1] *A. N., C., Sér.* C^{13}, vol. xxviii, fols. 269-270.

[2] *Ibid.*, vol. xxx, fol. 249; vol. xxxi, fol. 188.

[3] *Ibid.*, vol. xxxii, fol. 70.

[4] *A., B. N., Joly Coll.*, vol. 1726, fol. 242.

[5] Margry, vol. vi, p. 180.

[6] *Ibid.*, p. 181; *A. N., C., Sér.* C^{13}, vol. i, fol. 502.

For a while no further efforts were made there. In 1721, however, interest in the project was revived by the news from the Indians of the area that 200 Spanish soldiers had tried to make an expedition overland, with the object, as the French surmised, of seizing the Illinois country. They were driven back and finally destroyed by hostile Indians. As soon as the commandant of the Illinois country heard of the expedition he sent out a party of men in search of the route traversed by the Spaniards, hoping that it would lead to New Mexico.[1] Though unsuccessful, the attempt suggested to Governor Bienville the desirability of constructing Fort Orleans on the Grand river.[2] In 1723, some trade with the Spaniards, probably a mere exchange of merchandise for horses effected through Indian agents, was carried on at this post.[3] Nevertheless there is a possibility that the traffic in horses was entered upon directly with the Spaniards themselves, for they very early brought horses to sell to the French at Natchez.[4] Whatever its nature, the commerce at Fort Orleans did not prosper, and it was even thought advisable to abandon the post altogether or to make of it simply a mission station.[5]

For a while there seems to have been no interest among the French of the Illinois country in finding the way to New Mexico. On July 24, 1739, however, a party of men from that part of Louisiana reached Santa Fé. The route was long and difficult, nine pack-horses and their burdens being lost in making the trip. The French still had merchandise enough left to make the experiment that had brought them to New Mexico, and to assure for themselves

[1] *A. N., C., Sér.* C^{13}, vol. i, p. 386.

[2] *Supra*, p. 30.

[3] *A. N., C., Sér.* C^{13}, vol. vi, fol. 287; Margry, vol. vi, p. 387.

[4] Dumont, vol. i, p. 81.

[5] *Supra*, p. 30.

friendly treatment during their stay. They were lodged in Spanish homes and were invited to eat at Spanish tables.[1]

While no great advance in the trade was effected, some interest in it was aroused. The vicar and ecclesiastical judge of the province soon after the departure of the Frenchmen wrote to the priest at Natchitoches declaring that the idea appealed to him. He said that his people were without money, but that if there were a possibility of securing merchandise from Louisiana he felt certain that he could induce them to obtain the silver needful to be given in exchange. He remarked there were rich mines of that metal at a place called " Chihuahua ", only 200 leagues from his mission, where Spanish settlers of the province went to trade. If they could procure French goods he was positive they could easily be persuaded to work these mines for all the silver that might be required. On his own account he observed that he had 4,000 piastres ready to make a beginning in the traffic.[2]

Just what the influence of this expedition on commerce between New Mexico and Louisiana was, it is impossible to say with any definiteness. Some of the men engaged in it returned by water to New Orleans, the remainder went back to the Illinois country over the same route by which they had come. The French, therefore, succeeded in finding the way overland from the Illinois to New Mexico, but so long as they were in possession of Louisiana the route apparently was not used again. Just at the end of the French period, however, they rediscovered the eastern terminus of what later became the famous Santa Fé trail.[3]

[1] Margry, vol. vi, pp. 455-464, 466-468.

[2] *Ibid.*, pp. 464-465.

[3] *Ibid.*, pp. 460, 466, 467, 468, 472.

CHAPTER XXIII

Trade with Florida

Shortly after Iberville planted this colony, he suggested to the Spanish commandant at Pensacola the desirability of entering into commercial relations. As the garrison there was not any too well supplied with food, the proposition was readily accepted. By 1702, therefore, the traffic was fairly well under way, the commodities for the purpose being drawn from the royal storehouse.[1]

On March 10, 1704 the French supplied Pensacola with 4000 pounds of flour.[2] Notwithstanding the quantity sent the governor of that post was at Mobile, April 6, beseeching Bienville to send a boat to Vera Cruz for the purpose of procuring foodstuffs for him. The vessel was dispatched May 18, but before its return a ship from Havana arrived with flour on board, 75 sacks of which were hurried off at once to Pensacola.[3] Again on December 20, the French furnished supplies to the amount of 100 barrels of flour, 30 quintals of lard and some munitions of war.[4]

In September 1706 Mobile provided Pensacola with 100 quintals of flour.[5] It was at this time asserted that

[1] *A. N., C., Sér. B*, vol. xxxii, pt. 2, fol. 47; Margry, vol. iv, pp. 502, 552; La Harpe, pp. 71, 72.

[2] La Harpe, p. 83.

[3] *Ibid.*

[4] *Ibid.*, p. 86.

[5] *A. N., C., Sér. C[13]*, vol. i, fol. 472.

the reason why Louisiana was always so short of food was because the brothers of Iberville drew so freely on the royal supplies to promote their own private trade at Pensacola. Moreover it was claimed that 1217 livres, 16 sols, 8 deniers of government funds thus far had been expended in boats that were used chiefly in furthering these family transactions.[1]

For two months, Bienville asserted on February 20, 1707, the food supply for the province had been short. Nevertheless he was obliged to share what there was with the garrison at Pensacola, where the scarcity was much greater.[2] In June he made a consignment of 40 quintals of flour.[3] The following year the report to the home government showed that the Louisiana officials, since 1702, had furnished Pensacola with something more than 692 piastres' worth of such provisions.[4] In August, 1709, the future looked dark. There were rations at Mobile for the soldiers for only two months, and the Indians' harvest had been very light. The Pensacola settlement was again facing starvation; therefore, Bienville, out of his meagre amount of provisions, sent it twenty barrels, which was all that could be spared.[5]

The next year, 1710, before the vessels from France arrived to replenish the royal storehouse, Bienville sold to Pensacola 150 barrels of corn, at from four to five piastres each, thereby forcing the French soldiers and settlers into the woods in search of food.[6] In 1711 the

[1] *A. N., C., Sér.* C^{13}, vol. i, fols. 472-501; *Sér. B*, pt. 2, vol. xxxii, fol. 47.

[2] *Ibid., Sér.* C^{13}, vol. ii, fol. 5.

[3] *Iberville's Journal*, Lib. of Congress, Washington, D. C.

[4] *A. N., C., Sér.* C^{13}, vol. ii, fols. 519-527.

[5] *Ibid.*, vol. ii, fols. 427-438.

[6] *Ibid.*, fols. 519-527.

Louisiana officials secured at Vera Cruz 100 quintals of flour for their distressed Spanish neighbors,[1] who had as yet made no clearings of any kind. Besides the supplies thus provided, the settlers of Louisiana also had developed a small traffic with Pensacola in vegetables, corn, poultry and other local products. Through it the French colonists obtained a certain amount of silver with which to provide themselves with French goods.[2]

During the period under discussion, 1702–1712, there were times when Pensacola was in a position to furnish foodstuffs to the French settlement on the Mobile. In 1703 the governor of the former post, learning of the dearth of provisions at the latter, despatched messengers thither with the information that three vessels laden with food from Vera Cruz had just reached him and carried sufficient in quantity for both garrisons. The French were filled with joy at the news. For some time they had been forced to subsist chiefly upon fish and clams. A boat was at once sent to Pensacola where Governor Andrés de la Riola provided them with what they wished. On August 16, 1705, also, the Louisiana officials learned from the captain of a French ship that had stopped at Pensacola on the way to Mobile that the Spanish governor had just received a large consignment of food from Vera Cruz and expressed a desire to share it with his French neighbors.[4] In 1706 and 1707 both garrisons were short of rations. In 1708 a shipment of foodstuffs was dispatched from Mobile[5] to Pensacola; in April a cargo of such commodities went from the latter

[1] *A. N., C., Sér.* C^{13}, vol. ii, fols. 641-645.

[2] *Ibid.*, vol. iii, fols. 513-515.

[3] La Harpe, p. 80.

[4] *Ibid.*, pp. 91-92.

[5] *Supra*, p. 419.

to the former post;[1] in June the direction of the cargoes was again reversed.[2]

On his arrival in the province, Governor Cadillac at once ordered trading on the part of the colonists with any one but the Crozat agents stopped. The effect of the mandate, if any, was to stimulate it. Under the Crozat rule, furthermore, the French at Mobile began to deal secretly with Spanish ships on their way to or from Pensacola. The transactions took place in the lower bay, sometimes off Dauphin Island. On the other hand the Louisiana officials continued to provide the garrison at Pensacola with food.[3] In September 1714 Crozat's agents received 150 quintals of flour from France and sold 30 barrels (200 lbs. each) of it to the Spaniards.[4] Early in 1716 the Louisiana officials sent merchandise to Pensacola to be sold to Spanish vessels from other ports or to the garrison itself.[5] The neglect of the post by the Spaniards, in fact, caused it to become a fairly good market for the Louisiana settlers as well, who by 1717 were selling supplies there to the amount of about 12,000 piastres annually.[6]

The Company of the West from the first considered the trade between Pensacola and Mobile prejudicial to the growth of the province as a whole, and in order to check it, proposed to make settlements upon the Mississippi.[7] The war that broke out between France and Spain in 1719, however, provided a much more effectual

[1] La Harpe, p. 102.

[2] *Supra*, p. 420.

[3] *A. N., C., Sér.* C^{13}, vol. iii, fols. 469-476, 511-513, 568-570.

[4] *Ibid.*, fols. 513-515.

[5] *Ibid.*, vol. iv, fol. 69.

[6] La Harpe, p. 140.

[7] Margry, vol. v, pp. 547-549.

means of destroying it.[1] In 1723 the traffic was resumed, and some of the larger landowners in Louisiana were making plans to increase it by the addition of a "balandre" and a half-galère to the boat service on the river and along the coast.[2] Whether this was done is not clear. In 1725 at all events it is stated that the commerce was being carried on partly by sea and partly by land, and since the close of the war had grown considerably.[3] Governor Périer was favorably disposed toward it, and on October 2, 1727, had a talk with the "pagador" of Pensacola, who was at Mobile, on ways and means of furthering such a traffic.[4]

As commerce had not advanced with sufficient rapidity, the crown instructed the Louisiana officials, in 1731, to put it on the freest possible basis. Through such a course of action presumably much Spanish silver and many Spanish vessels would find their way to the province.[5] On December 5, the governor and "ordonnateur" informed the home government that the commandant at Pensacola was opposing the new policy.[6] In view of this situation, and of the fact that the inhabitants of Mobile were not raising products of sufficient value to attract the Spaniards, the government now proposed to use flour and brandy as the chief articles of the traffic.[7] The bait proved to be effective, at least to some extent. Pensacola may have been an outpost against possible encroachments on Florida, but its garrison apparently

[1] Margry, vol. v, p. 569; Le Page du Pratz, vol. i, p. 93.

[2] La Harpe, p. 346.

[3] *A. N., C., Sér.* C^{13}, vol. ix, fols. 9-10; *A., A. É., Am.*, vol. i, fol. 26.

[4] *A. N., C., Sér.* C^{13}, vol. x, fol. 188.

[5] *Ibid., Sér. B*, vol. lv, fol. 596.

[6] *Ibid., Sér.* C^{13}, vol. xiii, fol. 13.

[7] *Ibid.*, fol. 17.

could not survive without provisions from its French neighbors. Whether they liked it or not, the viceroy and local commandant had to tolerate what, from the Spanish legal standpoint, was certainly illicit trade.[1]

In 1733 the Louisiana officials received 5,000 livres in freight charges for a cargo of supplies carried on one of the French royal ships from Vera Cruz to Pensacola.[2] On the whole, however, the commercial relations between the two posts in question were too scanty to arouse strong opposition from Spanish officials or great enthusiasm on the part of the French.[3] In 1735 the trade was worth only about 5,000 or 6,000 piastres a year. It was carried on, as before, partly by Spaniards who came to Mobile; partly by the French who went to Pensacola in the hope of doing business with Spanish vessels that touched there, and more commonly by the colonists of Mobile themselves who met the Spaniards at designated places on the coast and there exchanged their products for silver.[4]

With the employment of all these methods the garrison, at times, was not able to keep itself above extreme want. Such periods of distress were apt to occur when Mobile itself was very short of food; even in such cases the French felt impelled to share their scant supplies.

Ties of friendship made it impossible to turn a deaf ear to the Spanish appeals. During these years, also, the soldiers at Pensacola were quite as short of money as they were of provisions:[5] accordingly in 1736 when the commandant received his allowance from the viceroy, amounting to between 7,000 and 8,000 piastres, it was

[1] *A. N., C., Sér. C*^{13}, vol. xvi, fols. 82-88. [2] *Ibid.*

[3] *Ibid.*, vol. xvii, fols. 36-38; vol. xviii, fols. 41-44.

[4] *Ibid.*, vol. xx, fols. 52-56.

[5] *Ibid.*, vol. xxi, fols. 7-11, 25-30.

not enough to pay the debts of something more than 35,000 livres already contracted at Mobile.[1] At this time also, the French officials held a bill for 500 piastres against the same post for freight charges on supplies carried by French ships from Vera Cruz to Pensacola.[2] For several months the garrison had lived on what it could procure at Mobile; accordingly the French had about reached a point where their financial condition would no longer allow them to advance food to the Spaniards on credit. The settlers themselves were interested in keeping the traffic alive: at this juncture one of the well-to-do men there began to furnish supplies to the Spaniards. With consignments of this sort he sent small quantities of tar and pitch to Pensacola which the Spaniards sold to merchants of their nationality who came to the post.[3] The commandant was thus enabled to ward off the danger of famine.

During the next two years owing to the somewhat unfriendly feeling existing between France and Spain, the viceroy had made it difficult for the commandant at Pensacola to meet the bills as they fell due. In 1737, therefore, the only person in the province who would venture to advance corn on credit was the commandant at Mobile. He also had taken over for collection the debts the Spaniards had contracted with private persons at Mobile.[4] In spite of the indebtedness, on May 9, 1739 a further request for provisions came from Pensacola. A Spanish vessel soon appeared at Mobile; but its captain, having no money with which to pay for what he bought, procured the signatures of the commandant and commissaire of Pensacola as security for the pay-

[1] *A. N., C., Sér.* C^{13}, vol. xxi, fols. 94-100. [2] *Ibid.*, fol. 100.

[3] *Ibid.*, fols. 25-30.

[4] *Ibid.*, vol. xxii, fols. 37-41, 233-243.

ment of the bill.[1] On being informed of the circumstance, the home government cautioned the colonial officials to insist upon good security for whatever was furnished in future to the Pensacola garrison, lest the Spaniards be led to believe that anythng so easily procured might be paid for entirely at their own convenience, if at all.[2]

In 1741 from the supplies delivered in 1737 the treasury at Mobile could boast of 4,500 piastres obtained from guns, powder, and cordage furnished to the garrison at Pensacola.[3] Meanwhile the relations between France and Spain had improved, and the Spaniards were meeting their obligations more promptly. Spain now being at war with England was well disposed to renew its friendship with France and to obtain military supplies from the French colonies.[4] Though the conflict made trade conditions easier between Mobile and Pensacola, the possibilities of greater development remained very small. For the time being the traffic of the Spanish post centered almost exclusively at the French village.[5] The year following, the opening of hostilities changed the situation again. This was evident enough when the commandant at Pensacola received instructions from the viceroy of New Spain to confiscate all vessels from Louisiana coming thither to trade. The orders, to be sure, were not obeyed, because the Spanish officer found it necessary to continue drawing supplies from Mobile, as the viceroy had made no arrangements for him to obtain them elsewhere. That functionary appears to

[1] *A. N., C., Sér.* C^{13}, vol. xxiv, fols. 246-249.

[2] *Ibid., Sér. B,* vol. lxx, fol. 6.

[3] *Ibid., Sér.* C^{13}, vol. xxvi, fol. 149.

[4] *Ibid.,* fols. 149, 181.

[5] *Ibid., Sér. B,* vol. lxxiv, fols. 17-18.

have made no effort to punish his subordinate for the disobedience shown, except possibly to render payment difficult.[1]

In 1743, at all events, the governor of Louisiana informed the home government that the collection of bills due from Pensacola had caused a great deal of trouble. On this account he had decided to forbid the despatch of any more supplies to that post, and notified its commandant accordingly. The latter thereupon wrote to the officer in charge at Mobile declaring that in future he would be ready to pay cash or give food security for anything furnished him from the French province. This assurance, it seems, was not to take effect immediately, for he stated that the allowance from the viceroy had not yet arrived. As the Spanish soldiers undoubtedly were in need, the commandant at Mobile sent on some provisions notwithstanding.[2] The governor's ordinance, issued on August 14, therefore, was not heeded from the outset; nor was much effort made to enforce it,[3] in spite of the royal approval.[4]

From 1743 to 1749 Pensacola continued to be provisioned largely from Mobile, but the payments for what was procured became so much prompter that the merchants at the French village began to hope that a considerable increase in trade would result.[5] During these years the relations between the French and the Spanish were cordial and the value of the traffic rose to more than 14,500 livres annually.[6] In other respects the

[1] *A. N., C., Sér.* C^{13}, vol. xxviii, fols. 62-63. [2] *Ibid.*

[3] *Ibid., Sér. A,* vol. xxiii, Aug. 14, 1743.

[4] *Ibid., Sér. B,* vol. lxxxiii, fol. 11.

[5] *Ibid., Sér.* C^{13}, vol. xxx, fol. 273.

[6] *Ibid.,* vol. xxxii, fols. 68-71; *A., B. N., Joly Coll.,* vol. 1726, fol. 242.

situation at Pensacola remained much as it had been: a period of plenty followed closely by one of want. In May 1749 a vessel came to Mobile with information that the post was virtually in a state of famine; whereupon the French furnished 25 barrels of flour, half of the amount asked for, together with some lard, beans and rice, amounting in all to 2,785 pounds. The merchandise brought good prices, but as was usually the case the French were forced to wait a long time for their money.[1]

Because of the abuses in the traffic which worked injury to the province, Governor Kerlérec suspended commerce with Pensacola and demanded the commandant at Mobile to see to it that he enforce the order.[2] To what extent and for what length of time this official followed the instructions from his superior is not evident. Certain it is that before the war was long in progress the old relations between the two posts were much the same as they had been, and remained thus during the remainder of the French régime.[3]

Although the trade between Louisiana and Florida centered naturally at Pensacola, St. Augustine was not entirely overlooked. In 1702 the governor of that post besought the French on the Mobile to aid him in his struggle with the English by sending him ammunition. To this request Bienville replied by providing him with 100 guns, 500 pounds of powder and some bullets.[4] The next year the latter official despatched to Vera Cruz a boat bearing the news to the viceroy of New Spain that St. Augustine was besieged and in need of succor.[5]

[1] *A. N., C., Sér.* C^{13}, vol. xxxiii, fols. 7, 65.

[2] *Ibid.*, vol. xxxix, fol. 51.

[3] *Ibid.*, vol. xxxvi, fol. 270; Bossu, vol. i, p. 221.

[4] La Harpe, p. 74.

[5] *Ibid.*, p. 75.

Before help from the latter source could arrive, the governor of this hard-pressed Spanish post again appealed to the Louisiana officials for munitions of war, and secured enough to bring the value of the amount thus far procured there to 7,009 livres, 5 sols.[1] In July the boat that had gone to Vera Cruz to carry the news to the viceroy of the conditions at St. Augustine returned, bearing to Bienville the thanks of that official for the munitions he had provided, but apparently nothing more substantial.[2]

During the years 1709–1710 Louisiana settlers furnished St. Augustine with food worth 8,140 livres, 10 sols. The home government was requested to send to the province provisions equal in quantity to make good to the colonists the amount they had advanced.[3] For a number of years the French records contain no reference to the traffic. In 1715, however, the Carolinians claimed that since their war with the "St. Augustine Spaniards," the inhabitants of Mobile had enjoyed a trade with the post in question worth about £30,000 sterling.[4] What probably happened was that vessels passing from Mobile to Vera Cruz for food supplies sometimes carried part of the cargo to St. Augustine.[5]

In 1727 when Governor Périer was at Mobile he asked certain Spaniards whom he met there whether it would be possible for Louisiana to procure cattle from among the large herds in Florida. They answered in the affirmative, and ventured the opinion besides that the governor

[1] *A. N., C., Sér.* C^{13}, vol. i, fols. 387-396.

[2] La Harpe, p. 80.

[3] *A. N., C., Sér.* C^{13}, vol. ii, fol. 524.

[4] *Coll. S. C. Hist. Soc.*, vol. ii, p. 223; *B. of T. Papers, Prop. No. 10*, Penn. Hist. Soc. Trans.

[5] *A. N., C., Sér.* C^{13}, vol. ii, fols. 387-396; vol. xxxiii, fols. 166-173.

of the province would not be averse to the scheme. A Frenchman was at once sent thither to establish the traffic through Indian agents. He carried with him presents for the savages and also a small gift for the governor of that province. The French officials hoped to secure 700 or 800 head of cattle.[1] The number actually acquired from this quarter is not given.

The friendliness of the governor of Florida was again turned to account by the Louisiana officials, in June 1729, when they sent a vessel to Vera Cruz under the pretext of informing the viceroy of New Spain of the danger that threatened the Florida coast, but in reality to carry on trade with the merchants of that town.[2] Of this scheme the commandant at Pensacola and the governor at St. Augustine had full cognizance and in fact were instigators of it.[3]

The governor of Florida on his part was not slow to draw every possible advantage from his friendship with the French. To this end in 1736 he requested the officials at Mobile to send him a supply of 400 guns. On October a vessel left with one half that number and proceeded first to Campeachy, where, the captain pleading that he had been driven thither by a storm, tried to get in touch with the local merchants whom he hoped to induce to visit Louisiana. The excuse failed to impress the governor who ordered him to leave the harbor at once. The French boat thereupon set sail for St. Mark's where, according to the agreement with the Florida governor, he was to deliver the guns. This Spanish officer in charge refused to pay for them at the rate of five piastres each,

[1] *A. N., C., Sér.* C^{13}, vol. x, fol. 189.

[2] *Supra*, p. 397.

[3] *A. N., C., Sér.* C^{13}, vol. xii, fols. 61-63.

the price fixed by the governor himself. Instead he paid only 800 piastres in the form of a bill of exchange on Havana.[1]

In 1746 it was claimed that the Spaniards of St. Augustine came frequently to Mobile in search of flour, corn, rice and all sorts of European goods, for which they paid cash.[2] Again in 1749 it was asserted that they made visits to New Orleans on similar errands.[3] Since St. Augustine was on the route of the Spanish ships making the circuit of the Gulf of Mexico, this trade with Louisiana, though insignificant, gave the French opportunity to come into contact with Spanish merchants and for that reason seems to have been encouraged. What it actually amounted to is not shown in the French records.

[1] *A. N., C., Sér. C*[13], vol. xxi, fols. 94-100; vol. xxii, fols. 37-41.

[2] *Ibid.*, vol. xxx, fol. 273.

[3] *Ibid.*, vol. xxxiii, fols. 166-167.

CHAPTER XXIV

TRADE WITH CUBA

TRADE with Havana was also one of Iberville's schemes, and as early as November 24, 1701 he was investigating ways and means of establishing it. That port was located conveniently enough at a distance of only about 15 days sail from Biloxi, but Spanish regulations constituted a formidable bar to traffic. Iberville had been most careful to show the Spaniards of Pensacola certain favors[1] which he hoped in the end to turn to advantage at Havana.[2] With this object in mind he sent a vessel for a cargo of domestic animals, only to have it peremptorily excluded. The founder of the Louisiana colony therefore wrote to the home government asking it to induce Spain, if possible, to revise its regulations sufficiently to permit of an exchange of such animals for French merchandise.[3] France took no action in the matter apparently. In 1704[4] and again in 1706 Bienville despatched a vessel to Havana for a cargo of food supplies. These were furnished, but no domestic animals were forthcoming.[5]

The visits seem to have created some interest among the Havana merchants, who, on January 30, 1707, had a

[1] *Supra*, p. 418.

[2] Margry, vol. iv, p. 502.

[3] *Ibid.*, p. 552.

[4] *Ibid.*, vol. v, p. 441.

[5] *A. N., C., Sér.* C^{13}, vol. i, fols. 502-513.

vessel in Louisiana with a cargo of wine from the Canary Islands.[1] The arrival of the ship encouraged the French in the following year to instruct the captains of vessels making voyages to Louisiana to call at Havana on the return to France with the object of stimulating the interest further. At all events, on January 9, 1708, a small ship from Havana sold at Dauphin Island a cargo of brandy, lard and tobacco.[2]

The officials of Louisiana now ventured to ask the home government for a boat of about 80 tons on which to transport domestic animals from Cuba.[3] In 1711 a vessel of some 50 tons was purchased at Martinique for this purpose at a cost of 2,000 livres. On its way to Louisiana it was wrecked by a storm.[4] The outlook for the trade at this time was especially gloomy, since the Spanish colonists appear to have entertained a certain amount of jealousy toward Louisiana, arising from a belief that the better climate and soil of the French possession would soon enable it to become too powerful for their safety. This sentiment, added to the force of the existing commercial relations, strengthened the unwillingness of the functionaries at Havana to sell the domestic animals so much sought after.[5]

In spite of such obstacles, the "ordonnateur" of Louisiana recommended to the home government, in 1713, the desirability of procuring hogs at "Matance" (Mantanzas), since they could be obtained there at from six reaux to two livres a head. The profit of 100 per

[1] La Harpe, p. 101.

[2] *A. N., C., Sér. B*, vol. xxxix, Louisiane, 1C, fols. 44-46.

[3] La Harpe, p. 104.

[4] *A. N., C., Sér. C*[13], vol. ii, fols. 89, 600.

[5] *Ibid.*, fols. 803-809.

cent made on French merchandise given in exchange would lower the ultimate cost of the animals to 30 or 40 sols each. There, also, and at Havana, cattle could be bought at from seven to eight piastres a head, and if similarly acquired, the resultant price would be three or four piastres. The animals, in fact, could be purchased even cheaper perhaps at Tampico. Accordingly the "ordonnateur" requested permission to use the boat of 70 tons that had been acquired at Vera Cruz[1] in promoting the trade. It was thought that the English ships that during the war had closed these ports would no longer disturb vessels entering them. No reply to the request was made by the home government.[2] So thoroughly did the "ordonnateur" believe in the possibilities of the traffic that, before the end of the year, he, in conjunction with Bienville and a nephew of the governor of Pensacola, fitted out a vessel and despatched it to Havana for the purpose of their own private trade. No details, however, are given as to the results of the venture.[3]

The commercial activities of the "ordonnateur" caused a clash between him and the Crozat agents. On his own behalf that officer informed the crown that the agents in question had violated their agreement in charging far too much for the domestic animals that they had sold to the settlers.[4] His contention was upheld, for in reply the government stated that no profits should be derived from the sale of such animals to the colonists, because enough could be made on the French

[1] *Supra*, p. 283.

[2] *A. N., C., Sér.* C[13], vol. iii, fols. 245-248.

[3] *Ibid.*, fol. 355.

[4] *Ibid.*, fols. 695-696.

merchandise given in exchange to warrant disposing of them at their cost in Havana.[1] Thc crown also instructed the officials to send thither a vessel three times a year for livestock.[2] The royal command, however, does not seem to have been heeded by Crozat's representatives.[3]

Fortunately for Louisiana, persistency was a strong element in the character of the man who was "ordonnateur" of the province during these years. In March 1716 he despatched a vessel to Havana, instructing the captain to enter that port on the pretext of shortage of food and while there to purchase a cargo of cattle. The plan worked and the shipmaster was allowed by the Spanish governor three days in which to secure the supply he needed. In that time he succeeded in putting on board 60 head of cattle. Just as he was about to set sail, one of his sailors, on being asked what they were going to do with so many cows, inadvertently replied that they were going to take them to Louisiana. On receipt of this information the governor ordered all but 15 of the animals to be taken off, after which the vessel was commanded to leave the port at once.[4] The Louisauna athorities were not yet disposed to give up the idea of securing cattle from Havana, and on October 26, 1717, a ship was again sent to that place to buy them but, with even less satisfactory results.[5]

The change made at this time in the administration caused a lull in all activities, yet French interest in the

[1] *A. N., C., Sér. F³*, vol. ccxli, M. S. S. M., Dec. 27, 1715.

[2] *Ibid., Sér. C¹³*, vol. iv, fols. 660-661.

[3] *Ibid.,* fol. 736.

[4] La Harpe, pp. 132-133; *A., M. des C., Sér. G¹*, vol. 464.

[5] *A. N., C., Sér. C¹³*, vol. v, fol. 46.

trade with the Spanish West Indies was in some way kept alive. On June 5, 1721, at all events, a vessel from Havana reached Louisiana where a cargo of tobacco at three quarters of a real a pound payable in French merchandise was disposed of. Considerable quantities, also, of brandy, powder, flour, paper and groceries were purchased and paid for in cash. Though the merchandise in question was greatly needed at home, the colonial officials evidently believed it to be good policy to sell them to the Spaniard, inasmuch as any temporary embarassment would be counterbalanced in future by an increase in trade. Whatever may have been the Spanish merchant's intention in the matter, his work came to a sudden end on his return to Havana, where he was seized and imprisoned on a charge of smuggling.[1]

The next year Bienville renewed the attempt to establish trade relations with Havana. Under the pretext of a desire to exchange prisoners of war, his vessel, with a cargo of merchandise amounting to about 2,000 piastres in value, effected a landing and the captain sold the entire consignment for more than 200,000 piastres. So great was the demand for French goods that the local merchants came in small boats and begged him "for the love of God" to sell them what he had on board. They brought with them in fact, 300,000 piastres from which liberal presents were given to the captain and sailors as an inducement to make them speedily return.[2]

This venture naturally intensified Louisiana's interest in the Spanish West-Indian commerce. On February 11, 1727 a representative of the provincial government held a conference at Cape Français with some Cuban

[1] La Harpe, pp. 252-253.

[2] Béranger, *Mémoire de la Louisiane*, 1722, p. 103. Newberry Lib., Chicago.

merchants who agreed to send agents to the colony with piastres to exchange for French merchandise. Letters also were despatched to France asking to have the storehouse replenished with articles suited to the Spanish trade, and ready for the merchants in question who agreed to make a journey thither in about six months.[1] The response to the call was so slow that on January 30, 1729, when the goods finally arrived there were no Spaniards there to buy them. The Louisiana authorities thereupon sent out letters in triplicate[2] to merchants in Havana lists of the merchandise then available; but the action elicited no response.[3]

After the resumption of royal administration the task of developing trade with the Spanish West Indies was more difficult than ever. Incapacity on the part of the Company's agents had brought the traffic into disfavor with the Spanish merchants, but the Louisiana officials believed that under the new régime the evil would be remedied. They felt sure, in 1733 at all events, that they could find people at Havana willing to put vessels into the service, if only the crown would supply the storehouse at the Balise with merchandise that was sufficiently attractive.[4] The next year the home government again was informed that trade with Havana could be established through Spanish merchants as they made the circuit of the Gulf ports by inducing them to touch at the Balise.[5] There was little possibility of building up such traffic by means of French boats; since in 1735 the governor of Havana was instructed by the viceroy of New Spain to

[1] *A. N., C., Sér.* C^{13}, vol. x, fol. 310.

[2] *Supra*, p. 404.

[3] *A. N., C., Sér.* C^{13}, vol. xi, fol. 309.

[4] *Ibid.*, vol. xvi, fols. 82-88.

[5] *Ibid.*, vol. xviii, fols. 41-44.

allow no French vessels, whether from the colonies or from France itself, to enter that harbor. The enforcement of the command, it was asserted, caused the loss of two French boats before the end of the year, as well as great damage to many other vessels and cargoes. A protest was made against such an order, especially in the case of ships bound for that harbor because of some pressing need.[1]

For some time the obstacles seem to have been too formidable to be overcome. By 1743, however, trade became fairly active. Numerous vessels from France bound for Louisiana called en route at Havana where they disposed of a large part of their cargoes.[2] The governor again being ordered to allow no French ships to enter, in October confiscated a boat of that nationality with a cargo on board worth 100,000 livres, notwithstanding it had put in there by reason of heavy seas.[3] The change of policy toward the French vessels affected those from Louisiana itself, some of which could obtain no trading permits whatever, and others were granted them at such exorbitant rates that the business could not be made profitable. Before the end of the year the governor of Cuba received orders to exclude all ships from Havana, as no prohibitions against them had been removed.[4]

In spite of the heightened risk of confiscation, many boats from France and Louisiana found their way to Havana or vicinity. Some, to be sure, were seized, but others succeeded in carrying on a very lucrative trade.[5]

[1] *A., B. N., Fr.*, vol. 10769, fol. 88.

[2] *A. N., C., Sér.* C[13], vol. xxviii, fols. 62-63.

[3] *Ibid.*, fol. 44.

[4] *Ibid.*, fol. 62.

[5] *Ibid.*, vol. xxviii, fols. 271-272, 277, 281.

In October 1744, for example, a ship left Louisiana with a cargo of French merchandise to be exchanged for one of powder.[1] By December Governor Vaudreuil through his correspondence with the governor at Havana, had brought about in that official a different attitude toward trade with the French. He was now lenient to both Spanish and French merchants who desired to trade with one another.[2] Moreover France now being at war with England, naturally the, Spanish port was not so tightly closed as usual. Therefore many Spaniards from there passed to Louisiana. Some of the traffic was carried on by the "Royal Company of Havana" for the purpose of securing lumber, pitch and tar. By 1746 it had become quite extensive and brought to the province large sums of Spanish money.[3]

Since the beginning of hostilities, the vessels sailing from France in larger convoys had found it safer to touch at Havana, and thence to proceed singly or in smaller convoys. The practice was very prejudicial to existing commercial relations: first, by depriving the colony of the greater part of its European merchandise, sold en route; and secondly, by providing that town with so much material of the sort as to remove any inclination to send vessels to Louisiana for it. This in turn lessened correspondingly the number of boats available to take local products to Cuba.[4]

Even before the opening of the war, the rigidity of the Spanish officers in enforcing the rules of trade had caused

[1] *A. N., C., Sér.* C^{13}, vol. xxviii, fol. 279.

[2] *Ibid.*, fols. 271-272.

[3] *Ibid.*, vol. xxix, fol. 41; vol. xxx, fol. 273; *Sér. B*, vol. lxxxiii, fols. 11, 19.

[4] *Ibid., Sér.* C^{13}, vol. xxx, fols. 25, 144.

new methods to be inaugurated by the merchants. Vessels from Campeachy, Vera Cruz, Tampico and other Spanish settlements on the western part of the Gulf coast, on their way to Havana with cargoes of salt, flour and other articles, touched at the Balise and exchanged the commodities for French merchandise and Louisiana products that were wanted in Cuba. The goods thus obtained were placed in the empty packages, which were again fastened and labeled just as they had been when taken on at the original port of departure. At Havana the stuff from Louisiana was exchanged for sugar and molasses, which, on the return trip, in turn were exchanged in similar fashion at the Balise for another cargo of local or French products to be carried back to Mexico. These processes appear to have been carried on with the full knowledge and consent of the officials at the various places concerned, and yet enabled them to make a plausible report to their superiors. Perhaps no one thing contributed more to the success of the arrangement than the clever correspondence of Vaudreuil with the various influential Spaniards involved.[1]

By 1747 he had so ingratiated himself with the governor at Havana, through skilful letter-writing, that the opposition to trade with the French had been removed. Vaudreuil next turned his attention to the "Royal Company of Havana," whose trade with his province he hoped to increase. Nothing of importance was accomplished, chiefly because of a difference of opinion on prices.[2] Traffic with other merchants at that port, how-

[1] *A. N., C., Sér.* C^{13}, vol. xxx, fols. 145-146; *A., B. N., Fr.*, vol. 12224, fols. 126-127; *A., A. É., Am.*, vol. i, fol. 19; vol. ii, fols. 119-120; vol. x, fol. 44.

[2] *A. N., C., Sér.* C^{13}, vol. xxxii, fols. 31, 57, 70; vol. xxxiii, fols. 64-66.

ever, had gone on in defiance of the risk of capture by the English.[1]

Nor were the skippers of the French vessels averse to other expedients that might enable them to avoid the Spanish trade regulations. Some of them have already been noted. Besides the "stress of storm" and "heavy seas" they found "sprung a leak," "broken mast," "shortage of wood and water" and similar excuses quite as effective, according to circumstances.[2] In general, however, during the war and for a considerable period afterward, French vessels were seldom denied admission to Havana at least. Nevertheless for two months in 1748 this port was closed to commerce by an English man-of-war.[3]

Encouraged by the activity of commerce with Cuba, a Louisiana official proposed to the home government, in 1749, that it sound Spain on the possibility of concluding a treaty permitting pitch, tar, lumber and other building materials to be sold in its colonies openly. On each of these articles, also, the crown was to fix the price.[4] The suggestion is simply a repetition of the proposal in 1746 and like it similarly received no further consideration.

The return to peace brought about marked changes in the trade with Havana. In 1750 the number of Spanish vessels coming to Louisiana fell off considerably. This decrease was due in part to the vigorous way in which

[1] *A. N., C., Sér.* C^{13}, vol. xxxii, fols. 88-90; *A., B. N., Joly Coll.*, vol. 1726, fols. 145-146.

[2] *A., B. N., Fr.*, vol. 12224, fols. 133-136; *A., A. É., Am.*, vol. ii, pp. 111-120.

[3] *A. N., C., Sér.* C^{13}, vol. xxxii, fol. 132.

[4] *A., A. É., Am.*, vol. ii, fols. 119-120; *A., B. N., Fr.*, vol. 12224, fols. 133-136.

the Spanish governor enforced the commercial regulations. Another contributing factor lay in the circumstance that the adjacent Spanish colonies had become overstocked with French merchandise which sold there more cheaply than in Louisiana itself. Until adjustment of demand and supply could be reached, therefore, it was unlikely that Spanish vessels would soon appear on the scene.[1] On the other hand the hope for an admission of French ships at Havana harbor was equally improbable of realization, unless the traffic restrictions were abated in some measure.[2] The obstructions, it was hoped, would be the means of bringing Spanish boats again to Louisiana.

At this time, 1752, the trade with Havana was crippled still further by the recall of Governor Vaudreuil and the appointment of a successor far less skilled in colonial affairs and possessed of much less cleverness and tact. Moreover the new incumbent was scarcely installed in office when France became involved in the Seven Years War. During the early years of the conflict Havana remained absolutely closed to French ships. In 1758 it was asserted by a merchant at Mobile that the Spanish trade which for the past seven years had been about 500,000 livres annually had dwindled to almost nothing. Every one engaged in it desired to sell out and leave the place.[3] The next year the Louisiana officials requested the home government to take up the matter of the closed ports with Spain on the ground that, since France and Spain were at peace, the attitude of the Spanish governor

[1] *A. N., C., Sér.* C^{13}, vol. xxxiii, fols. 64-66; *A., A. É., Am.*, vol. ii, fols. 107, 119-120.

[2] *A. N., C., Sér.* C^{13}, vol. xxxiv, fols. 250, 277.

[3] *Ibid.*, vol. xl, fols. 246-247.

seemed not only incomprehensible but was in fact a violation of treaties subsisting between the two nations.[1] Since Louisiana at the time was short of food supplies, in December the "ordonnateur," without waiting for a reply from France, sent a boat to Havana for a cargo of powder.[2] The venture was entirely fruitless. The ship was not allowed in the harbor nor was permission granted to buy the desired commodity outside.[3]

The French government meanwhile called the attention of Spain to the treatment of its vessels at Havana and succeeded in re-establishing trade relations. In order to open the Spanish ports it became necessary to pay some very questionable bills of exchange drawn in favor of Spanish merchants. As a further encouragement to the process Governor Kerlérec of Louisiana was allowed to draw bills of exchange in favor of such merchants to the amount of 400,000 livres a year.[4] The work of restoration, however, was too long delayed to be of any considerable importance to the French.

[1] *A., B. N., Fr.*, vol. 10769, fols. 96-97.

[2] *A. N., C., Sér. C*[13], vol. xli, fol. 323.

[3] *Ibid.*, vol. xliii, fol. 93.

[4] *Ibid., Sér. B*, pt. 1, vol. cxiii, fols. 276-277; *A., B. N., Fr.*, vol. 10764, fols. 243-244.

CHAPTER XXV

Trade with the English

Since one of the aims of the French in establishing Louisiana was to keep the English out of the Mississippi valley, it could hardly be expected that the latter would be encouraged to come thither to trade. From the outset, therefore, not much cordiality was displayed between the officials of the French settlements on the Gulf coast and those of the English on the Atlantic seaboard. Each feared and distrusted the other. For example, Iberville, on his way from Louisiana to France in 1700, touched at New York. The visit gave rise to considerable speculation and some uneasiness there as to its object. According to rumor, James II had presented New York to France, and this Frenchman had been ordered to make the stop for the purpose of examining the channel and the harbor. Some specific purpose, the English felt certain, must have turned so clever a seaman and colony-builder out of the direct route to France. Moreover, this opinion was reinforced by the further belief that Frenchmen in general were individuals of too great perspicacity to let an advantage slip or to make a voyage having no significance.[1] So far as the English colonial merchant of the time on his part was concerned, neither fear nor repugnance entered into his commercial relationships. To him business was business, not sentiment or hatred,

[1] *Calendar of State Papers, Colonial Series, Am. and West Indies*, p. 602. Penn. Hist. Soc. Trans.

and he, too, was as active and alert as his French neighbors, if not more so.

In any case the possibilities of trade with the little French colony on the Gulf of Mexico seemed promising enough. At the time of the founding of Biloxi, English merchants knew the field fairly well. They already had carried on a commerce with the West Indies in direct violation of existing regulations. Restrictions upon traffic with Louisiana, therefore, would be nothing new for an English sea captain.[1]

Accordingly it might be supposed that English vessels would soon participate in the trade of the province. It was not to be presumed, however, that a suggestion to that effect would come from the French themselves; yet in 1706 the provincial authorities proposed to the crown to invite the sending of ships from Maryland with cargoes of food for the reason that French boats could not provide the colony with more than half of the commodities needed.[2] To be sure the proposal received no consideration on the part of the home government. Nevertheless in June 1707 an English vessel appeared on the Gulf coast with an appropriate cargo.[3]

The traffic thus begun was soon interrupted by the war then prevailing between England and France.[4] One of the boats that Bienville sent to Havana with a cargo worth more than 1,524 livres was seized and confiscated by the English, and the crew landed at Havana.[5] Up to the end of the war repetition of this procedure was

[1] Pub. of the Prince Soc., vol. xxviii, pp. 231, 268, 285; *Coll. Maine Hist Soc.*, vol. ix, pp. 254-256; vol. xi, p. 38.

[2] *A. N., C., Sér. C*[13], vol. i, fols. 472-501.

[3] *Ibid.*, vol. ii, fols. 57-69.

[4] *Ibid.*, fol. 471.

[5] *Ibid.*, vol. iii, fol. 66.

always to be expected.[1] In 1710, furthemore, an English privateer made an attack upon Dauphin Island and destroyed or carried off property valued at upwards of 50,000 livres.[2]

After the restoration of peace in 1713 the French had an advantage over the English in the colonial trade. Spain closed her ports to the latter and the French saw to it that the command was enforced.[3] The French similarly refused to admit English and Dutch ships to its provincial ports.[4] While official agencies both of Louisiana and Carolina kept a close watch, and in their communications to the respective mother countries exaggerated the power and importance of their adversaries, private individuals from either province were not averse to carrying on trade surreptitiously.[5] Governor Cadillac himself appears not to have objected to the practice of French vessels on the homeward voyage to touch at Carolina, where they exchanged such things as wine, brandy, cloth and paper for rice, tobacco, silk and silver.[6]

In July 1717 an English vessel came to Dauphin Island, presumably for wood and water, but in reality to dispose of its cargo. The following month a second ship of that nationality arrived on apparently the same quest. Permission to take on wood and water was granted on an agreement from the captain that he should not engage in trade, the penalty for violation of the agreement being confiscation of the cargo. Notwithstanding this under-

[1] *A. N., C., Sér.* C^{13}, vol. iii, fols. 245-248.

[2] La Harpe, p. 107.

[3] *Pub. Rec. of S. C.*, 1711-1716, vol. vi, p. 279.

[4] *A. N., C., Sér.* C^{13}, vol. iii, fols. 248-251.

[5] *Ibid.*, fols. 446, 522-523; vol. iv, fols. 241-242.

[6] *Ibid.*, vol. iii, fol. 421.

taking he exchanged his shipload for another. The commodities thus obtained were welcome enough, since the local storehouse at the time was quite empty. They made it possible, also, for the officials to allay discontent among the soldiers over the shortage.[1]

The Company of the Indies was not at all opposed to trade with the English. On the contrary, it was decidedly willing, and was granted permission by the crown to procure 1,500 slaves[2] from that source.[3] The favorable attitude was speedily appreciated. In April, 1719, three more English ships appeared on the Gulf coast ready to exchange their cargoes of flour and cloth for new ones of peltry. An offer of the Company's bills, however, was declined.[4] Earlier in the year, in fact, the superior council of Louisiana had notified the governor of Carolina of its desire to buy cattle, paying for them in bills of exchange or deerskins, a suggestion that was not accepted.[5] In July the ensign of the Company was sent to Carolina to reclaim some French deserters and to make an agreement with the governor to furnish Louisiana with 2,000 cows. He accomplished neither of the tasks assigned; instead, on his arrival he was seized as an undesirable alien, made a prisoner and sent to England, whence he was allowed to go to France.[6]

In May, 1722, an English vessel reached Mobile. The captain, having been there before on a similar errand, was so sure of his reception that he made no excuse for his coming. Nevertheless, he informed the authorities

[1] *A. N., C., Sér. C*[13], vol. v, fols. 48-49; *Sér. F*[3], vol. ccxli, M. S. S. M., July 27, 1717.

[2] *Supra*, p. 231.

[3] *A. N., C., Sér. C*[13], vol. v, fols. 301-302.

[4] *Ibid.*, fol. 209.

[5] *Ibid.*, fol. 344.

[6] La Harpe, p. 149.

that a French ship, putting into Havana harbor for wood and water, had been confiscated and its crew landed.[1] He asserted also that he knew some of the French officers and had loaned them a boat to make their escape to an English island where they could secure passage to France by way of England. The Mobile authorities naturally expected to be requested to pay for the boat. The captain was apparently too well satisfied with winning their favor and being able to sell a cargo for 1,500 piastres to make any such demand.[2]

Since the Carolina officials were apt to be alarmed at any report describing Louisiana as a prosperous province, it was not to be supposed that they would consent to provide a possible rival with anything that would promote its development.[3] In 1724, when a British sloop entered Charleston harbor with a load of pitch and tar from Mobile, they dispatched a letter to the home government in which they declared that the French of Louisiana were a menace to their local market in those commodities. They asserted that, unless these articles were taken out of the enumerated list, the French at Mobile in particular would be able to supply Europe with them at rates cheaper than was possible under existing English restrictions. The higher price of Carolina products was due entirely to the "double charge of risque, landing and shipping, besides loss of time."[4]

The next year two English ships reached Mobile and did some trading with private parties. St. Denis who was in charge at the time gave the visiting merchants permission to go to New Orleans by way of Lake Pont-

[1] *Supra*, p. 435.

[2] La Harpe, p. 324; *A. N., C., Sér. C*[13], vol. vi, fols. 318-320.

[3] *B. of T. Papers*, vol. x, pt. 2, 1718-1720. Penn. Hist. Soc. Trans.

[4] *Pub. Rec. of S. C.*, vol. xi, p. 204.

chartrain, while he sent their vessel to the Balise where the captain examined the mouth of the Mississippi and sold the remainder of the cargo, the officials at New Orleans having refused to enter into trade with them.[1] Although refusing these advances, these same officers in 1727 were attempting to induce Englishmen to come to the province from Virginia or Carolina to teach the French to grow tobacco. To this end Governor Périer, while on his way to Louisiana, had met some Carolina tobacco growers at Cape Français and had persuaded them to come to Louisiana, where they were to live on the plantations belonging to the Company at Natchez and Capitoulas in order to oversee the culture in question. They agreed on their return to Carolina to send to Louisiana some tobacco seed, which promise they seem never to have fulfilled,[2] due no doubt to the fact that the officials of the former province in 1730 had forbidden trade with the French.[3]

Aside from an unsuccessful attempt on the part of an English trader to secure a contract for the construction and delivery of a boat for the service with the French West Indies[4], the chief item in the commercial relations of 1733 was the supply of limbourg. As the Indians showed a decided preference for the English article[5], the French at Mobile were not slow in securing it. Merchants from the Carolinas and other English provinces were encouraged accordingly to bring it. Three vessels of that nationality soon appeared with cargoes of limbourg, flour, cider and beer, all of which were quickly

[1] *A. N., C., Sér.* C^{13}, vol. ix, fol. 62.

[2] *Ibid.*, vol. x, fols. 171, 310.

[3] *Pub. Rec. of S. C.*, vol. xiv, p. 211.

[4] *A. N., C., Sér.* C^{13}, vol. xvi, fols. 84-85; *Sér. B*, vol. lix, fols. 573-574.

[5] *Ibid., Sér.* C^{13}, vol. xvi, fol. 70.

sold. With this traffic Governor Bienville had hesitated to interfere because of the risk of a rupture with the savages if they were not provided with what they wanted. On the other hand he had some fear that it would weaken the French influence over them, since it was the natives' policy to carry on no trade with enemies. Such double-dealing on the part of the French might have an unfortunate effect, as in reality it did. Eventually, however, Bienville decided to discourage the traffic, requesting the English traders at Mobile to inform their compatriots that nothing more of the sort would be permitted.[1]

What word the traders actually passed along can perhaps be guessed from the nature of what occurred during the next few years. The French at Mobile, it seems, had been forced by the governor to reject part of the peltry offered by the savages, on the ground that the home market would accept skins of the best quality only. Rejection of the inferior grades naturally threw them into the hands of the English who took all varieties of pelts at the same price.[2] If, therefore, the French should wish to find a market for inferior skins it could be furnished solely through dealing with the English. As it could hardly be presumed that the governor's disapproval would end a traffic popularly considered to be advantageous to all concerned, the English traders continued to bring cargoes of flour, beer and goods for the Indian trade from New England, New York, Pennsylvania, Virginia and the Carolinas to exchange them at Mobile for peltry and other products.[3] Informed of the prac-

[1] *A. N., C., Sér.* C^{13}, vol. xvi, fols. 281-282; vol. xvii, fols. 271-275.

[2] *Supra*, p. 350.

[3] *A. N., C., Sér.* C^{13}, vol. xviii, fols. 3-7, 8-12; *Pub. Rec. of S. C.*, vol. xvi, pp. 392-393.

tice, the crown declined to admit the evidence of its value, and accordingly ordered all English vessels found trading in Louisiana confiscated.[1] When the provincial officials, obedient to the royal command, began to deal more severely with the English, a struggle was inevitable.

In February, 1734, an English vessel of about 29 tons, pretending to be on its way from Carolina to Jamaica, touched at Mobile on the plea that it had been forced to do so on account of violent winds. The story not being credited, the ship was confiscated and the cargo, consisting chiefly of Indian goods, was sold for between 13,000 and 14,000 livres. Of the six members of the crew two were allowed to make their way overland to the Carolinas, four were sent to New Orleans for transportation to France, and the captain requested to be allowed to go to Pensacola there to get passage to an English port.[2] In April a second English vessel arriving at Mobile, its captain asked for supplies and for permission to make certain repairs caused by a severe storm. As its appearance so strongly corroborated the story, the French commandant granted the request. It was not permitted to depart, however, until the status of the ship had been ascertained, which took a number of months. At the end of the investigation the captain was allowed to have his property.[3]

The continued appearance of these vessels on doubt was due in a measure to the fact that the commandant, Diron, at Mobile and Governor Bienville held different opinions concerning commerce with the English. The former continued to allow the traders there to secure

[1] *A. N., C., Sér. B,* vol. lxi, fol. 631.

[2] *Ibid., Sér.* C^{13}, vol. xvii, fols. 3-7, 8-12; vol. xx, fols. 67-70.

[3] *Ibid.,* vol. xviii, fols. 55-57; vol. xix, fols. 148-149.

quantities of English goods in exchange for peltry.[1] In July 1734 an English captain brought to Mobile a cargo of flour which he exchanged for deerskins that could not be sold to the French merchants. The people of the village, thereby, were spared further suffering due to lack of food. Bienville now joined Diron in an effort to have the captain of the boat bring there at once another such cargo to be similarly exchanged. Moreover the governor defended the proceeding to the home government.[2]

Opposition from the Louisiana officials certainly did not put an end to the trade with the English. On April 28, 1735, an English captain entered Mobile Bay on the plea that he had come to collect a number of debts contracted at a time when commerce with his nation was not considered illicit. He was allowed to settle his affairs, and meanwhile succeeded also in selling his entire cargo of flour, salt meat, beef and staves.[3] Another English ship appeared in July. On this occasion the captain was allowed 24 hours to take on wood and water, but he was not granted the privilege of trading. Presumably, in order to supervise the loading of these commodities, the "entrepreneur" of public works remained two days on board the English ship. With him was a local settler who managed to procure two "quarts" of flour in return for peltry. Convinced that illicit trade was in progress, the commandant sent a company of 55 soldiers to stop it. They did not reach the boat until the last of the merchandise had been taken on, and the "entrepreneur's" boat had left, carrying only a small amount of flour that the captain had given in exchange for some

[1] *A. N., C., Sér.* C^{13}, vol. xviii, fols. 138-141, 203.

[2] *Ibid.*, fol. 205.

[3] *Ibid.*, vol. xx, fols. 93-94.

food supplies. An encounter with the English cost the government 453 livres, 12 sols, 8 deniers, and the loss of a number of sailors.[1] In August a vessel from Carolina took away 5,000 deerskins, though its captain was officially informed that the traffic was not allowed. The home government, nevertheless, was notified that the transaction was allowable because it helped Louisiana by depriving the English of a large part of their fur trade.[2] During the same month the captain of a ship from Jamaica entered the harbor under the pretext of adjusting certain matters connected with the confiscation of 1734.[3] Thus, employing one device or another, the English skippers pushed their way to Louisiana ports, where they usually were able to sell their cargoes.

In April, 1736, two vessels of that nationality were at Mobile, one claiming refuge from heavy seas, the other a shortage of water. Bienville was there at the time of the arrival of the first ship, and allowed its captain to sell flour; Diron made a similar concession in the case of the second, who had come from New York. The privilege was given because of a shortage at the time of that commodity.[4] This leniency could have but one result. In May a vessel arrived from Carolina with a plea for necessary repairs. It had cheese, flour and beer on board, which the captain was permitted to sell, bringing him 5,000 livres, payable in four months. Credit had to be offered because neither cash nor peltry was available. The sale, however, was made only on the condition that the captain be allowed to return within the period stipulated. He

[1] *A. N., C., Sér. C*[13], vol. xx, fols. 93-100; vol. xxii, fol. 270.

[2] *Ibid.*, vol. xx, fols. 160-167; vol. xxi, fols. 94-100.

[3] *A., B. N., Nouvelle Acquisition*, vol. 9311, fol. 32.

[4] *A. N., C., Sér. C*[13], vol. xxi, fols. 7-11; vol. xxii, fol. 223.

was told also that, if he would bring to Mobile a cargo of flour, he might be allowed to sell it. The French commandant justified his action in this respect, though a direct violation of royal orders, on the ground of extreme scarcity of supplies.[1] Later the crown gave its approval to the buying of flour from the English, but forbade absolutely any other form of trade with them on any pretext whatever.[2]

Early in January, 1737, two English vessels were at Mobile. Bienville, who at the time was at that post, commanded the captains to leave at once or have their boats and cargoes seized and confiscated. One of the ships was wrecked on an island near by, but part of the load, 300 barrels of flour, with some barrels of lard and salt meat, was saved. It was sold to the "entrepreneur" of public works and various settlers, the captain and the crew being given passage on a Spanish boat bound for the Carolinas. The ship-master requested permission to return by sea to secure payment for the merchandise, but it was denied on pain of confiscation of the vessel. He was, however, to be allowed to return by land. Notwithstanding the prohibition, the officials at Mobile were assured by one of the settlers that the Englishman, who, it was asserted, had made a secret arrangement with the "entrepreneur" and some of the traders at the village to return with another cargo of flour and some negroes, would soon be there again. The prediction came true. In the following March the captain arrived in the harbor.

Since his departure the commandant had found out the details of the agreement with the Frenchmen, and at this

[1] *A. N., C., Sér. C^{13}*, vol. xxi, fols. 346-351; vol. xxiv, fol. 33.

[2] *Ibid., Sér. B*, vol. lxiv, fol. 509.

time proceeded to carry it out as prearranged, in order to trap the captain and capture the vessel, which proved to have on board a crew of sixteen men and five negroes, and was armed with ten cannon. Following a signal, the captain steered the ship for the "Isle of Vessels," where he supposed his confederates were to meet him and buy his goods. The commandant forced the "entrepreneur" to write and sign a dictated letter to the Englishman asking him to come on shore with some of his men in order to secure a certain quantity of deerskins. On the arrival of the unsuspecting Englishmen at the meeting-place designated, they were seized and taken to the local fort by a company of soldiers. At the same time another party of soldiers was sent after the remainder of the crew left in charge of the boat. Under pretext of bringing some fresh meat, they attempted to board it. The English, however, were too wary for this, and at once opened fire. In the skirmish the French, with the loss of only two negroes, succeeded in capturing the ship, which was later sent to the Balise and sold for 10,000 livres and the money given to the church. Bienville learned through the papers in the possession of the Englishman, and from some of the settlers in a position to know, that such meetings at different places along the coast were frequent. The tremendous amount of limbourg at Mobile bore out this information. Only severe treatment, the Louisiana officials believed, therefore, would put an end to the coming of the English to Mobile.[1]

Because of the punishment or for some other reason, no English boats, in fact, came to Louisiana in 1738. The Carolinians possibly may have thought that their traffic by this time was in no danger of competition from

[1] *A. N., C., Sér. C*[13], vol. xxii, fols. 28-29, 107-110, 173-175, 198-203, 223-232.

the French. The English government, however, did not appear to be so confident on this point. A treaty between England and France made in 1686, had prohibited trading and fishing by the natives of either in the territory of the other. Accordingly trading boats found in Carolina waters were ordered to be confiscated. Govnernor Glenn, was instructed to take particular care to enforce the exclusion rigorously.[1]

Neither the severity of the French officials nor the prohibition in question kept the English merchants out of Louisiana commerce very long. In January, 1739 an English captain who had previously worked as a carpenter in that province reached Dauphin Island in a vessel from the Carolinas. He presented to the commandant at Mobile a permit that Bienville had given him in 1735 allowing him to bring to Louisiana other English carpenters. The document presented was considered to be only an excuse to engage in illicit trade; therefore he was ordered to leave the port at once or have his ship confiscated. The inhabitants of Mobile, also, were warned against going on board. Finding it impossible to do anything in the face of this opposition, the Englishman set sail.[2]

For several years after this episode there seem to have been no English vessels at Mobile. During the period England at first was busied in the war with Spain, which disturbed Louisiana traffic to the extent of involving the seizure of French ships suspected of carrying contraband.[3] Some of the French merchantmen, were

[1] *Pub. Rec. of S. C.*, vol. xx, pp. 118-119; *The Weston Documents of South Carolina*, p. 97.

[2] *A. N., C., Sér.* C^{13}, vol. xxiv, fols. 247-248.

[3] *Supra*, p. 194.

held for as long as two months.[1] During the conflict, moreover, the Carolinians became more inclined than ever to believe that the possible competition from Louisiana trade was not important enough to give them the least concern. A French prisoner, it seems, told the governor that there were only six or seven small vessels engaged in it and their activities were insignificant.[2]

The French on their part would tolerate no trade with the English. A vessel from Londonderry in 1742 was wrecked off the coast of Louisiana, and the part of the cargo that was saved the French confiscated and sold for 8,912 livres, 10 sols.[3] It is not known whether the ship had entered the Gulf of Mexico for the purpose of trade with that province, but it is fair to assume that such was the intention.

The outbreak of war between France and England in 1744 made it very difficult for merchants of the latter nation to carry on trade by sea with Mobile. In April 1746 a Dutch ship from Caracas anchored at Mobile. The captain, a Frenchman, made a declaration that he was on his way to Campeachy, but was forced to enter the harbor because of contrary winds. The boat in fact had such a bad leak that within 24 hours after it hove to, the cargo of flour, wine, beer, cloth and other goods was damaged to the extent of more than a thousand écus. Accordingly the skipper asked permission of the governor then at Moblie to land the merchandise. He was permitted so to do and later he was allowed to sell it at a moderate price.[4]

[1] *A. N., C., Sér.* C^{13}, vol. xxv, fol. 143; vol. xxvi, fols. 94, 130; vol. xxvii, fols. 78, 122,

[2] *Journal of the Minister of the Colony,* from Dec. 17, 1743, to Dec. 6, 1744. Penn. Hist. Soc. Lib.

[3] *A. N., C., Sér.* C^{13}, vol. xxix, fol. 106.

[4] *Ibid.*, vol. xxx, fols. 110-112, 145; *Sér. B*, vol. lxxxiii, fol. 39.

The Louisiana officials were fearful lest the selling of the flour would affect the price of the article expected at the time from the Illinois country. The defense to the home government was on the ground of extreme need of foodstuffs. The crown approved the action, but instructed its agents in the province in future to be less lenient to Dutch traders.[1]

In June 1748 a ship appeared off the "Isle of Vessels" with a letter from the governor of Pennsylvania requesting an exchange of certain prisoners of war he had on board. On this proposition Governor Vaudreuil declined to take action before he had received instructions from the home government. The captain, on his own part, asked to be allowed to take on a supply of wood and water. The request was granted and the people living along the shore were delegated to furnish what was requested and to receive flour in payment. Such quantities of merchandise changed hands, however, as to justify suspicion that illicit traffic was in progress. If so, nothing seems to have been done about it.[2]

An exchange of prisoners of war now became a common excuse among English sea captains for the appearance of their vessels in Louisiana. On June 28 Governor Vaudreuil informed the home government that an English ship had arrived at the Balise for that purpose. The local authorities promptly searched the vessel for prohibited merchandise. They found none, simply because the captain, the night before, had landed 33 negroes and some goods from Jamaica on a small island in the river not far away. By this maneuver he hoped to outwit the authorities and later deal directly with the colonists

[1] *A. N., C., Sér.* C^{13}, vol. xxxii, fols. 32-33; *Sér. B, Louisiane,* vol. lxxxv, fol. 3.

[2] *Ibid., Sér.* C^{13}, vol. xxxii, fols. 88-89.

along the coast, just as had probably been done by his predecesssor. Learning of the presence of the negroes and the merchandise on the island, the officials sent a detachment thither, seized the negroes and two Englishmen on guard and confiscated the goods on the spot, together with some beer and tafia found on board the vessel. The proceeds from the sale of the entire cargo amounted to 63,197 livres, 14 sols.[1]

The home government strongly approved of the action, partly, it would seem, because England granted a bounty of six shillings a pound on indigo which worked to the presumptive detriment of Louisiana, and partly because of the general necessity of suppressing illicit trade with the Carolinas. As the French saw the situation, English merchants would be able to buy indigo in Louisiana, carry it to the Carolinas and send it thence to England as a Carolina product. Traffic of this sort would be able to command a good price for the commodity, and hence Frenchmen would easily be induced to enter upon illicit transactions. Whatever the wisdom of this reasoning, the governor of Louisiana was instructed henceforth to prohibit absolutely all English and Dutch vessels visiting the province under any pretext whatever.[2]

Ere long France and England were again at war, and the English, as usual, seized every French ship encountered on the seas. In 1755, furthermore, England instructed the provincial governors to take particular care to prohibit trade with the French.[3] Almost from the beginning of the war certain persons in Louisiana, in a

[1] *A. N., C., Sér.* C^{13}, vol. xxxii, fols. 20-22, 200-201.

[2] *Ibid.*, vol. xxxiii, fol. 156; vol. xxxiv, fols. 5-7; *Sér.* F^{3}, vol. ccxli, M. S. S. M., Jan. 2, 1749.

[3] *Pub. Rec. of S. C.*, vol. xxviii, 1754-1755, p. 336; *R. I. Col. Rec.*, vol. v, p. 516.

position financially to do so, had sent out from time to time "vaisseaux parlementaires," or cartel-ships, in order to secure foodstuffs. Under the guise of a flag of truce these boats tried to traffic with ships at sea, or entered the ports of colonies belonging to other nations. Many of them, to be sure, were taken by the English, who later used them in trade with the province. It was the policy of the "ordonnateur" to confiscate them in case the persons in possession refused to give them up.[1]

On the principle that absolute necessity justified unusual action, Governor Kerlérec believed it to be permissible under the French law to get supplies even from enemies. This attitude, in fact, had led yearly to an increase in the number of English vessels.[2] It was, however, a mooted question whether the colony was really in a condition that would warrant the policy adopted by the governor.

Whether or not the governor was justified in his decision did not matter, since it had the result he intended to produce. On January 9, 1759, an English ship of 50 tons reached New Orleans with a cargo of flour, lard, beer, hams, cheese, cordage, iron, cider and cloth. It also had on board nine negroes and two French prisoners of war who were seized by the "ordonnateur."[3]

In March another English boat appeared bringing a cargo of dry-goods that had been bought in Jamaica for 200,000 livres. It was disposed of in New Orleans for 600,000, the captain being accorded the privilege of selling at both retail and wholesale.[4] As these cargoes were

[1] *A. N., C., Sér.* C^{13}, vol. xli, fols. 175-177; *Sér.* F^{3}, vol. xxv, fols. 130-131.

[2] *Ibid., Sér.* C^{13}, vol. xli, fols. 191-196.

[3] *Ibid.*

[4] *Ibid.*, fols. 175, 247-248; *Sér.* F^{3}, vol. xxv, fols. 201-205.

not large enough to relieve the needs of the province, Governor Kerlérec, on May 3, 1759, before leaving the capital on a tour of inspection to Mobile and the other posts, ordered the major situated at the Balise to allow any vessel that might come during his absence with a supply of food, to sell what it had regardless of the flag under which it sailed.[1] Scarcely had the governor departed when an English boat arrived. Its captain forthwith requested to be allowed to dispose of the cargo at retail. Meanwhile a French prisoner of war had offered to purchase the entire consignment, but as the price he mentioned was very low his proposal was rejected. The offer no doubt was prompted by the "ordonnateur" who now proceeded to confiscate the cargo instead. This procedure threw New Orleans into great excitement because for months the troops had been on half-rations, the negroes were almost without food altogether, and every one in the province was more or less in need.[2] Governor Kerlérec, however, on his return suspended the major at the Balise and arrested the secretary of the "ordonnateur" for the part they had taken in the affair, and in this action he was later upheld by the crown.[3]

In June 1759 the commercial situation of New Orleans was worse than it had been since the war began. The English had a ship carrying 36 guns and a smaller one having between 16 and 20 cannon stationed at the mouth of the Mississippi in order to prevent supplies of any kind from being carried up the river. The colonial officials accordingly were forced to have food and munitions landed at Pensacola and thence trans-

[1] *A. N., C., Sér.* C13, vol. xli, fols. 20-29.

[2] *Ibid.*

[3] *Ibid., Sér. B,* vol. cix, fols. 25-26.

ported to Louisiana.[1] This expedient being ineffective, the French government made an arrangement with a merchant of Amsterdam to carry what was needed. At the same time it instructed the local officials to receive consignments from that source and allow their sale.[2] In order to make it possible for the Dutch boat to reach New Orleans, an armed vessel was despatched to drive the English war-ship from the mouth of the Mississippi and succeeded in doing so.[3]

The French, indeed, were able to give the English considerable cause for disquiet. Governor Bull of South Carolina wrote to the Board of Trade May 29, 1760, that Louisiana was procuring supplies for the Indian trade from the northern colonies, chiefly Rhode Island, the goods being carried to Pensacola or elsewhere for purchase.[4] This trade was highly offensive to some of the English colonial officials who believed that it was prolonging the war. The governor of Pennsylvania was especially strong in his denunciation of the traffic; yet nothing apparently could be done to stop it.[5]

In this connection Governor Colden of New York admitted that only too many traders from that colony had been engaged in the business, but declared that those from Philadelphia were still more numerous and active. Merchants from both localities shipped large cargoes of merchandise to New England, where any particular captain concerned would obtain the needful papers in accordance with the navigation acts. He could then put his

[1] *A, N., C., Sér. C*[13], vol. xli, fol. 71.

[2] *Ibid., Sér. B,* vol. cxi, fols. 2, 3.

[3] *Ibid., Sér. C*[13], vol. xlii, fols. 56-57, 93-96.

[4] *N. C. Col. Rec.,* vol. vi, p. 260; Beer, *British Colonial Policy,* p. 103.

[5] Beer, p. 105.

cargo ashore at any port he saw fit; yet to the officials of the port from which he set sail he could give the appearance on his return to Philadelphia or New York, of having delivered the ship-load at the first landing-place visited. With a cargo of sugar probably taken on at a French or Spanish settlement, the captain went first to some point on the New Jersey coast or back to New England, where he procured other papers, in order to make it look as if the merchandise had been embarked at some one of the ports last named. So far as Colden knew, no New York boats had gone to Louisiana, but he was told that some from the New England colonies had done so. English colonists, however, were not lacking who claimed that traffic of the sort with the French province was an advantage, since it afforded an outlet for products that otherwise would have a poorer market or none at all, and on this ground advocated its official approval.[1]

Throughout the war a small number of English sloops from one colony or another, and from Rhode Island in particular, carried on trade with Mobile and some of the bolder captains transported cargoes directly to New Orleans.[2] The traffic, nevertheless, was managed so skilfully that it had the appearance of legality. So cleverly indeed was the work done that captains tried in the admiralty court of Charleston for bringing to that port cargoes undoubtedly procured in Louisiana were able, by the papers in their possession, to prove, judicially at least, that the stuff had been taken on at a Spanish settlement. The collector accordingly was obliged to

[1] *Colden Papers*, vol. i, Oct. 27, 1760, in *N. Y. Hist. Soc. Pub.*, Fund Ser., vol. ix, pp. 26-30. N. Y., 1877.

[2] Beer, p. 103.

clear any vessel sailing to a Spanish port under the rules of trade. It would simply get a clearance from Charleston for such commodities as it was known the Louisiana colonists would want, and depart for Pensacola or Monte Cristo; but instead would carry the goods to Mobile or New Orleans as the circumstances would warrant. One such boat in particular was seized and taken to Charleston, in March 1761, and notwithstanding the rigid examination the captain underwent at the hands of the governor and other officials there, he was able to prove his innocence of either high treason or smuggling. By the end of the war the illicit traffic with Louisiana had become public and notorious. However it was kept within the appearance of the law. Through it the French at Mobile were receiving a considerable quantity of supplies for the Indian trade from Pensacola. English vessels also dealt directly with New Orleans, either as supposed cartel-ships or by other elusive devices.[1]

Governor Bull roundly declared that the voyages were made wholly for commercial objects. In 1761, an English sloop was seized at Boston for trafficking with New Orleans. The examination of the captain brought out the information that at the time two other English vessels—one from Rhode Island, the other from Jamaica—also were regularly trading at that port.[2] Records of the transactions, however, are necessarily limited to the vessels that in some way got into trouble with the officials, for the practice was opposed by both the English and French governments, and hence had to be carried on secretly. When the war ended in 1763, the illicit trade had not lost any of its significance.

[1] *Pub. Rec. of S. C.*, vol. xxix, p. 42.

[2] Beer, p. 103.

BIBLIOGRAPHY

(Titles of Works Referred to in the Text)

Contemporaneous Manuscript Material

Archives, Bibliothèque du Departement des Affaires Étrangères, Paris.
Amérique,
Mémoires et Documents, 1712 à 1718, vol. 1.
Mémoires et Documents, 1716 à 1752, vol. 2.
Mémoires et Documents, Indes Occidentales, Saint Domingue, 1630 à 1772, vol. 12.
Mémoires et Documents, Indes Occidentales, Canada, Acadie, 1518 à 1759, vol. 24.
Mémoires et Documents, vol. 7.
Mémoires et Documents, de 1753 en 1771, vol. 10.
Espagne,
Mémoires et Documents, Commerce, 1698 à 1752, vols. 81, 153.
France,
Commerce,
Mémoires et Documents, 1700-1730, vol. 1990.
Mémoires et Documents, 1700-1740, vol. 1991.
Mémoires et Documents, 1700-1742, vol. 1992,
Mémoires et Documents, 1712-1728, vol. 2004.
Mémoires et Documents, 1745-1820, vol. 2006.
Mémoires et Documents, 1717-1755, vol. 2009.
Mémoires et Documents, 1730-1748, vol. 2019.
Finances et Monnaies, Mémoires et Documents, vol. 225.
Sur le Sr. Jean Law Écossais, devenu Contröleur Général des Finances du Roïaume de France au tems de la Régence du Duc d'Orléans, vol. 140.

Archives, Bibliothèque de l'Arsenal, Paris.
Mémoire pour servir à l'histoire du sisteme de Law, présenté à M. Le Duc d'Orléans en l'année 1719, vol. 3724.
Pièces Fugitives Concernant le Commerce au Nouvel establissement du Biloxi, vol. 4497.
Poem en Vers Touchant l'établissement de la province de la Louisiane Connuée sous le nom du Missisipy avec tout ce qui sy est passé de depuis 1716 jusqu'a 1741. Le Massacre des Français au passe des Natchez, Moeurs des sauvages leur dances, leur Religion, enfin ce qui concerné le pays en général. (Il parait

que l'auteur de ce Poeme était un M. Dumont. Ses vers sont detestables, mais il y a des choses singulières.) The part in parenthesis was written in the margin of the front page. There are some good cuts and maps in the book. vol. 3459.

Recueil de Pieces Curieuses et Intéressantes, vol. 3459.

Archives, Bibliothèque du Departement des Colonies, Paris.

Série G[1], vol. 464, *Les Recensements de la Louisiane*, 1706-1741.

Transcripts of Série G[1], vol. 464, in Louisiana Historical Society Library, Tulane Library, New Orleans.

Archives, Bibliothèque Nationale, Paris.

Fonds Français,

Détail du Mississipi, de son commerce et de celui qui sy pourrait faire, de ses produits et la façon de pouvoir les mettre a profit, vol. 12224.

Journal de Correspo., 1758 à 1766, vol. 10764.

Journal du Voyage fait par Deux frégattes du Roy, La Badine Commandée par M. d'Iberville, et Le Marin par M. Le Chevalier de Surgères, qui partirent de Brest, le Vendredy 24 Octobre 1698, vol. 9097.

Mémoire sur la Louisiane, vol. 12105.

Mémoires sur la Marine, vol. 11342.

Ordonnances et Arrêt du conseil, vol. 7220.

Règlemens, Traités, Mémoires raport au Service de la Marine, Commerce Maritime aux Colonies, etc. et fait depuis 1715 jusqu'en 1730, vol. 11332.

Régistre des Déliberations de Mrs. les Commissaires nom'és par Arret du Conseil du 18 Obre. 1758 pour procéder à l'examen et vérification des dettes de la Marine depuis le 21 Obre. 1758 Jusqu'a et compris le 25 Septembre 1759, vol. 11334.

Régistre des Déliberations de Mrs. les Commissaires, nommée par Arrest du Conseil du 18 Ober. 1758 po. procéds à l'examen et Vérification des Dettes de la Marine depuis le 13e Obre. 1759 jusques et compris le 8 Obre. 1760, vol. 11335.

Régistre des Déliberations de Mrs. les Commissaires nommée par Arrest du Conseil du 18 Obre. 1758 pour procéds a l'Examen et Vérification des Dettes de la Marine depuis 18 Obre. 1760 jusqu'a et compris le 24 Septembre 1761, vol. 11336.

Relations de la Louisiane, Penicaut, vol. 14613.

Table Générale des Édits et Ordonnances Concernant la Marine, 1714-1718, vol. 14273.

Table Générale des Édits et Ordonnances Concernant la Marine, 1718-1725, vol. 14274.

Table Générale des Édits et Ordonnances Concernant la Marine, 1728-1734, vol. 14376.

Table Générale des Édits et Ordonnances Concernant la Marine, 1740-1756, vol. 14278.

Fonds Français, Nouvelle Acquisition.

Collection, Joly de Fleury,

Louisiane, Colonie de la, Minute d'une Mémoire, par M. Béletrus, ancien commis de la Marine à Versailles. (Without date but written about 1749.) Vol. 1726.

Amérique du Nord, Entreprises de Cavalier de la Salle, 1669-1684, vol. 9288.

Amérique du Nord, Index Louisiane, vol. 9311.

Recueil sur la Marine, XVII-XIX Siècles, vol. 5399.

Archives Nationales, Colonies, Paris.

Série A,

Édits, Arrets et Ordonnances Concernant la Louisiana, 1712-1754, vol. 22.

Édits, Lettres-Patentes, Déclarations, Arrêts, Ordonnances et Reglémens Concernant la Colonie de la Louisiane depuis le 24 Septembre 1712 jusques au 27 Aoust 1746, vol. 23.

Série B, *Registre des Dépêches des Colonies Septentrionales, Dépêches et Ordres du Roy Concernant la Colonie la Louisiane*, vols. 25-117.

Série C^{13}, *Correspondance Générale*, Louisiane, 1679-1763, vols. 1-45.

Transcripts, selections, Louisiana Historical Society Library, Tulane Library, New Orleans, 2 vols.

Transcripts, Public Record Office, Jackson, Miss. This is a good selection of documents, the work is well done and is accurate, 19 vols. in 1910.

Transcripts, Private Library of Peter J. Hamilton, Mobile, Ala.

For the most part the letters are from the governor and "ordonnateur", jointly or separately, and are signed and dated. There are also letters and communications from other officials.

Série F^3, Colonies,

Description et Historique Louisiane, 1680-1755, M. S. S. M., vol. 24.

Description et Historique Louisiane, 1756-1803, M. S. S. M., vol. 25.

Code Louisiane, 1682-1723, M. S. S. M., vol. 241.

Code Louisiane, 1724-1746, M. S. S. M., vol. 242.

Lettres, M. S. S. M., vol. 243.

Arrêt du Conseil d'État du Roy, du Mai, 1720, New York Public Library.

Arrêt du Conseil d'État du Roy, 13 Octobre, 1750, New York Public Library.

Bancroft Papers Relating to Carolina, New York Public Library.

Baptismal and Death Registers, 1704-1740, Cathedral Archives, Mobile, Alabama.

Béranger, *Mémoire de la Louisiane,* 1722. Newberry Library, Chicago, Illinois.

Colonial Entry Book. Public Record Office, Columbia, South Carolina.

Concessions. Louisiana Historical Society Library, Tulane Library, New Orleans. Transcripts.

Cotte G. Louisiana Historical Society Library, Tulane Library, New Orleans. Transcripts.

French MSS., Mississippi Valley, 1676-1869. Louisiana Historical Society Library, Tulane Library, New Orleans.

Indian Book, 1710-1718, vol. i, Public Record Office, Columbia, South Carolina.

Journal Historique de la Louisiane. Library of Congress, Washington, D. C.

Journal de Penicaut, Louisiane, 1699-1721. Newberry Library, Chicago. A Transcript.

Journal of the Minutes of the Council, 1743-1744. Public Record Office, Columbia, South Carolina.

Kaskaskia Papers, 1737-1784. Chicago Historical Society Library, Chicago.

Notes et Documents Historiques de la Louisiana. Louisiana Historical Society, Tulane Library, New Orleans.

Register, 1737-1762. Court House, Belleville, Illinois. Local name, "Old Hog-Hide Register".

Rémonville, *Lettres Touchantes le Mississippi,* Paris, Aoust, 1702. Newberry Library, Chicago.

Transcripts, Board of Trade Papers. Public Record Office, London. In Public Record Office, Columbia, South Carolina.

Transcripts, Board of Trade Papers. Public Record Office, London. In Pennsylvania Historical Society Library, Philadelphia.

Transcripts, Calendar of State Papers, Colonial Series. America and West Indies, Public Record Office, Columbia, South Carolina.

Vent de Maison, 1755. Court House, Belleville, Illinois.

Weston Documents, Reports to the Lords of Trade, 1739-1755. Public Record Office, Columbia, South Carolina.

CONTEMPORANEOUS PRINTED MATERIAL

Adair, James, *The History of the American Indians,* London, 1775.

American State Papers, Documents, Legislative and Executive, of the Congress of the United States, Class VIII, Public Lands, vol. 2, Washington, D. C., 1834.

Anderson, Adam, *Historical and Chronological Deduction of the Origin of Commerce from the Earliest Accounts*, 6 vols., Dublin, 1790.

Bartram, John, *Observations on the Inhabitants, Climate, Soil, Rivers, Productions, Animals and other matter worth notice*, London, 1751.

Bartram, William, *Travels through North and South Carolina, Georgia and West Florida, The Cherokee Country, the Extensive Territories of the Muscogulges, or Creek Confederacy, and the Country of the Choctaw: Containing an account of the Soil and Natural Productions of those Regions, together with Observations on the Manners of the Indians*, Philadelphia, 1791.

Baudry des Lozières, *Second Voyage a la Louisiane, Faisant suite au Premier de l'Auteur de* 1794 à 1798, Paris, 1803.

Bernard, Jean Frederic (editor), *Recueil de Voyages au Nord Contenant Divers Mémoires très-utiles au Commerce et à la Navigation*, Troisiéme Edition, Tome x, Amsterdam, 1738.

Boone, Daniel, *Autobiography.* In Hartley, Cecil B., *Life and Times of Colonel Daniel Boone*, Appendix, Philadelphia, 1859.

Boston Gazette or Country Journal, October 20, 1755; November 15, 1756. Boston Public Library.

Bossu, N. (Captain in the French Marines), *Travels through that part of North America formerly called Louisiane.* Translated by John Reinhold Foster, 2 vols., London, 1771.

Carver, Jonathan, *Travels through the Interior Part of North America in the Years 1766, 1767, and 1768*, London, 1778.

Charlevoix, P. F. X., *A Voyage to North America: Undertaken by Command of the present King of France, Containing the Geographical Description and Natural History of Canada and Louisiana*, 2 vols., Dublin, 1766.

Charlevoix, P. F. X., *History and General Description of New France*, Translated by J. G. Shea, 6 vols., New York, 1866-1872.

Chaville, Franquet de, *Le Voyage en Louisiane*, 1720-1724, in *Journal de la Société des Américanistes de Paris*, Tome iv, 1903.

Colden, Cadwallader, *The History of the Five Indian Nations of Canada*, 2 vols., New York, 1904.

Coxe, Daniel, *Description of the English Provinces of Carolana by the Spaniards call'd Florida, and by the French, Louisiane*, London, 1741.

Croghan, George, *Journal.* In Butler, Mann, *A History of the Commonwealth of Kentucky*, Appendix, Louisville, Ky., 1836.

Delisle's Map. 1718. New York Public Library.

Documents Relating to the Colonial History of the State of New York, edited by E. B. O'Callaghan, 11 vols., Albany, 1856-1881.

Dumont, Butel, *Mémoires Historiques sur la Louisiane*, 2 vols., Paris, 1753.

Early Western Travels, edited by R. G. Thwaites, 32 vols., Cleveland, 1904.

Force, Peter, *Tracts and Other Papers relating principally to the Origin, Settlement and Progress of the Colonies in North America, from the Discovery of the Country to the Year 1776*, 4 vols., Washington, 1836-1846.

Gist, Christopher, *Colonel Christopher Gist's Journal of a Tour through Ohio and Kentucky in 1751*. In Filson Club Publications, No. 13, Louisville, Ky., 1898.

Goodman, Alfred T. (editor), *Journal of Captain William Trent from Logstown to Pickawillany, A. D. 1752*, Cincinnati, 1871.

Gravier, Gabriel (editor), *Relations du Voyage des Dames Religieuses Ursulines de Rouen, a la Nouvelle-Orléans*, Paris, 1872.

Hennepin, Louis, *A Description of Louisiana*, (Paris, 1683), edited and translated by J. G. Shea, New York, 1880.

Hennepin, Louis, *A New Discovery of a Vast Country in America*, (London, 1698), edited and translated by R. G. Thwaites, Chicago, 1903.

Hennepin, Louis, *Nouveau Voyage d'un Pais plus grand que l'Europe, avec les reflections des enterprises du Sieur de la Salle*, Utrecht, 1698.

Hutchins, Thomas, *An Historical Narrative and Topographical Description of Louisiana and West Florida*, Philadelphia, 1784. Also found in Imlay, Gilbert, *A Topographical Description of the Western Territory of North America*, London, 1797.

Jefferys, Thomas, *The Natural and Civil History of the French Dominions in North and South America*, Part I, containing a Description of Canada and Louisiana, London, 1760.

Journal de la Guerre du Micissippi contre les Chicachas en 1739 et finie en 1740, le 1er d'Avril. Par un Officier de l'Armee de M. de Nouaille, Nouvelle York, 1859.

Joutel, *A Journal of the Last Voyage Perform'd by Monsr. de la Salle to the Gulf of Mexico to find out the Mouth of the Mississippi River*. Written in French by Monsieur Joutel, a commander in the expedition. Caxton Club, London, 1896.

Kalm, Peter, *Travels in North America: Containing Its Natural History and a Circumstantial Account of its Plantations and Agriculture in General with the Civil, Ecclesiastic and Commercial State of the Country, the Manners of the Inhabitants, and Several Curious and Important Remarks on Various Subjects*, translated by John Reinhold Foster, 3 vols., London, 1771.

Keith, Sir William, *A Collection of Papers and other Tracts Written occasionally on Various Subjects to which is prefixed by way of Preface an Essay on the Nature of a Public Spirit, London*, 1740.

Ker, John, *The Memoire of John Ker, Esq., of Kersland in North Britain, Relating to Politicks, Trade and History,* 3 parts, 3 vols., London, 1726.

Kerlérec, *Report of 1758,* New Orleans, 1758.

La Harpe, Bernard de, *Journal Historique de l'Établissement des Français a la Louisiane,* Nouvelle-Orléanes, 1831.

Le Gac, Charles, (Director of the Company of the Indies), *Mémoire d'apres les Voyages sur la Louisiane, la Géographie, la Situation de la Colonie Française ou 25 Aoust 1718 au 5 Mars 1721 et des moyens de l'améliorer,* 1722. Boston Public Library.

Le Page du Pratz, *Histoire de la Louisiane,* 3 vols., Paris, 1758.

Margry, Pierre, *Découvertes et Établissements des Français dans l'Ouest et dans le Sud de l'Amérique Septentrionale,* 6 vols., Paris, 1879-1888.

Pennsylvania Archives, series 1, 12 vols., 1852-1856; series 2, 19 vols., Harrisburg, Pa., 1879-1893.

Pennsylvania Colonial Records, Minutes of the Provincial Council of Pennsylvania, 10 vols., Philadelphia, 1852.

Pittman, Captain Philip, *The Present State of the European Settlements on the Mississippi* (London, 1770), Hodder, F. H. (editor), Facsimile edition, Cleveland, 1906.

Pownall, Thomas, *The Administration of the Colonies,* 2nd edition, London, 1765.

Public Records of South Carolina. Transcripts from the English Public Record Office, America and West Indies, 5 vols., Charleston, S. C., 1889.

Radisson, Peter Esprit, *Voyages of Peter Esprit Radisson, Being an Account of his Travels and Experiences among the North American Indians from 1652-1684.* In The Prince Society Publications, vol. 16, Boston, 1885.

Raynal, G. T. F., *A Philosophical and Political History of the Settlements and Trade of the Europeans in the East and West Indies,* translated by J. O. Justamond, 6 vols., London, 1784.

Records of the Colony of Rhode Island and Providence Plantations in New England, 10 vols., Providence, 1856-1865.

Shea, John Gilmary, *Early Voyages up and down the Mississippi by Cavelier, St. Cosme, Le Sueur, Gravier and Guignas,* Albany, 1861.

The American Weekly Mercury, Facsimile by the Colonial Society of Pennsylvania, (1719-1721), 2 vols., Philadelphia, 1898.

The Colden Papers, 2 vols., in Coll. of N. Y. Hist. Soc. Pub., N. Y., 1877-1878.

The Colonial Records of North Carolina, edited by William L. Saunders, 10 vols., Raleigh, N. C., 1886-1890.

The Jesuit Relations and Allied Documents, edited by R. G. Thwaites, 71 vols., Cleveland, 1896-1901.

The Present State of the British and French Trade to Africa and America, Considered and Compared with some Propositions in Favor of a Trade of Great Britain, London, 1745. In John Carter Brown Library, Providence, R. I.

The Present State of the Country and Inhabitants, European and Indians of Louisiana on the North Continent of America, by an officer at New Orleans to his Friend at Paris, London, 1744.

The South Carolina Gazette, Jan. 26, 1758. Boston Public Library.

Umberville, Edward, *The Present State of Hudson's Bay, Containing a full Description of that Settlement, and the Adjacent Country; and Likewise of the Fur Trade with hints for its improvement*, London, 1790.

Walker, Dr. Thomas, *Journal of an Exploration of Kentucky in 1750, being the First Record of a White Man's Visit to the Interior of that Territory*, now first Published Entire with Notes and Bibliographical Sketches. In Filson Club Publications, No. 13, Louisville, Ky., 1898.

Year Book, City of Charleston, South Carolina, 1894.

Zeisberger, David, *Diary of David Zeisberger, a Moravian Missionary Among the Indians of Ohio*, 1781-1798, 2 vols., Cincinnati, 1885.

LATER PUBLICATIONS CONTAINING SOURCE MATERIAL

Albach, James R., editor, *Annals of the West, Embracing a concise Account of Principal Events which have occurred in the Western States and Territories from the Discovery of the Mississippi Valley to the Year Eighteen Hundred and Fifty-six. Compiled from the most authentic Sources*, Pittsburgh, 1857.

Andreas, A. T., *History of Chicago, from the Earliest Period to the Present Time*, 3 vols., Chicago, 1884-1886.

Austin, Moses, *A Summary Description of the Lead Mines in Upper Louisiana, also an Estimate of their Products for Three Years*, Washington, 1804.

Baker, George A., *The St. Joseph-Kankankee Portage, Its Location and Use by Marquette, La Salle and the French Voyageurs*. In the Northern Indiana Historical Society Publications, No. 1, South Bend, Indiana, 1899.

Bancroft, George, *History of the Colonization of the United States*, 10th edition, 10 vols., Boston, 1844.

Bancroft, George, *History of the United States from the Discovery of the American Continent*, 9th edition, 3 vols., Paris, 1842.

Bancroft, Hubert Howe, *History of Arizona and New Mexico*, 1530-1888, San Francisco, 1889.

Beck, Lewis C., *A Gazetteer of the States of Illinois and Missouri: Containing a General View of Each State; A General View of their Counties, and a Particular Description of their Towns, Villages, Rivers, etc., etc., with a Map and Other Engravings,* Albany, 1823.

Beer, George Louis, *British Colonial Policy, 1754-1765,* New York, 1907.

Begg, Alexander, *History of the Northwest,* 3 vols., Toronto, 1894-1895.

Benton, Elbert Jay, *The Wabash Trade Route in the Development of the Old Northwest.* In J. H. U. Studies, History and Political Science, vol. 21, nos. 1-2, Baltimore, 1903.

Biggar, H. P., *The Early Trading Companies of New France,* University of Toronto Library, 1911.

Billon, Frederick, *Annals of St. Louis in its Early Days under the French and Spanish Dominations,* St. Louis, 1886.

Blanchard, Rufus, *History of Illinois,* Chicago, 1883.

Breese, Sidney, *The Early History of Illinois, from its Discovery by the French, in 1673, until its concession to Great Britain, in 1763, including the Narration of Marquette's Discovery of the Mississippi,* Chicago, 1884.

Buffalo Historical Society Publications, 17 vols., Buffalo, 1870-1914.

Bunner, E., *History of Louisiana from its First Discovery and Settlement to the Present Time,* New York, 1841.

Bureau of American Ethnology, Bulletin 43, *Indian Tribes of the Lower Mississippi Valley and Adjacent Coast of the Gulf of Mexico,* Washington, 1911.

Butler, Mann, *A History of the Commonwealth of Kentucky,* Louisville, Ky., 1834.

Butterfield, C. W., *Discovery of the Northwest by Jean Nicolet,* Cincinnati, 1881.

Chicago Historical Society Collections, 5 vols., Chicago, 1884-1890.

Chittenden, Hiram Martin, *The American Fur Trade of the Far West,* 3 vols., New York, 1902.

Claiborne, J. F. H., *Mississippi as a Province, Territory and State, with Biographical Notes of Eminent Citizens,* Jackson, Miss., 1880.

Collections of the Georgia Historical Society, 6 vols., Savannah, 1840-1904.

Collections of the Illinois State Historical Library, 10 vols., Springfield, Ill., 1903-1915.

Collections of the Maine Historical Society, series 1, 9 vols.; series 2, 5 vols., Portland, Me., 1831-1914.

Collections of the Massachusetts Historical Society, Boston, 1792—.

Collections and Researches made by the Michigan Pioneer and Historical Society, 38 vols., Lansing, Mich., 1874-1912.

Collections of the Minnesota Historical Society, 15 vols., St. Paul, Minn., 1872-1914.

Collections of the South Carolina Historical Society, 5 vols., Charleston, S. C., 1857-1897.

Collot, General Victor, *Voyage dans l'Amérique Septentrionale,* 2 Tomes, Paris, 1826.

Corthell, C. E., *A History of the Jetties at the Mouth of the Mississippi River,* 2nd edition, New York, 1881.

Dillon, John B., *A History of Indiana, from the Earliest Exploration by Europeans to the close of the Territorial Government in 1816,* Indianapolis, Ind., 1859.

Dubroca, Louis, *L'Itinéraire des Français dans la Louisiane,* Paris, 1802.

Dunn, J. P., *Indiana, A Redemption from Slavery,* American Commonwealths, Boston and New York, 1905.

Ellet, Charles, *The Physical Geography of the Mississippi Valley, with Suggestions for the Improvement of the Navigation of the Ohio and Other Rivers.* In Smithsonian Contributions to Knowledge, vol. 2, Washington, 1899.

Filson Club Publications, 26 vols., Louisville, Ky., 1884-1911.

French, B. F., editor, *Historical Collections of Louisiana,* 5 parts, New York, 1846-1853.

French, B. F., editor, *Historical Collections of Louisiana and Florida,* New Series, 2 vols., 1869-1875.

Gayarré, Charles, *Histoire de la Louisiane,* 2 vols., Nouvelle Orléans, 1846-1847.

Gayarré, Charles, *History of Louisiana, The French Domination,* 4 vols., New Orleans, 1885.

Gayarré, Charles, *Louisiana: Its History as a French Colony,* New York, 1852.

German American Annals, vol. 7, New York, 1909.

Gordon, Thomas F., *The History of Pennsylvania, from its Discovery by Europeans to the Declaration of Independence,* Philadelphia, 1829.

Guénin, Eugène, *La Louisiane,* Paris, 1904.

Hall, James, *Notes on the Western States: Containing Descriptive Sketches of their Soil, Climate, Resources and Scenery,* Philadelphia, 1838.

Halsey, Francis Whiting, *The Old New York Frontier,* 1714-1800, New York, 1901.

Hamilton, Peter J. Colonial Mobile. *An Historical Study, largely from Original Sources, of the Alabama Tombigby Basin from the Discovery of Mobile Bay in 1519 until the Demolition of Fort Charlotte in 1821,* Boston and New York, 1898.

Heinrich, Pierre, *La Louisiane sous la Compagnie des Indies,* 1717-1731, Paris, 1906.

Hildreth, S. P., *Pioneer History. Being an Account of the First Examination of the Ohio Valley and Early Settlements of the Northwest Territory,* Cincinnati, 1848.

Historical Papers and Addresses of the Lancaster County Historical Society, 18 vols., Lancaster, Penn., 1896-1914.

Howe, W. W., *Municipal History of New Orleans.* In J. H. U. Studies, History and Political Science, vol. 7, Baltimore, 1889.

Hulbert, Archer Butler, *Historic Highways of America,* 16 vols., Cleveland, 1902.

Hunt, F., editor, *The Merchant's Magazine and Commercial Review,* 63 vols., New York, 1839-1870.

Indiana Historical Society Publications, 3 vols., Indianapolis, Ind., 1895-1897.

Kennedy, Howard Angus, *The Story of Canada,* London, 1898.

King, Rufus, *Ohio, The Fruits of the Ordinance of 1787,* American Commonwealths, Boston and New York, 1888.

Kingsford, William, *The History of Canada,* 10 vols., London, 1888-1889.

La Revue Canadienne Religioni, Patriae, Artibus sous la Direction de M. Alphonse Leclaire, vol. 29, Montreal, 1893.

Leverett, Frank, *The Lower Rapids of the Mississippi River.* In Proceedings of the Iowa Academy of Science, vol. 6, Des Moines, 1899.

Logan, John H., *A History of the Upper Country of South Carolina from the Earliest Periods to the close of the War of Independence,* Charleston, S. C., 1859.

Lowery, Robert and McCardle, William H., *A History of Mississippi from the Discovery of the Great River by Hernando de Soto, including the Earliest Settlement made by the French under Iberville to the Death of Jefferson Davis,* Jackson, Miss., 1891.

MacPherson, David, *Annals of Commerce, Manufactures and Navigation,* 4 vols., London, 1805.

Magazine of Western History, 14 vols., New York and Cleveland, 1844-1891.

Martin, François-Xavier, *The History of Louisiana from the Earliest Period,* 2 vols., New Orleans, 1827.

Monnette, John W., *History of the Discovery and Settlement of the Valley of the Mississippi, by the Three Great European Powers, Spain, France, and Great Britain, and the Subsequent Occupation, Settlement, and Extension of Civil Government by the United States until the year 1846,* 2 vols., New York, 1848.

Montagne, Charles, *Histoire de la Compagnie des Indes,* Paris, 1899.

Moses, John, *Illinois, Historical and Statistical,* 2 vols., Chicago, 1889-1892.

Neill, Edward Duffield, *The History of Minnesota: from the Earliest French Explorations to the Present Time,* Philadelphia, 1858.

New England Magazine, vol. 33, Boston, 1858.

Ohio Valley Historical Series, 7 vols., Cincinnati, 1870-1873.

Parkman Club Papers, Milwaukee, 1896.

Parkman, Francis, *A Half-Century of Conflict,* 2 vols., Champlain edition, Boston, 1897,

Parkman, Francis, *The Old Régime in Canada,* 2 vols., Champlain ed., Boston, 1897.

Parkman, Francis, *Count Frontenac and New France under Louis XIV,* Champlain edition, 2 vols., Boston, 1897.

Parkman, Francis, *La Salle and the Discovery of the Great West,* Champlain edition, 2 vols., Boston, 1897.

Parrish, Randall, *Historic Illinois, The Romance of the Earlier Days,* Chicago, 1905.

Perkins, James H., *The Annals of the West: Embracing a Concise Account of Principal Events which have Occurred in the Western States and Territories, from the Discovery of the Mississippi Valley to the Year Eighteen Hundred and Fifty,* St. Louis, 1850.

Pickett, Albert James, *History of Alabama and Incidentally of Georgia and Mississippi from the Earliest Period,* 2 vols., 3rd edition, Charleston, S. C., 1851.

Proceedings and Transactions of the Royal Society of Canada, 26 vols., Montreal, 1882-1909.

Proceedings of the State Historical Society of Wisconsin, 21 vols., Madison, Wis., 1874-1914.

Ramsey, J. G. M., *The Annals of Tennessee to the End of the Eighteenth Century: Comprising its Settlements, as the Watauga Association, from 1769-1777; A Part of North Carolina, from 1777-1784; The State of Franklin from 1784-1788; A Part of North Carolina from 1788-1790; The Territory of the United States, South of the Ohio, from 1790-1796; The State of Tennessee from 1796-1800,* Charleston, S. C., 1853.

Records of the American Catholic Historical Society of Philadelphia, 25 vols., Philadelphia, 1884-1914.

Reports and Collections of the State Historical Society of Wisconsin, 20 vols., Madison, Wis., 1855-1911.

Reynolds, John, *The Pioneer History of Illinois,* Belleville, Ill., 1852.

Roberts, Ellis H., *New York. The Planting and Growth of the Empire State,* American Commonwealths, 2 vols., Boston and New York, 1893-1896.

Shea, John Gilmary, *The Catholic Church in Colonial Days,* New York, 1886.

Shea, John Gilmary, *Discovery and Exploration of the Mississippi Valley,* New York, 1853.

Speed, Thomas, *The Wilderness Road. A Description of the Route of Travel by which the Pioneers and Early Settlers first came to Kentucky.* In Filson Club Publications, No. 2, Louisville, Ky., 1886.

Sulté, Benjamin, *Mélanges d'Histoire et de Littérature*, Ottawa, 1876.

Taylor, James W., *History of the State of Ohio*, 1650-1687, Cincinnati, 1854.

The Magazine of American History with Notes and Queries, 30 vols., New York and Chicago, 1877-1893.

The North American Review, vol. 49, Boston, 1839.

The Olden Times, edited by N. B. Craig, 2 vols., Pittsburgh, 1846-1848.

The Publications of the Prince Society, 31 vols., Boston, 1865-1909.

The Virginia Magazine of History and Biography, 22 vols., Richmond, Va., 1894-1914.

Thwaites, Reuben Gold, *Wisconsin, The Americanization of the French Settlements*, American Commonwealths, Boston and New York, 1908.

Topographical and Statistical Account of the Province of Louisiana, Baltimore, 1803.

Transactions of the Illinois State Historical Society, Nos. 8-14, Springfield, Ill., 1904-1914.

Transactions of the Alabama Historical Society, 2 vols., Tuscaloosa, Ala., 1897-1898.

Transactions of the Literary and Historical Society of Quebec, New Series, Part 9, Quebec, 1871-1877.

Vergennes, M. de, *Mémoire Historique et Politique sur la Louisiane*, Paris, 1802.

Villiers du Terrage, Bon Marc de, *Les Dernière Années de la Louisiane Française*, Paris, 1903.

Wallace, Joseph, *The History of Illinois and Louisiana under the French Rule, etc.*, 2 vols., Cincinnati, O., 1900.

Walton, Joseph S., *Conrad Weiser and the Indian Policy of Colonial Pennsylvania*, Philadelphia, 1900.

Willson, Beckles, *The Great Company. Being a History of the Honourable Company of Merchants—Adventurers Trading into Hudson's Bay*, New York, 1900.

Winsor, Justin, editor, *A Narrative and Critical History of America*, 8 vols., Boston and New York, 1889-1890.

Winsor, Justin, *Cartier to Frontenac, Geographical Discovery in the Interior of North America in its Historical Relation*, 1534-1700, Boston and New York, 1894.

Winsor, Justin, *The Mississippi Basin, The Struggle in America between England and France*, 1697-1763, Boston and New York, 1895.

Winsor, Justin, *The Westward Movement, The Colonies and the Republic West of the Alleghanies*, 1763-1798, Boston and New York, 1897.

Zay, E., *Histoire Monétaire des Colonies Françaises d'après les Documents Officiels, avec 276 figures*, Paris, 1892.

INDEX

www.ingramcontent.com/pod-product-compliance
Lightning Source LLC
LaVergne TN
LVHW050554110926
847619LV00018B/58
* 9 7 8 0 8 1 7 3 5 2 9 6 7 *